The Quest For
Q

The Quest For Q

David R. Catchpole

T&T CLARK

EDINBURGH

T&T CLARK LTD
59 GEORGE STREET
EDINBURGH EH2 2LQ
SCOTLAND

First published 1993

ISBN 0 567 09616 5

British Library Cataloguing-in-Publication Data
A catalogue record for this book is available from the British Library

Typeset by Datix International Ltd, Bungay, Suffolk
Printed and bound in Great Britain by Bookcraft (Bath) Ltd.

To
Helen and Kate

Contents

Acknowledgements

This volume incorporates a series of previously published articles, which have been extensively supplemented and in some cases very drastically revised. I am grateful to the editors and publishers of the journals and books in question for their kindness in giving me permission to use the material.

Those parts of Chapter 1 which discuss the beatitudes and the call to avoid anxiety draw upon two articles, one published in *SUNT* 6/7 (1981/82) 77–87, and the other in *A Dictionary of Biblical Interpretation*, edited by R. J. Coggins and J. L. Houlden (London: SCM, 1990) 79–82. Chapter 2 was published in *NTS* 38 (1992) 205–21. An earlier version of Chapter 3 was delivered as the Manson Memorial Lecture in the University of Manchester in 1985, and subsequently published in *BJRL* 68 (1986) 296–316. Chapter 4 is based on an article originally published in *SUNT* 8 (1983) 79–90. Chapter 5 was a contribution to a symposium on *Early Christianity, Q and Jesus*, edited by J. Kloppenborg and L. Vaage, and published in *Semeia* 55 (1992) 147–74. Chapter 6 was included in the Festschrift in honour of Otto Knoch, edited by J. J. Degenhardt, *Die Freude an Gott – unsere Kraft* (Stuttgart: Katholisches Bibelwerk) 89–101. Chapter 7 is an adaptation of two articles published in *JTS* 34 (1983) 407–424 and *JTS* 40 (1989) 377–88. A substantial part of Chapter 8 was delivered as a paper at the British New Testament Studies conference in London in 1986 and subsequently published in the Festschrift for E. Earle Ellis, edited by G. F. Hawthorne and O. Betz, *Tradition and Interpretation in the New Testament* (Grand Rapids, Michigan: Eerdmans, 1987) 95–109. Chapter 9 was a contribution to *Templum Amicitiae. Essays on the Second Temple presented to Ernst Bammel*, edited by W. Horbury (JSNTSup 48; Sheffield: JSOT, 1991) 305–29. Finally, Chapter 10 appeared in *The Four Gospels 1992: Festschrift for Frans Neirynck*, edited by C.

M. Tuckett, F. Van Segbroeck, G. Van Belle, and J. Verheyden (BETL 100; Leuven: University Press/Peeters, 1992) 517–40.

The completion of the task of writing this book brings an acute awareness of help received and debts owed. My sincere thanks go to to my friends and colleagues in the Department of Theology in the University of Exeter for their support and encouragement; and in a very special way to my wife and daughters for their tolerance and understanding during what turned out to be an extended period of distraction.

Exeter   David Catchpole

Abbreviations

AB	Anchor Bible
AnBib	Analecta biblica
ANTJ	Arbeiten zum Neuen Testament und Judentum
ASNU	Acta seminarii neotestamentici upsaliensis
BBB	Bonner biblische Beiträge
BETL	Bibliotheca ephemeridum theologicarum lovaniensium
BEvT	Beiträge zur evangelischen Theologie
Bib	*Biblica*
BibS(F)	Biblische Studien (Freiburg, 1895–)
BibS(N)	Biblische Studien (Neukirchen, 1951–)
BZ	*Biblische Zeitschrift*
CBQ	*Catholic Biblical Quarterly*
CNT	Commentaire du Nouveau Testament
Ebib	Etudies bibliques
EKKNT	*Evangelisch-katholischer Kommentar zum Neuen Testament*
FB	Forschung zur Bibel

FRLANT	Forschungen zur Religion und Literatur des Alten und Neuen Testaments
HNT	Handbuch zum Neuen Testament
HTKNT	Herders theologischer Kommentar zum Neuen Testament
IBS	*Irish Biblical Studies*
JBL	*Journal of Biblical Literature*
JSNT	*Journal for the Study of the New Testament*
JSNTSup	Journal for the Study of the New Testament – Supplement Series
JTS	*Journal of Theological Studies*
NCB	New Century Bible
NovT	*Novum Testamentum*
NovTSup	Novum Testamentum, Supplements
NTAbh	Neutestamentliche Abhandlungen
NTD	Das Neue Testament Deutsch
NTL	New Testament Library
NTS	*New Testament Studies*
RGG	*Religion in Geschichte und Gegenwart*
RHPR	*Revue de l'histoire et de philosophie religieuses*
RNT	Regensburger Neues Testament
SANT	Studien zum Alten und Neuen Testament
SBLMS	SBL Monograph Series
SBS	Stuttgarter Bibelstudien
SBT	Studies in Biblical Theology

SJT	*Scottish Journal of Theology*
SNTSMS	Society for New Testament Studies Monograph Series
SUNT	Studien zur Umwelt des Neuen Testaments
TDNT	G. Kittel and G. Friedrich (eds), *Theological Dictionary of the New Testament*
THKNT	Theologischer Handkommentar zum Neuen Testament
WMANT	Wissenschaftliche Monographien zum Alten und Neuen Testament
WUNT	Wissenschaftliche Untersuchungen zum Neuen Testament
ZNW	*Zeitschrift für die neutestamentliche Wissenschaft*
ZTK	*Zeitschrift für die Theologie und Kirche*

I

Did Q Exist?

The study of Q, the hypothetical second source used by Matthew and Luke alongside Mark, has rarely flourished as exuberantly as it does now. Monographs abound, articles jostle with one another in the scholarly journals, ever more sophisticated and nuanced proposals concerning its development arise. And yet at the same time Q is experiencing a mid-life crisis, with wounding attacks being made on its identity, indeed its existence, the intention being to kill the hypothesis stone dead. Something therefore needs to be said in its defence.

To start at the very beginning is, however, beyond the scope of this book. Some results will have to be taken as read. The first of these is the priority of Mark over Matthew and Luke. This is not the place for engagement with the contemporary successors of Griesbach, the adherents of the hypothesis that Mark used both Matthew and Luke, a proposal which leaves open the pre-history of the Matthaean traditions.[1] In any case, the priority of Mark is a conviction shared by advocates and opponents of Q, as the work of Michael Goulder, one of the most persistent and formidable of contemporary critics of the Q hypothesis, demonstrates.[2] The second issue, which will only be touched on lightly when it becomes necessary to relate the Q traditions to Mark, is that of the 'minor agreements' between Matthew and Luke against Mark. These have been canvassed more than adequately elsewhere.[3] For present purposes it is necessary simply to note that the conclusion of the debate about

---

[1]For a full critique, see C. M. Tuckett, *The Revival of the Griesbach Hypothesis* (SNTSMS 44; Cambridge: CUP, 1983).

[2]*Midrash and Lection in Matthew* (London: SPCK, 1974); *Luke. A New Paradigm I-II* (JSNTSup 20; Sheffield: JSOT Press, 1989).

[3]See especially F. Neirynck, *Evangelica II* (BETL 99; Leuven: University Press, 1991) 1–138.

these 'minor agreements' does not foreclose the question of a second source alongside Mark.[4] If Luke were proved to have used Matthew, who in turn used Mark, the origin of the non-Marcan material in Matthew would still need clarification.[5] One pattern of clarification, though by no means the only possible one, was developed by Austin Farrer in the years just before redaction-criticism effectively took root in British scholarship. He set Matthew 'in the stream of a living oral tradition' and attributed to him a free reshaping and enlargement of the work of his predecessor, Mark, in the light of practical, doctrinal and liturgical influences.[6] In this tradition, though with many distinctive features, Michael Goulder has argued that the origin of the non-Marcan material in Matthew is to be found in the liturgically shaped and theologically creative work of Matthew, and the challenge he has posed is a serious and powerful one. Whether or not he is right will be a concern of much that follows. But at this stage it is the underlying logic of the situation which needs to be exposed. To accept a chain of Mark-Matthew-Luke dependence would still leave open in principle the question of where the non-Marcan material in Matthew originated. Instead of Q we would be discussing 'M', assessing the extent of Matthaean creativity, attempting to distinguish pre-Matthaean tradition and Matthaean redaction in each of the little 'm's which might or might not have been associated in pre-Matthaean collections. The discussion would simply be more difficult than is the case with the Q hypothesis. For one thing, Luke could never be a witness to the pre-Matthaean wording. For another, no appeal to the common order of double traditions in Matthew and Luke would be possible, and thus the establishing of pre-Matthaean collections would be more speculative. Those matters apart, the discussion of M would be not dissimilar to the discussion of Q. Whether that which we call Q would,

[4]T. A. Friedrichsen, 'The Matthew-Luke Agreements against Mark. A Survey of Recent Studies: 1974–1989', *The Gospel of Luke* (ed. F. Neirynck; BETL 32; Leuven: University Press, 1989) 335–92, esp. p. 391: 'Even if the minor agreements were to demonstrate convincingly that Luke depended on Matthew, the Q hypothesis would not automatically fall, for that is quite another discussion.'

[5]Logically, even though the discussion has not paid much attention to this possibility, Matthew's use of Luke ought not to be excluded.

[6]A. M. Farrer, 'On dispensing with Q', *Studies in the Gospels. Essays in Memory of R. H. Lightfoot* (ed. D. E. Nineham; Oxford: Blackwell, 1957) 58–88.

like a rose, by any other name like M smell as sweet to specialists in gospel criticism might be doubted, but having been chopped down on the basis of Lucan use of Matthew it would still have the potential to bloom again.

The contemporary argument between advocates and opponents of the Q hypothesis has moved beyond the need to establish a literary relationship between Matthaean and Lucan material in the non-Marcan parts of those gospels. This is quite right, partly because of the intensity of the verbal agreement in individual traditions, partly because of very frequent agreement in the ordering of units which might have been arranged in any number of other sequences, and partly because identical secondary editorial additions appear in both versions. Where the noise of battle sounds most loudly is in the discussion of priority when, within the overall Matthew/Luke verbal agreement, discrepancies of wording and often therefore of meaning are confronted. Advocates of Q are in general less uneasy about making a judgment about probable priority, whereas opponents of Q have often criticized such judgments as fragile and subjective.[7] However, both sides in the debate can perhaps agree that when a writer changes a text we would normally expect the change to be in harmony, rather than disharmony, with the writer's theological outlook and intention, and with such evidence as we have from a reading of his work as a whole concerning its setting and purpose. The word 'normally' is important: on a few very rare occasions Mark is treated, and therefore some other source might be treated, in surprising ways by Matthew and/or Luke – rarely, but not regularly. The possibility of surprises cannot therefore be eliminated in advance, but perhaps all can agree that a life *full* of surprises would be a life full of strains. Therefore, the charitable presumption of consistency ought to govern our approach to what the evangelists were doing, and for both sides an accumulation of evidence will be important.

There is another respect in which an accumulation of data

---

[7]Farrer, 'Dispensing', 64: 'There is scarcely an instance in which we can determine priority of form without invoking questionable assumptions.' Similarly, M. D. Goulder, 'The Order of a Crank', *Synoptic Studies* (JSNTSup 7; ed. C. M. Tuckett; Sheffield: JSOT Press, 1984) 111–30, esp. p. 111: 'criteria have varied, and often seemed slippery'.

may be expected to be helpful, indeed may be required as necessary. The decision about priority during the discussion of any tradition will ultimately have to be part of an overall reconstruction of the history of the tradition concerned. Alternative and competing reconstructions may, of course, emerge. If so, a judgment will simply have to be made as to which is the more convincing, though made with full awareness that the history of gospel study does not encourage us to think that any one view will achieve over a rival view a crushing and final victory.

Protracted skirmishing between advocates and opponents of Q arises also from another difficulty faced on all sides, one which again affects decisions about priority but which sometimes has more to do with the shape than the substance of a tradition. Sometimes, though not always, the *way* something is said is powerfully determinative of *what* is said. What should we do, then, if what is recognizably the same tradition exists in two versions, of which one is balanced or polished or clear, and the other unbalanced or rough or unclear or in some other way awkward? Should we lay down a general rule *lectio difficilior placet*? Sometimes this will probably be appropriate, but not invariably. The reason is that the written traditions will often, though again not always, have been orally transmitted traditions. If they were such, they will have had to be self-contained enough, smooth enough, straightforward enough to survive. Subsequently, they may have been made to interlock with other traditions, made rough, made obscure. And we do not always know for sure when this has happened. Nevertheless it is perhaps *on balance* safe to proceed by accepting the likelihood of a tendency at the written stage to interfere with, and even to mar, that which made a tradition capable of surviving at the oral stage.

Advocates of the Q hypothesis are sometimes harried with the argument about 'lostness'. Would it not be better to abandon the frail argument that something existed and then was lost, in favour of the argument that because it remains 'lost' it probably never existed? This, one has to say, is an extraordinary question. There may or may not be collections of pre-Marcan collections waiting to be exposed by the textual archaeology of Marcan specialists. There may or may not be pre-Pauline tradition quoted without acknowledgement (contrast 1 Cor 7:10; 11:23; 15:3) in the text of Rom 1:3–4 or Rom 3:25 or Gal 3:26–28 or Phil 2:6–11. There may or may not be pre-Johannine tradition quoted in parts of the Johannine prologue or the signs material. But no one seems to feel obliged to dismiss the possibility in principle simply because those traditions have never been found existing separately. The challenge represented by the harrying question is therefore only of value to the extent that it goes on to ask whether there existed more than a diffused set of little 'q's, that is, rather less than a substantially sized and somehow unified collection of different units of tradition. An answer would require the clarification of the sort of evidence for which one might look and which, if it were found, would prove convincing.

At this point it is worth observing that we should not ask too much. If all the pieces which presently fit together to form the jigsaw of the gospel of Mark were separated out and presented to us in a heap we would have the greatest difficulty in establishing that all of them came from one document. That said, two sorts of evidence which would work in favour of a unified Q can be suggested.

First, if Luke were regarded as independent of Matthew, and if we succeeded in establishing the existence of a set of 'q's, as distinct from a set of 'm's, then agreement in order when combined with proximity would suggest a belonging together of the different traditions. Proximity would be important: the agreement in order of the three traditions in Matt 11:2–6/Luke 7:18–23; Matt 11:7–11/Luke 7:24–28; Matt 11:16–19/Luke 7:31–35 would say more than the agreement in order of, say, Matt 5:1–12/Luke 6:20–23; Matt 6:25–33/Luke 12:22–31; Matt 13:33/Luke 13:20–21. However, not all the traditions will be covered by agreement in order combined with proximity.

Second, if we succeeded in establishing a congruence of concerns and emphases between secondary editorial additions made to a series of individual traditions, then the possibility of literary unity would be enhanced. Of course, not all traditions exhibit internal evidence of strata, and there will remain some uncertainty about whether they might be associated on the basis of an identity of concern alone. The problem then will resemble that raised by the use of the criterion of coherence in the quest of the historical Jesus: does coherence imply a common source or a consistent development? It could mean one. It could mean the other. But what it must mean is that there will not be, just as there never has been, reluctance on the part of the advocates of Q to accept that the boundaries of this hypothetical document remain indistinct.[8] And that in turn means that it is inappropriate, even illogical, to oppose the Q hypothesis on the grounds that (i) there are traditions, usually those with less intense verbal overlap, which no one can be sure about assigning to Q; (ii) advocates of Q do not agree among themselves about whether these traditions should be so assigned; and therefore (iii) because no one knows precisely the extent of the supposed Q document, the supposed Q document did not exist.

Two main concerns dominate the agenda of the present chapter. First, the discovery in directly related Matthew/Luke traditions of a substantial number of examples of verbal variations in which Luke has preserved the original form. The implication of such a discovery is pointedly set out by B. H. Streeter, 'Sometimes it is Matthew, sometimes it is Luke, who gives a saying in what is clearly its original form. This is explicable if both are drawing from the same source, each making slight modifications of his own; it is not so if either is dependent on the other.'[9] The more such discoveries pile up, the less sustainable is the notion that Luke used Matthew. Second, the discovery of some sort of space between the theology of Q and the theology of Matthew. I say 'some sort of space' advisedly. The Q hypothesis does not demand that the theology of Q should be at odds with the theology of Matthew, for the obvious reason that Q and Matthew may well have been, as it were, on the same theological trajectory.[10] Nevertheless, Michael Goulder's argument that Q and Matthew are source-critically

---

[8]Thus, A. Harnack, *The Sayings of Jesus* (London: Williams & Norgate, 1908) xi; J. C. Hawkins, 'Probabilities as to the So-called Double Tradition of St. Matthew and St. Luke', *Studies in the Synoptic Problem* (ed. W. Sanday; Oxford: Clarendon, 1911) 95–138, esp. 113–17; B. H. Streeter, *The Four Gospels* (rev. ed.; London: Macmillan, 1930) 185: 'While the phenomena make the hypothesis of the existence of a written source Q practically certain, its exact delimitation is a matter of a far more speculative character.' In similar vein more recently, M. Sato, *Q und Prophetie. Studien zur Gattungs- und Traditionsgeschichte der Quelle Q* (WUNT, 2/29; Tübingen: Mohr, 1988) 17–28.

[9]*Four Gospels* 183. Cf. also W. D. Davies & D. C. Allison, *The Gospel according to Matthew I* (ICC; Edinburgh: T. & T. Clark, 1988) 116.

indistinguishable because they are theologically indistinguishable[11] deserves to be taken seriously, and in what follows an attempt will be made to do so. I shall argue that space is indeed visible between the two on key issues such as poverty, the Gentiles, the debate about the status of the law, the kingship and Davidic lineage of Jesus, the relationship of Jesus to Wisdom, and the gift of the Spirit.

From general principle we can now move to specific traditions. We shall consider in a series of test cases how well the hypothesis that Luke used Matthew works, how well the theory that all the material was created by Matthew works, and how well the Q hypothesis might explain the data. The approach will be essentially a combination of the form-critical and the redaction-critical for the purpose of clarifying the source-critical situation. The suggestion will be that all traditions in the sample provide evidence that Luke gives us access to an earlier version than that in Matthew, and that in different ways they undermine the theory of Matthaean creativity. Some in addition provide very important evidence of the space between the theology of Q and the theology of Matthew.

I. The Baptist's Preaching. Matt 3:7–12/Q 3:7–9, 16b–17.

Matt 3:7–12, as it stands, contains two notable incoherences. First, v. 9, 'Do not presume to say . . .', is a warning against

---

[10]In this vein U. Luz, *Matthew 1–7* (Edinburgh: T. & T. Clark, 1990) 74–6, 82–3, has recently put forward the following discrepancies in outlook between Q and Matthew: (i) The Q tradition was formed by wandering prophets and sages, whereas Matthew adopted the perspective of a resident community to whom 'the wandering charismatics are only transient visitors'. (ii) The concern of the Q tradition with judgment on Israel was shared by Matthew, but the latter spoke about it differently and 'many a Q minatory saying against Israel becomes with him a threat which is directed at the church'. (iii) Q had not travelled the Marcan route of criticizing the law and liberating Christians from the ritual law, indeed 'almost all Jesus traditions critical of the law are missing, . . . Jesus' proclamation was understood rather as a new accenting of the law which is always valid (cf. Matt 23:23–26; Luke 11:39–42)'. Matthew, on the other hand, made the question of the law central. (iv) Q registered 'Jesus' pointed openness toward Gentiles in individual cases' but nowhere presupposed the existence of a Gentile mission. Matthew, by contrast, stressed that mission. Each of these proposals is doubtless arguable, but what is important is the principle that development rather than dissonance may be the nature of the theological relationship between Q – as reconstructed by those who believe in it! – and Matthew.

[11]*Luke I* 52–70.

covenant-based complacency, and the hypothetical speech, 'We have Abraham for our father', is suitable for anyone in Israel and not just for a particular group of hypocrites.[12] It makes plain indeed that the audience consists neither of opponents nor of those who have decided to be baptized (over against Luke 3:7a) but of those who have to be warned, those whose sinful state permits the use of prophetic hyperbole concerning their poisonous parentage ('offspring of vipers', v. 7b),[13] those who, it is hoped, *may* be baptized. The speech as a whole is a call for repentance, a call to baptism. Consequently, Matthew's 'many Pharisees and Sadducees' (v. 7a) do not really fit as an audience for the speech, nor do those who have already responded by being baptized (vv. 5–6/Mark 1:5). Matthew's introduction gives us a polarized audience which the speech does not fit.

Second, in striking a note of prophetic warning the speech as a whole (vv. 7b–12) consists of sub-units each of which concludes appropriately with a warning about judgment. Thus, the 'coming wrath' is the theme (v. 7b), repentance is the way of escape (v. 8), but lack of repentance means 'the fire' (v. 10b). Similarly, the person with the winnowing-fork will naturally separate off some for good, but the final and emphatic warning is the separation of others for ill, indeed for 'the unquenchable fire' (v. 12b). Similarly again, the saying about the two baptisms envisages a route to safety via the first ('I baptize you with water', v. 11a), and a warning of the route to ruin via the second ('he will baptize you with .. fire', v. 11a). Rudolf Laufen urges that this last saying requires a salvific reference in its second part, on the grounds that (i) after John's salvific baptism is mentioned there must be an upward movement (as it were) to a second baptism that is also salvific, and (ii) that an expectation of a future eschatological figure without salvific function would be without precedent.[14] The better alternative would be (i) that this saying implies a remarkable status for John's work from an eschatological perspective, in that the standard expectation of a division in the final judgment is indeed

[12]Against Goulder, *Luke I* 273.

[13]Cf. W. Foerster, 'ἔχιδνα', *TDNT* 2.815–16.

[14]*Die Doppelüberlieferungen der Logienquelle und des Markusevangeliums* (BBB 54; Königstein/Ts.-Bonn: Hanstein, 1980) 102–3, cf. H. Schürmann, *Das Lukasevangelium I* (HTKNT 3/1; Freiburg: Herder, 1969) 175–6.

adopted, and then that division is said to be determined by whether or not a person submits to the baptism of John, and (ii) that it does not deprive the coming one of salvific function but rather, in terms of its own function, serves to underline the urgent judgment-based necessity of submitting to John's baptism. It is not giving a panoramic and systematic view of *all* that the coming one will do, but rather focussing on just that *part* of what he will do which will underline the authority of, and reinforce the need to submit to, John's baptism. The reference to 'the Holy Spirit', which both Paul Hoffmann[15] and Michael Goulder[16] from their different points of view quite rightly recognize as neither appropriately positioned to describe a refining process[17] nor supported by any evidence anywhere as a sign of judgment, is therefore an intrusion, not because John did not offer the prospect of salvation[18] but on strictly formal grounds. This understanding enables the 'you' who are addressed throughout vv. 7b–11 to be understood consistently, i.e. not as hypocrites in vv. 7b–10 and (?) some other persons in vv. 11–12. In the last saying the 'you' are those who, if they respond in repentance and submission to baptism, will be safe, but who, if they do not, will be anything but safe. So Matt 3:7b–12 has an underlying consistency but at the same time two notable internal dislocations, and these dislocations in non-Marcan material do not favour the view that Matthew used Mark alone.

If Matthew used Mark he introduced several significant changes, among which were: (i) the addition of the phrase εἰς μετάνοιαν to the description of the first baptism; (ii) the sandwiching of the saying about the coming one between the two halves of the saying about the two baptisms, and its firm attachment by means of μὲν . . δέ to the description of the second baptism; (iii) the change from aorist ἐβάπτισα to present βαπτίζω; (iv) the introduction of the preposition ἐν in connection with both baptisms; (v) the addition of καὶ πυρί to the

---

[15]*Studien zur Theologie der Logienquelle* (NTAbh NF 8; 2nd ed.; Münster: Aschendorff, 1972) 29–31.

[16]*Luke I* 277–8.

[17]Similarly, Laufen, *Doppelüberlieferungen* 104.

[18]This is rightly stressed by Laufen, *Doppelüberlieferungen* 101–2, and by Goulder, *Luke I* 278.

description of the second baptism, together with the following saying about the one with the winnowing fork.

Every one of these 'changes' other than (i) is adopted by Luke, so that his version is not solely formed under Marcan influence. In passing, why would he omit εἰς μετάνοιαν? Statistics (2–1–5 + 6) show his fondness for the repentance theme, and in 5:32 diff Mark 2:17 he introduces the very same phrase (cf. also 24:47, and the direct quotation of, or indirect allusion to, baptistic tradition in Acts 5:31; 13:24; 19:4; 26:20). Although he has already referred to it in 3:3, 8 it is unlikely that he would resist pressure to emphasize it again in the definitive statement about John's mission. This small straw in the wind does not favour Luke's use of Matthew.

The alternative reconstruction of the history of the tradition could take seriously the dislocations mentioned above and then go on to see the Matthew/Luke agreements against Mark, that is, (ii)–(v) listed above, as evidence of a variant version of the tradition. With the implausible alliance of 'Pharisees and Sadducees' assigned to MattR, and a neutral and unspecific audience mentioned at the outset instead,[19] and with a 'baptism with fire' towards the end, the tradition would hold together consistently. It could certainly survive in the setting of the prophetic preaching to Israel of judgment and repentance.[20] If the presence of the theme of salvation is the *sine qua non* condition for survival, that condition is satisfied (fruit, baptism in water, wheat) but not so obtrusively as to prevent the tradition from functioning as it was intended to do in the setting of a mission to the covenant people. Only at one point would there be any hiatus in this tradition, that is, the definition of the baptizer with fire as someone to whom John is markedly inferior. This definition, as long as it was inserted within the two baptisms saying, did not disturb the balance of that saying or shift its concern away from a prophetic warning of judgment to an announcement of christology: it merely superimposed a third figure, probably the Son of man, on the original duo, John and God.[21]

This reconstruction, it will be noted, relieves us of the rather drastic and unpersuasive suggestion that all non-Marcan material

[19]Hoffmann, *Studien* 17; Luz, *Matthew 1–7* 170.
[20]*Pace* Goulder, *Luke I* 278.
[21]Hoffmann, *Studien* 28–33.

in Matthew is Matthaean midrash. It also enables us to establish a multi-stage history of the tradition. On the basis of what we have seen already it is plainly not necessary to separate Q 3:7b–9 from 3:16b-17 on the basis of a distinction between 'a threat of imminent judgment and a call for repentance' in the former, and 'an apocalyptic prediction concerning a figure who will effect both fiery judgment and salvation of the elect' in the latter.[22] Nor is it necessary to separate Q 3:8bcd as an unoriginal addition, by distinguishing an attack on the idea that baptism itself will save and an attack on the different idea that national privilege will exempt from judgment.[23] Rather, the whole address is united by its urgent concern to achieve repentance in those who need to be stirred and awakened. So we can envisage a first pre-Q stage, Q 3:7–9, 16b–17 (minus 3:16c), and then a Q stage (at which 3:16c was introduced). From there wholly explicable progress was made to the next stage represented by Mark 1:7–8. Mark's interests were christological and soteriological. He removed all the prophetic warning material, shifted to a controlling position the saying about John's successor (Mark 1:7), changed the programmatic statement about the present (cf. βαπτίζω) baptism of John into one which placed that baptism in a past era of salvation history (cf. ἐβάπτισα), and under the influence of a theology of Christian initiation changed the baptism with fire to a baptism with Holy Spirit (Mark 1:8).[24] Thereafter Matthew and Luke proceeded by merging the two Marcan and Q versions, though with a little more inconsistency on Matthew's part than on Luke's. In both cases judgment almost regained its proper place.[25] And in both cases the christological concern at both Marcan and Q stages was picked up and taken even further: in Luke's case by insisting that the status of Χριστός does not belong to John (Luke 3:15),[26] and in Matthew's case (i) by the implicit recognition of the superiority of Jesus in

---

[22]J. Kloppenborg, *The Formation of Q. Trajectories in Ancient Wisdom Collections* (Studies in Antiquity and Christianity; Philadelphia: Fortress, 1987) 102–3.

[23]Schürmann, *Lukasevangelium I* 181–3; Kloppenborg, *Formation* 102–4 hesitantly.

[24]Hoffmann, *Studien*, 18.

[25]In spite of the Lucan Pentecost it remains highly unlikely that the tongues of fire, Acts 2:3, were in Luke's mind in his 3:16 (thus, Goulder, *Luke I* 277) in view of the immediate context, 3:9, 17, and the subsequent sayings about the fire of judgment, Luke 9:54; 12:49; 17:29.

the conversation with John (Matt 3:14–15) and (ii) by the making public of what had in earlier tradition been a private and personal announcement of Jesus' sonship (Matt 3:16–17 diff Mark 1:10–11).

The two major dislocations in Matt 3:7–12 are therefore to be found in the introductory reference to the Pharisees and Sadducees, and in the definition of the coming baptism as 'in Holy Spirit'. In the first case it would be odd that Luke, using Matthew, should drop the personnel reference. He is not short on anti-Pharisaic polemic, and he adopts the sole Marcan allusion to Sadducees (Mark 12:18/Luke 20:27) as well as presenting them negatively several times in Acts (4:1; 5:17; 23:6–8). In the second case we have a Matthew/Q theological discrepancy of some importance. Matthew communicates a sense of the Holy Spirit as an endowment conveyed by Jesus in baptism, whereas Q does no such thing. Q emphasizes the Spirit as the endowment *of* Jesus (Q 11:20; 12:10) but not an endowment *by* Jesus.[27]

2. The Temptations. Matt 4:1–11/Q 4:1–13.

The formal structure of the temptations tradition is determined by the so-called 'law of three'. Two temptations begin with 'If you are the son of God . . .', and a third brings a climax with a different beginning, 'I will give you . . . if . . .'. With apparent uniformity all three temptations are resisted with Deuteronomic quotations, carefully chosen to follow the reverse order of the biblical text (8:3; 6:16; 6:13). Only one feature prevents the Matthaean scheme from exhibiting another schematic arrangement of two negative statements, 'Man shall not . . . you shall not', followed by a climactic positive statement 'You shall . . .'. That is the presence of 'but by every word that

---

[26]This probably reflects dialogue with the disciples of John (Hoffmann, *Studien* 16), a dialogue which arguably was already being carried on by Q: see below, pp. 67–8.

[27]This presumes that ἐν πνεύματι (Matt 12:28) stood in Q, rather than ἐν δακτύλῳ (Luke 11:20). This is likely, because (i) the 'finger of God' Exodus allusion (cf. Exod 8:19) suits Lucan theology; (ii) the LukeR removal of a 'Spirit' reference is paralleled in Luke 20:42; 21:15; (iii) a Spirit reference is more appropriate in an exorcistic context; (iv) a reminiscence of the original Spirit reference in Q 11:20 is probably present in the nearby LukeR 11:13.

proceeds from the mouth of God' (Matt 4:4b). If Luke knew it, as on Goulder's view he did, he dropped it. That he knew it is not confirmed by the presence of the phrase ἐκπορευομένοις ἐκ τοῦ στόματος αὐτοῦ shortly afterwards in Luke 4:22.[28] The latter is more likely to be a straight LukeR construction, a combination of terms well-attested in LukeR activity elsewhere,[29] than such a reminiscence. If he knew it his reason for dropping it would not have been sensitivity to the overall structure of the tradition, for which he showed little respect in reversing the order of the second and third episodes. But if he had known it, would he have dropped it?

Reception of the word of God is throughout Luke-Acts a major theme. That word is a word of divine disclosure,[30] ultimately expressed through the word of Jesus[31] and the gospel.[32] Intended to be heard, guarded and done, it represents 'words of life' (Acts 5:20). And life in the ultimate sense includes for Luke an existence which is not defined by what is owned or, for that matter, eaten (Luke 12:15, 19). Given this very heavy Lucan emphasis, which would be served well by the inclusion of the final part of Deut 8:3, it is extremely difficult to envisage a Lucan excision from an original Matt 4:4b.

Are there any other supports for the hypothesis of Lucan use of Matthew? Goulder believes that there are two such, one verbal, the other thematic.[33]

In the first case he argues that Luke 4:8 quotes word for word the MattR modification of Deut 6:13 in Matt 4:10, following the LXX(B) reading φοβηθήσῃ and explaining the LXX(A) reading προσκυνήσεις . . μόνῳ as an assimilation to the gospels. With MattR usage of προσκυνεῖν and μόνος in the background, the case is for Lucan dependence on MattR and therefore on Matthew.

Long ago Krister Stendahl warned that the LXX(A) reading 'cannot simply be dismissed as a correction from the NT; it may render the Greek text as the NT knew it'.[34] This is supported

---

[28]*Pace* Schürmann, *Lukasevangelium I* 210 and Goulder, *Luke I* 292.

[29]ἐκπορεύομαι: Luke 3:7; 4:37, and in narrative statements in Acts 9:28; 19:12; 25:4; ἐκ(ἀπὸ) τοῦ στόματος αὐτοῦ(σου): Luke 11:54; 19:22; 22:71.

[30]Luke 1:38; 2:29; 3:2.

[31]Luke 5:1; 8:11 diff Mark 4:14; 8:21 diff Mark 3:35; 11:28.

[32]Acts *passim*.

[33]*Luke I* 294–6.

by the undisputed occurrence of the pairing προσκυνεῖν/λατρεύειν elsewhere in the LXX of Deuteronomy.[35] But more important than that is the fact that προσκυνεῖν in the quotation in Matt 4:10 is demanded by προσκυνήσῃς in the temptation itself in Matt 4:9 – in just the same way, in fact, as ἄρτος in the quotation in Matt 4:4 is demanded by ἄρτος in the temptation in Matt 4:3. In both cases the words concerned were not optional extras, to be included if the evangelist so chose, and are therefore not analogous to the MattR cases of προσκυνεῖν.[36] They are of the very fabric of the tradition. Consequently the occurrence of προσκυνεῖν in Luke 4:8 only demonstrates Lucan use of Matthew if the whole of the tradition is a Matthaean creation. This conclusion is, of course, the one which Goulder favours, but this means biting off rather more than many advocates of Luke's indebtedness to Matthew may wish to chew. As far as the word μόνῳ is concerned, it expresses a contrast which Deut 6:14 originally articulated; an exclusive worship would seem to be demanded by the context in Matt 4:8–10/Luke 4:5–8, and therefore essential to the form of the quotation; and already in Matt 4:4/Luke 4:4 the word has been used in the interest of the idea of exclusiveness.

The thematic argument runs as follows: Matt 4:1–11 contrasts Israel's failures and Jesus' victories. This is 'a theme which is not of great significance on its own (but which) does gain greatly in point if it is part of a larger canvas in which Jesus fulfils Israel's history; and it is this larger picture which is supplied in Matthew's Gospel'.[37] Fulfilment is here understood as repetition or recapitulation: like Israel Jesus went down to Egypt, escaped a tyrannical king's slaughter of the innocents, received the divine word to return home after the death of those who threatened his life, and fulfilled the prophecy of Hos 11:1. In short, what Matt 4:1–11 says is what Matthew 2 says, indeed what Matthew himself creatively says.

But is the Jesus/Israel parallelism what Matt 4:1–11 is about? In order to reach that conclusion Goulder declares that the order of the Exodus events, by virtue of its conformity to Matthew's

---

[34] *The School of St Matthew* (ASNU 20; 2nd ed.; Lund: Gleerup, 1967) 89.
[35] See 11:16; 17:3; 30:17.
[36] Matt 8:2; 9:18; 14:33; 15:25; 20:20.
[37] *Luke* I 295–6.

14

order, is more important than the Deuteronomic citations which are 'in reverse order, and so probably not significant'.[38] But the situation of Jesus (and remember that it was the situations of Jesus which were said to match the situations of Israel in Matt 2) – the situation of Jesus only matches that of Israel in the first temptation. Therefore it is the open appeal to Deuteronomy rather than some hidden appeal to Exodus which is formative for the three episodes involving Jesus. It is, as Ulrich Luz rightly emphasizes,[39] Jesus' obedience as the Son of God to the word of God in the Old Testament which is presented in those episodes. His testing at the outset of his activity serves, as in other parallel cases,[40] to define and establish his status and his fitness to perform his designated function. He personally is therefore the focus. His temptations are neither those of Israel nor those of Christians (the latter point, but not the former, is rightly stressed by Goulder), but emphatically *his* temptations. We must add that the third episode, which must on formal grounds be the most critical, gives no encouragement to a Jesus/Israel correspondence, for the gift of the kingdoms and their glory is appropriate, and only appropriate, for a distinct individual and a potentially kingly figure. Israel simply does not come into the reckoning. And the tradition which matches that of the third temptation is the secondary editorial stratum of the *Jubelruf*, not a passage attested by Matthew alone, but a double tradition passage: 'All things have been delivered to me by my Father . . .' (Matt 11:27). Just as Matt 11:27 picks up, and goes far beyond, ideas present in 11:25–26, providing not only a christological commentary [41] but such evidence of layers as will prevent Matt 11:25–27 being regarded as a single-stage creation, so also Matt 4:1–11, however closely the evangelist may have kept to a source, cannot be so assimilated to Goulder's understanding of the theology of the evangelist as to derive from no other source at all.

We have been discussing a tradition in which Matthew and Luke are very close to one another, and therefore one whose Q

[38]*Luke I* 295.
[39]*Matthew 1–7* 185.
[40]Cf. the survey by Kloppenborg, *Formation* 256–62.
[41]J. Wanke, 'Kommentarworte. Älteste Kommentierungen von Herrenworten', *BZ* 24 (1980) 208–33, esp. p. 218.

version will, as set out by advocates of that hypothesis, inevitably be close to Matt 4:1–11. That closeness cannot therefore be a handicap. What is a help is the evidence of an underlying structure which Matthew has disturbed by extending an OT quotation and which Luke has damaged by transposing its second and third sections. In short, the Q hypothesis does more justice to the data than the theory of Matthaean creativity.

3. The Beatitudes. Matt 5:3–12/Q 6:20b–23.

For both Matthew and Luke the beatitudes serve to introduce, and therefore to control, the first extended discourse by Jesus. The word 'extended' must be emphasized, because of course the announcement in Nazareth (Luke 4:18–21) is programmatic for the third evangelist, yet in itself it is the briefest indication of major themes for the mission as a whole. For Luke, as for Matthew, the detailed unfolding of the teaching of Jesus has still to begin. For him therefore, as for Matthew, it is to be expected that the balance and the priorities of Jesus' teaching for their respective communities will be disclosed by means of the beatitudes. Any definition of either evangelist's redactional activity which does not give this fact due recognition will be problematic.

Advocates of the Q hypothesis not infrequently introduce at this point the additional refinement of Q^{Mt}. The effect of this is to assign four of the five beatitudes which are unique to Matthew, namely those concerned with the meek, the merciful, the pure, and the peacemakers (vv. 5, 7, 8, 9), to a later version of Q and not to the original version nor indeed to MattR.[42] This refinement is a second-order development of the Q hypothesis, and may or may not be required by the evidence. The first-order question whether the Q hypothesis itself is inferior to the alternative view that Luke used Matthew must first be answered. And the nub of the problem is this. If Luke used Matthew we are required to view as credible an extremely drastic shortening and the removal of several themes which one might have

[42]See Davies-Allison, *Matthew I* 121; Luz, *Matthew 1–7* 226–9; Sato, *Prophetie* 48.

expected Luke to favour. In the form proposed by Goulder we are asked to accept that Matthew was responsible for creating a tradition marked by serious internal tensions, and that Luke only partly corrected them.

The internal tensions in Matthew should first be noted. First, the eight short beatitudes are clearly intended to be clasped by the two sayings which share the apodosis 'for theirs is the kingdom of heaven' (vv. 3, 10). But those two sayings are divided from one another by their protases' treating in the one case a state to which anyone would aspire, being 'poor in spirit', and in the other case a state to which no one would aspire, and from which everyone would seek release, being 'persecuted for righteousness'. This tension is not unrelated to another oddity, the unnecessarily repeated coverage of persecution (vv. 10, 11–12). Second, the collection as a whole is not uniform: sometimes piety and principled action are treated (vv. 3, 5–9), sometimes adverse and unhappy human experiences (vv. 4, 10). Third, within the six describing approved conduct there is an overlap, since meekness (v. 5) is the same as poverty in spirit (v. 3). Fourth, there is a discrepancy between those sayings whose apodoses envisage the future experience of the age to come (vv. 3, 4, 7, 8, 10) and those which envisage an experience in the present age (vv. 5, 6, 9). To these tensions must of course be added that between all the short beatitudes and the subsequent long one. The short sayings have no reference to the person of Jesus, but the long one (vv. 11–12) does. Such tensions are normally accepted as evidence of editorial interference, maybe even a sign that more than one literary level or stage of development is discernible, but certainly not that one writer has been engaged in single-stage creative work.

Tension is also observable between Matt 5:3–12 and material elsewhere in Matthew. In Matt 11:5 a summary of Jesus' activity is provided, a summary so important to Matthew that all the miracles listed have been assembled in the preceding narrative. The only preceding material which feeds into the statement that 'the poor have the gospel preached to them' is Matt 5:3 where, contrary to Matthew's normal implication that poverty really is poverty (cf. 19:21; 26:9, 11), we are faced with something different, 'poverty in spirit'. Goulder argues that Matthew is glossing, not Q but Isaiah 61, to 'make sure that all this is taken on the proper spiritual level',[43] but Isaiah 61 is in mind in Matt 11:5, and poverty there cannot be taken on a spiritual level as if the preaching of the gospel were directed at the poor in spirit. In short, if Matt 5:3 is a glossing of Isaiah 61 it is an *improper* spiritual glossing, and the problem of the tension between 5:3 and 11:5 remains. It seems to call for a rather obvious, though different, literary solution.

The three beatitudes in Luke 6:20b–21 create at first sight a different impression. As they stand they are thematically homogeneous, not merely in dealing with aspects of human suffering rather than aspects of virtue and piety, but above all in dealing with the single problem of poverty viewed from three angles. For the hungry and the sorrowful repeatedly emerge as none other than the poor.[44] So far, so good. But when we ask who the poor are, we begin to discover a further set of tensions. Under the influence of Luke 6:20a, 'he lifted up his eyes on his disciples, and said . . .', it would be possible to follow Goulder's suggestion that the poor are disciples, and even that poverty is in Luke's view an inevitable characteristic of disciples.[45] This suggestion is part of an extended argument that the Lucan version of the beatitudes is part of a unified section, 6:20–38, 'about the poverty and the persecution which a disciple must expect'.[46] But here we encounter a major inconsistency. Disciples are not for Luke confined to the ranks of the poor. Even those addressed elsewhere in 6:20–38 are told: 'give to every one who begs from you; and of him that takes away your goods do not ask them again' (6:30). In an indisputably LukeR section this point is pressed relentlessly by the evangelist: 'And if

[43]C. M. Tuckett and M. D. Goulder, 'The Beatitudes: A Source-critical Study', *Nov T* 25 (1983) 193–216, esp. p. 209.

[44]See below, p. 18.

[45]*Luke I* 349.

[46]*Luke I* 348–9. Goulder asserts at this point that the first part of the sermon, 6:20–38, 'proceeds in a series of fours: four Beatitudes; four Woes; the response to enemies, those who hate, curse, abuse; to those who hit, take, beg and take; the Golden Rule, loving, benefiting, lending; judging, condemning, releasing and giving. The end takes up the beginning, 6:20, 38.' This neat quartet-defined structure is not quite how the text turns out: v. 31 does not belong with vv. 32–34, which are shown by v. 35 to form a trio picking up vv. 27ab and v. 30; v. 36 has been overlooked; the correspondence suggested between v. 20 and v. 38, (cf. also *Luke I* 366–7), is obscure, as is the proposed *inclusio* between the fall of the blind, v. 39, and the fall of the house, v. 49, (*Luke I* 348).

you lend to those from whom you hope to receive, what credit is that to you? Even sinners lend to sinners, to receive as much again. But ... lend, expecting nothing in return ...' (6:34, 35b). This evidence, of precisely the sort which Goulder assembles a little later on to urge that the disciples of Jesus and the members of the early Church were not poor,[47] suffices to show here that the Christians addressed by Luke, just like many Christians portrayed in Acts, are not all poor. Equally, there is no evidence that Luke sees discipleship as a life of hunger and sorrow.[48] So Goulder's suggestion that the Lucan beatitudes are 'restricted to the demandingness of discipleship' falters. But if there is one tension between the Lucan beatitudes and their context there is another actually within the beatitudes themselves. The protases have, as Goulder rightly observes,[49] to be understood as third-person formulations, whereas the apodoses are in the second-person form. The third-person form is much more suitable for a general and unspecific audience, the second-person form necessarily for a very specific and defined one. The tension between the two suggests some ambivalence about the equation between poverty and discipleship. Not all poor persons are disciples, and not all disciples are poor persons. Some may be, but some are not. To those who are, the beatitudes on the poor are a message of hope. But to those who are not, there is scope for something else to be said. And this makes it all the more necessary to press the point made by Christopher Tuckett that 'Luke appears to have an interest in many of the themes of these extra (Matthaean) beatitudes, and hence it is not easy to see why he should have omitted them'.[50] This point merits being spelt out more fully.

If the disciples addressed by the discourse are not exclusively the poor there is room in the discourse, *and most suitably in the beatitudes*, to say something about topics other than poverty. And for all that Luke is concerned about the gospel for the poor, he has other concerns as well. The study of those concerns reveals

[47]*Luke I* 357.

[48]Cf. Luke 8:1–3; 10:5–8. The principle about guest lists set out in Luke 14:13–14 for the benefit of the ruler of the Pharisees, 14:1, is shown by 14:21 to be of wider applicability, doubtless among Christians, who are therefore shown to include persons in a position to provide help for the hungry as well as for the poor.

[49]*Luke I* 350–1.

the high value he places on some of the attitudes and actions applauded so loudly by the beatitudes he does not include.

Take the theme of righteousness, so prominent in Matt 5:3–12. Goulder declares that 'Luke elsewhere lacks Matthew's zeal for righteousness'.[51] Not so: even the statistics tell the story of Luke's preoccupation with this theme: 17–2–11 + 6 for δίκαιος, 7–0–1 + 4 for δικαιοσύνη, 2–0–5 + 2 for δικαιόω, and 6–0–16 + 3 for the δίκη group. It represents for him the traditional piety which he prizes (Luke 1:6, 17; 2:25; 23:50) and which is rewarded by the experience of the gospel (Acts 10:35), indeed it *is* the gospel (Acts 13:10). It is the relationship established by God through the gospel (Acts 13:38–39), it is epitomized by that Jesus who is the centre of the gospel (Luke 23:47; Acts 3:14; 7:52), it is the essence of those divine actions which are recognized by the spiritually alert and receptive (Luke 7:29, 35). To exert oneself in terms of rightousness or, as it might be put, to hunger and thirst for righteousness reflects the supreme religious priority as far as Luke is concerned. How extraordinary that he should remove it, not once but twice (Matt 5:6, 10)! But did he?

---

[50]'Beatitudes', 200. Goulder, 'Beatitudes', 208, detects a typical Lucan tendency to shorten and diversify long Matthaean structures – here by splitting Matthew's eight beatitudes into four beatitudes and four woes. But Matt 5:3–12 and Luke 6:20b–26 each occupy 20 lines of Greek text, and 'splitting' – a quite appropriate word to use for the subdivision of woes in Luke 11/Matt 23 – is hardly the right word when the Lucan beatitudes and woes are symmetrical in content 'four and four'. Goulder also points to the shortening of the Marcan collection of seed parables in Luke 8:4–18, the omission of Marcan teaching on two Lucan favourite topics of prayer and faith, and the omission of the whole Long Omission in spite of some of its contents, e.g. Mark 7:24–30, being very congenial. But (i) the seed parables dropped from Mark 4 consist of the mustard seed parable which almost certainly came as one of a pair to Luke 13:18–21 by a non-Marcan and non-Matthaean route, while the seed growing secretly is just as likely to have been regarded as inessential by Luke as by Matthew. In any case, trios of parables occur elsewhere in Luke in extended teaching sections, cf. 12:22–59, so the example given is not significant. (ii) The omission of teaching on prayer and faith presumably means that there is no place found for Mark 11:20–25. But it would have been surprising if a place had been found. The equivalent of the cursing of the fig tree, to which the sayings about faith and prayer are attached, had already been used, 13:6–9, and matching sayings about prayer and faith have also already been used, 11:9, 10; 17:5–6. (iii) It is not at all difficult to understand why Luke might omit Mark 7:24–30 as being a good deal less congenial to a participant in the Gentile mission than the variant tradition in Matt 8:5–13/Luke 7:1–10.

[51]'Beatitudes', 209.

Take the theme of meekness, present only in Matthew's gospel (3–0–0 + 0), but represented also by its synonym humility for readers of that gospel, among whom we are bidden to include Luke. The divine reversal of the situation of the humble, particularly if it stemmed from humiliation, was eloquently acclaimed in the magnificat (Luke 1:48, 52). So important was the humiliation of the proud and the exaltation of the humble that such an affirmation was twice attached to key parables (Luke 14:11; 18:14). Unsurprisingly, humility is the ideal demeanour of the Lord's servant (Acts 20:19). Against that background one has to observe that the excision of the idea of meekness would be an odd thing for Luke to carry out. But did he?

Take the theme of mercy, unmistakably a Lucan favourite and for him the equivalent of love (10:37, cf. 10:27; 11:42 diff Matt 23:23). Drawing upon tradition he constructs four pleas for mercy (16:24; 17:13; 18:38, 39; cf. Mark 10:47, 48) and highlights in his canticles the prospect of the merciful action of God (1:50, 54, 72, 78; cf. 1:58). Mercy as human action is specially expressed in almsgiving (ἐλεημοσύνη, 11:41; 12:33; Acts 9:36; 10:2, 4, 31), which God 'remembers' in the most approving and dynamic fashion. The correlation of human and divine acts of mercy is plainly woven into the very fabric of the Lucan understanding, and in just the way envisaged by Matt 5:7. That Luke should remove such an essential theme from the beatitudes is almost inconceivable. But did he?

Take the theme of the cleansed heart (Matt 5:8). Repeatedly concerned in his gospel with the cleansing of lepers (4:27; 5:12, 13; 7:22; 17:14, 17), the evangelist uses one such case, Naaman, as a powerful illustration of surprising divine freedom in choosing the beneficiaries of grace.[52] Passing by the extended discussion of external and internal cleanness in Mark 7:1–23, he nevertheless shows that he knows it by echoing Mark 7:1–2 in Luke 11:37–38, and proceeds to move the woe concerning cleansed vessels to the first position in the sequence of woes (11:39–41/Matt 23:25–26). Fuller treatment was being held back until the dramatic test-case of Cornelius. Here was exhibited a

---

[52]See D. R. Catchpole, 'The Anointed One in Nazareth', *From Jesus to John. Essays on Jesus and New Testament Christology in honour of M. de Jonge* (ed. M. C. de Boer; Sheffield: JSOT, 1993) 229–49, esp. pp. 245–6.

divine cleansing which set aside the traditional Jewish definition (Acts 10:15 = 11:9). Precisely as a commentary on that incident it became possible to legitimize the Gentile mission by the principle that God had '*cleansed* their *hearts* by faith'. This same Luke, who does not keep everything to do with the Gentile mission in reserve for Acts, would hardly have set aside the beatitude of Matt 5:8.

Take the theme of peacemaking (Matt 5:9). No evangelist emphasizes peace more than Luke does (4–1–14 + 7). No evangelist so equates peace with the gospel (Acts 10:36), or so clearly sees the work of Jesus as epitomizing a peace transcending that which is exchanged in normal everyday human greetings (10:4b-6). For him, in spite of the divisions which are intrinsic to the work of Jesus (Luke 12:51), and indeed (though he wishes to play them down) the life of the church, it is peace which is at the heart of the gospel's penetration of the world (Luke 2:14; 19:38, 42). The overcoming of enmity by action is precisely what the carefully structured section 6:27–35 is about. That being so, it is hard to envisage Luke's discarding of Matt 5:9.

We have seen that Matt 5:3–10, 11–12 as it stands is internally dislocated and replete with themes which Luke would be unlikely to pass by, especially in the first extended discourse he presents. We have also seen that Luke's parallel version shows evidence of a certain amount of stress and strain, most notably in the relationship between the three short beatitudes and the narrative setting (Luke 6:20a) and the long beatitude which follows (Luke 6:22–23). On the other hand, the Lucan trio of short beatitudes is marked by an impressive homogeneity and harmony. It would be an extraordinarily happy coincidence that Luke should find in his dislocated and inconsistent source the raw material for so integrated a proclamation as Luke 6:20b, 21ab contains. That being so, one has to ask whether there might be 'a better way', speaking tradition historically, than that which opponents of Q are compelled to choose. And indeed there is. Detailed arguments for an alternative treatment will be presented at a later stage, but we already have sufficient evidence to favour the view that (i) Luke 6:20b-21 represents the earliest stratum in the tradition;[53] (ii) Matt 5:11–12/Luke 6:22–23 is the first of the superimposed strata; (iii) Matt 5:5, 7–9 constitute either a pre-Matthaean expansion in advance of the MattR addition in Matt 5:10, or, together with Matt 5:10 and other small adjustments, a more sweeping MattR revision; (iv) Luke has for his part made minor changes of no great moment. The incoherence of the data within the tradition, the inconsistency of the reconstruction of the history of the tradition on the basis of Luke's use of Matthew, and the coherence and consistency of the alternative reconstruction on the basis of the Q hypothesis, may all be fairly claimed as support for that hypothesis.

Before we leave the beatitudes one further point should be underlined. It should not be forgotten that on the matter of poverty a gap has been found separating the outlook of Q from the outlook of Matthew. Q was concerned about the poor: the position of the trio of beatitudes (Q 6:20b, 21) at the start of the inaugural discourse puts that beyond doubt. But where is there any sign of Matthaean energy and commitment in this area? True, he adopts here a tradition, there a tradition, on poverty. But he does nothing constructive with any of them and is clearly happier with piety than with poverty. He even slides past Jesus' own words, 'Whenever you will, you can do good to them.'[54]

4. Turning the Other Cheek. Matt 5:38–40/Q 6:29.

This is a classic case of confused presentations by both Matthew and Luke, neither of whom can be regarded as preserving the earliest form of the tradition. On the other hand, both combine to enable us to reach back to an unconfused version which must have been in a shared source.

A suitable starting point is the fact that Matt 5:38–39a alone

[53]It is no necessary part of the literary analysis that the three short beatitudes in that earliest stratum derive from Jesus, and therefore no argument against the Q hypothesis that they do not: against Goulder, *Luke I* 356. However, if those beatitudes were a summary of the gospel of Jesus there is plenty of evidence of the sort of economic exploitation and poverty which would give relevance to that gospel, cf. R. A. Horsley, *Bandits, Prophets, and Messiahs* (New York: Harper & Row, 1988).

[54]E. Bammel, 'πτωχός', *TDNT* 6.888–915, esp. p. 904, put the matter precisely and perceptively thus when commenting on Matt 5:3, 5: 'The emphasis is shifted from the material sphere to the spiritual and hence the religious sphere. The beatitude is the first and programmatic πτωχός saying of the Evangelist; it shows that he is not greatly interested in the problems of actual want.'

uses plural forms, while Matt 5:39b does not. Therefore more than one level of tradition is involved. In what follows, Matt 5:39b describes one of the most serious forms of insult, a blow on the right cheek. The background texts are not just those which describe in general terms an insulting blow on the cheek (1 Kgs 22:24; Isa 50:6; Lam 3:30; Mic 5:1), but rather more significantly those which speak of the blow with the back of the hand (so, 1 Esdr 4:30). This insult is rated one of the most serious possible, along with tearing a person's ear, pulling out his hair, spitting so that the spittle touches him, loosening a woman's hair in public, and pulling someone's cloak off him (*m. B. Qam.* 8:6).[55]

The structure of Matt 5:39b–42 is important. Verses 39b, 41 have the form ὅστις σε + present/future indicative verb, leading to an imperative. The intervening verses 40, 42 have the form τῷ + dative participle, leading to an imperative. This suggests an attempt to achieve some kind of unified structure. However, it does not really work, for v. 42 stands apart from vv. 39b–41: it is not linked to the preceding trio by καί in the way that they are linked to one another, and it does not follow the pattern 'if one, then a second' as they do. But it does contain two demands in some sort of parallelism, the second of which refers to ὁ θέλων ἀπὸ σου. With this there corresponds the similar reference to ὁ θέλων σοι in v. 40, which may indicate indirectly a Matthaean awareness that, as with v. 42ab, so also with vv. 39b, 40, there was an original linkage and parallelism which has been obscured somewhat by the presence of v. 41. When allowance is made for the Matthaean effort to integrate that which should not be integrated, it is possible to recognize that the first two statements, those concerning the physical blow and the clothing, are properly regarded as a separate pair. They should be isolated not only from what follows but also from what precedes, namely v. 39a which was intended editorially to set the scene for v. 39b in legal process. Nevertheless, as it stands, v. 40 is in crucial respects in no sort of harmony or parallelism with v. 39b. The problem is not insult, and the person addressed is not the offended person but the offender, that is, the poor debtor whose refusal of the pledge, the shirt (χιτών) envisaged in Exod 22:26–27

---

[55]For the full text, see p. 111.

and Deut 24:10–13, causes the creditor to go to court to obtain it.

When we turn to Luke 6:29a we find that the insult is described in less precise terms as simply a blow on the cheek, that is, not clearly one of the most serious offences listed in *m. B. Qam.* 8:6.

The four constituent parts of Luke 6:29, 30 are also intended to form a unity. This is clear from the initial phrases which run dative participle/ καὶ ἀπὸ τοῦ αἴροντος . . ./ dative participle/ καὶ ἀπὸ τοῦ αἴροντος . . . This time it is a genuine unity up to a point. For in both halves the person addressed is the offended party. But what sort of offence? The primary action involves the cloak (ἱμάτιον), and uses the verb αἴρειν, which is suggestive of violence, cf. Cant 5:7: 'They beat me, they wounded me, they took away (LXX: ἦραν) my mantle.' And such a violent snatching of someone's cloak appears in the list of most serious insults assembled in *m. B. Qam.* 8:6!

The situation is therefore as follows. The content of the first part of a bipartite saying in Matthew matches the content of the second part of the comparable saying in Luke. Both Matthew and Luke have in different ways marred it. If Luke used Matthew he reduced the significance of the insult in his 6:29a, but contrariwise introduced *de novo* the most serious form of insult in his 6:29b. He, the evangelist who is said by Goulder[56] to be fashioning this part of his discourse with the poor in mind, removed a reference to the situation of the poor man faced with legal procedure.

Contrary to such a reconstruction, it is more likely that we have chanced upon an original saying which was concerned with the subject of insult and treated it by focussing on two of the most damaging forms that insult might take. Of course, for the parallelism in Q 6:29 to work, we require Matthew's δεξιός to have stood in Q. That has been disputed[57] on the grounds, first, that after an initial and so extremely hostile attack as a blow on the right cheek the second and less serious follow-up blow on the left cheek becomes anticlimactic, and, second, that a secondary addition of the word δεξιός would be in line with

---

[56]*Luke I* 348.
[57]Luz, *Matthew 1–7* 324–5.

the tendency in the development of tradition towards greater precision (cf. Matt 5:29–30 diff Mark 9:43, 47). These arguments should be set aside. First, the word δεξιός gives the bipartite saying a technical meaning which Matthew himself was obscuring rather than exploiting; second, while Matt 5:29–30 attests a tendency to introduce the word δεξιός, that change is shown by the parallel Matt 18:8–9 to be unnecessary, and the proximity of Matt 5:29–30 and 5:39b to one another suggests that the one is a reminiscence of the other, in this case that the former is a reminiscence of the latter; third, the right-left order is itself the conventional one; and, fourth, the word δεξιός allows Q 6:29 to conform to the recurrent pattern of Jesus' teaching, which often takes as its starting-point the most trivial offence *by* the Christian disciple or the most extreme offence *against* him. On this basis we can go on to note that Matthew has set the saying in a new legal context and at the same time partially adapted it to deal with a quite different problem. Luke, for his part, has made a less far-reaching change, but he has shown in the process his lack of understanding of the original concern of the saying. The Q hypothesis enables us coherently to reconstruct the history of the tradition in a way that the hypothetical Lucan use of Matthew does not.

5. Love of Enemies. Matt 5:43–48/Q 6:27–28, 32–36.

The demand for love and prayer is set out in absolute terms without any supporting argument (vv. 44–45). The significance, but not the incentive or the reward, is presented in v. 45 as sonship. That sonship is almost certainly not eschatological or a matter of becoming:[58] it is a matter of being and the open realization of that which *is*. Those who act lovingly show themselves to be sons of God in that they behave as he does (Ps 146:9). Just as Sir 4:10 sees sonship in very practical terms as the imitation of God's care for the widow and the orphan, so Matt 5:44–45 sees sonship in very practical terms as the imitation of God's benevolence towards the wicked.

The saying in vv. 44–45 is so complete in itself that the

---

[58]Against Luz, *Matthew 1–7* 343.

addition of extra material in vv. 46–47 suggests the existence here of strata of tradition, specifically that the former is earlier than the latter. That means that vv. 44–45 are on the whole pre-Matthaean, though one feature immediately arouses suspicion as possible MattR interference, namely, the references to the good and the righteous. For one thing, the logic of the saying demands only the evil as the beneficiaries of divine action, since only the enemies and persecutors are the beneficiaries of human action; for another, MattR is plainly responsible for a similar and even more artificial formulation in 22:10, 'both bad and good'.

The sayings in vv. 46–47 are strikingly discordant with what precedes them. (i) An argument is produced in support of the behaviour demanded, whereas previously there had been no argument. (ii) A future perspective is introduced for the first time in the form of a reward for those who behave better than certain despised groups of persons, the tax collectors and the Gentiles. The last named will soon be encountered again in another saying which looks gratuitous and secondary in its own setting (Matt 6:32a).[59] (iii) Special problems are introduced by the saying about 'greeting only your brothers'. First, failure to greet is scarcely on a par with enmity and persecution. Second, if love is the theme of v. 46 in the light of v. 44a, prayer should be, but is not, the theme of v. 47 in the light of v. 44b. Third, it makes little sense to speak of Gentiles greeting only their brothers, since brotherhood presumes a religiously defined community as in the usage of Lev 19:17–18. Fourth, not greeting '*only* your brothers' is of a piece with the suspicious element in v. 45, the presence of the good and the righteous alongside the evil and the unrighteous. So, all in all, vv. 46–47 are confirmed as secondary in relation to vv. 44–45, and in the case of v. 47 a singularly maladroit addition.

A sideglance at Luke 6:27–28, 32–35 at this point brings into view several features which are extremely likely to be LukeR: the punning χάρις ... χρηστός ... ἀχάριστοι over against Matthew's μισθός (cf. Luke 6:35) and his 'concrete pictures';[60] the third example of lending, provoked not by vv. 27–28 but by the originally separate v. 30/Matt 5:42; the uniform allusion

[59]See p. 34.
[60]Luz, *Matthew 1–7* 339.

to sinners over against Matthew's Gentiles and tax collectors; the transformation of present sonship into that future sonship which can count as a reward. But several other Lucan features appear more primitive than their Matthaean counterparts. Thus, first, 'doing good' is appropriate as a synonym for 'loving'[61] at just the point where 'greeting' is so inappropriate.[62] Second, the relevant range of God's action includes the ungrateful and evil and not the good as well – a much more startling and restrictive reference. One can understand a Luke to Matthew movement but scarcely one from Matthew to Luke. Correspondingly the matching absence of 'only' is more primitive.

The situation in Matt 5:44–47 is therefore that there is a primary layer (vv. 44–45), which cannot be attributed to Matthew's creativity, and a secondary layer (vv. 46–47) which is at crucial points preserved in a more primitive form by Luke, and cannot be attributed to Matthew's creative activity either. And Luke's distinctiveness over against Matthew cannot be accounted for in terms of Luke's use of Matthew. Once again, is there 'a better way'? Yes, a development from a pre-Q stage to an editorial-Q stage and then subsequently to MattR and LukeR stages.

6. The Lord's Prayer. Matt 6:9–13/Q 11:2–4.

The Lord's Prayer is set in Matthew within a paraenetic section directed positively to disciples and polemically against hypocrites who are allegedly concerned only with the outward appearance of righteousness. Three topics are discussed – almsgiving, prayer and fasting – and each of the three units comes to a conclusion with the assurance that 'the Father who sees in secret will reward you' (Matt 6:4, 6, 18).

Within this tripartite scheme the section 6:7–15 reads as an interruption, and this would normally lead us to infer the presence of source material. Further, there is within 6:7–15 additional

---

[61]Luz, *Matthew 1–7* 341: 'One must think not primarily of friendly feelings but of concrete deeds.'

[62]Goulder, *Luke I* 364, in an effort to assign ἀγαθοποιεῖν to LukeR, argues that the evangelist inserted the word in Luke 6:9. But the source of Luke 6:9 is Mark 3:4: ἀγαθὸν ποιῆσαι . . . κακοποιῆσαι. The argument is not secure.

evidence of strata. Matt 6:14–15 is evidently derived from Mark 11:25, but there remain the prayer and its introduction. The paraenetic introduction (6:7–8) also has a polemical thrust, though it criticizes a different group of persons from the hypocrites of 6:1, 5, 16, and it is directed at a different problem, that is, verbosity towards God rather than creating an impression among men. Not only so, it must be a secondary addition to the prayer itself, since the original purpose of the prayer can hardly have been to serve as a model of a certain simple style of praying – that would be to trivialize it – but rather as instruction on what should be prayed. Indeed, Matthew's introductory 'Pray then like this (οὕτως)' is rather less suitable than Luke's 'When you pray, say . . .' (Luke 11:2). Consequently different layers of pre-Matthaean material seem to be before us, and certainly not a uniform creation by the evangelist himself.

When the two versions of the Lord's Prayer are set alongside one another, how easy is it to regard Luke's version as simply an edited version of Matthew's text? Some of the distinctive details of Luke 11:2–4 are readily explicable as LukeR. A change from δὸς .. σήμερον to δίδου . . . τὸ καθ' ἡμέραν would fit Lucan usage elsewhere.[63] Such a change adjusts the prayer to life during an indefinite period of time and removes the urgent tone of Matthew's petition for food. Similarly the prayer for forgiveness prefers the present form ἀφίομεν and relinquishes the symmetry of the two references to debts for the sake of clarifying at the outset that sins are in mind. That which Matthew achieved by adding 'trespasses' to the Marcan saying about forgiveness Luke achieves by internal editing of the prayer itself. In these respects LukeR activity can be discerned, and moreover no sign is conveyed that the Lord's Prayer was to Luke some kind of unalterable holy text. That being so, the crucial question is whether Luke would have reduced the address to the Father, removed the petition for God's will to be done, and removed also the final petition for deliverance from evil.

We have no evidence from Luke's use of Mark that he preferred short references to God as Father. Such an inference can only be made on the basis of Luke's use of Matthew, which is not a given but an opinion.[64] The omission of ἀββᾶ, Mark

---

[63]Cf. 9:23 diff Mark 8:34; 19:47 diff Mark 11:18.

14:36/Luke 22:42, has more to do with the removal of an Aramaism[65] than a dislike of wordiness. The one Marcan reference to 'your Father who is in heaven' (Mark 11:25) occurs in a saying which Luke does not retain. That saying is transferred by Matthew to his 6:14 as a commentary on the prayer for forgiveness in the Lord's Prayer. This makes it easy to see the initial and lengthy invocation of 'our Father who art in heaven' (6:9) as preparation for that same commentary saying. We know that in a different but also closely associated saying Luke was content to retain a reference to 'the heavenly Father' (Matt 7:11/Luke 11:13), just as elsewhere he was content to retain a rather formal and extended invocation of the 'Father, Lord of heaven and earth' in prayer (Matt 11:25/Luke 10:21). So there is no reason to suppose that Luke would have shortened Matt 6:9, had he known it, and every reason to suppose that Matthew is responsible for lengthening an earlier short version.

No opportunity is lost by Matthew in stressing that 'doing the will of my Father who is in heaven' is the ultimate test of religious authenticity.[66] Once again there is a single Marcan reference which proved stimulating to the later evangelist: 'Whoever does the will of God . . .' (Mark 3:35). And it was a modest Matthaean modification of the prayer of the Marcan Jesus in Gethsemane (Mark 14:36) which produced exactly the same wording as in Matt 6:10, 'thy will be done' (Matt 26:42). Since Luke also adopts with slight verbal adjustments the prayer of Mark 14:36, and shows himself elsewhere to be concerned about 'doing the will of the Lord' (Luke 12:47), it is again difficult to see Luke excising the petition that the Father's will be done. It is not a matter of 'dropping this hint of fatalism',[67] and even if it were it would be curious that an evangelist with so strong a sense of the divine should find such a hint unattractive. Although Mark 14:36 and also Acts 21:14 contrast sharply submission to the will of God and what is preferable in human terms, this is not the case in Matt 6:10. So it is hard to see Luke dropping this petition and extremely easy to see Matthew introducing it.

[64]Against Goulder, *Luke II* 496.
[65]Cf. Mark 5:41/Luke 8:54.
[66]Cf. 7:21; 12:50; 18:14; 21:31.
[67]Goulder, *Luke II* 497.

References to evil come easily from Matthew. He is well aware of the opposition of 'the evil one' (Matt 13:19 diff Mark 4:15) and of the constant battle with evil in a variety of forms which is waged in the experience of Jesus and his followers.[68] Here is a threat from outside, yes, and a danger within the community (7:17; 22:10). It is more than credible that the petition 'deliver us from evil' derives from the evangelist. But the same concern for deliverance is clear in Luke's approach, for Jesus brings freedom for the prisoners (4:18; 13:16), that is, deliverance from supernatural evil.[69] The petition in Matt 6:13b would have been very congenial to him.

We conclude that the shorter Lucan version of the Lord's Prayer is more original than the Matthaean version, which was therefore not created by Matthew.[70] The phenomena in Matt 6:1–18 suggest that MattR was responsible for weaving into the anti-Pharisaic fabric of the section as a whole a secondarily extended version of the Lord's Prayer (6:9–13) with a Marcan saying (6:14–15) attached as commentary. The original short form had already received an artificial editorial introduction (6:7–8).[71] Once again the Q hypothesis permits a coherent and consistent reconstruction of the history of a tradition in a way not achieved by the hypothesis that Luke used Matthew.

7. Cares about Earthly Things. Matt 6:25–33/Q 12:22–31.

If the Matthaean version of the tradition is taken as base we can again test whether it contains one stratum or more.

First, Matt 6:25 begins διὰ τοῦτο λέγω ὑμῖν and needs therefore to be a concluding inference from what went before. Yet this it cannot be, since (i) the contrast between the service of God and that of mammon (v. 24) is no counterpart of the contrast between recognition of the superiority of the ψυχή/σῶμα on the one hand and concern about food and clothing on the other (v. 25); (ii) formally v. 25 is not the conclusion of one section but the beginning of another, as is shown by the

[68]Matt 5:45; 9:4; 12:39; 13:38; 16:4.
[69]Luke 7:21; 8:2; 11:26; Acts 19:11–12.
[70]Against Goulder, *Luke II* 496.
[71]On this, see further, pp. 225–6.

31

recurrence of its characteristic terminology in v. 31. So there comes into view a line of demarcation between traditions at vv. 24/25, and an unsuccessful attempt to achieve linkage in v. 25a. If that attempt to achieve linkage is to be credited to Matthew in one sense, it was a debit in another sense.

Second, Matt 6:25a issues a demand to avoid anxiety about ψυχή/σῶμα in respect of food and clothing, and v. 25b supports the demand with an argumentative question: 'Is not the ψυχή more than food, and the σῶμα than clothing?' Food and clothing here represent the absolutely basic necessities of life,[72] and ψυχή/σῶμα represents the human person as an indivisible whole.[73] The connection between v. 25a and v. 25b is, however, defective. (i) In the former, concern about food and clothing is an expression of anxiety about the ψυχή/σῶμα, whereas in the latter it is an antithetical alternative. (ii) As an antithetical alternative, concern for the ψυχή/σῶμα becomes the basis of a painfully weak argument, for recognition that the person is more important than the means of subsistence does not by any means exclude concern about the latter.[74] Even supreme concerns with Torah on the part of the rabbis, or the gospel on the part of Paul (1 Thess 2:9), did not preclude activity designed to secure ordinary human subsistence.[75] (iii) The overlap between v. 25a and v. 31 is too strong to be discounted. It extends to common terminology and formal agreement in being followed by an argument (v. 32) and a hint of what should be the higher concern (v. 33). But vv. 32, 33 do not overlap at all with v. 25b in the content of their argument, which means that either v. 25b or vv. 32, 33 (in whole or in part) may excite suspicion as a secondary development. Of the two v. 25b is the more vulnerable, since v. 32 at least picks up the logic of the preceding argument from the natural world and the care of God (as does v. 31 with οὖν), thus permitting v. 31 to introduce a concluding summary which matches an introductory demand in v. 25a. So v. 25b looks like a secondary addition and further evidence of the existence of strata.

[72] Cf. Sir 29:21; 39:26 – the term used there is ζωή.
[73] K. H. Rengstorf, *Das Evangelium nach Lukas* (NTD 3; Göttingen: Vandenhoeck & Ruprecht, 1966) 161.
[74] D. Zeller, *Die weisheitlichen Mahnsprüche bei den Synoptikern* (FB 17; Würzburg: Echter Verlag, 1977) 86–7.
[75] H.-J. Degenhardt, *Lukas Evangelist der Armen* (Stuttgart: Katholisches Bibelwerk, 1965) 84.

Third, Matt 6:27 deals with man's inability, not to add the massive extra amount of a cubit (=0.52m) to his height, but to add the smallest length of time to his life-span. In commenting on a person's life-span v. 27 links up with the subordinate and ancillary reference in v. 30 to the grass of the field with its fleetingly brief period of existence,[76] though the point of emphasis is different. V. 27 envisages a small addition to a life-span of unspecified length, while v. 30 refers to a life-span which is short *in toto*. Now vv. 26, 28–30 match one another very neatly in that (i) both deal with examples from the natural world, in which (ii) none of the normal human activities are involved, on which basis (iii) an appeal can be made by way of the *a minore ad maius* principle, to (iv) the provision of God for certain human persons. On the other hand, v. 27 is a distraction and a deviation away from a straight movement from v. 26 to vv. 28–30. Its man-centred appeal to the ineffectiveness of anxiety is to be contrasted with the God-centred appeal to the inappropriateness of anxiety in the surrounding material. Once again, therefore, evidence of strata within the Matthaean tradition comes into view.[77]

Fourth, Matt 6:30 has Jesus rebuking his audience for ὀλιγοπιστία. But is the tradition as a whole designed to encourage and fortify those who are making a leap of faith in their commitment to Jesus, or to chastise verbally those who are falling short? Nothing in the rest of the material suggests the latter, indeed everything favours the former. The address ὀλιγόπιστοι belongs rather to a secondary stage when every possible form of pressure is proving necessary in order to achieve obedience to an astonishing and unnatural demand.

Fifth, Matt 6:31 introduces a section which corresponds remarkably with the content of what precedes. First, an identical demand is voiced by vv. 25a, 31. Second, when vv. 26, 28–30 affirm God's care in the provision of food and clothing they

[76]Cf. Pss 37:2; 90:5–6; 102:11; 103:15–16; Isa 40:6.

[77]Goulder, *Luke II* 546, counters this by means of a comparison with Matt 5:36 'you cannot make your hair white or black', and Matt 10:30 'but even the hairs of your head are numbered'. It is difficult to see how these examples help his case, for they are indeed in both cases interruptions whose removal leaves visible an earlier layer of tradition. In the first case Jas 5:12 is closer to the pre-Matthaean form, and in the second case the smooth transition from Matt 10:29 to 10:31 is clear for all to see.

lead directly into v. 32, the comparable affirmation of divine awareness of need, now seen as a function of divine Fatherhood. Thus a rounded and complete tradition begins to emerge, comprising at least vv. 25a, 26, 28–30, 31, 32b. The concluding summary has, however, been amplified in v. 32a. (i) Its reference to πάντα τὰ ἔθνη is new and unprovoked by anything that has gone before. (ii) Its logic is alien, in that previously there had been no hint of a requirement to preserve a higher standard of behaviour than that of another less than highly regarded category of persons. (iii) Its position is totally wrong, in that the time for a concluding summary is not the time to introduce another argument. So the presence in v. 32a of another second-ary addition provides yet more evidence of strata within the tra-dition.

Sixth, Matt 6:33 introduces a positive concern which is to take the place of those activities which constitute anxiety in the preceding material. This too should be regarded as secondary.[78] (i) The language of ζητεῖν, as well as πάντα and προστιθέναι, is the language of the secondary additions in v. 32a and v. 27 respectively. (ii) Formally, the unit of tradition which we have isolated reached its conclusion with v. 32b. This is made all the more obvious by the duplication of v. 32b in v. 33b. (iii) Although there are very good reasons for reading the underlying tradition in terms of an implicit expectation of the near kingdom, such a presupposition is only made explicit in v. 33.

To sum up, an essentially form-critical investigation suggests that we have in Matt 6:25a (minus διὰ τοῦτο λέγω ὑμῖν, τῇ ψυχῇ ὑμῶν and τῷ σώματι ὑμῶν), 26, 28–30, 31, 32b a pre-Matthaean unit of tradition. This has at some stage been extended by means of an attempted but poor connection with preceding material (διὰ τοῦτο λέγω ὑμῖν, v. 25a), three extra arguments (vv. 25b, 27, 32a, with the first contributing τῇ ψυχῇ ὑμῶν and τῷ σώματι ὑμῶν v. 25a), and a positive balancing demand (v. 33). It may fairly be claimed that if a form-critical sensitivity to overlaps, interruptions, poor connections and the like produces such a coherent source-critical outcome it will not suffice methodologically to set such evidence aside as Goulder does with the observation that 'weak arguments and connections

[78]Zeller, *Mahnsprüche* 86–7.

are to be found in many writers'.[79] The history of the synoptic tradition was not reconstructed thus, and form-criticism will not go away!

No form-critical investigation is complete without attention being given to the question of a tradition's *Sitz im Leben*. In this case the natural starting point is the pair of illustrations concerning the birds and the lilies. An appeal, typical of the wisdom tradition, is here made to the natural world. The illustrations make contact with the situation of the hearers by referring to activities which are normal and necessary if the basics of human existence are to be produced, male activity in the case of σπείρειν ... θερίζειν ... συνάγειν (v.26), and female activity in the case of κοπιᾶν ... νήθειν v. 28).[80] Yet these activities are seen as expressions of that anxiety which the hearers are required to avoid! This involves a resounding clash with the wisdom tradition which lavishly praises the worker and severely chides the non-worker.[81] Only one explanation seems ready to hand for such a clash. That is, the tradition belongs to a situation which is special in character and short in duration.[82] It belongs to that period of time conditioned by the expectation of an imminent eschatological crisis.[83] It applies to such persons as have abandoned self-sufficiency and independence for the sake of attachment to Jesus – not those who just respond to the message, but those who also associate themselves with the prophetic messenger.

The study of Matt 6:25–33 has served to show that Goulder's proposed Matthaean midrash is not viable.[84] Had it been viable, the very extensive Matthew/Luke verbal overlap would have made Lucan dependence on Matthew an inevitable corollary. Since it is not viable we have two options still open: either Lucan dependence on Matthew, or common dependence on

[79]*Luke II* 547.

[80]Luz, *Matthew 1–7* 405.

[81]See Prov 6:6–8; 10:26; 12:24, 27; 13:4; 15:19; 18:9; 19:15, 24; 20:4; 26:13–16; Sir 2:12; 7:15. In Prov 10:3 it is the righteous that the Lord does not let go hungry, and in 10:4–5 it is made clear that such righteousness involves diligence and is exemplified in harvesting.

[82]See the telling summary by Luz, *Matthew 1–7* 402–3, of the criticisms called forth by this tradition when it is set in any other context.

[83]Hoffmann, *Studien* 41.

[84]*Midrash* 302–4.

earlier material. The balance of probability will be tipped in favour of the latter option if there is evidence of independent Lucan access to the pre-Matthaean stratum, in other words, evidence of greater Lucan primitiveness at points of Matthew/ Luke overlap.

First, within the symmetry of the two illustrations in Matt 6:26, 28–30, several disturbances can be detected. (i) A very specific example 'the lilies of the field' (v. 28) became the basis for a broad generic reference to 'the grass of the field' in the clinching *a minore ad maius* question (v. 30), but the symmetrical section (v. 26) began with a broad generic example, 'the birds of the heaven', and in its corresponding and clinching question used the simple word 'them'. (ii) The person who clothes the flowers was simply 'God' (v. 30), but in the symmetrical section that person was more amply described as 'your heavenly Father'. How should these asymmetries within the symmetry of the tradition as whole be evaluated? An injudicious hankering after cast-iron canons of criticism which can be applied in all circumstances might produce the answer that asymmetry is always more primitive than symmetry, and therefore that in Matt 6:26, 28–30 the asymmetries must be earlier. But that would be to neglect the inseparability of form and content and, in this instance, the consideration that it is of the essence of the tradition that it should originally have been symmetrical. Therefore a different approach is needed. First, then, we would expect a specific example to lie behind 'the birds of the heaven' which would then be evaluated as a redactional generalization shifted from its proper place in the final clinching question, where in turn it had been replaced by 'them'. Given the evidence for such a tendency the words 'of the field' (v. 28), which are wholly unnecessary as definition of 'the lilies', also fall under suspicion. Second, the term 'your heavenly Father' (v. 27) introduces into the discussion of the birds a quite unnecessary and complicating idea which the corresponding 'God' (v. 30) does not. While this reference to God as the Father of those addressed prepares for the similar reference in v. 32, in so doing it robs the latter of a measure of climactic forcefulness. Consequently, one would suppose that the one who provides for birds and flowers would be named as God, and the one who provides for certain human persons would be named as Father.

36

The striking reality which emerges from this discussion is that on the basis of Matthew alone we would reconstruct an earlier version of the tradition which, it turns out, matches exactly what we find in Luke. A specific example is there, that is, the ravens. This citation of the case of the ravens shows that the tradition echoes Job 38:41 and Ps 147:9, where again divine provision of food is the theme. Finally we must note that in Luke the references to the divine provider take precisely the required form 'God . . . God . . . the Father' (Luke 12: 24, 28, 30).

Second, within Matt 6:33 two secondary defects can be detected. One concerns the emphasis laid on what should be sought 'first'. The other concerns the search which is to concentrate on both kingdom and righteousness of God. Now the presence of 'first' indicates priority rather than exclusivity of concern. In context that means that, provided it is kept at a subordinate level, concern about food and clothing remains permissible.[85] Yet the underlying tradition said precisely the opposite, and the whole argument was dedicated to the assertion of an exclusive claim. The word πρῶτον articulates a concern to blunt the sharp edge of eschatological radicalism under the influence of non-eschatological everyday life, and as such it must be classed as secondary. Not only so, we can understand the realism which brings about the insertion of that word, but we can scarcely understand a Lucan move to remove it. Then, next, there is the reference to 'his kingdom and his righteousness'. Talk of 'God's kingdom' is at least at home in this context, even if the saying as a whole is a secondary addition. But talk of 'God's righteousness' certainly is not. As noted in the discussion of the beatitudes,[86] it is an idea which would be superfluous in the underlying tradition, but one which Matthew is happy to add and Luke unlikely to subtract.

Third, the incidence of greater originality in the Lucan version, as outlined in the preceding two sections,[87] might

---

[85]Degenhardt, *Lukas* 85: 'Das Bemühen um anderes is nicht ausgeschlossen.' Goulder, *Luke II* 546, criticizes the view that πρῶτον is 'introduced to lessen the radicalism of Q/Luke' by appealing to Matt 20:16; 21:31; 23:26 as examples of Matthew's use of first/before without such a suggestion. The relevance of the first two is not clear, but the third case is very relevant: Matthew does not wish to suggest in 'first cleanse the inside of the cup and of the plate' that the cleansing of the outside is excluded.

[86]See p. 20.

conceivably be taken as Luke's having recovered, rather than preserved, earlier tradition. But Luke does not appear to have been so alert and sensitive, as can be seen in a further list of examples of his moving away from and (to a degree) spoiling other features of the tradition which have the stamp of originality and have been preserved by Matthew. Thus (i) in a tradition which is commenting upon activity Luke's 'they have neither storehouse nor barn' is less original than Matthew's 'they gather into barns'. (ii) Following the interruption in Matt 6:27 the Matthaean transition, 'And why are you anxious about clothing?' is more likely to be the basis of Luke's 'If then you are not able to do as small a thing as that, why are you anxious about the rest?' than vice versa. Word statistics could point to MattR for ἔνδυμα (7–0–1 + 0), especially in view of 3:4; 7:15; 22:11, 12; 28:3, but in this particular case ἔνδυμα links up with ἐνδύσεσθε (Matt 6:25/Luke 12:22). The Lucan version, on the other hand, makes a far more concerted attempt to integrate the πῆχυς/ ἡλικία saying into the surrounding tradition. The clarification of πῆχυς by means of ἐλάχιστος, the verbal linkage via δύναται-δύνασθε, the extra employment of the *a minore ad maius* argument – all these represent an awareness of a problem, a more considered attempt at solving it, a blurring of the clear line of demarcation between traditions, but a further distraction from the main line of the earliest tradition's argument. (iii) Luke's καὶ ὑμεῖς μὴ ζητεῖτε is less primitive than Matthew's μὴ οὖν μεριμνήσητε (Matt 6:31). Luke has here integrated 12:29, 30, 31 with one another more than was the case in Matthew, but at the cost of damaging the symmetry between the initial and final demands (thus, μὴ μεριμνᾶτε ... μὴ ζητεῖτε). Here then are three examples of LukeR activity, each of which has done some damage to the earliest version of the tradition. Thus it becomes necessary to work back to that earliest version, not only on the basis of Matthew and Luke but also at times in spite of Matthew or Luke.

The better conclusion from all the data therefore seems to be

---

[87]One might add the absence of ἁπάντων (Matt 6:32) and πάντα (Matt 6:33) from Luke 12:30, 31 as further examples of Lucan primitiveness. Matthew has probably added them under the influence of Matt 6:32a/Luke 12:30; Luke with his well known tendency to insert πᾶς formulations would be unlikely to drop either.

that Luke did not depend on Matthew for this tradition. The Q hypothesis sets up a more coherent reconstruction of the history of the tradition. On this showing, both evangelists used and modified an earlier tradition which had itself passed through two stages on its way to both of them. The first, the pre-Q stage, belongs to the setting of discipleship and short-term expectation and incidentally has a strong claim to stem from Jesus himself.[88] It is at home with him and with the disciples who had left their work to follow him. It is most particularly at home with them when they left behind the supports for human life which they might have taken on mission (Q 10:4), and instead went out as itinerant charismatics – here both male and female! – to preach the kingdom, trusting that the divine Father would make provision through the 'sons of peace' (Q 10:5–7). Then there was the second, the Q-editorial stage in the history of the tradition. At this stage we detect a sense that though the original tradition remained authoritative it was clearly posing problems. It remained relevant because the preserving community was a base for further itinerant charismatic mission,[89] but it needed to be bolstered. So a series of additional supporting arguments (and probably also ὀλιγόπιστοι, Q 12:28, since the original tradition was designed to encourage rather than to rebuke) was brought in to bolster instruction and stiffen commitment.

8. The False Prophets. Matt 7:15–20, 21–23/Q 6:43–45, 46; 13:26–27.

The whole section Matt 7:15–20 is carefully constructed out of a number of sayings, each of which is capable of sustaining a separate existence. Together they show every sign of having been brought together with some care and attention to structure.[90] The complementary sayings relating the quality of a tree and the quality of its fruit (vv. 17, 18) are appropriately ordered, so that first the true situation is described (v. 17) and then the opposite and untrue situation (v.18). These sayings are

[88]Luz, *Matthew 1–7* 402.
[89]See pp. 159–60.
[90]Luz, *Matthew 1–7* 439–40.

then suitably framed within the repeated 'You will know them by their fruits' (vv. 16a, 20). Within this structure there are set two further sayings, the first a question concerning grapes/thorns and figs/thistles (v. 16b), whose line of logic is the same as the bad tree/good fruit affirmation (v. 18b), and the second a quotation from John the Baptist (Matt 3:10), which introduces the theme of judgment for the first and only time within this unit. Just as v. 18b is somewhat alien and interruptive, so also the matching v. 16b creates in formal terms an unnecessary disturbance. But in terms of content it, like v. 19, serves Matthew's purpose, in that he is tackling the problem of persons who in his view do not have a record of good deeds. Such persons are destined for the fire of judgment.

It is already apparent in the repeated reference to 'them' (vv. 16a, 20) that Matthew has specific persons in mind, and these persons are defined in v. 15 as prophets who may visit the community. A prediction put into the mouth of Jesus probably represents a present reality for Matthew and his community[91] and one which the evangelist understands as part of the pre-eschatological programme. So these persons *have* now visited the community. The prospect of judgment on them, introduced initially in v. 19, is amplified in vv. 22–23, as is their prophetic profile. It is thus clear that vv. 15–20 and vv. 21–23 are ultimately intended by Matthew to form a single whole.[92] But vv. 21–23 are not entirely smooth running. The overlap between 7:21 and 5:20 suggests heavy MattR involvement, and the singling out of the cry, 'Lord, Lord', a reference to the basic confession made by any Christian rather than the special claim of a particular set of Christians. Correspondingly, the words 'Lord, Lord' are merely incidental in the self-defence of the prophets which follows in 7:22. In that defensive statement the presumption is that an adverse judgment has already been pronounced, but in fact it has not. So the unity of 7:21–23 turns out to be pretty much artificial. Matthew is clearly less worried about that than about bringing 7:21–23 alongside 7:15–20 in order to deal with the threat posed by those Christian prophets

[91]G. Barth, 'Matthew's Understanding of the Law', in G. Bornkamm, G. Barth and H. J. Held, *Tradition and Interpretation in Matthew* (NTL; London: SCM, 1963) 73; Davies-Allison, *Matthew I* 703.
[92]Davies-Allison, *Matthew I* 693–4.

who can claim success in exorcisms and mighty works, but whose deeds belie them and ultimately bring their ruin. While the word ἀνομία (cf. Ps 6:8) could mean simply that internal alienation which does not necessarily prevent hypocritical external attractiveness (cf. Matt 23:28), Matthew seems to understand it more intensely in view of the association with 'scandal' (Matt 13:41; 24:10–12) and 'leading astray' (24:4–5, 11). Within the structure of the sermon on the mount it is almost inevitable that 5:19 should be drawn in, and indeed the controlling unit 5:17–19. This ensures that ἀνομία refers not only to practice but to teaching which undermines the law in the name of the gospel.[93]

We have the impression that a good deal of the material in Matt 7:15, 16–20, 21–23, which is used in various ways in Matt 12:33–35 and Luke 6:43–45, 46; 13:26–27, could exist not simply as separate units but for a different purpose, the exhortation to obedience rather than warnings against the disobedient. Typical, first, is the saying about calling Jesus 'Lord, Lord', which seems to need an unrestricted audience of persons who are being reminded to 'do'. That, as a matter of fact, is how Luke 6:46 works.[94] Typical, second, is the saying about being known by one's fruits, a general saying which can naturally function in a quite unrestricted context and with no necessary relevance to the judging of one group of persons by another. In the form adopted in Matt 12:33b/Luke 6:44a, using γινώσκεται rather than ἐπιγνώσεσθε, the transferred sense of the proverbial saying is likely to have been God's knowledge in the ultimate judgment, and the function of the saying therefore the encouragement to good deeds. But Matthew has a different concern. That concern makes the denunciation and dissociation voiced by Jesus the judge the real thrust of the section as a whole. But how do the two versions of the claim by those under judgment compare in terms of originality? Is Matthew's statement by the charismatic and miracle working prophets more primitive or less than Luke's 'We ate and drank in your presence, and you taught in our streets' (13:26)? Would Luke have had some purpose which made him less interested in a threat to the community posed by itinerant charismatics meriting(?) scathing

[93]Barth, 'Law', 74–5.
[94]On the priority of Luke 6:46 over Matt 7:21, cf. Davies-Allison, *Matthew I* 711–13.

dismissal as 'wolves in sheep's clothing', and more interested in Jesus' Palestinian contemporaries and the warning that 'one needs more than the superficial acquaintance of a contemporary'?[95] It is not impossible that Luke should have done this; that he should have shifted the focus of the saying to the situation of the earthly Jesus; that he should have, as Goulder argues, adapted Matthew's words to apply to the Jewish people at large, who had not responded to Jesus' ministry'.[96] But the community situation is so much more evident in Matthew than in Luke that a decision in favour of the Lucan version seems preferable.[97] Indeed one may add that Luke has his anxieties about a community threatened by incoming 'wolves' (Acts 20:29), for whom the warning of Matt 7:15 would be apposite. And it is also relevant that the Lucan version does not make so much of the confession of Jesus as 'Lord', and it does presume that an adverse judgment has already been passed. Finally, the reliance upon mere acquaintance with Jesus (Luke 13:26) has a close parallel in the double tradition when Jesus denounces Capernaum (Matt 11:23/Luke 10:15) for closeness to him combined with closedness against his call. So there are small straws in the wind pointing towards the conclusion that Matthew has constructed a not so unified whole out of disparate traditions which have in certain respects been preserved in more original form by Luke. In short, the Q hypothesis copes rather better with these complex data than Lucan dependence upon the work of a creative Matthew.

The study of Matt 7:15–23 and related Matthaean texts has served to bring out into the open another discrepancy between Matthew and Q. For Matthew the controversy about the status of the law in the light of the gospel is a key issue on which the evangelist is compelled to reflect actively and to fight vigorously with opponents. His gospel contains a very extensive and careful engagement with this problem. In Q, on the other hand, there is only the slightest trace of any awareness of such a problem. Q 16:17 stands alone, and by itself cannot possibly suffice as an apologia for the conservative cause. It looks as if the problem of

[95]J. A. Fitzmyer, *The Gospel according to Luke II* (AB 28A; New York: Doubleday, 1985) 1023.

[96]*Luke II* 574.

[97]Davies-Allison, *Matthew I* 714; Luz, *Matthew 1–7* 441.

law is known to be vexing Christianity in general, but it is not menacing the Q community in particular. For the conservative Christians of Q it is 'their problem'; for the conservative Christians of Matthew it is all too painfully 'our problem'.

9. The Baptist's Question. Matt 11:2–6/Q 7:18–23.

Matthew has carefully set the scene for 'The Baptist's Question' by ensuring that every sort of miracle listed in Matt 11:5 has indeed occurred (the blind: 9:27–31; the lame 9:1–8; the leper: 8:1–4; the deaf: 9:32–34; the dead: 9:18–26). Only in respect of the poor has he outmanoeuvred himself by editorial interference (5:3).[98] As far as explicit christology is concerned, the titles ranging from Son of God (8:29) and Son of man (9:6) to Son of David (9:27) have been placed on view. It is therefore natural that the phrase τὰ ἔργα τοῦ χριστοῦ should be used to sum up all that has gone before. And it would be equally natural for Luke to retain it if he were using Matthew.

Luke has included some but not all of the miracles listed in Matt 11:5 prior to his story of 'The Baptist's Question' (the lame: 5:17–26; the leper: 5:12–16; the dead: 7:11–17). Others might be intended in summary statements (4:40; 5:15; 6:17–19), but that is not made explicit. Partial amends are made by including the opening of the eyes of the blind in Luke 7:21, though the deaf have to wait till 11:14. The LukeR introduction of Mark 3:10–11 in Luke 7:21 serves to give content to 'what you have seen and heard'. But it involves more than that: the adoption of a tradition which had already contributed to Luke 4:40–41/Mark 1:32–34 the demonic announcement of Jesus' being the Son of God, explained by Luke as his being the messiah. The reader is in no doubt, well before reaching Luke 7:18–23, that the evangelist regards the activities listed as 'the deeds of the messiah'. Not only so, for as Fitzmyer has remarked, 'though not the most frequently used title for Jesus in the Lucan writings, Χριστός has to be regarded as the most important'.[99] As such, the term is never dropped by Luke from

---

[98]See above, pp. 17–8.
[99]*Luke I* 197.

Marcan traditions adopted by him. Michael Goulder quite rightly bids us take notice of how Luke handles Mark. We are doing so!

First, it takes little perspicuity to notice how tight is the connection in Luke's mind between miracle working and the status of the messiah. The Petrine confession of Jesus as messiah is the answer to questions raised by Jesus' activity just as much in Luke (9:18–20, cf. 9:7–9) as in Mark (8:27–29, cf. 6:14–16), and all the more insistently because of the closeness in Luke of two traditions which are somewhat distanced in Mark. When the comment of Herod is mentioned it is amplified by Luke's statement that 'he sought to see him', that is, 'he was hoping to see some sign done by him' (23:8). Miracles clearly point to 'the messiah'. In similar vein, it is only Luke who grounds the crowds' acclamations of the king, Jesus, at the time of the entry in 'all the mighty works that they had seen' (19:37 diff Mark 11:9).

Second, Matt 11:5 also refers to how how 'the poor have good news preached to them', and for Luke that phrase evoked Isa 61:1 and the recollection of the one whom God 'anointed' (ἔχρισεν: 4:18). When Luke 4:43 diff Mark 1:38 replaces κηρύξω . . . ἐξῆλθον with εὐαγγελίσασθαι . . . ἀπεστάλην the reader gets the message very loud and clear that Isaiah 61 is being kept firmly in mind. Now the activities of the anointed one, as set out in Luke 4:18–19, include miracle and are underlined as doing so when Acts 10:38 describes the anointing as 'with the Holy Spirit and power' issuing in 'doing good and healing all that were oppressed by the devil'.

Third, immediately before 'The Baptist's Question' Luke inserted 'The Widow's Son of Nain' (7:11–17), with its Elijah/ Jesus parallelism and its choral ending, 'A great prophet has arisen among us!'. Luke is quite happy with the idea of Jesus as a prophet, whether in parallel with Elijah (cf. 9:51–56) or with Moses (Acts 3:22; 7:37). But he finds it appropriate elsewhere to superimpose on the status of the prophet (Luke 24:19) that of the messiah (Luke 24:26). It would have been very appropriate to accept the invitation to do so in Luke 7:18/Matt 11:2. For some unknown reason he has not.

Fourth, the curious notion that John might be the messiah was introduced redactionally in Luke 3:15, and then put down by the saying about the stronger one who 'comes' (3:16–17). In

Matt 11:2–6 the superiority of Jesus and his identity as 'the coming one' are both in focus again. It would be quite extraordinary if in such a context Luke had dropped the phrase 'the deeds of the messiah'.

The natural inference from the presence in Matthew, and the absence from Luke, of 'the deeds of the messiah' is that Matthew added it, Luke did not subtract it, and Q existed. Various other Matthew/Luke discrepancies in 'The Baptist's Question' may well derive from LukeR: the 'two' disciples (cf. Luke 10:1), the description of the arrival of the messengers and their posing of the question, the typical Lucan reference to Jesus as the κύριος, as well as the occurrence there and then of miracles. John's hearing 'in prison' would probably have been retained by Luke[100] in continuity with his report of John's captivity in 3:20; the tradition does not presuppose it, and nothing has so far been said to Matthew's readers about it. It looks secondary, but it is too small a detail to be relied on – not at all comparable to 'the deeds of the messiah'!

One final point relates to the theological relationship between Matthew and his source. Hints of a kingly destiny for Jesus are dropped by a few Q traditions (Q 4:5–8; 10:22a; 22:30). But his future kingship is not connected with his present miracle working, as is often the case in Matthew, nor is the term χριστός itself used, as is also often the case in Matthew. The suggestion that, theologically speaking, Q is Matthew, does not here find support.

10. Violence to the Kingdom. Matt 11:12–13/Q 16:16.

In its Matthaean setting this saying is evidently alien. First, Matt 11:10 has already affirmed a John = Elijah equation, but Matt 11:14 does so again. In doing so again, 11:14 not only appears a clumsy reduplication but, rather worse, it behaves as if 11:12–13 were essentially a saying about John, which it is not. Second, the kingdom of heaven in 11:11 represents the new order within which Jesus is preeminent. As such it can scarcely be attacked. In 11:12 it is vulnerable to attack, and therefore has to be understood not as the new order itself but as the preaching

---

[100]Cf. Acts 5:21, 23; 16:26.

about that order. Hence, however consonant 11:12–13 may be in this or that respect with its Matthaean context, these two factors show that it is also dissonant and therefore no creation by Matthew.

When we turn to the content of the saying we find no fewer than four Matthaean features which seem to be less primitive than their Lucan counterparts.

First, the Matthaean word πάντες would not only fit with the Lucan tendency to generalize, but would also in association with οἱ προφῆται fit a well-established Lucan trend.[101] Mark nowhere, and Matthew nowhere apart from 11:13, uses the phrase πάντες οἱ προφῆται, but we would have expected Luke to have adopted it with enthusiasm if it had been in his source. That he did not suggests that it was not.

Second. the word γάρ is present only in order to make Matt 11:13 explain 11:12. But the sequence from 11:12, describing the post-Johannine period, to 11:13, describing the pre-Johannine period, must be secondary. No such bipartite saying would exist in isolation in so artificial a form, and its existence thus in the Matthaean context clearly derives from a redactional concern with the John/Elijah equivalence affirmed in 11:14. Again Luke's rendering is more primitive.

Third, the order οἱ προφῆται καὶ ὁ νόμος must be secondary since it serves the MattR purpose of highlighting the prophets, whereas Luke's phrase ὁ νόμος καὶ οἱ προφῆται is more conventional.[102]

Fourth, the verb προφητεύειν again fits the purpose of Matthew, but it is artificial when its subject includes the law. Luke's version without any verb at all appears more original.

A discussion of the one remaining Matthew/Luke discrepancy, i.e. ἕως/μέχρι need not be undertaken here.[103] Nor is this the place for a consideration of Matt 11:12/Luke 16:16b, in which there are very probably Matthaean features more original than their Lucan counterparts. What is important for our present purpose is the evidence, first, of the existence of a pre-Matthaean saying, and second, of the Lucan retention of some of the original features of that saying which Matthew modified for theological reasons.

[101]Luke 11:50 diff Matt 23:35; Luke 13:28 diff Matt 8:11; Luke 24:27; Acts 3:18, 24; 10:43.
[102]Cf. 4 Macc 18:10; Matt 5:17; 7:12; Luke 24:44; John 1:45.
[103]See p. 233.

11. The Children in the Marketplace. Matt 11:16–19/Q 7:31–35.

The infrequently used term ἔργον enters the gospel of Matthew from Mark in Matt 26:10/Mark 14:6 and is employed redactionally at 5:16 and 23:3, 5. In all these passages it refers to conduct in general, but in the two remaining cases, 11:2, 19b, it is different. In the first, τὰ ἔργα τοῦ χριστοῦ are plainly miracles. In the second, τὰ ἔργα τῆς σοφίας are again defined clearly by the following tradition (Matt 11:20–24) as miracles. This has a double effect. On the one hand, the suspicion is aroused that the messiah/Wisdom parallelism is intended to produce a Jesus/Wisdom equation, a suspicion which is confirmed shortly afterwards by 11:28–30 in which Jesus echoes 'the preaching of wisdom in self-commendation'.[104] On the other hand, it tends to divorce Matt 11:19b from what immediately precedes it, for in Matt 11:16–19a there is no reference, either explicit or implicit, to miracles. Yet that divorce cannot be pressed through, since the new narrative introduction in 11:20 has the effect of pushing the saying in 11:19b back into liaison with the other sayings preceding it. Consequently, Matt 11:19b plays a very awkward part in the total collection of units of tradition brought together here, at least to an extent, by Matthew.

Over against the deeds of Wisdom in Matthew stand all the children of Wisdom in Luke. Formally, a new narrative introduction in Luke 7:36 forces 7:35 to function as the conclusion of the preceding section, but this time it is admirably suited to doing so. The 'children of Wisdom' are traditionally those who hear, receive and act upon her teaching. In Luke 7:31–32 there figured certain persons who refused to respond to verbal invitations. Worse still, in 7:33–34 the refusal took active form in scathing dismissals of two prophetic figures. Over against the obdurate and the dismissive are now set in 7:35 those who respond and recognize the presence of Wisdom in those invitations and in the conduct of the prophetic figures whose actions were the epitome of their missions. Consequently, Luke 7:35 fits very

---

[104]U. Wilckens, 'σοφία', *TDNT* 7.496–528, esp. pp. 516–17. Cf. Prov 1:20–33; 8:1–36; Sir 24:19–22; 51:23–30.

smoothly and naturally into its present context. Is this smoothness the product of sensitive Lucan redaction?

One must ask whether a movement from the form of the
tradition in Matthew to Luke is more plausible than a movement
from the form of the tradition in Luke to Matthew. It is no
coincidence that there is almost a unanimous consensus among
gospels specialists in favour of the second position. And there is
a theological reason which far outweighs the combination of
literary considerations and Matthaean theology, and it is this: If
Luke redacted Matthew here he reduced the status of Jesus from
Wisdom to the messenger of Wisdom. This is simply unbeliev-
able.[105] Of course, it would not be the only occasion on which
he did this if he knew Matthew. The variety of view in Matt
23:34–36/Luke 11:49–51 and the omission of Matt 11:28–30
come to mind. But in a similar way those two instances are
more believably assessed as new MattR developments than as
Lucan revisions of the Matthaean text.

Finally, in this setting, another Matthew/Q theological
discrepancy becomes sharply focussed. Matthew is plainly
convinced that Jesus and Wisdom are the same, though he does
not exploit this equation with reference to pre-existence or
responsibility for creation. Q, on the other hand, sees the earthly
Jesus as the emissary and mouthpiece of Wisdom.

12. The Pharisees' Accusation. Matt 12:22–24/Q 11:14–16.

This unit of material introduces the extended tradition of the
Beelzebub controversy, which was used rather effectively by
Gerald Downing[106] as a test case of the consequences of 'dispensing with Q'. Downing drew attention to the major and unappealing consequence that Luke would have omitted Marcan material
from his rendering of material similar to that which Matthew
conflated with Mark. This is odd but not impossible: faced with
a choice between Mark and Matthew it is perfectly possible that

---

[105]Note the observation by Davies-Allison, *Matthew I* 104, when discussing
the Matthew/Mark relationship, an observation which applies equally when
Luke comes into the reckoning: 'The general direction of early Christology
cannot be gainsaid. It was from the lesser to the greater.'

[106]'Towards the Rehabilitation of Q', *NTS* 11 (1964) 169–81, esp. pp. 170–6.

he chose at this point to give an overwhelming vote of confidence to Matthew. He could have de-conflated the Matthaean account and preferred that with which Matthew conflated Mark. But that decision to stick close to Matthew makes it all the more important to impose another test: how closely has the contact with Matthew been maintained in matters of theological substance, and has Luke acted with consistency?

We note that the Beelzebub controversy is provoked by no specific miracle in Mark, by the healing of a blind and dumb demoniac in Matthew, and by the healing of a dumb demoniac in Luke. In Mark, because there is no healing, there is no acclamation; in Matthew there is astonishment voiced in the acclamation of the crowds, 'Can this be the Son of David?' (Matt 12:23); and in Luke there is amazement and no acclamation at all (Luke 11:14).

On the basis of Lucan use of Matthew, there is precedent for what seems eccentric editorial behaviour here by Luke. Matt 9:27–31 had told of the healing of two blind men who had acclaimed Jesus as Son of David, and the story was apparently ignored by Luke. Similarly, Matt 9:32–34 had told of the healing of a dumb demoniac, and this story also was apparently ignored by Luke, unless one is going to say that he preferred it to Matt 12:22–24 here.[107] But simply to affirm that Luke did this will not do, for we want to know why, given the theologically more significant content of the 'comprehensive exorcism', the 'simpler exorcism'[108] should have been preferred. If Luke, by such preference, effectively reduced both the problem solved by Jesus and the acclamation of Jesus, this extraordinary procedure needs to be shown to be ordinary on the basis of Luke's use of Mark. Otherwise an alternative explanation of the data is readily available.

In fact a comparative Luke/Mark study signally fails to reduce the extraordinary to the ordinary. First, Luke never scales down the size of a problem presented to Jesus the miracle worker in the gospel of Mark. Second, he never removes Son of David christology, and indeed the frequency with which it is presented in Luke and the first half of Acts makes his commitment to it crystal clear. Third, the only precedent for the exclusion of the

[107]Thus, H. B. Green, 'Matthew 12:22–50 and Parallels: An Alternative to Matthaean Conflation', *Synoptic Studies* (JSNTSup 7; ed. C. M. Tuckett; Sheffield: JSOT Press, 1984) 157–76.
[108]Green's terms.

healing of the blind is the dropping of Mark 8:22–26, a story so odd and so lacking in any basis for theological interpretation[109] that Matthew also dropped it. Luke's exclusion can hardly be significant. Since the opening of the eyes of the blind is given explicit programmatic status in the opening sermon in Luke 4:18, and the blind included among those who represent a divine and human priority (Luke 14:13, 21), it is very hard indeed to view Luke 11:14–16 as either an edited version of, or an alternative substitute for, Matt 12:22–24.

The implausibility of one scheme requires, and is in turn reinforced by, the plausibility of the alternative which runs as follows: Just as Matthew brought forward the Marcan traditions of the healing of the leper (Matt 8:1–4/Mark 1:40–45) before the healing of Peter's mother-in-law (Matt 8:14–15/Mark 1:29–31) and the healing of the sick at evening (Matt 8:16–17/Mark 1:32–34); just as he brought forward the stilling of the storm (Matt 8:23–27/Mark 4:35–41) and the exorcism of the Gadarene demoniac (Matt 8:28–34/Mark 5:1–20) before three of the Marcan controversy stories (Matt 9:1–8, 9–13, 14–17/Mark 2:1–12, 13–17, 18–22), and then attached the sole remaining member of the Marcan miracle complex, the raising of Jairus' daughter (Matt 9:18–26/Mark 5:21–43); so too Matthew brought forward the healing of the blind from Mark 10:46–52 to Matt 9:27–31, at the same time touching it up with details drawn from Mark 1:40–45. He also brought forward the Q tradition of the healing of the dumb demoniac, editing it lightly by reference to Mark 2:1–12 (προσήνεγκαν . . . οὐδέποτε . . . οὕτως) and Q 7:1–10 (ἐν τῷ Ἰσραήλ). Thus it was in position as the sole miracle of healing of a deaf person in advance of the summary in Matt 11:5. The Q tradition itself can, on the basis of Matt 9:32–34/Luke 11:14–16 agreements, be seen to have included the following elements: (i) a demoniac, whose problem (ii) was dumbness, and who (iii) spoke after his cure by Jesus, so that (iv) the crowds 'marvelled', while (v) others referred to the agency of Beelzebub. When he came to use it a second time (compare his double use of Mark 10:46–52) he added blindness to the problem, and the acclamation 'Can this be the Son of David?' to the

[109]H. J. Held, 'Matthew as Interpreter of the Miracle Stories', G. Bornkamm, G. Barth and H. J. Held *Tradition and Interpretation in Matthew* (NTL; London: SCM Press, 1963) 210.

solution of the problem. In so doing he was behaving entirely in character. Is this not made clear by the MattR introduction of 'Son of David' to the Syro-phoenician woman's call for the exorcism of the demon from her daughter (Matt 15:22 diff Mark 7:25), and the healing of the blind and the lame in the temple to accompanying cries of 'Hosanna to the Son of David' in spite of negative criticisms from other sources (Matt 21:14–16).[110] In short, the Q hypothesis allows Matthew and Luke to have acted consistently and meaningfully, whereas the alternative hypothesis has Luke acting oddly.

13. The Sign for this Generation. Matt 12:38–42/Q 11:29–32.

Matt 12:38–42 as it stands is a curious formation, one which, if it were treated as an isolated tradition, would almost certainly be thought to contain more than a single stratum of tradition produced by one person.

First, vv. 38, 39 contain three elements which point towards the refusal of a sign: (i) the fact that the demand for one stems from the standard representatives of the opposition to Jesus, 'some of the scribes and Pharisees'; (ii) Jesus' own denunciation of those who press such a demand as 'an evil and adulterous generation'; and (iii) the formulation 'no sign shall be given except . . .', which indicates that the demand will, in its own terms, be rejected, but that such 'sign' as will be forthcoming will, from the point of view of the questioners, be adverse. But the content of v. 40 does not match these expectations at all, for the Jonah/Son of man parallelism in the three days and nights experience is plainly designed to point towards the appearance of the Son of man risen from the dead,[111] and this must constitute a sign in the most positive sense.[112]

If we were to draw in 3 Macc 6:8, this would be precedent for

[110]Held, 'Miracle Stories', 247–8.

[111]U. Luz, *Das Evangelium nach Matthäus II* [*Mt 8–17*] (EKKNT 1/2; Zürich-Branschweig: Benziger/Neukirchen-Vluyn: Neukirchener Verlag, 1990) 277.

[112]Jeremias, ''Ιωνᾶς,' *TDNT* 3.406–10, esp. p. 409, takes the *tertium comparationis* as the three days/nights in the belly of the fish in Matt 12:40, and as the deliverance from death in the parallel Luke 11:30. In fact the three days/nights in Matt 12:40 are almost certainly mentioned strictly with a view to the idea of deliverance from death, and the meaning of Luke 11:30 may well be quite different.

taking Jonah as a sign in that positive sense. For there Jonah is associated with two other examples of divine intervention to rescue faithful servants, the three young men (v. 6: Dan 3) and Daniel himself (v. 7: Dan 6), and it is significant that both the other two are categorized as σημεῖα (Dan 3:32 LXX; 6:27(28) Θ). The provision of a sign of the Jonah/Son of man variety can scarcely count as the refusal of a sign.

Second, the relationship between vv. 38–40 and what follows is strained. Jonah is the connective to v. 41, but any association between vv. 38–40 and v. 41 leaves v. 42 stranded, which, in view of the close correspondence between v. 41 and v. 42, it manifestly should not be. But in any case a clearcut differentiation between the two complexes vv. 38–40 and vv. 41–42 is forced upon us. (i) The first has a personal focus, especially if by σημεῖον is to be understood a confirmation of Jesus' own status,[113] and the second (note the neuter πλεῖον) does not. (ii) The first involves a refusal to give any sign of heavenly authorization, and the second (by virtue of πλεῖον) probably presumes visible manifestations of the near kingdom in the form of acts of power. (iii) The first is concerned only with Jonah, and fits awkwardly with a Solomon + Jonah pairing, particularly when that pairing is more likely to have been in biblical order to survive during transmission. (iv) The first gives no detail of the response of the Ninevites, whereas the second is very specific. (v) The second assigns to the Ninevites a role in the last judgment, whereas the first does nothing of the sort.

A study of Matt 12:38–42 therefore suggests internal stresses both within vv. 38–40 and between that section and the following vv. 41–42.

At this point we naturally turn to Luke 11:29–32. How easy is it to understand this as an edited version of Matt 12:38–42? The different order of the sayings in Luke 11:31–32 could certainly be attributed to LukeR, a thoroughly appropriate reversion to what would seem to be the more suitable and biblical sequence. But a movement from Matt 12:38–40 to Luke 11:29–30 is more problematic. No hint is dropped in the Lucan text that the sign is the presentation of someone rescued from death.[114]

---

[113]Luz, *Matthäus 8–17* 276.
[114]Against Jeremias, *TDNT* 3.409.

Indeed, as the tortured discussion of this tradition by commentators amply confirms, there is no clear hint at all of what the sign involves – only that it is in a sense a happening which, because it is the refusal of a sign, must involve the redefinition of the very term itself. One might well take Luke 11:29–30 as pointing to the eschatological manifestation of the Son of man, but Luke scarcely makes this clear. So our question narrows into one about the likelihood of a clear, passion-oriented version, whose meaning is congenial to Luke, being replaced by another version whose meaning is unclear. All the normal considerations suggest that the process worked in the reverse direction. (i) The Matthaean allusion to Jesus' passion is less easily regarded as original than as a typical OT insertion by the evangelist. Matthew often inserts OT quotations into Marcan blocks; Luke never drops those he finds in Marcan blocks unless at the same time he drops the whole block. Why should he drop such a quotation from a Matthaean block which he retained? (ii) The allusion is distinctly artificial, since no one, including the Ninevites, could witness the proposed sign. (iii) Luke would hardly have discarded it, had he known it, bearing in mind his insertion of an edited version of Mark 8:31 in Luke 17:25. He never drops Marcan passion sayings unless they figure in blocks which he elects not to use *in toto*. (iv) The originality of the allusion is not established by the time note 'three days and three nights' over against 'on the third day'.[115] Luz is therefore surely right when he declares that 'Luke would certainly have taken over the christological text in Matt 12:40 if he had known it'.[116] That being so, we merely need to add that the final Lucan phrase 'to this generation' (Luke 11:30) is probably more original and has been supplanted.

The Q hypothesis once again turns out to be a better basis for the reconstruction of a tradition history.[117] The full detail of how Q 11:29–32 evolved we reserve for a later discussion.[118]

---

[115]Cf. MattR at 27:63, and acceptance of traditional formulations 'in/through three days' at 26:61; 27:40.

[116]*Matthäus 8–17* 273.

53

14. The Blessedness of the Disciples. Matt 13:16–17/Q 10:23–24.

Matt 13:16–17 owes its present position to the evangelist's concern to develop the ideas contained in 'The Reason for Parables' (Mark 4:10–12). The disciples (v. 10) have been given the mysteries (v. 11). The crowds (v. 2), however, have not, so seeing and hearing take place, but it is sightless seeing and deaf hearing which lacks understanding (v. 13). This is in accord with the text (now quoted *in extenso*) Isa 6:9–10. The fact of seeing and hearing is not in itself significant: only understanding makes it so.

Into this setting Matt 13:16–17 fits only partially. The fact of seeing and hearing is the cause of celebration (v. 16), and in the light of what has gone before it is to be assumed that the disciples (no new introduction, and emphatic ὑμῶν, therefore the μαθηταί of v. 10, also addressed with emphatic ὑμῖν, v.11) are seeing and hearing with understanding. But if so, v. 17 immediately causes trouble. Seeing and hearing remain the topic under discussion, but (i) the contrast is between two groups, one of which is defined quite differently from that mentioned previously; (ii) the separation between the groups is one of time rather than understanding; (iii) correspondingly there are not in v. 17 two different levels of seeing and hearing; (iv) the absence of seeing and hearing in v. 17 derives solely from the fact that the things to be seen and heard were not available to be seen and heard, rather than being available but not disclosed. All four differences, which do not figure in the discussion by Goulder,[119]

---

[117]Green, 'Matthew 12:22–50', 167–8, mounts a series of arguments against a Q-based treatment of Luke 11:29–30. (i) Scholars are assuming that a fuller version is as such later, and he here appeals to the work of E. P. Sanders, *The Tendencies of the Synoptic Tradition* (SNTSMS 9; Cambridge: CUP, 1969) 46ff. Answer: Not so. The issue is not the size but the substance of Matt 12:40/Luke 11:30. (ii) The argument for 'Lucan priority' has to assume that the clause 'except the sign of Jonah' was added at an early stage of the oral tradition. Answer: Not so. Q specialists are not agreed about how Luke 11:29 relates to Mark 8:12 in the history of the tradition, cf. later, pp. 244–7. It is perfectly possible within the parameters of the Q hypothesis to view the exceptive clause as a piece of literary redaction. (iii) Luke 11:30 is not traditional but a redactional bridge, indeed a contrived and artificial bridge between 11:29 and 11:31–32. Answer: Very likely, and readily viewed as such by advocates of Q.

[118]See pp. 241–7.

[119]*Luke II* 480–1.

stem from the essential distinction between ὅτι (v. 16) and ἅ (v. 17). Now that distinction drives a wedge into Matt 13:16–17, but it simply does not arise in the Lucan counterpart, Luke 10:23–24. Put another way, Matt 13:17/Luke 10:24 is about salvation history. So is Luke 10:23 (note the connecting γάρ). But the counterpart, Matt 13:16, is about a theology of hardening. Yet both parts of Matt 13:16–17/Luke 10:23–24 need to be about the same topic.

In the light of these considerations Matt 13:16 is secondary over against Luke 10:23. It is a tradition which Matthew did not invent. This opens the way for further conclusions about (i) Matt 13:16b, the reference to hearing ears, which is more probably a MattR insertion than a LukeR omission, and (ii) Matt 13:17/Luke 10:24, the righteous men so beloved of Matthew over against the kings, here seen rather unusually in a positive light as those looking forward to the fulfilment of hope for the future. In three crucial respects, therefore, the Lucan version appears more primitive than the Matthaean. Another success for the Q hypothesis can be registered.

15. The Woe about Unmarked Tombs. Matt 23:27–28/Q 11:44.

Whereas several of the woes against the Pharisees make perfect sense in their Matthaean form, and the Lucan version is readily explicable as secondary in comparison, this is not the case in the woe which compares the Pharisees with tombs.

The application in v. 28 accuses the Pharisees of a discrepancy between an attractive exterior ('you outwardly appear righteous to men') and an exceedingly unpleasant interior ('full of hypocrisy and iniquity'). That which is applied must therefore be externally attractive by intention and designed to hide internal corruption. Specially marked tombs will not serve, for the external marking is not intended to make attractive, and it is not intended to hide the nastiness within but rather to draw attention to it. In other words v. 27 provides no basis for v. 28 and is dissonant with it.

There is no doubt that Luke 11:44 is intended to be the Lucan counterpart, for its position is almost identical. This time there is no failure of logic. It is factually true that an unmarked grave is such that persons may unwittingly walk over it. It is quite straightforward, even if unappealing, to apply this to a human situation. 'You are like . . .' expresses the message very plainly that those addressed are morally defiling, even though those who come into contact with them do not realise it.

Both versions of this woe show an awareness of a traditional Jewish concern which leads to the marking of graves. Luke picks up ideas expressed in, for example, Num 19:16, 'Whoever in the open field touches . . . a grave shall be unclean seven days.' Luke's version is logical and consistent; Matthew's version is illogical and inconsistent. The illogical version is unlikely to contain a single stratum of material, and therefore the existence of a pre-Matthaean version is likely. If the pre-Matthaean material is to have been capable of surviving it must have been logical. Luke's version satisfies that requirement. Finally we can easily understand a change from the Lucan to the Matthaean version, because Matt 23:28 in particular bears the marks of Matthaean style and interests, and probably some indebtedness to the 'inside . . . outside' scheme of the immediately preceding woe about the washing of vessels (Matt 23:25–26). So the most obvious inference is that the earlier of the two versions of the woe referring to graves is preserved by Luke.

16. The Parable of the Watchful Householder.
Matt 24:43–44/Q 12:39–40.

In Matt 24:42–25:13 a trio of parables is designedly framed within a double demand for watchfulness: 'Watch therefore, for you do not know on what day your Lord is coming . . . watch therefore, for you know neither the day nor the hour.' The cue for this double demand is provided by Mark 13:32 (Matt 24:36), 'But of that day or that hour no one knows . . .', and by Mark 13:35, 'Watch therefore for you do not know when the master of the house will come . . .'. That same theme of not knowing, furthermore, controls the intervening saying about the flood and the parousia of the Son of man: 'They did not know until . . .' (Matt 24:39).

Manifestly, the frame in 24:42 and 25:13 is artificial and

secondary. The parable of the so-called watchful householder is misnamed, for protection against burglary is not watchfulness but prevention. Therefore 24:42 does not fit with 24:43.[120] Equally, the parable of the ten virgins is not about watchfulness, for the opposite of watchfulness is sleeping (cf. Mark 13:35–37), and the wise slept along with the foolish (Matt 25:5). Therefore 25:13 does not fit with 25:1–12. As for the intervening parable (24:45–51), the servant if he had been faithful and wise would have shown those qualities in obedience: he is not a failure on the ground of failing to watch. So all three parables are parables about ignorance of the time of a coming, but they are not parables demanding watchfulness. That being so, the theme of watching inside the so-called parable of the watchful householder (24:43) is a damaging addition to a pre-Matthaean parable, and it happens that Luke does not have it and is therefore more original. Its absence from Luke cannot be attributed to LukeR for another reason. In Luke 12:35–38 Luke has used a parable which, because it contains a dislocation (12:37b: 'Truly, I say to you, he will gird himself and have them sit at table, and he will come and serve them.'),[121] derives

---

[120]By a significant accident, Goulder, *Luke II* 545, omits the words 'would have watched' from his intended verbatim quotation of Matt 24:43–44.

[121]Fitzmyer, *Luke X-XXIV* 986–7, sees here a 'reversal of roles' which gives the servants a share in the master's banquet. But v. 37b breaks into the simile, which otherwise runs smoothly; it describes something unusual, when the exhortation is based on what usually happens; it clashes with the content of the simile, in that the returning one has come *from* a meal-type celebration, and the possible time of his return (the second or third watch) is no time for a meal; it functions as a climax, with ἀμὴν λέγω ὑμῖν, but leaves the original climax, v. 38, hanging loose; in terminology it matches Luke 17:7c-8, which also appears secondary in its present context. Goulder, *Luke II* 544, treats the Lucan tradition as a rewriting of Matt 25:1–13, with details drawn from Matt 6:22; 24:46. He sees v. 37b as an echo of the idea of Jesus as the humble servant, overturning human norms (cf. Luke 14:11; 22:26–27). However, his scheme does not permit a recognition of the discrepancy between v. 37b and its context. The parallel with Luke 17:7–9, which Goulder, *Luke II* 547, wishes especially to stress, is indeed a significant parallel: a parable arguing from common experience ('Which of you . . .?') that thanks are neither in order nor to be expected when a servant has done what he has been ordered to do, and superimposed upon it the alien and overloaded allusion to the meal situation. His correct observation that the waiting (male servants) and the return home of the bridegroom after the wedding are normal details does not, however, require Luke's material to be secondary over against Matthew's.

from pre-Lucan tradition. At the pre-Lucan stage it exhorted to watchfulness (12:37a), and Luke was happy to include that theme. There would therefore be no reason for him to exclude the idea of watchfulness from Matt 24:43, had he known it.

It is worth adding that within this complex of eschatological parables there are other distinctive Lucan features which appear more original. First, 'they did not know that' (Matt 24:39) is something of a distraction in the description of the strikingly normal everyday activities of the generation of the flood. Luke is more original in lacking this detail. Second, the description of the servant as 'wicked' (Matt 24:48) is less appropriate than no description at all.[122] Indeed if an adjective were to be used at this stage it would better have been 'foolish' (contrast 'wise', 24:45). Luke is again more original. Third, the punishment of the unfaithful servant with a 'share with the unfaithful (οἱ ἄπιστοι)' is more original than a 'share with the hypocrites'. The Lucan wording respects the symmetry of the parable (cf. πιστός, Matt 24:45/Luke 12:42).[123] Fourth, 'the weeping and gnashing of teeth' (Matt 24:51b) is clearly unnecessary in formal terms, and its alleged omission by Luke fits ill with its retention shortly afterwards in Luke 13:28. It is more likely that it did not originally feature at the end of the parable (so, Luke) but was added subsequently (so, Matthew).

An already lengthy discussion needs no further lengthening except to the extent that implications must be drawn out. What have these sixteen test cases demonstrated? Four results at least, it may fairly be claimed. First, a methodology which pairs form-critical attention to the shape of a tradition with redaction-critical alertness to the consistent theological intentions of editorial change turns out to be source-critically fruitful. Second, attention to the Matthaean versions of the sixteen traditions serves to show the presence of strata within them and thus to establish that these were not the product of a single-stage creative action by the evangelist. Third, at crucial points, though naturally not at all points, space can be seen between the theol-

[122]Fitzmyer, *Luke X-XXIV* 990, rightly declares that the word is 'a bit strange, since it is not yet clear why he is "evil"'. Goulder, *Luke II* 550, attributes to Luke an improvement in the logic.
[123]Fitzmyer, *Luke X-XXIV* 990.

ogy of Matthew and the theology of the traditions Matthew adopted and adapted. Fourth, the Q hypothesis not only permits flexibility in decision-making about the relative priority of this version or that, and thus liberates the discussion from the compulsion always to find that Matthew's version is earlier than Luke's or (in theory) vice versa, but it also repeatedly permits a sensible reconstruction of the tradition history as a whole. Of course, not even sixteen swallows make a summer, but they certainly do drop a strong hint that it is time to replace one perspective with another. And, of course, to the sixteen there can be added many other traditions where Matthew may well have the priority. Often these other traditions are closely associated with the sixteen by virtue of order: thus, 'on treasures' (Matt 6:19–21/ Luke 12:33–34) with the warning against anxiety, or 'hearers and doers of the word' (Matt 7:24–27/Luke 6:47–49) and 'the centurion's servant' (Matt 8:5–13/Luke 7:1–10) with the warning against false prophets, or 'Jesus' testimony to John' (Matt 11:7–11) with the Baptist's question and the parable of the children in the marketplace, or the Beelzebub controversy (Matt 12:25–37, 43–45/Luke 11:17–26) with the Pharisees' accusation and the sign of Jonah, or the rest of the sequence of woes against the Pharisees (parts of Matt 23:1–36/Luke 11:37–53) with the unmarked tombs denunciation, or the parable of the faithful and wise servant (Matt 24:45–51) with the parable of the watchful householder. Clusters begin to emerge, once it is recognized that again and again the double tradition is not patient of the explanation that Luke used Matthew, or vice versa. Whether all the 'q's add up to form a composite Q depends on whether there is general theological congruence between the diverse traditions and, most importantly, agreement of outlook between those parts of the traditions which appear to be editorial. That conclusion cannot be reached except by a further series of studies, which it will be the concern of the rest of this volume to provide.

2

The Beginning of Q

Recent discussion of the genre of Q suggests that a consensus is not yet emerging. On the one hand there is the view of John Kloppenborg that the wisdom literature provides the key. In detail, several stages in the development of Q are envisaged: first, the assembling of a number of wisdom speeches; second, an expansion by various groups of sayings, many formed as chriae; then, third, a move in the direction of a βίος by means of an historicizing tendency and the addition of the temptation story (Q 4:1–13).[1] Within this approach, traditions which seem at first sight to exhibit prophetic form or content are strictly subordinated to, or at least controlled by, their setting in a wisdom collection. That is, the wisdom *Makrogattung* determines how any prophetic *Mikrogattungen* are to be viewed. On the other hand, there is the view of Migaku Sato that Q should be compared with the prophetic literature, and that it grew in several redactional stages, each of which was informed by the prophetic tradition and conditioned by prophetic mission.[2] On this view the prophetic *Makrogattung* determines how any sapiential *Mikrogattungen* are to be viewed.

These two views are sharply divided in their treatment of the beginning of Q. Kloppenborg is hesitant about anything before Q 3:7–9 and merely notes in passing an historicizing tendency in the introductory reference to John in Q 3:7a.[3] In his discussion of the genres of instruction, chriae collection, and biography, he collects much evidence of how titles, prologues and narrative introductions occur as devices for the legitimation of the speaker.[4] This is the role he assigns to Q 4:1–13. But that only

[1] *Formation* 317–28.
[2] *Prophetie* 406–11.
[3] *Formation* 84–5, 102.
[4] *Formation* 262–316.

makes all the more noticeable the presence of Q 3:7–9, 16–17, traditional material positioned before Q 4:1–13 and concerned not with Jesus but with John. Sato by contrast suggests, and provokes stern reservations from Kloppenborg for doing so,[5] that one of the six prophetic features of Q which set it apart from wisdom collections is its beginning. This beginning, so runs the argument, included Luke 3:2–4, 21–22, that is, the narrative of the appearance of John and the baptism of Jesus. The suggestion about the baptism tradition is markedly more confident than that concerning the appearance of John[6] and there are several references to '3:2–4/6?', but access to 'die Urgestalt des Anfangs der Quelle' is no longer possible.[7] The presence of 3:21–22, however, is 'nicht völlig sicher, aber wahrscheinlich', and a basis for argument.[8] Sato's forms of words convey a sense that a proposal which is in general strong may in this particular be fragile. It may not be quite 'game, set and match' against Sato, but it might be 'advantage Kloppenborg'. It certainly seems worth investigating whether we can know more about how Q began.

From Q 7:18–35 it is evident that the Q community maintained a lively interest in John the Baptist. Indeed material which can be split into several separate units by form criticism is here very probably assembled and edited in order to be both appreciative of John and also, in the strict sense, Christian. There is keen interest in the work and status of John. Nevertheless there is never any doubt that Jesus, not John, is supreme and the focus of faith. This balance of purpose is achieved by placing an earlier traditional list of activities reminiscent of key prophetic texts (Q 7:22) in a frame which sets up an equation between Jesus and 'the coming one' (Q 7:19),[9] a person whose existence is disclosed to the reader only by Q 3:16c, 'One who is stronger than I is coming . . .'. The natural *Sitz im Leben* of all this editorial activity would arguably be a Christian community which is, at one or more stages in its own development (depending on how many editorial strata are discernible in Q 7:18–35),

[5] See his review in *CBQ* 52 (1990) 362–4.
[6] The presence of 3:2–4 is said to be 'möglich aber unsicher', *Prophetie* 21.
[7] *Prophetie* 78.
[8] *Prophetie* 21, 111.
[9] Cf. *Prophetie* 140–4.

in direct contact with the continuing Baptist movement. The sensitivity of such contact, not to mention the editorial dependence of 7:19 on 3:16c, would suggest that the way in which Q introduces the Baptist himself would be of crucial importance. Yet here we encounter a problem. If the Baptist was introduced, and if Q began, with 3:7–9, 16–17 alone, then that beginning was abrupt indeed. The readers, whether Q community members or we ourselves, start to bristle with questions: Who is this John? What is this baptism? What is the basis of the call to repentance? Where are 'these stones' out of which God could produce children of Abraham?

In asking such questions it is worth recalling a similar difficulty which arises if we take Q 4:1–13 as the first tradition in the Q sequence which introduces us to Jesus. That too would seem extremely abrupt, and all the more so when we observe that the structure of the temptation tradition is, as already noted,[10] determined by the so-called 'law of three', with the two preparatory units, Q 4:3–4, 9–12, presuming that something has been said to provoke the repeated challenge, 'If you are the Son of God, . . .'. Of course, one might follow Kloppenborg's argument that the presupposition of a Son of God christology is in itself 'no reason to posit a special narrative justifying that christology any more than there is reason to posit a narrative which grounds the Son christology of 10:21–22 or the Son of Man christology observed elsewhere in Q'.[11] But this does not quite meet the point about how the challenge, 'If you are the Son of God, . . .' is formulated. Elsewhere when this challenge appears there is indeed something preceding it upon which it can lean. That is the case in Wis 2:18 where the opponents of the righteous servant of God are able to formulate their hostile challenge, 'If the righteous man is God's son, he will help him', precisely because they have just quoted his own claim, 'He calls the last end of the righteous happy, and boasts that God is his father' (Wis 2:16). This is also the case in Matt 27:40 where the redactional insertion of 'if you are the son of God' within the Marcan 'Save yourself and come down from the cross' (Mark 15:30) presumes an explicit claim to that effect. In the redactional

[10]See p. 12.
[11]*Formation* 84–5.

Matt 27:43 the explicit claim is quoted, and a little earlier in Matt 26:64 the claim is made. When we travel back from Wisdom and Matthew to Q 4:3, 9 we become uncomfortably aware of the inadequacy of Q 4:1–13 standing alone as the introduction of Jesus to the readers of Q.

Given such awkwardnesses as these if the beginning of Q consisted simply of Q 3:7–9, 16–17; 4:1–13, it is worth investigating the possibility that there was more there than that. In what follows we shall first check Q 7:24–28 for layers of tradition, and then examine Mark 1:1–11 for matching evidence of such layers. It will be argued that the correspondence between redactional material in both settings suggests that Mark depended upon Q, and therefore that we may be able to find in Mark some evidence of how Q originally began.

1. Jesus' Testimony to John. Q 7:24–28.

Q 7:24–28 is controlled by a trio of questions about the status of John (vv. 24b–26). By the usual 'law of three' convention we expect the third stage to be climactic, and this is confirmed by other formal evidence. Each question beginning with 'What did you go out . . . to see?' is followed by another question supplying a possible object of sight. But after that there is in the first case no further comment, in the second case a further comment, though not one which clarifies Jesus' own view of John, but in the third case a comment which does express Jesus' view: 'What did you go out to see? A prophet? Yes, I tell you (ναὶ λέγω ὑμῖν), and more than a prophet' (v. 26). The formulation of Jesus' own view is important in two ways. First, the phrase ναὶ λέγω ὑμῖν brings together the particle ναί, 'denoting affirmation, agreement, or emphasis'[12] and equivalent to ἀμήν (cf. Luke 11:51; Rev 1:7), and the affirmation λέγω ὑμῖν, which Sato has shown to be varied in both origin and Q usage but unvarying as a formula of intensification of the authority of the speaker (from Q 3:8b onwards).[13] Prefacing a repetition of what has just been said (as in Luke 11:50–51; 12:5), ναὶ λέγω

[12] W. F. Arndt and F. W. Gingrich, *A Greek-English Lexicon of the New Testament* (4th ed.; Cambridge: University Press, 1957) 534.
[13] *Prophetie* 226–46.

ὑμῖν in v. 26b ensures an unequivocal endorsement of the crowds' view set out in vv. 24b–26a. There can therefore be no question of that view's being criticized, or of the crowds' having received a setback,[14] or of their having been uncertain what they wanted.[15] On the contrary, Jesus sets out their opinion, establishes common ground with them by agreeing with that opinion,[16] and then declares that its validity stems not from human opinion but from divine disclosure: John is indeed a prophet. Second, when Jesus builds on this common ground the phrase he uses, 'more than a prophet', is forceful but lacks the definition which is necessary to conclude a unit of tradition. This inconclusiveness is recognized even by those who are reluctant to find an original conclusion within vv. 27–28.[17] But vv. 27–28 are all we have available, and when we ask which part or parts of those two verses could form the original definitive ending, the most promising answer seems to be v. 28a. But before that promising answer becomes convincing two associated questions have to be tackled.

First, are we at liberty to consider v. 28a without v. 28b attached? In favour of the original unity of v. 28 are cited the antithetical parallelism of its two parts, together with the overlap between both parts and *Gos. Thom.* 46.[18] Against this, it is hard to see *Gos. Thom.* 46 as an earlier or independent version of the saying, and direct dependence upon synoptic tradition can scarcely be excluded. Furthermore, if we can demonstrate that vv. 24b–26, 28a cohere thematically in one way, and that vv. 27, 28b cohere thematically in another way, the possibility of an editorial creation of the antithetical parallelism will grow in strength.

Second, does the double ἀμὴν λέγω ὑμῖν in vv. 26b, 28a

---

[14]M Dibelius, *Die urchristliche Überlieferung von Johannes dem Täufer* (FRLANT 15; Göttingen: Vandenhoeck & Ruprecht, 1915) 10.

[15]J. Ernst, *Das Evangelium nach Lukas* (RNT; 5th ed.; Regensburg: Pustet, 1977) 249–50.

[16]Hoffmann, *Studien* 217; Schürmann, *Lukasevangelium I* 416.

[17]Thus Schürmann, *Lukasevangelium I* 417: 'V.26b verlangt nach eigenen Kommentierung.' Similarly Kloppenborg, *Formation* 109–10: 'Q 7:26b requires further explication.'

[18]Schürmann, *Lukasevangelium I* 417, 419; D. Lührmann, *Die Redaktion der Logienquelle* (WMANT 33; Neukirchen: Neukirchener Verlag, 1969) 27; S. Schulz, *Q. Die Spruchquelle der Evangelisten* (Zürich: Theologischer Verlag, 1972) 232; Kloppenborg, *Formation* 108–9.

prevent a close association between the two sayings and favour instead the original discreteness of v. 28?[19] Again, it must be thematic correspondence which is determinative, but in any case λέγω ὑμῖν is essential in v. 26b and inessential in v. 28a. The latter instance could easily be redactionally designed to echo the former so that, although the editor regards v. 27 as important, the remarkable implications of vv. 26b, 28a should not be lost. This, I take it, is what Kloppenborg means by 'a redactional clasp'. We therefore return to v. 28a in its own right.

Within Q 7:28a two terms carry great weight. The first is ἐγήγερται, contributed by Matt 11:11a. A biblicism,[20] only rarely used in the synoptics[21] in the sense of divine appointment to some function,[22] its presence in Matt 11:11 diff Luke 7:28 and in the nearby Luke 7:16 is best explained in terms of original Q wording in the former and Lucan reminiscence in the latter.[23] The second weighty term is ἐν γεννητοῖς γυναικῶν, which recurrently points to man in his/her humanness, often with a strong sense of human separation from God.[24] When ἐγήγερται and ἐν γεννητοῖς γυναικῶν are brought together in Q 7:28a, the end product is truly astonishing. Jesus surveys the whole of human history and declares that at no time has anyone been appointed by God to a more significant mission than that of John! While one might justifiably linger over the authenticity of such a remarkable saying, which could not possibly be a Christian construction and which must demonstrate that the Jesus who speaks had been a disciple of John,[25] the more important observation to be made is that form-critically it is the only element in vv. 27–28 which will define and complete v. 26. Both v. 26 and v. 28a affirm unreservedly John's greatness; both evaluate him

[19]Kloppenborg, *Formation* 109.
[20]Cf. Judg 2:16, 18; 3:9, 15; Isa 41:25; 45:13; Sir 10:4.
[21]Cf. Matt 24:11, 24/Mark 13:22; Luke 1:69.
[22]The persons 'raised up' (note the 'divine passive') may be for the benefit of Israel, as in the texts just cited, or for judgment upon Israel, cf. 1 Kgs 11:14, 23; Isa 10:26; Jer 50:9; Josephus, *Ant.* 8.7.6 §199.
[23]The use of ἐγήγερται is unlikely to have been provoked by Mark 6:16, as proposed by Goulder, *Midrash* 356, in view of the quite different meanings attached to the verb in the two texts.
[24]Cf. Job 14:1; 15:14; Sir 10:18;1QH 13:13–14; 18:10–13, 23; *b. Sabb.* 88b.
[25]P. Vielhauer, 'Johannes der Täufer,' *RGG* 3.807; J. Becker, *Johannes der Täufer und Jesus von Nazareth* (BibS(N) 63; Neukirchen: Neukirchener Verlag, 1972) 12, 15; Hoffmann, *Studien* 223.

in terms of divine mission; both stress his supreme status without reference to current schemes or titles;[26] both have to be understood in terms of John's relationship to the impending and ultimate crisis of judgment and his consequent insistence on repentance.[27] Above all, v. 28a causes the graph of assessment to rise, as it were, beyond vv. 24–26, whereas vv. 27, 28b both cause it to fall by insisting on John's inferiority to someone else.[28]

Since our main interest is in secondary editorial elements it is on vv. 27, 28b that we must now concentrate. The less complicated of the two additions is v. 27, which combines two OT texts, Exod 23:20 and Mal 3:1. The verbal overlap between the two texts makes such a combination entirely unsurprising (an undated midrash on Exod 23:20 in *Midr. Exod.* 32:9 also draws on Mal 3:1 in describing the revelation of God in the millennium and the coming of salvation to Israel), and the inference that Q was using an already established combination is precarious.[29] Q, unlike the midrash, causes the texts to interpenetrate and to form a new composite whole. In the main clause Q agrees with Exod 23:20 LXX and against Mal 3:1 in ἀποστέλλω (diff ἐξαποστέλλω), in the positioning of πρὸ προσώπου, and in the definition of the face by σοῦ (diff μοῦ), while agreeing with Mal 3:1 on the absence of ἐγώ. In the subordinate clause Q agrees with Mal 3:1 and against Exod 23:20 in making ὁδός the direct object, and in including at this point ἔμπροσθέν σου, a counterpart of πρὸ προσώπου σου, while agreeing with Exod 23:20 on the continued use of the you-forms. The verb κατασκευάζειν derives from neither OT passage. The combination of choices which has brought about the Q version has defined John in relation to *two* other persons rather than *one*, i.e. God

[26]F. Hahn, *The Titles of Jesus in Christology* (London: Lutterworth, 1969) 366–7.

[27]Cf. Schürmann, *Lukasevangelium I* 418; Lührmann, *Redaktion* 28; Schulz, *Spruchquelle* 232.

[28]Some confirmation of this analysis is probably to be found in Matt 21:32/ Luke 7:29–30. Doubtless this material has been substantially redacted into its present forms, but the overlap between the two versions supports the presence of an original Q narrative conclusion at this point. Rightly, G. Schneider, *Das Evangelium nach Lukas 1–10* (Gütersloh: Mohn, 1984) 172; otherwise, Sato, *Prophetie* 20, 55.

[29]Thus, K. Stendahl, *School* 50.

who speaks and sends, and the person to whom God speaks, rather than God alone. Exod 23:20, plainly the more dominant influence, had done the same, whereas Mal 3:1 had not. In two respects, however, Exod 23:20 needed to be adapted for use in its present Q context. First, the definition of the ἄγγελος was supplied by Mal 3:1, namely Elijah. Second, the person addressed had to be someone other than Israel. This modification could not be achieved by Mal 3:1, and it probably explains why κατασκευάζειν was employed. That verb's sole occurrence in the synoptics, apart from here and in Mark 1:2, is in Luke 1:17, a passage which defines the function of John/Elijah in relation to God as ἑτοιμάσαι κυρίῳ λαὸν κατεσκευασμένον.

Two final observations need to be made about the redactional Q 7:27. First, this saying has links with the Q temptation story in its use of the OT with a γέγραπται introduction, and its John/Elijah parallelism is unique in Q. In the context of a multi-stage redactional process that link tends to locate Q 7:27 in the final stage.[30] As the basis for an *ad hominem* argument this may have its uses! On the other hand, the proposed multi-stage process may not be entirely convincing. Second, one must ask whether this redactional insertion preserves any earlier tradition. This brings one back again to Luke 1:17. In the initial section of the Lucan infancy narrative (1:5–25) the role of John is defined by the angel with reference to God, and to God alone: greatness before the Lord, turning the sons of Israel to the Lord their God, going before the Lord in the spirit and power of Elijah, and making ready for the Lord a people prepared (1:15–17). Since the evangelist is concerned to relate John to 'the coming one', whom he equates with Jesus, the material in 1:15–17 should probably be added to the stock of pre-Lucan traditions which quite conceivably formed a consecutive Baptistic source.[31] Whether or not the latter hypothesis commends itself, it remains likely that the view that John was the prophetic preparer for the Lord (that is, God) was the view maintained by the Baptist himself and retained by those who belonged to his circle. It is this view which is recognized, at the same time as it is revised,

---

[30]Kloppenborg, *Formation* 108–10; Sato, *Prophetie* 35–6.
[31]P. Vielhauer, 'Das Benedictus des Zacharias', *ZTK* 49 (1952) 255–72; J. A. Fitzmyer, *The Gospel according to Luke I-IX* (AB 28; New York: Doubleday, 1981) 316–21.

by Q 7:27. Given the evidence of considerable contact between the Q group and the surviving disciples of John,[32] this is not surprising. The revision, however, is important. For all the material in Q 3:7–9, 16–17, except for 3:16c (which, as we have seen, is picked up by the redactional 7:19, and to which we shall return), is coherent with the view that John looks for the coming of God. The shift from God to Jesus in the identity of 'the coming one' is carried out equally by the framing of 7:18–23 around 7:22 and by the insertion of 7:27. It looks as if both Q-editorial interventions belong together and were influenced by the conviction that John's task was the renewal of the people of God, a renewal which was seen as the prelude to the coming, not of God, but of someone else.

That other person, mentioned neither by name nor by title, is the preoccupation of Q 7:28b: ὁ μικρότερος ἐν τῇ βασιλείᾳ τοῦ θεοῦ μείζων αὐτοῦ ἐστιν. In the face of the notorious ambiguities of this saying it will be argued below that ὁ μικρό-τερος is a strict comparative, rather than a superlative, and that it has an individual, rather than a generic, sense; that ἡ βασιλεία τοῦ θεοῦ here refers to the future end-time order, rather than a present period of fulfilment; that ἐν τῇ βασιλείᾳ τοῦ θεοῦ functions adjectivally to define ὁ μικρότερος, rather than adver-bially to define ἐστίν; and that ἐστίν itself is a Semitic future, rather than a strict present.

The reasons for taking ἐν τῇ βασιλείᾳ τοῦ θεοῦ as a description of the future order[33] are as follows: First, that is the sense of the only other Q saying using this phrase, Q 13:29. Second, this interpretation fits the contrast between the transcendent divine world and the limitations of human existence which is implicit in the term ἐν γεννητοῖς γυναικῶν.[34] Third, that same phrase ἐν γεννητοῖς γυναικῶν would serve ill as a definition of one period of salvation-history which has now been succeeded by another period, since participants in the latter period are just as much 'born of woman'. The corollary will necessarily be a future

[32]Sato, *Prophetie* 371–2.

[33]F. Dibelius, 'Zwei Worte Jesu', *ZNW* 11 (1910) 188–92, esp. p. 191; A. Polag, *Die Christologie der Logienquelle* (WMANT 45; Neukirchen: Neukirchener Verlag, 1977) 159.

[34]Dibelius, 'Worte', 190. The introduction of the scheme used in John 3:3, 5 is inappropriate in this particular context: rightly, Schürmann, *Lukasevangelium I* 419.

sense for ἐστίν, but for that there is precedent elsewhere in Q.[35]

Next, to interpret ὁ μικρότερος as a superlative and a generic term would be to place John lower than the lowest participant in the future order, that is, to exclude him from it.[36] Such an exclusion would be at variance first of all with Q 7:18–23, where, as a result of redaction,[37] John and his disciples 'see and hear' and thus qualify for the blessing announced in Q 10:23–24. An exclusion would also be at variance with Q 13:28–29, where the presence of the patriarchs at the promised celebration is clear and can scarcely be harmonized with the absence of the Baptist. Hence ὁ μικρότερος is better taken to refer to an individual and to involve a contrast with Jesus.[38] Functionally John's exalted role in human history is contrasted with Jesus' role in the ultimate eschatological order.

This interpretation is facilitated by several relevant considerations. First, it brings v. 28b alongside v. 27 to exhibit a unity of christological and future-eschatological concern, and it thus becomes unnecessary to attribute v. 27 and the whole of v. 28 to different redactional stages. Second, it allows those two statements in vv. 27, 28b to recognize and respond to the serious problem posed for Christian theology by what has been said in vv. 24b–26, 28a: Jesus' declaration that John has a quite unique status creates a problem which is strictly *christological*.[39] Third, a dominant christological concern in Q 7:24–28 is supported by the presence of that same dominant concern in the surrounding passages, both of which address the christological issue in a setting which is fundamentally appreciative of John: Q 7:18–23, with its secondary christological framework focussed on 'the coming one', and Q 7:31–35, with its secondary

[35] See 3:9b; 6:20b.

[36] The serious problem involved in such an interpretation is widely recognized, cf. Schürmann, *Lukasevangelium I* 419; Ernst, *Lukas* 249; Polag, *Christologie* 159.

[37] See Sato, *Prophetie* 141.

[38] See Dibelius, 'Worte', 191; O. Cullmann, 'ὁ ὀπίσω μου ἐρχόμενος,' *The Early Church* (London: SCM, 1956) 177–82; O. Michel, 'μικρός', *TDNT* 4.648–59, esp. pp. 653–4; Hoffmann, *Studien* 219–24. Otherwise, Hahn, *Titles* 367; Schulz, *Spruchquelle* 233–4. The description of the disciple or taught one as μικρός in relation to the teacher is not without precedent (1 Chr 25:8, cf. the similar use of other diminutive terms for those needing instruction, 1 Kgs 3:7; Q 10:21; Rom 2:20).

[39] See Hoffmann, *Studien* 223.

christological expansion focussed on him who 'has come', the Son of man.

The conclusion is therefore that Q 7:27, 28b are editorial statements designed to define the person of Jesus by reference to his eschatological function. These statements achieve their purpose by contrasting Jesus with John, and also by putting Jesus in the position which in earlier tradition had been reserved for God.

2. The Beginning of the Gospel. Mark 1:1–8.

We now transfer our attention to the earliest section of the gospel of Mark with a view to demonstrating that Mark knew Q. Such a relationship has been discounted by Sato as 'unprovable and improbable' in view of two critical considerations: the difficulty of explaining secondary features of the *Doppelüberlieferungen* in Mark as the evangelist's editorial work on Q, and the further difficulty of explaining why Mark would have ignored the rest of the Q material if he had known it.[40] In response, the first difficulty may not be so daunting, as Wolfgang Schenk has indicated,[41] and Sato himself has sketched in some considerations which potentially reduce the second.[42] With particular and, for our purpose, significant reference to 'the account of the beginning (Mark 1:(2), 3–15 and Luke 3:(2–4?), 7–9, 16–17, 21–22; 4:1–13; (6:20) par.)' he suggests contacts and correlations between the Q-group and pre-Marcan traditions. That is at the very least entirely plausible, but it points to a knowledge, and consequent setting aside, of a good deal of Q material at that pre-Marcan stage. If it is conceivable at the pre-Marcan stage, it is conceivable at the Marcan stage as well, particularly if the Marcan genre, special interests and comparative lack of concern with the content of the teaching of Jesus are borne in mind. In short, while a series of special studies is needed to establish an overall conclusion, nothing predetermines the outcome of any one of them. To the one which is most important for this investigation we now turn.

[40]Sato, *Prophetie* 383.
[41]'Der Einfluss der Logienquelle auf das Markusevangelium', *ZNW* 70 (1979) 141–65.
[42]*Prophetie* 384.

First, Mark 1:2b interprets the work of John by means of the composite OT quotation, 'Behold, I send my messenger before your face, who shall prepare your way.' Apart from the absence of ἔμπροσθέν σου this is exactly the combination Exod 23:20 + Mal 3:1 which appears in Q 7:27, to the extent of even employing the verb κατασκευάζειν which has no basis in any version of either text. Not surprisingly, opponents of the Q hypothesis have fastened on this overlap and attempted to establish alternative explanations.[43] Clearly, it will not do for supporters of the Q hypothesis to play down this quite remarkable correspondence, and they are in some difficulty if they suppose Mark and Q to have been wholly independent. However, v. 2b is very awkward in its Marcan context, as is evident from the introductory reference 'as it was written in Isaiah the prophet' (v. 2a), which leads into the Isa 40:3 quotation (v. 3) but into nothing else. This awkwardness is confirmed, of course, by the proliferation of manuscript variants for v. 2a and the removal of v. 2b by both Matthew and Luke. When the smoothness of the transition from vv. 1–2a to v. 3 is taken into account, it becomes possible not only to see in v. 2b evidence of MarkR based on Q-redaction, and therefore of Marcan use of Q, but also evidence of an emergent pre-Marcan tradition consisting of vv. 2a, 3. What is not yet clear is the provenance of this tradition.

Second, Mark 1:7 employs the saying about the stronger one who is coming. Another version of this saying appeared in Q 3:16c. As we have already noted, everything else said by John suggests that he is anticipating the coming of God. This would by no means be excluded by the anthropomorphic reference to the sandals (cf. Pss 60:8; 108:9),[44] but it must be admitted that an assertion of God's great superiority to John would be a trifle overdone.[45] Therefore the suspicion takes root that in this saying someone other than God is in mind, a corollary of which would be that the saying is itself an editorial intrusion.

In Q 3:16c John employs two ideas as measures of the superiority

[43]M. D. Goulder, 'On putting Q to the test', *NTS* 24 (1978) 218–34, esp. pp. 224–5; E. P. Sanders and M. Davies, *Studying the Synoptic Gospels* (London: SCM, 1989) 95–6.

[44]Against C. H. H. Scobie, *John the Baptist* (London: SCM, 1964) 66.

[45]Hoffmann, *Studien* 24: 'Der Sitz im Leben für einen solchem Vergleich war erst in einer Situation gegeben, die Johannes und Jesus einander gegenüber stellte.'

of the coming one, namely strength and the carrying of sandals. It may be significant that the idea of strength is used elsewhere in Q in the context of miracle (11:21–22), which would interlock with Q 7:22, but this should probably not be pressed. What has a more obvious bearing is the recurrent equivalence in Biblical material of ἰσχυρός and μέγας, and therefore the equivalence of ἰσχυρότερος (Q 3:16c) and μείζων (Q 7.28b). In such material the much laboured themes are irresistibility,[46] judgment,[47] and salvation.[48] The sandals allusion very probably has to be understood in terms of discipleship in the light of R. Joshua b. Levi's famous dictum that 'all manner of service that a slave must render his master a student must render to his teacher, except that of taking off his shoe' (*b. Ketub.* 96a). If Q 3:16c uses the disciple/teacher relationship as a yardstick of the extreme inferiority of John to the coming one, it matches the corrective effect of Q 7:28b on 7:28a. That is, the erstwhile relationship of the disciple (Jesus) to the teacher (John) is reversed and more than reversed. It is perhaps fair to add that 'to carry the sandals' may be more directly an allusion to the slave/master relationship, which *b. Ketub.* 96a also envisages. In that case the coming one is the κύριος of Q, the central figure of the future eschatological parables, the Son of man (Q 12:39–40, 42–46). By whatever means, a unity of construction and conviction is exhibited in Q 3:16c and the secondary stratum in Q 7:18–35. Like the latter the former needs to be credited to Q-editorial intervention.[49]

When Mark 1:7 is set alongside this Q-editorial saying all Mark/Q discrepancies are readily explicable in terms of Marcan interests. (i) The indicative ἔρχεται, by contrast with the original Q term ὁ ἐρχόμενος,[50] makes John announce *that* a certain person is coming, not *what* such and such a coming person is

---

[46]Josh 23:9; Job 36:22; Eccl 6:10; Jer 1:18, 19; 20:11.

[47]2 Kgdms 22:48; Job 9:19; 22:13; and with storm imagery in context: Job 37:5; Isa 28:2.

[48]2 Chr 25:8; Isa 50:2; 59;1.

[49]Hoffmann, *Studien* 32–3. Kloppenborg, *Formation* 104–5, opposes Hoffmann by deducing the great age of the saying from its widespread occurrence in Q, Mark, John 1:26 and Acts 13:25. But Mark's knowledge of Q, Luke's knowledge of Mark, and John's probable knowledge of both Mark and Luke would set the objection aside.

[50]Hoffmann, *Studien* 23–4.

like. That logically means that the sequel must be an identification of *who* that certain person is, an identification achieved by the baptismal tradition affirming, 'You are my beloved Son . . .', which Mark places next. (ii) The phrase ὀπίσω μου is symmetrical with the phrase ἔμπροσθέν σου, dropped by Mark from the composite Exod 23:20 + Mal 3:1 quotation. (iii) Fluctuation between 'loosing' and 'carrying' sandals is just as easily explained in one direction as in the other, and the unique κύπτειν coheres with the Marcan form here, as well as with the Marcan tendency elsewhere to refer to such gestures of respect (cf. 1:40; 5:22; 7:25; 10:17). (iv) The replacement of a future baptism in fire[51] by one in holy spirit belongs to the tendency to scale down the theme of judgment as John inaugurates the preaching of the Christian gospel and the fulfilment of the time (cf. 1:1, 14–15; 13:10; 14:9), and prepares for the next event described by Mark, the event in which the one who endows is himself endowed with holy spirit (1:9–11). In sum, the evidence once again points to Marcan use of Q-editorial material, that is, to Marcan use of Q.

We are now in a position to explore the possibility that other Marcan material may derive from Q. For a particular piece of Marcan material to be accepted as an edited version of a Q tradition three conditions should ideally be met. The first is that other indubitably Q material should make more sense with such a tradition in the background than without it. The second is that within the Marcan context there should be some evidence of literary seams. And the third is that there should be some Matthew/Luke 'minor agreements' against Mark. The hypothesis here advanced is that these conditions are met by a combination of elements drawn from Mark 1:2a, 3, 4, 5.

The first condition, which engages with the questions mentioned at the beginning of this chapter, is met by v. 4. John is mentioned, and indeed defined, by the contemporary title ὁ βαπτίζων (cf. Josephus, *Ant.*, 18.5.2 §116: ὁ βαπτιστής). His

[51]The original Q version may have referred to 'spirit and fire', though this must remain conjectural. It would have certain advantages, such as (i) respecting the lack of differentiation within ὑμῖν between those experiencing judgment and those experiencing salvation; (ii) providing some basis within the tradition for Mark's '*holy* spirit'; (iii) allowing a natural progression to the wind allusion in Q 3:17; and thus (iv) drawing upon traditional storm imagery for judgment, cf. Job 21:18; Isa 17:13; 33:11; Hos 13:3; Wis 5:21–23; 1QH 7.22–23.

baptism is introduced by the traditional formula κηρύσσων βάπτισμα μετανοίας εἰς ἄφεσιν ἁμαρτιῶν. The final phrase could conceivably be a MarkR addition to a shorter formula (cf. Acts 13:24; 19:4), but this is unlikely since all other Marcan instances of ἄφεσις (3.29) and ἀφιέναι (2:5, 7, 9, 10; 3:28; 4:12; 11:25–26) are traditional. Finally, 'the phrase ἐν τῇ ἐρήμῳ provides the same setting for the stones as in the temptation sequence (Q 4:1, 3), as well as agreeing with the content of Q 7:24.

The second condition, evidence of literary seams, is satisfied by the sequence already discussed in vv. 1–3, and by the sequence still to be discussed in vv. 4–6. As it stands, v. 4 introduces John and defines his mission. There then follows in v. 5 an expansion of the circle of interest to include those affected by John's activity. After that, when we would on formal grounds have expected some specific details of his preaching or his interaction with his audience, v. 6 comes as something of a surprise. It causes the circle of interest to contract by giving instead an ample description of John's clothing and diet. This literary evidence is corroborated in two ways. First, the MattR and LukeR decisions confirm awkwardness by, in the one case, re-ordering v. 6/Matt 3:4 and v. 5/Matt 3:5–6, and, in the other case, omitting v. 6 altogether. Second, by promoting the John = Elijah equation v. 6 coheres with the Marcan interest (9:11–13) and the secondarily added v. 2b. A seam therefore divides vv. 4–5 from v. 6, and the implication is again that beneath the surface of vv. 4–5 there lies pre-Marcan source material.

The third condition, the existence of 'minor agreements', serves to direct attention to Matt 3:5/Luke 3:3 πᾶσα ἡ περίχωρος τοῦ Ἰορδάνου over against Mark 1:5 πᾶσα ἡ Ἰουδαία χώρα καὶ οἱ Ἰεροσολυμῖται πάντες.[52] In Luke this phrase describes *where* John worked, but in Matthew it describes some of those who went out to where John worked, and the MattR combination of it with τότε ἐξεπορεύετο πρὸς αυτὸν Ἰεροσόλυμα καὶ πᾶσα ἡ Ἰουδαία is awkward: it hardly makes sense to say that the surrounding area of Jordan went *out* to the Jordan. Hence,

---

[52]The possibility that this derives from Q has been viewed sympathetically by a number of writers: Harnack, *Sayings* 41; Hoffmann, *Studien* 17; E. Schweizer, *The Good News according to Matthew* (London: SPCK, 1976) 48; Luz, *Matthew 1–7* 165; Schneider, *Lukas I* 82.

within the Matthew/Luke agreement in wording there must be a preference for the Lucan setting of the phrase. This would require that Mark 1:5 should itself have modified the Q rendering and introduced the movement of personnel from Judaea-Jerusalem to Jordan as well as their response to the call for baptism. That is easily envisaged. First, Mark could draw from Q 7:24 the idea of persons going *out* into the desert to see John. Second, it is typical of Mark to depict an extremely large audience or sphere of influence (cf. 1:28, 33, 37, 39, 45; 3:7, etc.). Third, similar movements from Jerusalem are introduced redactionally in Mark 3:22; 7:1. This leads to the question of the provenance of v. 5b. Again there are reasons to invoke MarkR. First, this description of wholehearted response is in tune with Mark's tendency towards acclamation or 'choral ending' (cf. 1:27; 2:12; etc.). Second, it can also without difficulty be viewed as a Marcan inference from the appreciative view of John described in Q 7:24–26. Third, it does not lead smoothly into Q 3:7–9, where the implied attitude of John is more detached and critical.

Last of all in the process of reconstruction, it is notable that Matthew and Luke agree in introducing John before quoting Isa 40:3, and that both quote that text by itself and in a form which makes ἐν τῇ ἐρήμῳ define the location of the herald and not that of 'the way of the Lord'.

It now becomes possible to assemble all the separate conclusions and thus to produce one major result, namely that beneath the surface of Mark 1:2–5 the original beginning of Q can be found waiting to be uncovered. When the introduction to John's preaching (Q 3:7a)[53] is attached, the following consecutive and coherent text emerges as that beginning:

Ἰωάννης ὁ βαπτίζων ἦλθεν εἰς πᾶσαν τὴν περίχωρον τοῦ Ἰορδάνου κηρύσσων βάπτισμα μετανοίας εἰς ἄφεσιν ἁμαρτιῶν, καθὼς γέγραπται ἐν τῷ Ἠσαΐᾳ τῷ προφήτῃ·
    φωνὴ βοῶντος ἐν τῇ ἐρήμῳ·
    ἑτοιμάσατε τὴν ὁδὸν κυρίου,

---

[53]Only in one detail does the reconstruction by Schulz, *Spruchquelle* 366–7, perhaps need modification. Matthew's 'Pharisees and Sadducees' are certainly redactional, cf. Matt 16:1, 6, 12 diff Mark 8:11, 15, but Luke's ὄχλοι may be pre-Lucan since it is both more typical of Q, cf. 11:14, 29, and also present in Q 7:24.

εὐθείας ποιεῖτε τὰς τρίβους αὐτοῦ.
ἔλεγεν δὲ τοῖς ὄχλοις ἐρχομένοις ἐπὶ τὸ βάπτισμα ...

From there the Q text will have continued with John's eschatological and christological preaching (3:7b-9, 16–17), and probably too Jesus' baptism and acclamation as son of God (3: 21–22),[54] and his testing (4:1–13).

3. Theological Implications.

The above reconstruction imposes two obligations. The first is to set the beginning of Mark alongside the beginning of Q and to check inductively whether a redaction-critical movement to the one from the other coheres with the evangelist's theology and purpose. The second is to describe the relationship between the beginning of Q and the rest of the document.

Mark took from the beginning of Q the quotation of Isa 40:3, together with its introduction (Q 3:4), inserted the Exod 23:20 + Mal 3:1 quotation from Q 7:27, and attached all these biblical allusions to his own formulation ἀρχὴ τοῦ εὐαγγελίου Ἰησοῦ χριστοῦ υἱοῦ τοῦ θεοῦ. The resultant 1:1–3 is a heading, not a sentence. It has been shown by Robert Guelich[55] to be unified and, in view of the usage of the word ἀρχή, 'a heading for the 'beginning' section of the Gospel rather than for the work as a whole'. The ideas which Mark deliberately included in this heading must therefore be matched and developed in ideas which he has introduced and developed in the 'beginning'. The activity of John is presented in two subsections (vv. 4–6, 7–8), each introduced by κηρύσσειν.

In the first of these subsections Mark picked up Q 3:3 and made four interpositions of his own: First, he added ἐν τῇ ἐρήμῳ, thus confirming the fulfilment of the same reference in

---

[54]The Matthew/Luke minor agreements exist, i.e. ἀνοίγειν diff σχίζειν; the aorist participle of βαπτίζειν; the phrase ἐπ' αὐτόν. They are not sufficient in themselves as evidence of non-Marcan source material, but can play a small part in conjunction with other arguments. See Sato, *Prophetie* 25–6.

[55]'The Gospel Genre', *Das Evangelium und die Evangelien* (ed. P. Stuhlmacher, WUNT 2/28; Tübingen: Mohr, 1983) 183–219, esp. pp. 204–7.

Isa 40:3. Second, he modified the περίχωρος idea in order that John's impact on Judaea and Jerusalem might be signalled (cf. Mark 3:22; 7:1). Third, instead of taking his cue from the confrontational sense of Q 3:7–9, he made the reception of John by the Judaeans wholly favourable, partly no doubt as a signal to the reader of the status of what was happening, partly in order that their response in baptism might be the factual fulfilment of the pluralized call to 'prepare the way of the Lord, make ready his paths', and partly to prepare for a contrast between the people at large, who receive John as a prophet, and the authorities who do not believe (Mark 11:31–32). Fourth, he developed the Elijah pattern in Mark 1:6, a pattern which would be explained in greater detail later on, and indeed made to incorporate the suffering theme (Mark 9:11–13) in a way which suggests that Mark 1:14a should be read in the same way.

In the second of the subsections (1:7–8) Mark changed the chiastic structure of Q 3:16. He thus gave special prominence to the announcement of the coming one, the preliminary character of his baptism which the hearers have undergone, and the prospect, not of judgment (hence the omission of 'fire' from Q 3:16d and all of Q 3:7b–9, 17) but of salvation. From there John becomes little more than a background figure (Mark 1:9, cf. 1:14a), and the end of the beginning of Mark is dominated by the person of Jesus (Mark 1:9–11, 12–13, cf. 1:14–15). In short, although Mark's account has on any showing its internal tensions, as an introduction to key Marcan ideas, it makes excellent sense as a redacted version of the beginning of Q.

The beginning of Q gives some support to the proposal that a prophetic text is before us. While Jesus dominates the document as a whole, it is John who briefly dominates its beginning. Here is someone who is identified with prophecy (Isa 40: 3), who is due to be acknowledged later as a prophet (Q 7:24b-26), whose demands echo the prophets (3:7–9, 17), and whose proclamation is subtly adapted to become prophecy of the coming Son of man. All this is initiated by the introductory quotation.

Two significant features of the Q quotation of Isa 40:3 invite reflection. They are the agreement with the LXX text in omitting the second 'in the desert', and the substitution of αὐτοῦ for 'of our God'. These changes permit the first 'in the desert' to define 'the voice of one crying', and also the term 'Lord' to be freed from its more natural reference to God. Whereas for Isaiah 'the train of thought demands not the ringing out of the voice in the wilderness, but that in the wilderness – which, of course, separates the people of Israel from their homeland – the way should be prepared',[56] for the Q editor, as for the LXX translator, the people of Israel are in their homeland, and the content of the announcement must differ. It is not necessary to go to the desert to make preparation. Yet going to the desert was a live option in the time and environment of Q. It was there that some of the popular prophetic movements of the thirty year period before the war with Rome were drawn (Q 17:23).[57] In Matt 24:26/Q 17:23 it is the version, 'Lo, he is in the desert . . . lo, he is in the inner rooms' which is likely to be original: it reflects the situation before the war with Rome and is unlikely to have been added by MattR afterwards. That being so, the Q critique of this option is centred on the coming Son of man (Q 17:24–30), the very person who was introduced redactionally into the speech of John in Q 3:16c and 7:19. Thus the beginning of Q is formed in such a way that it can introduce that perspective to the reader.

The κύριος of Isa 40:3 stands no longer for God, but now for the Son of man. With his 'way' and his 'paths' in mind Q/Isa 40:3 issues the call: 'Make ready the way . . . make straight his paths.' Later in Q the term 'ready' occurs with heavy overtones of eschatological fulfilment, maybe in 14:17 but certainly in 12:40: 'Therefore you also must be ready, for the Son of man (*sic*) is coming at an hour you do not expect'. Hence, whatever may have been the message of the historical John for his contemporaries, the message of the John of Q for his audience is clear. That message recurs in Q and is there at the beginning. It is that the people of God must be prepared in the fullest sense for the eschatological crisis which will, in spite of delay, occur imminently and centre on the coming of the Son of man to judge and save.

---

[56]C. Westermann, *Isaiah 40–66* (OTL; London: SCM, 1969) 37.
[57]R. A. Horsley, ' "Like One of the Prophets of Old": Two Types of Popular Prophets at the Time of Jesus', *CBQ* 47 (1985) 435–63.

3

The Inaugural Discourse

A collection of material chiefly comprised of the sayings of Jesus might conceivably attach no more importance to one saying than to another. Once some of the sayings, however, show signs of having been collected together according to some design, once they are set in a narrative sequence which suggests attention to order, then the situation changes. A narrative beginning, as well as sporadic narrative connections, a tendency to produce interactions between particular sorts of sayings, preoccupation with certain apparently favourite ideas, a final discourse – such features suggest that the collection is more than a mere assembly of bits and pieces. And this is the setting in which an inaugural discourse will have a special part to play. In Q that is plainly so. Set in the sequence after the mission of John and the temptations of Jesus, and framed by a short definition of an audience of disciples (Q 6:20a) and a story about an officer's faith (Q 7:1–10), the inaugural discourse in Q may be expected to yield very sensitive and significant evidence of the major concerns of the Q editor and the self-understanding of the community with which he identifies. If, in one sense, all the sayings of Jesus in Q are in status and authority equal, this initial collection will be more equal than the others.

Just two preliminary observations are necessary before the process of uncovering these vital concerns is attempted. The first concerns the broad trend in contemporary Q discussion which is to accept that Luke has more or less faithfully preserved the Q sequence. This will be accepted here as on the whole a reasonable working hypothesis. Occasionally, though, in various parts of Q there is evidence of exceptions to the rule. And at one point in the inaugural discourse in Q 6:20–49 there is a strong suspicion that Luke has intervened. That is probably by the insertion of v. 40: 'The disciple is not above his teacher . . .'.

The somewhat unnecessary, and probably Lucan,[1] introduction in v. 39a, 'He also told them a parable . . .' does not by itself mean that the following saying in v. 39b about the blind leading the blind owes its present position to Lucan redaction.[2] There are counter-examples which demonstrate this,[3] and there are strong thought connections between v. 39b and the speck/log saying in vv. 41–42.[4] No such connections, however, link v. 40 to the sayings before and after it, and consequently this saying, although present somewhere in Q (cf. Matt 10:24–25), was probably not present in the inaugural discourse. That sole exception apart, it is probably true to say that while the words of Matthew are often the words of Q, the scheme of Q may safely be deduced from the scheme of Luke.

The second preliminary observation concerns the composition of the discourse. There are signs of deliberate and careful design. At the beginning are placed some beatitudes (Q 6:20b–23). This conforms to the trend in Jewish tradition to position beatitudes at either the start,[5] or the finish[6] of a literary unit, or to use them as 'choral endings',[7] that is, as summarizing acclamations of an impressive whole experience. In conforming to this trend the Q editor signals his conscious concern with design, his intention to place all that follows under the control of Q 6:20b–23. This must undoubtedly be inferred in respect of the discourse, and one must reiterate the point that since this is the first public utterance of the Jesus of Q it must also be understood to apply to anything and everything said by him in the source as a whole. Then there is the end of the discourse. At this point the parable of the two housebuilders (Q 6:47–49) sets before the reader an uncomfortable choice and a terrifying warning. Standing where it does it performs, as is often noted, the same function as the Mosaic warnings at the end of the holiness code in Leviticus 26 and the covenant discourse in Deuteronomy 28. These two signs of deliberate design at top and tail of the Q discourse represent an initial composition-critical investment

[1]Cf. Luke 12:16, 41; 13:6; 14:7; 15:3; 18:1, 9; 19:11.
[2]J. Dupont, *Les Béatitudes I* (Ebib; Paris: Gabalda, 1969) 127.
[3]Luke 5:36; 21:29.
[4]For details, see p. 127.
[5]Cf. Pss 1:1; 32:1–2; 119:1–2; Sir 26:1.
[6]Deut 33:29; Pss 2:11; 127:5; Isa 30:18; Sir 48:11.
[7]Cf. 1 Kgs 10:8–9/2 Chr 9:7–8.

from which redaction-critical activity may produce dividends. With these two traditions our study will begin.

1. The Beatitudes and Woes. Q 6:20b–23, 24–26.

Arguments have already been adduced in support of the view that the beatitudes in Q consisted only of those preserved by Luke 6:20b-23, and that those which confer blessedness on the meek, the merciful, the pure in heart, and the peacemakers are unlikely to have been known to Luke. Before further progress is made these arguments need to be reinforced, and the dependence of these beatitudes on Matthaean creativity established. All of them, and not only the beatitude acclaiming those who are persecuted for righteousness, express favourite Matthaean ideas and, in some cases, anticipate traditions which occur very shortly afterwards in the Q sequence.

The beatitude concerning meekness (Matt 5:5) is clearly a doublet of Matt 5:3, since the terms πτωχοί and πραεῖς are alternative renderings of one and the same Hebrew word (*anawim*) in the formative OT texts (Ps 37:11; Isa 61:1). At the same time the word πραΰς ensures that the words ἐν πνεύματι are successful in defining poverty as spiritual rather than material. The presence of the term πραΰς in Matt 5:5 corresponds to its redactional use in texts presenting Jesus as Wisdom (Matt 11:29) and messiah (Matt 21:4–5 diff Mark 11:3). As the meek Wisdom figure he imposes a burden whose lightness contrasts with that of others (Matt 11:28, 30, cf. Q 11:46), that is, of the Pharisees. In this way an implicit anti-Pharisaic tendency can be discerned in keeping with the theme of Matthew's sermon (5:20). As the meek messiah Jesus lays down the pattern for the new era and for all who share in it, and thus authorizes the Matthaean ethical principle of *imitatio Christi*. That Matthew is indeed keen on that principle is evident from the domination of his beatitude material as a whole by the theme of righteousness (5:6, 10), that is, conduct according to the will of God which has already been exhibited by Jesus himself in the MattR construction 3:14–15.

The beatitude concerning mercy (Matt 5:7)[8] looks very much like a combination of two features of the adjacent Q sayings

81

6:36, 37, namely the theme of mercy and the principle of 'measure for measure'. The supremacy of mercy over and above all other commitments, however good in themselves, is a deepseated Matthaean principle expressed in Matt 9:13; 12:7 and 23:23, texts which enable us again to discover an anti-Pharisaic subtext. In the evangelist's view, mercy received should be followed by mercy shown, mercy not shown will be followed by mercy retracted (Matt 18:23–34), and mercy defined is active care and forgiveness. So insistent is Matthew on this point that he adds the demand for forgiveness to both the Lord's prayer and the parable of the unmerciful servant (6:14–15; 18:35). And as he picks up from Mark 10:47 the cry of the needy for mercy from the son of David, and redacts it repeatedly into his versions of miracle stories (cf. 9:27; 15:22; 17:15; 20:30–31), it becomes plain again that he has in mind Jesus as exemplar.

The beatitude concerning cleanness of heart (Matt 5:8) is assuredly intended to echo Ps 24:4, but the psalm is not the sole influence on Matthew. It cannot be coincidental that two adjacent beatitudes dealing with mercy and purity articulate the ideas contained in two adjacent Q woes against the Pharisees (Matt 23:23–24, 25–26/Luke 11:39–41, 42), and in the Matthaean order as well, whether or not this was the original Q order. Here must be a formative influence, and as a consequence also a hint that a negative and anti-Pharisaic tendency is built into the positive affirmation contained in this beatitude, too. For the evangelist the heart of the human problem is the problem of the human heart, and he makes this abundantly plain in his assertion that adultery takes place there (Matt 5:28), evil criticisms of Jesus begin there (Matt 9:4 diff Mark 2:8), and the whole sorry assembly of defilements belongs there (Matt 15:18–20/Mark 7:21–23). Cleanness of heart is in his view a necessary condition of cleanness of the total person, as is evident not only in the woes but also in the minor modifications he makes to Mark 7:1–23. And attached to the achievement of such cleanness is the promise of the vision of God, which is doubtless to Matthew a mark of closeness to, and approval by, the God whose visibility it is the privilege of the angels to enjoy (Matt 18:10).

---

[8] The word ἐλεήμων is a *hapax legomenon* in the gospels, but since the ἔλεος word group is recurrent, and the idea even more so, this is not a pointer away from the evangelist himself.

The beatitude concerning peacemaking (Matt 5:9) in order that true sonship may be effected is most naturally seen as an anticipation of the Q 6:27–28, 35 saying calling for love of enemies. This respects the *imitatio Dei* principle, again with the status of sonship in mind. On the Matthaean level sonship probably describes a status attainable in the here and now (cf. Sir 4:10) rather than in the age to come, just as the satisfying of the hunger and thirst for righteousness (Matt 5:6 diff Luke 6:21a) must be understood as taking shape in present conformity to the will of God now.[9] Such sonship would undoubtedly in the light of Matt 4:1–11 also have been understood by the evangelist as *imitatio Christi*. Finally, with this beatitude acclaiming the defeat of enmity the evangelist begins to move towards the topic of the long beatitude (Matt 5:11–12/Luke 6:22–23), a movement which gathers pace in the concluding short saying.

The beatitude upon those persecuted for righteousness (Matt 5:10) is abnormal within the collection – apart from the promise to the mourners it is the only one spelling out openly an adverse situation, and the only one which does not refer to an admirable quality of character which is to be reproduced. As such it appears discrepant, but not because it derives from a pre-Matthaean source. Rather it unites in itself Matthaean themes by overlapping with Matt 5:3, 6 and 11 in respect of 'the kingdom of heaven', 'righteousness' and 'persecution'. Thus at one and the same time it rounds off the collection of short beatitudes and builds a bridge to the long one. For Matthew, that long one speaks to a situation in which fierce opposition is coming, doubtless from a Pharisaic direction.

To sum up, all the evidence supports the conclusion that we take no risk in attributing all the single tradition Matthaean beatitudes to the evangelist. They are all positive expressions of his theology. They are all loaded contributions to his critique of Pharisees. They are all explicable without recourse to pre-Matthaean tradition.[10] They thus contribute to the evidence that in Luke 6:20b-23 there is visible the complete range of Q beatitudes.

---

[9]This would mean that these two beatitudes reverse the development, cf. Luz *Matthew 1–7* 231, from wisdom parenesis to apocalyptic.

[10]Against G. Strecker, 'Die Makarismen der Bergpredigt', *NTS* 17 (1971), 255–75.

The Q version of the short beatitudes (Q 6:20b-21) has probably been modified by Matthew with the substitution of ἡ
βασιλεία τῶν οὐρανῶν for ἡ βασιλεία τοῦ θεοῦ, and the addition
of the phrases τῷ πνεύματι,[11] καὶ διψῶντες,[12] and τὴν
δικαιοσύνην.[13] Correspondingly, that Q version has been
preserved by Luke, except for just three modifying features.

Luke's first modification was arguably the insertion of νῦν.
The secondariness of this word is suggested overwhelmingly by
word-statistics (4–3–14 + 25), by its absence from the first
beatitude in spite of its presence in the second and third, and by
its effectiveness in sharpening the stark contrast between what is
and what will be.

Luke's second modification was probably a change from a
third-person to a second-person form. The former is the majority usage in Jewish tradition, a fact which does not by itself
establish that Matthew's form is the original. It does, however,
receive support from the protasis in each of the Lucan sayings,[14]
it is attested elsewhere in Q (e.g. 7:23), and it is somewhat at
variance with the tendency to address disciples (cf. Matt 5:1/
Luke 6:20a).[15] The latter second-person form can stem from an
attempt to assimilate to that audience of disciples as well as to
the last and longest beatitude (Q 6:22–23), and is supported by
several instances of Luke's having made the same sort of change
elsewhere (cf. 5:30, 34; 6:2; 9:50; 21:16, 19).

Luke's third modification was arguably a change from the
language of 'mourning' and 'being comforted' to that of 'weeping' and 'laughing'. The former pairing tends to be attributed to

---

[11]The Qumran parallels in 1QM 14:7; 1QH 18:14–15, etc., exhibit a similar
tendency to that of Matthew and do not confirm that the original saying
contained the phrase 'poor in spirit'. Against E. Bammel, 'πτωχός', *TDNT*
6.885–915, esp. pp. 904–5. Cf. Matt 27:50 diff Mark 15:37 for another redactional
reference to the human spirit.

[12]'Hunger and thirst' is of course an idiomatic combination, cf. Isa 49:10;
65:13, elsewhere in the synoptics only within Matt 25:31–46, and unlikely to
have been dropped by Luke in view of LukeR combinations of eating and
drinking, cf. 5:33; 10:7; 13:26.

[13]Statistics: 7–0–1 + 4. The matter is summed up by Dupont, *Béatitudes I* 220,
'L'omission de τὴν δικαιοσύνην serait incompréhensible, l'addition se comprend
d'elle même.'

[14]Dupont, *Béatitudes I* 281–2; Luz, *Matthew 1–7* 227.

[15]P. Hoffmann, 'Selig sind die Armen... Auslegung der Bergpredigt II
(Mt 5,3–16)', *Bibel und Leben* 10 (1969) 111–22, esp. p. 113.

redaction under the influence of Isa 61:2,[16] but there are arguments against this. First, Matthew's pairing is a point of agreement between Matt 5:4 and Luke 6:24, 25.[17] Second, although γελᾶν occurs nowhere else in the NT apart from Luke 6:21, 25 (no problem in view of the profusion of *hapax legomena* in Luke-Acts), the statistics for its obverse κλαίειν are 2–3–10 + 2, that is, quite sufficient to support LukeR here. Third, Luke's pairing is faintly inappropriate in view of the adverse connotation of derision conveyed by laughter (cf. Job 8:21; 22:19; Ps 52:6; Jer 20:7; Lam 1:7; 4 Macc 5:28).[18] It was probably part of a single Lucan plan that 'weeping' and 'laughing' should replace 'mourning' and 'being comforted', that this beatitude should be placed third, as had already happened in the reordering of the second and third parts of the temptations tradition (Q 4:1–12), and that a transition in thought should thus be effected to the theme of persecution covered by the fourth, last and longest of the beatitudes (Q 6:22–23). One final point may be added: Matthew's beatitude on the mourners accidentally confirms that Luke's overall scheme is original. Mourning here means real mourning, genuine anguish, authentic grief, not sorrow for sin. Ulrich Luz has observed[19] that mourning without further qualification is not interpretable as sorrow for sin. Not even 1 Cor 5:2 serves as a counter-example,[20] since there the context provides the required qualification. Therefore this is the one beatitude which cannot sustain an anti-Pharisaic tendency, and it is the one beatitude which is not internalized, not spiritualized, not deprived of concern for real human distress which God will rectify. It represents a small defeat for the Matthaean policy of

[16]Sato, *Prophetie* 47; Luz, *Matthew 1–7* 227.

[17]Particularly in the case of παράκλησις, Luke 6:24, it is natural to see a reminiscence of παρακληθήσονται, Matt 5:4. For, although the language of παρακαλεῖν and παράκλησις is predominantly Lucan in the NT (9–9–7 + 23; 0–0–2 + 4), it represents the reversal of ills in the context of the poverty/prosperity divide, cf. Luke 16:25, and never the original prosperity of the rich as such. An explanation has to be found for the naturalness of the παρακαλεῖν usage in Matt 5:4 and the contrivedness of the παράκλησις usage in Luke 6:24. If the one is an infelicitous echo of the other this explanation is found.

[18]See P. Humbert, '"Laetari et exultare" dans le vocabulaire religieux de l'Ancien Testament', *RHPR* 22 (1942) 185–214; K. H. Rengstorf, 'γελάω', *TDNT* 1.658–62, esp. p. 659.

[19]*Matthew 1–7* 235.

[20]Against Goulder, *Luke I* 350.

remodelling, but a significant victory for the original Q tradition which at this point stubbornly refused to be remodelled.

It is now possible to conclude that the original version of the short beatitudes ran as follows:

μακάριοι οἱ πτωχοί,
    ὅτι αὐτῶν ἐστὶν ἡ βασιλεία τοῦ θεοῦ.
μακάριοι οἱ πενθοῦντες,
    ὅτι αὐτοὶ παρακληθήσονται.
μακάριοι οἱ πεινῶντες,
    ὅτι αὐτοὶ χορτασθήσονται.

If this argumentation is correct we can go on to observe that the short beatitudes in Q consisted, not of three discrete declarations about the poor and the grief-stricken and the hungry, but of a single controlling declaration which was amplified or paraphrased by two others.[21] For in Jewish tradition the poor are themselves persons who experience at all times what others know only in times of bereavement.[22] They are also persons who struggle to obtain necessary food.[23] This being so, the future reversal envisaged in παρακληθήσονται and χορτασθήσονται enables us to interpret the verb ἐστίν in Q 6:20b as a Semitic future-type present, and ἡ βασιλεία τοῦ θεοῦ as the totality of God's design for the deprived. All this draws, not upon the wisdom tradition in the manner of many Jewish beatitudes, but upon the vision promoted by apocalyptic. Specifically, it draws upon the programme of Isa 61.1–2, as the answer of Jesus to John that 'the poor have good news preached to them' (Q 7:22) confirms.[24] Not only so: the choice of the beatitude form to articulate that programme draws its meaning from the frequency with which this very form had been used to reflect on the covenant and the blessings which stemmed from it.[25] In other words, the self-awareness of the people of God is concerned, and the concentration upon the poor reflects the conviction that the God of the covenant's concern for the

[21]Dupont, *Les Béatitudes II* (Paris: Gabalda, 1969) 13: 'un tout indissociable . . . la triple expression d'une déclaration unique'.

[22]Sir 4:1–2; 7:32–34; 38:19.

[23]Prov 22:9; Sir 4:1; 34:25.

[24]Cf. W. Grimm, *Die Verkündigung Jesu und Deuterojesaja* (ANTJ 1; 2nd ed.; Frankfurt am Main: Lang, 1981) 68–77, on the wide background of this presentation in Second Isaiah.

marginalized and vulnerable on the fringes of his people (humanly speaking), for those who found themselves at the wrong end of the socio-economic spectrum, for those who shared the defencelessness of the orphan and the widow,[26] for those who tended to be deprived of justice and victimized by the rich and powerful – for these persons the God of the covenant's concern remains unchanged. This then is the message of the first three beatitudes which, as we shall see, belong to the very earliest stratum of the material which was assembled to form Jesus' inaugural discourse.

Before we travel on to the fourth and last beatitude on the persecuted, a saying which arguably has its own distinct tradition history, we must pause to discuss the woes which Luke alone includes (6:24–25, 26). Might these have been derived by him from Q, and at the same time have been set aside by Matthew? There are several good reasons for supposing, in spite of the sharpness of the division among scholars, that this was indeed the case.[27]

First, it would be so impossible, in respect of both the structure of Matt 5 and the substance of the woes, for Matthew to have included them that their preservation by Luke alone cannot possibly be an argument against their original presence in Q. An evangelist who transformed and expanded the Q beatitudes so that they extolled spiritual qualities could not on any showing include such realistically material sayings as the woes, sayings which after all were not susceptible to the same sort of spiritualizing transformation. Matthew's distinctive presentation of money matters (see 10:9; 25:15) suggests that, however much he recognized the obligation to care for the poor, he instinctively identified with the prosperous and held the view that 'poverty and hunger *as such* have no ethical value'.[28]

Second, it is absolutely normal for Jewish traditions to balance

---

[25]See Deut 33:29; Pss 33:12; 89:15; 94:12; 106:3; 112:1; 144:15; 146:5, which is particularly close to the trio of Q beatitudes; Isa 30:18; 56:2; *Pss. Sol.* 4:23; 5:18; 17:44.

[26]See Job 29:12; Pss 10:14; 82:3–4; Sir 4:8–10.

[27]For the presence of the woes in Q: Schürmann, *Lukasevangelium I* 336–41; for their later attachment: P. Klein, 'Die lukanischen Weherufe Lk 6,24–26', *ZNW* 71 (1980) 150–9.

[28]Streeter, *Four Gospels* 252.

blessings on one group with woes and denunciations ostensibly directed at another group.[29] A profusion of examples can be called in aid.[30] It is important to note that the passage upon which the beatitudes draw, Isa 61:1–2, itself glances critically at the rich, and so does the Qumran text 11QMelch when providing a *pesher* exposition of Isaiah 61. Lest a division of target audiences be taken to imply the separateness of the traditions, it needs to be affirmed that the amplification of a speech to a primary and 'real' group by means of a denunciation of an 'opposition' group has a powerful effect of legitimation for the former. Negativity over against those who are only, as it were, hypothetically present has a deliberate and wonderfully reassuring effect on those who are really present (cf. Num 21:29; Jas 4:13–5:6). It may also be the case that the very emphatic αὐτῶν . . . αὐτοί in the three short beatitudes is intended to prepare for precisely the kind of contrast with the alternative group which the woes achieve. It is relevant at this point also to note that Luke's ἀλλὰ ὑμῖν λέγω τοῖς ἀκούουσιν is shown by Matt 5:43–44 to have been in Q, and it reads naturally as a conscious return to the immediate and actual audience and away from another group, that is, the group of rich persons addressed in most of 6:24–26.

Third, woes are a familiar phenomenon in Q (see 10:13; 11:42–52; 17:1) but never in LukeR material.[31]

Fourth, we shall see that within the Q discourse there is a strong thematic thread of continuity linking 6:22–23 to 6:27–36. Within vv. 27–36 the call to lend (v. 30) presupposes that those thus called are indeed in a position to lend. Lending is the one way in which a typical rich person can achieve blessedness, according to Sir 31:8–11. According to Q 12:33–34 as well, this

[29]Cf. C. H. Dodd, 'The Lucan beatitudes and woes, forming a unitary whole, are composed on a well established literary pattern.' 'The Beatitudes: A Form-Critical Study', *More New Testament Studies* (Manchester: University Press, 1968) 1–10, esp. p. 4. Dupont, *Béatitudes I* 326–35, is critical of the idea of a stereotyped literary formula. The important point, however, is that a combination of beatitudes and judgment/woe sayings is comfortable within a setting such as Q.

[30]See Pss 1:1–6; 146:5–9; Prov 8:34–36; 28:14; Eccl 10:16–17; Wis 3:13–15 within 3:10–19. Cf. also *b. Ber.* 61b: 'Blessed are you, Akiba, because you were arrested for words of Torah. Woe to you, Pappos, because you were arrested for idle words.'

[31]Schürmann, *Lukasevangelium I* 337.

is the only way to the heavenly treasure. Keeping an eye on the rich is an idea shared by the woes and the saying about lending, the one essentially negative in tone and the other more positive and constructive.

Fifth, there are some small but significant verbal straws in the wind. One is the commercial/accounting word ἀπέχειν, present in Luke 6:24 and in a matching trio of denunciations in Matt 6:2, 5, 16, and in each case using a present tense when describing the gain accruing to the group in question. This verbal overlap cannot be explained by Luke's knowing the Matthaean material, since nothing suggests that it belonged to Q. Therefore Matthew appears to know Luke 6:24. Another verbal straw in the wind is the common reference to something 'false' (Matt 5:11; Luke 6:26). References to falsity are rare in the gospels, and the coincidence of such a reference in the same context in Matthew and Luke may require explanation. The idea of falsity is vital in Luke's reference to 'false prophets', but it is not so in Matthew's reference to the falsity of slander which has with some justice been dismissed as 'a mincing addition'.[32] If so, Luke 6:26 would seem to have been known by Matthew.[33] Yet another verbal straw in the wind is the match between Matthew's 'they speak all kinds of evil against you' (Matt 5:11) and Luke's 'all speak well of you' (Luke 6:26). It is the Lucan counterpart of Matt 5:11, 'cast out your name as evil' (6:22), whose originality has commanded support as an 'obtrusive Aramaism',[34] an idiomatic Semitic way of referring to defamation or spreading an evil report about a person or persons, and a phrase for which there is no LXX equivalent which might permit its attribution to Luke. If that is the case, this part of the wording of Matt 5:11 is owed to MattR, and the match with Luke 6:26 supports the presence of the latter in Q.

The general probability that the woes figured in Q still leaves over the specific task of reconstructing their wording. It is likely that the effects of LukeR can still be detected, and that at an earlier stage there was a precise symmetry between beatitudes

[32]Schweizer, *Matthew* 96.

[33]H. Schürmann, *Traditionsgeschichtliche Untersuchungen zu den synoptischen Evangelien* (Düsseldorf: Patmos, 1968) 306.

[34]M. Black, *An Aramaic Approach to the Gospels and Acts* (3rd ed.; Oxford: OUP, 1967) 156.

and woes. Doubtless the introduction of νῦν and a change to second-person formulations can be posited. The one difficulty is the woe on the rich which ought to function as a heading for the other two woes and which is unlikely to have included the very Lucan word παράκλησις. The matching ἀπέχειν formulation in Matt 6:2, 5, 16 is worth considering as the solution to this problem. 'They have their reward' is general in the same way that the 'kingdom of God' reference in Q 6:20b is general, it uses a present tense with future meaning, and the term 'reward' itself can stand just as well for adverse punishment as for approved gain.[35] Given the dissonance between the first three and the fourth woes, we may speculate that the pre-Q tradition of the woes, matching the pre-Q tradition of the beatitudes, ran:

> οὐαὶ τοῖς πλουσίοις,
>   ὅτι ἀπέχουσιν τὸν μισθὸν αὐτῶν.
> οὐαὶ τοῖς (?γελῶσιν/χαίρουσιν),
>   ὅτι πενθήσουσιν.
> οὐαὶ τοῖς ἐμπεπλησμένοις,
>   ὅτι πεινάσουσιν.

All that was said about the pre-Q tradition of the beatitudes is now reinforced by what can be said about the pre-Q tradition of the woes. Q belongs to a community context in which it is felt appropriate to see this antithetical picture of poor and rich as essential to true religion and the epitome of the message of Jesus. The outlook of Q is just as much revealed by the preservation of these traditions as by the redactional alteration of others. This is a community which is acutely aware of the issue of poverty and of the peril of prosperity. Not surprisingly the woes in isolation sound very unguarded and unequivocal in their denunciation of the well off. There is, however, some slight softening. From related traditions such as Q 6:30 and Q 12:33–34 it emerges that the rich can participate within the movement, provided they learn to view their situation eschatologically and to disperse their wealth charitably.

This brings us to the fourth and last beatitude, Q 6:22–23, to

---

[35]H. Preisker – E. Würthwein, 'μισθός', *TDNT* 4.695–728, esp. p. 697. See Ezek 27:33; 2 Macc 8:33; Acts 1:18; Jude 11; Rev 22:12.

which we may now add the fourth and last woe (Q 6:26). The secondariness of the blessing of the persecuted is widely recognized and well grounded.[36] By contrast with the first three, it uses the second-person rather than the third-person form; it represents pastoral encouragement of disciples rather than unrestricted public proclamation; it is long and elaborate rather than short and pithy; it is christological while they are not. The corollary of this is that the saying must be interpreted on the Q level rather than being translated without more ado back into Aramaic and interpreted on some other level. But before we enter upon that process of interpretation it is worth checking exactly what was the content of the original Q version and whether any of that content can be assigned to Q redaction. On the first of these two issues, I would like to support the proposal of Günther Schwarz[37] that there was a pre-Q version of the underlying tradition which ran as follows:

μακάριοί ἐστε ὅταν ὀνειδισώσιν ὑμᾶς οἱ ἄνθρωποι.
 κατὰ τὰ αὐτὰ γὰρ ἐποίουν τοῖς προφήταις οἱ πατέρες αὐτῶν.
οὐαὶ ὅταν ὑμᾶς καλῶς εἴπωσιν πάντες οἱ ἄνθρωποι.
 κατὰ τὰ αὐτὰ γὰρ ἐποίουν τοῖς ψευδοπροφήταις οἱ πατέρες
 αὐτῶν.

This proposal takes seriously several factors. The first is the suggestion of a word-play in Aramaic involving the two main verbs, 'to insult' (= *qelal*) and 'to speak well' (= *qelas*). The second is the internal consistency achieved on the basis of statements made by Jeremiah, that arch-exponent of the deuteronomic view of Israel's history, about how insult is painfully woven into the fabric of the prophetic experience.[38] The third is that within Q 6:23 there is evident competition and rivalry between the two statements introduced by 'for', that is, 'for behold your reward is great in heaven' (Q 6:23b) and 'for so their fathers did to the prophets' (Q 6:23c). Of these two it is the former which appears to be secondary.[39] It is added secondarily

[36]Schulz, *Spruchquelle* 454–5; Hoffmann, *Studien* 73.
[37]'Lukas 6.22a, 23c, 26. Emendation, Rückübersetzung, Interpretation', *ZNW* 66 (1975) 269–74.
[38]See Jer 6:10; 15:15; 20:8.
[39]Otherwise Luz, *Matthew 1–7* 242.

(if the ensuing argument is correct) shortly afterwards in this discourse in Q 6:35. More importantly, it aligns the saying schematically to the suffering of the righteous one who is not restricted to the circle of the prophets. Now the inaugural discourse of Jesus is addressed to 'disciples' (Q 6:20a), that is, to anyone who 'confesses' Jesus the Son of man (cf. Q 12:8–9). It is not addressed restrictedly to those contemporary prophets who follow in the footsteps of the prophets of old and who represent a sub-group of those who confess Jesus. There is therefore a consistency and straightforwardness in the reconstruction of the history of the tradition in Q 6:20a, 22–23 if we assign to the Q editor the definition of the audience, the amplification and explicit Christianization of the description of the sufferings, and the call to rejoice with the great heavenly reward in mind.[40] Such consistency is further confirmed by recognizing that this is not the only pre-Q saying about insult in this context, since this will be the thrust of the argument about Q 6:29,[41] and that there are no signs in 6:27–35 that those who are to love their enemies are in any way restricted to latter day prophets. It will be noted that in reconstructing the history of the tradition in 6:22–23 no use has been made of 6:26 as a measure of the length of the underlying saying, but it happens to turn out rather neatly that the internal evidence in the former suggests an outcome in which there is a correspondence with the latter!

The argument has been that a saying which had its original *Sitz im Leben* in a prophetic mission – quite suitably the mission attested by the tradition underlying Q 10:2–16 – has been generalized and given a new and extended orientation towards the sufferings of a wider group of followers of Jesus. The mistreatment to which the followers of Jesus are subjected, according to the fourth beatitude, took several forms. The experience of 'separation' (Luke 6:22 diff Matt 5:11) was probably not involved: it is unlikely to have been dropped by Matthew as he breathed an unpleasant atmosphere in which echoed charges and counter-charges of deceit and apostasy, and is more likely to

---

[40]Matthew's χαίρετε, less firmly tied than Luke's χάρητε to the secondary LukeR ἐν ἐκείνῃ τῇ ἡμέρᾳ (so Schulz, *Spruchquelle* 454) is likely to be original. Luke's σκιρτήσατε was probably provoked by Matthew's ἀγαλλιᾶσθε, cf. the pairing of the two words in Luke 1:44.

[41]See below, pp. 109–12.

reflect a religiously polarized experience of rejection and exclusion in the latter part of the century.[42] For all that Q knows about confrontation, it remains within the relationship of brotherhood, cf. Q 6:41–42; 17:3–4. 'Persecution' (Matt 5:11 diff Luke 6:22) is uncertain and cannot safely be attributed to Q. By contrast, 'insult', agreed by Matthew and Luke, clearly was involved. So probably was the 'casting out of the name as evil', as we have already seen.[43] 'Hatred', attested only by Luke but not a word he normally employs when describing the sufferings of Christians, was yet another.[44] The agents of persecution are left undefined in Matt 5:12 over against 'their fathers' in Luke 6:23c. The general tendency is to invoke MattR,[45] but this is perhaps questionable in the light of the charge elsewhere that the Pharisees are the sons of the assassins of the prophets (Q 11:47–48). But as the Q editor amplified the portrayal of opposition what was most prominently in his mind was probably 'the Son of man'. That this term was used by him, possibly here, as in Q 12:8–9, as part of a deliberate word-play involving 'men' (Luke 6:22, but not Matt 5:11) is a justified inference, because (i) there is no precedent for Luke's introducing this term without any basis in tradition; (ii) there is precedent for Matthew's omitting explicit christological terms which he found in his source, cf. 10:32–33; 23:34; and (iii) elsewhere in Q a secondary appendix (Q 7:33–34) to primary tradition (Q 7:31–32) introduces the Son of man and at the same time, by careful choice of language, recalls the succession of the prophets who came and were rejected by verbal defamation and slander. That, as we have seen, is the horizon of the fourth beatitude.

Adding together the various decisions which have had to be made we can reconstruct the approximate content of the fourth beatitude, together with the matching woe, as follows:

[42]Schulz, *Spruchquelle*, 452. Cf. the use of such language in Neh 13:3; Isa 56:3; 1QS 2:16–17; 5:18; 6:25.

[43]Dupont, *Béatitudes II* 292.

[44]Dupont, *Béatitudes I* 229, correctly observes that this is not a term of which Luke is particularly fond. He employs it only under the influence of sources. His usage in fact clusters in the 'loving your enemies' complex and in texts influenced by Mark 13:13, but never extends to Acts, in spite of the presence of many persecution passages there.

[45]See Schulz, *Spruchquelle* 454; W. Schenk, *Synopse zur Redenquelle der Evangelisten* (Düsseldorf: Patmos, 1981) 25; Sato, *Prophetie* 258.

μακάριοί ἐστε ὅταν μισήσωσιν ὑμᾶς οἱ ἄνθρωποι καὶ ὀνειδίσωσιν
καὶ ἐκβάλωσιν τὸ ὄνομα ὑμῶν ὡς πονηρὸν ἔνεκα τοῦ υἱοῦ τοῦ
ἀνθρώπου. χαίρετε καὶ ἀγαλλιᾶσθε, ὅτι ὁ μισθὸς ὑμῶν πολὺς
ἐν τῷ οὐρανῷ· οὕτως γὰρ ἐποίουν τοῖς προφήταις οἱ πατέρες
αὐτῶν.

οὐαὶ ὅταν καλῶς ὑμᾶς εἴπωσιν οἱ ἄνθρωποι· οὕτως γὰρ ἐποίουν
τοῖς ψευδοπροφήταις οἱ πατέρες αὐτῶν.

Here, then, by employing the language of opposition which,
however, falls short of separation, and by building on earlier use
of the deuteronomic pattern of perpetually persecuted prophets,
which had often been employed (as it were) domestically within
Israel, the editor allows us a glimpse of a situation within the
community of Israel. That situation had developed 'because of
the Son of man'. What that means is not that other Israelites
object to the teaching of Jesus as such, for the Jesus of Q is
through and through orthodox (cf. Q 11:42; 16:17), and his
teaching again and again anticipated by Jewish precedents. What
is meant is the conviction that the Son of man is Jesus, an
equation established with some effort and care elsewhere in Q
(cf. 7:18–23), and an equation which conveys the heavenly status
and future coming in judgment of the Jesus who had been
known on earth. Originally, the experience of opposition in the
comparatively mild form of insult had been a possibility which
prophetic leaders of a renewal movement in Israel had been
warned to take seriously. Latterly, that possibility had had to be
entertained by any and every member of the movement. All
such persons were, in time-honoured fashion, offered comfort
in the form of the pattern of the suffering righteous one: in
place of earthly dishonour they would know heavenly honour
and reward, provided, of course, that they responded to suffering in the appropriate spirit. To a description of that spirit, with
the aid of the same language as had been employed in Q 6:22,
the discourse would move in 6:27–35. Shortly we shall examine
that section.

2. The Parable of the Housebuilders. Q 6:46, 47–49.

From the beginning of the discourse we turn now to its end,

the parable of the two housebuilders, with the preceding introduction.

The Matthew/Luke versions of the parable vary a little, but the Q original can be discerned fairly readily in Matt 7:24–27, once a few details are recognized as MattR and consequently pruned away. That applies to the adjectives φρόνιμος and μωρός which describe the two builders:[46] they are probably to be explained as a deliberate anticipation of the parables of the faithful and wise servant and the ten virgins.[47]. It may also apply to the statement that the first house 'did not fall', which to an extent anticipates and detracts from what is said about the second house: the final climax would be dramatically more powerful if Q had merely said, with Luke, that the storms 'did not shake' the first, but that under their impact the second 'fell, and its fall was great'. Put more positively, the capacity of the house to stand firm and not be 'shaken/moved' would match the comparable statement in one of the rabbinic parallels, *m. 'Abot* 3:18, that the soundly based tree (representing the person whose works are greater than his wisdom) 'even if all the winds in the world come and blow against it, cannot be stirred from its place'. That person is as secure as the many others whose firmness is expressed in terms of their 'not being moved' (cf. Pss 10:6; 15:5; 30:6). It might also be possible on such a basis for the parable deliberately to echo those OT texts where the notion of movement or being shaken is not only associated with the effects of any wind (1 Kgs 14:15; Job 21:18; Ps 18:42) but also included in imagery depicting the storm of divine theophany. This interpretation, which has attracted some support, will need to be tested. However that may be, after setting aside the Lucan interest in the manner of building rather than its location, we are in a position to set out the Q version:

πᾶς ὁ ἀκούων μου τοὺς λόγους καὶ ποιῶν αὐτούς ὅμοιός ἐστιν ἀνθρώπῳ ὃς ᾠκοδόμησεν οἰκίαν ἐπὶ τὴν πέτραν. καὶ κατέβη ἡ βροχή, καὶ ἦλθον οἱ ποταμοί, καὶ ἔπνευσεν οἱ ἄνεμοι καὶ προσέπεσαν τῇ οἰκίᾳ ἐκείνῃ, καὶ οὐκ ἐσάλευσαν αὐτήν.

[46]Schulz, *Spruchquelle* 312–4. Against Goulder, *Midrash* 309, it is hard to see why Luke would have dropped this traditional pairing (see Sir 21:14–26) when he was happy enough to retain φρόνιμος in Q 12:42, cf. also 16:8.

[47]Rightly, R. A. Guelich, *The Sermon on the Mount* (Waco, Texas: Word Books, 1982) 403–4.

ὁ δὲ ἀκούων μου τοὺς λόγους καὶ μὴ ποιῶν αὐτούς, ὅμοιός ἐστιν ἀνθρώπῳ ὃς ᾠκοδόμησεν οἰκίαν ἐπὶ τὴν ἄμμον. καὶ κατέβη ἡ βροχὴ καὶ ἦλθον οἱ ποταμοὶ καὶ ἔπνευσαν οἱ ἄνεμοι καὶ προσέπεσαν τῇ οἰκίᾳ ἐκείνῃ, καὶ ἔπεσεν, καὶ ἦν ἡ πτῶσις αὐτῆς μεγάλη.

The interpretation of this parable on the Q level has to take account of whether or not there may have been a shift away from its own intrinsic meaning. That meaning hinges on the contrast between the two ideas of rock and sand, together with the fact that in every other respect there is an exact correspondence between the two situations described. In other words, nothing is inherently true of the one house which is not true of the other, and nothing happens to the one house which does not also happen to the other.[48] As far as 'the rock' is concerned, the listener belonging to a specific religious tradition is bound to recall the definitive connotations of hardness and height (cf. Ps 27:5; 40:2; Isa 22:16; 33:16) and thus of complete security. He or she might recollect that only the overpowering force of theophany disturbs and breaks (Job 14:18; and by contrast, Isa 2:10, 19, 21). But such a recollection would serve only to point up a contrast: the 'rock' in Q 6:48 is not shattered, therefore the storm is not the theophanic storm of divine judgment, and therefore the parable is truly a parable whose details are not intended to be treated allegorically. As it is with the rabbinic parables, so it is with this parable. As far as 'the sand' is concerned, the tradition would recall the associations of the sea shore, of infinitesimal smallness as proverbial as that of the mustard seed (Sir 18:10), of lightness like that of dust (Gen 13:16; Ps 78:27; Jdt 2:20). The parable therefore draws upon a well understood tradition and sets up a telling contrast between height and sea level, between firm stability and shifting instability, between security and dangerous vulnerability. It is concerned

[48]Luke's interest was in the manner of the building process, and a discrepancy between the two buildings was thus introduced. Matthew and Q were interested only in the different locations of two otherwise identical buildings. The fact that the two houses are in every respect identical contrasts with the situation described in the rabbinic parallels. In *m. 'Abot*. 3:18 there is an inherent difference between 'a tree whose branches are abundant and whose roots are few' and 'a tree whose branches are few but whose roots are many'. In *'Abot. R. Nat*. 24:1–2 there is an inherent difference between constructions with 'stones below and bricks above' and 'bricks first and then stones above'.

with how to live in the present, not how to survive in the future. It is concerned with the true basis of human, i.e., disciples' existence in the present and under threat, but it is not concerned to narrow the definition of the threat which may come. By allowing for any threat, it accommodates every threat.

What is astonishing about this parable in and of itself is that whereas R. Eleazar b. Azariah had extolled the security of a life in which works are more abundant than wisdom, and Elisha b. 'Abuya had insisted upon good deeds over and above the study of Torah, Jesus is represented as claiming that performing, as well as listening to, what he himself says is the basis of that secure and ultimately stable existence. This is a more than ordinary teacher! Later on in Q another antithetically formed saying will be located at the end of its own discourse and make a similarly devastating claim: 'He who hears you hears me, and he who rejects you rejects me, and he who rejects me rejects him who sent me' (Q 10:16).

To this parable there is attached in Luke 6:46 an introduction, 'Why do you call me, 'Lord, Lord', and do not do what I say?' This Lucan introduction is probably the Q original, in spite of arguments to the contrary.[49] Such arguments are that Luke himself has intervened to deprive the text of its eschatological bearing, to substitute obedience to the words of Jesus for performance of the will of the heavenly Father, and to lose the primitive-sounding phrase 'enter the kingdom of heaven'. In fact, it will be argued in detail shortly that the eschatological nuance is firmly present in the invocation 'Lord, Lord', and the other two features are typically Matthaean. Given the distribution of references to 'my Father who is in heaven' (20–1–1), and the recurrent Matthaean insistence, not least in the sermon on the mount,[50] that performance of the will of the heavenly Father is the condition for entry to the kingdom of heaven,[51] the evangelist's own fingerprints are easily detected. Moreover,

---

[49]Rightly, Lührmann, *Redaktion* 56; Guelich, *Sermon* 398. Against F. Hahn, *Titles* 79–80; cf. also M. Krämer, 'Hütet euch vor den falschen Propheten', *Bib* 57 (1976) 349–77, esp. pp. 360–1.

[50]Cf. Matt 5:20; 7:13.

[51]Matt 6:10 diff Luke 11:2; 12:50 diff Mark 3:35; 18:14 diff Luke 15:7; 21:31; 26:42 diff Mark 14:39.

the question form of Luke 6:46 appears more primitive in view of Luke's tendency away from such questions.[52] It is therefore natural to infer that the Q saying has been preserved by Luke 6:46, and one is encouraged in this inference by noting that Luke 6:46 as it stands dovetails rather precisely with the parable in Q 6:47–49. Negatively in this connection one may set aside the proposal that vv. 43–46 constitute a unified section[53] by observing that there is no personal reference to Jesus in vv. 43–45 to link up with the 'Lord' language of v. 46, and that 'doing' in vv. 46, 47–49 stands for action in the broadest sense, whereas within vv. 43–45 the 'doing' of v. 43 is defined narrowly as speech in v. 45. Positively, both v. 46 and vv. 47–49 draw attention to the special status of Jesus, both are preeminently concerned with 'doing' as the only true response to his teaching, and both try to achieve that positive response by laying stress on the negative possibility of 'not doing'.[54]

Nevertheless, for all that Luke/Q 6:46 dovetails so precisely with what follows, it is not a necessary part of it. First, Matthew took the saying and merged it with additional material which appears in Luke 13:26–27 and thus formed a distinct unit, Matt 7:21–23. The effect was the isolation of, but no damage to, Matt 7:24–27. The latter stood, as it were, on its own feet without assistance. Second, the parable contains entirely within itself the key to its own meaning. Third, the two remarkably close rabbinic parallels for the parable lack any introduction. Since one can scarcely envisage this neat but unnecessary introduction in Luke 6:46 existing in isolation, the inference must be that, like the fourth beatitude, it is a secondary editorial attachment.[55] Fourth, the emphasis on 'doing' within the discourse and shortly after it (Q 6:27, 43, 45; 7:8) suggests that the attachment took place at the stage when the discourse was composed and set in its immediate context.

What then did Q 6:46 communicate on the Q level of meaning? First, we need to comment on the form of the saying:

[52]Schürmann, *Lukasevangelium I* 381.

[53]Thus, J. Schmid, *Das Evangelium nach Lukas* (RNT 3; 4th ed.; Regensburg: Pustet, 1960) 138; Ernst, *Lukas* 231.

[54]The parable, like *'Abot R. Nat.* 24:1–2, but unlike *m. 'Abot.* 3:18, emphasizes the negative second half within the antithetical parallelism.

[55]Similarly, Schenk, *Synopse* 35.

'Why do you . . . and not . . .?' This is the same as the form of Q 6:41, the speck and log saying, and this fact helps us to determine its intention. It is not an accusation about something which is already happening, and thus not, as has been suggested,[56] an attack on false teachers, any more than Q 6:41 is. The latter is intended to set out a fundamental principle, i.e., if one does *x*, then one must do *y*. So Q 6:46 did not condemn actual disobedience in the audience, but rather insisted that a spoken acknowledgement of the authority of the teacher required to be spelt out in action and obedience. Jesus as 'Lord' is to be recognized as such through 'doing', and there can be no room for what has been called 'deedless discipleship'.[57] It is important to observe how the 'doing' theme continues to be given prominence in the next Q unit, the healing of the centurion's servant (Q 7:1–10). Here it is christologically grounded in reflection on the theme of authority. The centurion is a person with understanding, and in respect of authority he detects a similarity between his position and that of Jesus. Yet there is also a dissimilarity: he addresses Jesus as the κύριος who, by virtue of his word, can bring about the healing for which he, the centurion, is obliged to plead. Jesus as κύριος is a healer, and his word is effective in healing because it is the word of authority, that is, his word is God's power decisively in action. Now in Q the person through whom the power of God is decisively exercised in miracle is 'the coming one' (Q 7:19), that is, the Son of man.

Second, elsewhere in Q κύριος denotes the person who has servants, gives them instructions, goes away, comes back, calls them to account, and exercises a fierce and final judgment upon those who have heard, but have either through disobedience done wrong (thus, the parable of the faithful and wise servant: Q 12:42–46) or through negligence done nothing (thus, the parable of the talents: Q 19:12–27). The κύριος figure of these parables has immediately beforehand in Q been defined (thus, the parable of the watchful householder: Q 12:39–40) as the one who comes, the Son of man. So Q is in line with other parts of early Christian tradition in which the idea of the Son of man

[56]Schürmann, *Lukasevangelium I* 380.
[57]J. Schmid, *Das Evangelium nach Matthäus* (RNT 1; 5th ed.; Regensburg: Pustet, 1965) 152.

lurks in the background behind the term κύριος.[58]

This finding allows us to discern the subtle way in which the Q discourse is deliberately designed and christologically controlled. Only twice within it does explicit christology surface, once at the start in the long beatitude (Q 6:22) and once at the finish (Q 6:46). On both occasions redaction is involved to produce a christological *inclusio*, articulating one central conviction, namely that the coming Son of man is the authoritatively speaking Jesus.

According to Q 6:22 the Son of man is acknowledged in a situation of acute stress and suffering, that is, just the sort of situation which gives rise to eager and intense longing of an apocalyptic sort. In Q 6:46 the double κύριε, κύριε acclamation indicates a call or appeal of intense longing, doubtless a longing for the coming of the Son of man. This future-oriented question inevitably had an effect on the interpretation of the following parable, which now had to be read eschatologically to a far greater extent than was legitimate when it existed in isolation. In Q, and only in Q, its imagery would as a result have recalled the imagery of theophanic texts in the biblical tradition. Such texts exploited the experience of rain (Ps 68:9) and flood (Job 22:16; Pss 93:3; 98:8; Hab 3:10) and wind (Isa 17:13; 57:13; 64:6) to warn about the ultimate storm-like appearance of God in judgment. 'Hailstones of wrath will be hurled as from a catapult; the water of the sea will rage against them, and rivers will relentlessly overwhelm them; a mighty wind will rise against them, and like a tempest it will winnow them away' (Wis 5:22–23). Such texts presented the effect of the storm of divine appearance as a moving and a shaking.[59] In Q, and only in Q, this had been the burden of the message of the Baptist, a message centred (by the editor) on 'the coming one' who now appears in the inaugural discourse in the person of Jesus, the Lord and the Son of man. The message of the editor for his audience is therefore rather carefully balanced. It is that the coming of the Lord and Son of man, whether it is expected to take place imminently and is thus a focus of intense and eager longing, or perhaps is hardly expected at all because of a sense of delay, has to be

[58]Schulz, *Spruchquelle* 429.
[59]Cf. Judg 5:5; Pss 18:7; 77:17–18; 97:4; Mic 1:4; Jdt 16:15; Wis 4:19; Sir 43:16.

anticipated in a spirit of obedience and with a commitment to make the present a time of dedicated 'doing'.

3. Love of Enemies. Q 6:27–35.

We turn now to Q 6:27–35, the section dealing with love of enemies. Once again there is evidence of deliberate design, including the positioning of sayings about insult, giving and the golden rule (vv. 29–31) inside the main tradition (vv. 27–28, 32–35). Students of Mark and John are familiar with such theologically motivated 'sandwich structures', but these are not a feature of Luke. His inclination is to smooth and refine away interruptions, and certainly not to create them.[60] Hence this one is likely to have been present in Q.[61] That leaves the surrounding main tradition consisting of three elements: first, an initial demand couched in positive terms: 'Love ... pray ...' (vv. 27–28); second, a pair of supporting illustrative arguments alluding to the taxcollectors and the Gentiles (vv. 32–33); third, a summary restating the positive demand with a promise of reward attached, together with the reinforcing reminder of the conduct of God (v. 35).

The most suitable entry point for a discussion of the history of this tradition and of its component parts is the pair of supportive arguments (vv. 32–33). Together they function in exactly the same way as the declaration (Q 12:30a) at the end of the tradition on anxiety about food and clothing: 'for all the nations seek these things'. We have already seen how in its own context that declaration calls for behaviour better than that of certain other persons. In its own context it is also manifestly intrusive. It employs a different argument (the ineffectiveness of anxiety) from that of the underlying tradition (the inappropriateness of anxiety), in which two examples from the natural world show that God provides food and clothing and can therefore be trusted as Father to do the same for his own people. With a concluding repetition of the initial demand to avoid anxiety (12:22, 29), and a final insistence on the knowledge of the

---

[60]Cf. Luke 22:54–71/Mark 14:53–72; Luke 23/Mark 15.
[61]Schürmann, *Lukasevangelium I* 345.

Father, that underlying tradition is internally consistent and complete. It is clear also that the argument referring to the Gentiles is badly positioned, in that it occurs within the concluding summary when the time for argument has passed. Therefore it is secondary. This throws light on what can be recognized as a counterpart in 6:27–35 – not this time an alien body pushed into the concluding summary (v. 35), but rather the two supporting arguments themselves (vv. 32–33). There, first, the identical demand, 'behave better than certain others', is employed, and, second, the certain others include (if Matthew preserves Q) identical persons, namely the Gentiles. That Matthew does indeed preserve Q may be inferred from the clash between Matt 5:47 and the evidence elsewhere of his positive attitude to Gentiles. For him they are the target audience and beneficiaries of the Christian mission (cf. 21:43; 28:19–20). The presumption must be that the mission has been successful, and therefore that there are Gentiles who belong to his church. The presence of 'Gentiles' in Matt 5:47 is unlikely therefore to be derived from MattR, just as its removal by LukeR is rendered plausible by Luke's own orientation to a mixed community consisting of Gentiles as well as Jews. In similar vein, Matthew's somewhat surprising openness to 'tax collectors' (cf. 10:3 diff Mark 3:18; 21:32) makes their presence in Matt 5:46 less likely to be derived from MattR than from the original text of Q. Luke's preference for 'sinners', on the other hand, is natural in a setting where traditional Jewish prejudices no longer apply: for him 'tax collectors' are included among, or are equivalent to, 'sinners'.[62] Finally, a disparaging comment about tax collectors is at home in Q, where there is not a single favourable reference to such persons: when Jesus is accused in Q 7:34 of being 'a friend of tax collectors and sinners' this insulting jibe by opponents has to be presumed to be as untrue as the initial smear that he is 'a glutton and a drunkard'.

It thus appears very probable indeed that 6:32–33, which could scarcely survive in isolation, should be assigned to Q redaction.[63] To strengthen this proposal it is worth observing at this point how difficult is the alternative suggestion of Paul

[62]Cf. Luke 5:30, 32/Mark 2:15–17; 15:1–2; 18:13; 19:7.
[63]This likelihood was already recognized by R. Bultmann, *The History of the Synoptic Tradition* (Oxford: Blackwell, 1963) 88.

Hoffmann[64] that these two sayings should be traced back to the historical Jesus. The argument is that the function of the Gentile and tax collector pairing here matches the function of the Samaritan in Luke 10:30–37, and that Jesus demands in both places the overcoming of all hostile thoughts about strangers and enemies, and their replacement with a universal openness which expresses itself in acceptance and goodness. Against that argument, the Samaritan makes his contribution precisely because the prejudice he provoked is attacked and overcome, whereas in Q 6:32–33 the prejudices provoked by tax collectors and Gentiles are unfortunately reinforced and exploited. We cannot, therefore, reject the secondariness of vv. 32–33 by an appeal to the historical Jesus.

We are now well on the way to a reconstruction of the history of the tradition which presently confronts us in Q 6:27–35. The next step is a clarification, first, of just what stood in vv. 27–28, and, second, of the original content of v. 35.

First, in vv. 27–28 a Matthaean pair presently vies with a Lucan quartet of injunctions, set out in two pairs exhibiting synonymous parallelism and concerned first with action and then with speech. The possibility that the quartet stood in Q is favoured in general by Luke's not being prone to expand and Matthew's being prone to reduce,[65] and in particular by some Matthaean echoes of Lucan language. Thus, (i) the MattR reference to 'you shall hate your enemy' (Matt 5:43) confirms the presence of the verb 'to hate' in the original tradition; (ii) the MattR reference to 'good works' (Matt 5:16) matches the idea of 'doing good', whose originality will be defended; (iii) the reference to greetings, whose origin in MattR will be proposed shortly, corresponds loosely with the verb 'to bless', just as the verbal attack represented by cursing picks up on the verbal attack described in Q 6:22–23.[66] The decision between the two Matthew/Luke versions therefore depends substantially on decisions about the second of the supporting arguments in vv. 32–33.

It seems overwhelmingly likely that Luke's 'doing good', far

---

[64]'Die bessere Gerechtigkeit. Die Auslegung der Bergpredigt IV (Mt 5,38–48)', *Bibel und Leben* 10 (1969) 264–75, esp. pp. 269–70.

[65]Dupont, *Béatitudes I* 155.

[66]See Schürmann, *Lukasevangelium I* 345–6.

from being (as has been claimed) part of a Lucan critique of a Hellenistic ethic based on reciprocity, is more original than Matthew's 'greeting'. For a start, greeting brothers and not greeting non-brothers is understandable in the context of some kind of community life where the boundaries are plain. It would work for Jews, it would work for Christians, but it would hardly work for Gentiles at large. Further, the purpose of these supporting arguments is to negate a reciprocity ethic in a setting of persecution. But the withholding of greetings is scarcely persecution, and it is surely correct to characterize a hypothetical original along the lines of 'If you only greet those who greet you ...' as 'strangely weak'.[67] The surprising thing is that the 'greeting' version should so often have attracted scholarly support.[68] The evangelist who (arguably) omitted the instruction to 'salute no one on the road' (Q 10:4), and who is most likely to be in touch with the increasing rabbinic interest in greetings,[69] would most easily be held responsible for a change away from 'doing good' and towards 'greeting'. When we bear in mind also that the greeting must be presumed to be *shalom sh^eelat*,[70] and that the notions of blessing and a real communication of peace in the context of a greeting can be shown to be equivalent (cf. Jdt 15:8–9), and that the 'peacemakers' of Matt 5:9 have already been shown to be derived from Q 6:27–28, 35 by MattR, then it is easy to explain the wording of Matt 5:47 as the evangelist's own drawing together of the calls to do good and to bless. To these arguments we may add a number of significant considerations which favour the 'doing good' version as the Q original. The verb ἀγαθοποιεῖν, occurring as it does in the gospels only at Luke 6:9/Mark 3:4 and Luke 6:33, 35, is without attestation as LukeR, but is abundantly attested in Jewish tradition: indeed, far from being the exclusive terminology of Hellenistic ethics, it represents a notion common to a variety of ancient ethical systems, including Jewish ones. Moreover, the term 'doing good' as the antithesis of evil and shame/offence/insult in the immediate context finds a precedent in Sir

[67]Schweizer, *Matthew* 114.
[68]For example, Schmid, *Lukas* 136; Schulz, *Spruchquelle* 129; Schenk, *Synopse* 29.
[69]See Billerbeck I.380–385.
[70]Billerbeck I.380.

42:14. Above all, the presence elsewhere in the Q discourse of strong emphases both on ποιεῖν[71] and on the ἀγαθός/πονηρός antithesis[72] makes it wholly consistent that at this point the two should be combined and ἀγαθοποιεῖν result. To draw together the implications of all these arguments, therefore, the Q tradition of the initial demand seems to have included all the Lucan quartet of demands.

Second, it is likely that in v. 35 Q originally referred to sun and rain. This is a much more vivid allusion than Luke's punning χάρις-χρηστός-ἀχάριστος combination. It is much more in tune with Q's regular approach to the created order (cf. 12:6–7, 24, 27–28). Above all, it makes possible the startling declaration – startling because it runs clean contrary to famous Old Testament evidence – that the wicked and the evil are beneficiaries of God's provision of sunshine and rain.[73]

(i) While it is true that the sun may rise upon the thief (Exod 22:2–3), and that in the full glow of sunlight godlessness may thrive (Job 8:16) and oppression flourish (Eccl 4:1, 3; 6:1; 8:9; 9:3; 10:5), it remains clear that it is emphatically a *problem* that this is so (cf. Job 8:16). The norm is that when death or judgment are envisaged this can be dramatically associated with darkness and the removal of sunlight (Eccl 12:2; Isa 13:10; Ezek 32:7). Normally the shining of the sun symbolizes a situation of majesty and glory (Sir 50:7), or prosperity because of the *righteous* rule of the king (2 Sam 23:4), whereas those who live in sin and persecute the servant of God can lament that 'the sun has not risen over us' (Wis 5:6).

(ii) While it is true that rain can be part of the flood, torrents and even fire sent down by God in judgment (Gen 19:24; Exod 9:23; Ps 105:32; Ezek 38:22), this is not the normal rain of the divine providential supervision of the world (cf. Gen 2:5). When that ordinary rain is in mind there is a sharp distinction drawn in several texts between rain as a sign of blessing (Ps 68:9; Joel 2:23) and the withholding of rain as a sign of moral displeasure (Isa 5:6). The Elijah saga (1 Kgs 17–18) comes to mind as a paradigm of this principle, a saga which we know Luke

---

[71]Q 6:22, 31, 33, 46, 47–49.

[72]Q 6:22, 26, 43–45.

[73]A similar conclusion is reached by Schulz, *Spruchquelle* 128; Zeller, *Mahnsprüche* 108.

remembered (Luke 4:25–26) and which may incidentally explain why he modified Q 6:35. A classic prophetic declaration of this scheme occurs in Amos 4:7–8, where the pointed and visible distinction between the provision of rain for one community, and the withholding of it from another, is meant to bring about repentance. Viewed from this perspective, Q 6:35 turns the tradition upside down. In this connection we should also infer that Q referred, by use of synonym, only to evil persons rather than to evil and good. The latter pairing is typical of Matthew (cf. 22:10) and is also the less starkly radical of the two, while Luke's version happens to agree with Q's sweepingly negative view of humanity at large: 'If you being evil . . .' (Q 11:13).

Within v.35 there is also the declaration that 'your reward shall be great' (v. 35b). This reference to reward is likely to have figured in Q, since the same term appears nearby in Matt 5:46, and its presence here in a context coloured by the thought of persecution is remarkably symmetrical with its presence in the immediately preceding context, again (as we have seen) probably secondary and again coloured by the thought of persecution (v. 23a). Moreover, the saying in which it is presently embedded (v. 35) is clearer and less cluttered without it, for it can then call without distraction for the imitation of God.

In the case of this material about love of enemies, the removal (as it were) of 6:29–31 would leave an introductory demand, two supporting arguments and a concluding summary. But the illustrations have also been assigned to the Q editor. If, then, the Q-editor is held responsible for the positioning of 6:29–31 and the creation of 6:32–33, as well as some modest interference in 6:35b, it necessarily follows that 6:27–28 and 6:35a, having been brought side by side, are doublets. In turn this means that the complex of material in 6:27–35 as a whole was spun out of the trio of sayings in 6:29–31, together with an original tradition which approximated to the following:

ἀγαπᾶτε τοὺς ἐχθροὺς ὑμῶν,
καλῶς ποιεῖτε τοῖς μισοῦσιν ὑμᾶς,
εὐλογεῖτε τοὺς καταρωμένους ὑμᾶς,
προσεύχεσθε περὶ τῶν ἐπηρεαζόντων ὑμᾶς·
   καὶ ἔσεσθε υἱοὶ ὑψίστου,
    ὅτι τὸν ἥλιον αὐτοῦ ἀνατέλλει ἐπὶ πονηροὺς
   καὶ βρέχει ἐπὶ ἀδίκους.

This striking saying deserves attention in its own right. The first pair of demands calls for human action: it conforms precisely to the observation that 'to exercise love is to do beneficent works'.[74] The second pair envisages divine action: those addressed will call down upon their opponents God's blessing and resort to God prayerfully. Such harmony between the actions of humans and of God makes fitting the concluding use of the *imitatio Dei* idea. The idea of imitative sonship is not the same as covenant-based sonship but can certainly be understood as an effective implementation of it.

The underlying thought is, by general consensus, that of Lev 19:18: 'You shall love your neighbour as yourself.' Absolutely no modification, still less contradiction or abandonment, of that principle is registered. Neither is any interest registered in the scholarly debate about the scope of the word 'neighbour'. The neighbour is and remains neither more nor less than a fellow-member of the community of Israel who has become estranged and hostile and offensive. Such offence is not to be reciprocated nor made the cause of smouldering hostility on the part of the offended person. Rather, the latter is to take steps to achieve a restoration of relationships. The intra-Israel situation presupposed here means that we are not dealing with community enemies, along the lines of the Israel/Gentiles confrontation, nor with the Christian church/world polarity of the sort which Matthew would secondarily insert. The problem being treated is internal to Israel and is simply and solely that of how to respond to the brother, *any* brother, who has acted as an enemy. And the treatment is starkly different from that recommended by certain texts where human restraint and even beneficence toward an enemy will stop the divine judgment's being deflected from him (cf. Prov 24:17–18; 25:21–22). For the God invoked by Q 6:28 is one whose disposition is to bless, and whose blessing will be an essential part of the restorative and healing process.

All of this is a far cry from the 'measure for measure' principle which deals in recompense and reward and sees a correspondence between good or evil treatment received and subsequent good or evil responses. No place can be found for strategic thinking

---

[74]*b. Sukk.* 49b; *b. Qidd.* 40a; cf. also *Jub.* 20:2; 36:4.

of the sort that led Demetrius to approach Jonathan Maccabeus and Lasthenes with the honeyed declaration that 'we will repay you with good for what you do for us . . . we have determined to do good because of the good will (the Jews) show to us' (1 Macc 10:27; 11:33). Inroads are even made into the principle of divine justice that God repays a person according to his or her deeds. Q 6:27–28 is not, however, entirely new. A partial precedent is provided by David's treatment of Saul (1 Sam 24:17–19): in Saul's words, 'You have repaid me good, whereas I have repaid you evil.' David's refusal to kill him had been a case of 'doing good' in the teeth of the normal principle: 'If a man finds his enemy, will he let him go away safe?' And for such an action there was the prospect of divine reward: 'May the Lord reward you with good for what you have done to me this day.' Here then we have an encounter between two recognized principles, first, that evil is normally and fittingly met with evil, and, second, that good action will receive divine reward. If it is true that in the David/Saul case the second principle had triumphed over the first, it is also true that the reason for such an outcome had been the special status of Saul as the Lord's anointed (1 Sam 24:6, 10), and thus *in general* the second principle remained intact. This leaves in a position of solitary eminence the case of Joseph. Small wonder that many years later the Testaments of the Twelve Patriarchs[75] would return with enthusiasm to the pattern of the man who calmed the fears that 'maybe he will hate us and pay us back for all the evil which we did to him' (Gen 50:15), who accepted the plea that evil should be met with forgiveness (Gen 50:17), and who declined to play the part of a judge: 'Fear not, for am I in the place of God?' (Gen 50:19). Reflection on the Genesis text led the writer to praise the very same combination of love, beneficence, prayer and blessing for which Q 6:27–28 calls, and, quite clearly, to do so on the basis of the Lev 19:18 text, since love of the 'brother' is love of the 'neighbour'.[76]

If all this is true of the pre-Q tradition it remains to describe the effect of the intervention of the Q editor. This, it will be recalled, consisted of the injection of the affirmation that ἔσται

[75]See Zeller, *Mahnsprüche* 106–7.
[76]See *T. Zeb.* 5:3; *T. Gad* 4:2; *T. Benj.* 3:3–4.

ὁ μισθὸς ὑμῶν πολύς in advance of the statement that 'you will be sons of the Most High', and also the creation of 6:32–33:

καὶ γὰρ ἐὰν ἀγαπήσητε τοὺς ἀγαπῶντας ὑμᾶς, τί περισσὸν ποιεῖτε; οὐχὶ καὶ οἱ τελῶναι τὸ αὐτὸ ποιοῦσιν;
καὶ γὰρ ἐὰν ἀγαθοποιῆτε τοὺς ἀγαθοποιοῦντας ὑμᾶς, τί περισσὸν ποιεῖτε; οὐχὶ καὶ οἱ ἐθνικοὶ τὸ αὐτὸ ποιοῦσιν;

The addition of vv. 32–33, first, is a tacit admission that the demand to love enemies so unconditionally is at odds with human instinct and needs persuasive support. The support provided serves to reinforce the strong sense of Israelite community which we have detected already. There is not the faintest tinge of distinctively Christian theologizing. So the editor and his readers are primarily conditioned by their Jewishness and their sense of separateness from other nations. They share a concern to live according to the covenant. Second, the theme of reward, which is naturally at home in sayings which assume that God will provide that justice for his people which outsiders or opponents may withhold, is unsurprisingly included in vv. 32–33 but rather more significantly introduced into vv. 27–28, 35. By positioning it before the statement about sonship, the writer gives a new twist to the latter. No longer does it serve to encapsulate a life of obedience in the present: instead, sonship becomes the future reward, a status tantamount to the vindication of the righteous sufferer (cf. Wis 5:5). Of course, that future status can be understood as confirmation of a relationship enjoyed in the present (cf. Wis 2:16, 18), but the latter does not have to bring the former in its train, and the original version of the 'love your enemies' saying did not have it in mind. The situation is much the same as that which became visible when Q 6:46 was recognized as a secondary addition to 6:47–49. Even more significant is the correspondence with 6:22–23, where an orientation to the future and an adoption of the pattern of the righteous sufferer were both introduced redactionally.

The pre-Q history of the traditions in vv. 29, 30 and 31, and their function within the Q context of vv. 27–35, now call for investigation.

First we consider v. 29. The two halves of this saying about the blow on the cheek and the removal of clothing must combine as two variations on a single theme. There is Matthew/ Luke agreement in the first half that the theme is insult: the blow on the cheek, whether literal or metaphorical, clearly had this sense when directed against Micaiah ben Imlah by Zedekiah (1 Kgs 22:24/2 Chr 18:23), or against the ruler of Israel by the enemies of Zion (Mic 5:1), or against God himself when he was contemptuously repulsed by his people (Hos 11:4 LXX), or against the penitent when bidden to 'give his cheek to the smiter, and be filled with insults' (Lam 3:30). There are two specific precedents which are specially relevant to Q 6:29. The first is that of the servant (Isa 50:6), whose literally shaming experiences are described in language which echoes through the saying of Jesus: blows on the cheek (ῥαπίσματα, cf. ῥαπίζειν, Matt 5:39) matching the shame of being spat upon.[77] The second is that of the king (1 Esdr 4:30), whose insolent concubine sat on his right hand side and struck him with her left hand, that is, on his right cheek with the back of her hand. Given the likelihood that the word δεξιός defined the cheek in the Q version,[78] it is evident that Q 6:29a had to do with one of the most serious forms of insult.

The second half of the bipartite saying presents serious problems. Matthew's version (Matt 5:40) is, for a start, in no sort of harmony with the first half, and is quite unfitted to function in parallel with it. The scene is set in possible legal process, the problem is not insult, and the person addressed is not the offended person but the offender. He is the debtor whose refusal of the pledge, the shirt (χιτῶν) envisaged in Exod 22:26–27 and Deut 24:10–13, causes the creditor to go to court to obtain it.[79] While this makes the two halves of the saying jarringly discordant, it conforms to the MattR tendency elsewhere in 5:21–48 to introduce formal legal procedure (cf.

---

[77]The verb ῥαπίζειν is probably derived from Q: it occurs in the NT only here and in Matt 26:67 diff Mark 14:65 (but cf. ῥάπισμα, Mark 14:65), while word-statistics suggest that the Lucan counterpart τύπτειν (2–1–4 + 5) is LukeR. The same may, incidentally, be said of Matthew's στρέφειν (6–0–7 + 3). This might be MattR, but it can also be derived by Matthew from his sources (cf. Matt 26:10/Mark 14:6), is related to the verb ἀποστρέφειν (Isa 50:6 LXX), and is more likely to be the Q term than the very probably LukeR counterpart παρέχειν (1–1–4 + 5).

[78]See above, pp. 25–6.

[79]See Billerbeck I.343.

vv. 22b, 25–26, 39a). Luke, by contrast, lacks any allusion to legal procedure, sees the primary action rather more naturally as affecting the cloak (ἱμάτιον), and uses the verb αἴρειν, which is not only suggestive of violence[80] but also normally used by him when under the influence of a source. In this light the double act of violence against the person has a single meaning, and all the more clearly so in view of the list of the most serious forms of insult carrying the maximum financial penalty, set out in *m. B. Qam.* 8:6:

> If a man cuffed his fellow he must pay him a *sela*. R. Judah says in the name of R. Jose the Galilean: One hundred *zuz*. If he slapped him he must pay him two hundred *zuz*. If with the back of the hand he must pay him four hundred *zuz*. If he tore his ear, plucked out his hair, spat and his spittle touched him, or pulled his cloak from off him, or loosed a woman's hair in the street, he must pay four hundred *zuz*. This is the general rule: all is in accordance with a person's honour.

The proposal is therefore that a consistent and meaningful Q original can be constructed. It ran somewhat as follows:

τῷ ῥαπίζοντί σε εἰς τὴν δεξιὰν σιαγόνα,
στρέψον καὶ τὴν ἄλλην·
καὶ τῷ αἴροντι σου τὸ ἱμάτιον,
ἄφες καὶ τὸν χιτῶνα.

If this is correct, the saying needs first a setting in life in which it can exist by itself. So drastic and wellnigh intolerable a demand must almost certainly derive from the historical Jesus. But it can hardly be supposed that all and sundry were bidden by him to subject themselves to the Isa 50:6 experience. On the other hand, it is perfectly possible that those who shared his prophetic mission might have to envisage sharing the prophetic experience of shame. If so, the incorporation of this saying in the Q discourse would be the third case we have so far uncovered of the editor's drawing on sayings which spoke of suffering and which were naturally addressed in the first instance to those who exercised a prophetic role in the style of Jesus. The

[80]Cf. Cant 5:7: 'They beat me, they wounded me, they took away (LXX: ἦραν) my mantle.'

ease with which this saying came to be incorporated into the discourse must by now be clear: while 6:22–23 recalled the precedents and affirmed the heavenly reward in store for the recipients of insult, and while 6:27–28/35 laid down a pattern of positive and beneficent response to hostility and reaffirmed the heavenly reward, 6:29 registered a complementary requirement to allow any one insult to be followed by a second. This is truly a policy for those whose hope of vindication is aligned to God, and to God alone. This may not have been a new thought in the mind of the Q editor, but it certainly acquired telling force as a result of his design of Jesus' inaugural discourse.

Next we consider v. 30. Once again Matthew and Luke agree the content of the first half of the saying, though not the second: Matthew repeats the importance of being willing to lend, whereas Luke requires that a previously made loan should not be retrieved. In this second half Matthew's δανίζειν is presupposed shortly afterwards in Luke 6:34–35 and is therefore original, which in turn means that the corresponding αἴρειν is LukeR and doubtless used under the influence of the first half of the saying in v. 29b. The effect of v. 29b upon v. 30 is to make the latter refer to a forceful taking of property, probably a theft. This in turn points to one argument in favour of the originality of ἀπαιτεῖν, namely that it is scarcely at ease with the notion of forceful theft. A second argument is that δανίζειν and ἀπαιτεῖν together have an association which helps us to understand the presence of Q 6:30 in this setting. So the Q original of this saying probably approximated to:

τῷ αἰτοῦντί σε δός, καὶ ἀπὸ τοῦ δανισαμένου μὴ ἀπαίτει.

Generous giving of the sort demanded by this saying is frequently and enthusiastically praised in the wisdom literature as an expression of righteousness and mercy (cf. Ps 37:26; Sir 29:1–2). This is how the poor should be treated (Prov 19:17). But a loan which is called back and which proves irretrievable tends to transform the lender into a reproachful or even cursing and reviling enemy (Sir 29:6, 28). Sir 20:15 therefore declares that true wisdom is the avoidance of the example of the fool who becomes hateful (μισητός) because 'he gives little and upbraids (ὀνειδίσει) much; today he lends and tomorrow he asks back (ἀπαιτήσει)'. In this light Q 6:30 articulates a policy which has both positive and negative aspects: the positive virtue of open-handed generosity, and the negative virtue of avoiding enmity.

The wisdom material which points so directly towards our saying has, however, to be supplemented by reference to two legal texts which in the LXX, the sacred text used by Q, use δανίζειν. One is Deut 24:11, which describes the problem of obtaining without compulsion a pledge that a loan will be repaid. That is the problem with which secondary MattR alterations to Q 6:29b were concerned, and doubtless there was an association of ideas here which stimulated the evangelist's (not entirely logical and enlightened) editorial intervention. On the Q level, however, much the more relevant material is to be found in Deut 15:1–6, 7–11. This is the sabbath year legislation, laying down the cancellation of debts within, but not outside, the brotherhood of Israel (v. 3), and recommending the abandoning of ἀπαίτησις (vv. 2–3), except in the case of the foreigner. Lest the existence of this legislation (which 4 Macc 2:8 recognizes as contrary to natural human instinct) discourage giving, even in the face of obvious poverty and proven need, an incentive is added, namely a return not of the loan itself but of a blessing from God (v. 10). Now Deut 15:1–11 is one of the texts upon which the programme and proclamation of Isa 61:1–2 is built; it is also one of the key texts drawn into a *pesher* exposition of Isa 61 by the author of 11QMelchizedek. And thus we find the clue to the presence of Q 6:30 within the discourse. It not only details conduct which is the very opposite of what disrupts human relationships, expresses reproach, generates hate, establishes enmity (compare vv. 27–28); it not only puts flesh on the bones of 'doing good' (see v. 27) and implicitly points to the divine recompense (see v. 35b); but it also spells out the didactic implications of the kerygma, proclaimed so simply but so majestically in the beatitudes.

Finally, we consider v. 31. Some would argue for the originality of Matthew's positioning of the so-called golden rule saying, on the ground that there is no reason to attribute it to MattR. This argument can be set aside on five counts. First, in the sermon on the mount it occurs between Matt 7:7–11 (Q 11:9–13) and Matt 7:13–14 (Q 13:23–24), neither of which belonged, as the golden rule did, to the inaugural discourse. That means Matt 7:12 has to be seen in relation to Matt 7:3–5 (Q

6:41–42) and Matt 7:15–20 (Q 6:43–45), with neither of which traditions it has any affinity. Second, Matt 7:12 occupies a notable and sensitive position in the sermon on the mount, especially with the concluding observation 'for this is the law and the prophets' attached: just as one saying about law and prophets introduces the first warning against ἀνομία (5:17, 18–19), so does another the second such warning (7:12, 15–23), and almost certainly as a result of MattR's being responsible for the concluding observation. Third, the verb θέλειν occurs in this discourse only in the golden rule and in Matt 5:40, 42 diff Luke 6:29, 30. Since the last two cases have both been found to be MattR, the likelihood is that the influence of Q 6:31 is responsible and that this saying was placed in Q where Luke has it. Fourth, the golden rule in Luke 6:31 is to a small extent separated from the preceding sayings in 6: 29, 30 by virtue of plural rather than singular formulations, the effect of which is to attach it a little more firmly to what follows. But that is the essential key. The rule correlates the actions of those addressed with the actions of others towards them, and so do the two following sayings about the taxcollectors and the Gentiles. Moreover, the Q form of the golden rule is positive (by contrast with Tob 4:15; *b. Sabb.* 31a), and lends itself to interpretation in terms of love: the sayings which follow talk about loving and doing good. Fifth, if Q 6:31 is so close to 6:32–33 it becomes rather unlikely that it had already attached itself to 6:30 at the pre-Q stage.[81] Instead, it functions as a sort of route back to the main road (6:27–28) after the detour or interruption (6:29–30).[82] We can conclude, therefore, that the saying was to be found in Q where Luke has it, placed there by the Q editor, and that the original wording was:

καθὼς θέλετε ἵνα ποιῶσιν ὑμῖν οἱ ἄνθρωποι,
   οὕτως καὶ ὑμεῖς ποιεῖτε αὐτοῖς.

That this saying came directly into the gospel tradition from Jewish tradition is perfectly possible. That it came via Jesus himself is quite conceivable, for it certainly fits the tenor of his

[81]Against Schürmann, *Lukasevangelium I* 351.
[82]It is possible to see Q-editorial activity of the same sort elsewhere: Q 12:26, after the inserted 12:25, smoothing the way on to 12:27–29 which originally belonged immediately after 12:24.

teaching. For our purpose, however, its function here in the discourse is what is important. First, as a variation on the theme of Lev 19:18, which we have found to be the unseen influence throughout the section 6:27–35, it is specially well placed. For both the golden rule and the love command the two foci are the neighbour and the self: the only difference is the implicit limitation of the horizon of the golden rule to the Israelite community alone. Second, in addition to its obvious links with 6:32–33, it connects easily and naturally to the editorial elements in 6:22–23, 26 and one of the traditional elements in 6:27–28/35. The fourth beatitude, with a word play on ἄνθρωποι and ὁ υἱὸς τοῦ ἀνθρώπου, spoke of persons engaging in enmity, and the golden rule, by speaking of that conduct which might be wished for from 'men', naturally hinted at their present conduct which would certainly not be wished. Also, the fittingness of the association of the golden rule and the *imitatio Dei* idea (v. 35c) is already anticipated in the saying in *Ep. Arist.* 207: 'As you wish that no evil should befall you, but to be a partaker of all good things, so you should act on the same principle . . . For God draws all men to himself by his benevolence.'

To sum up, a single mind seems to be at work in vv. 31, 32–33 and 35c. But what was the thought in the mind? Three elements combine to answer that question. The first is the controlling theme of love, mentioned first in v. 32 because it was dominant in the pre-Q saying about love of enemies. The second is the sense of Israelite, and exclusively Israelite, community in vv. 32–33, where the persons addressed clearly distinguish themselves from Gentiles and those who live like Gentiles. The third is the use of the self and the self's wishes as a criterion in v. 31, the golden rule. These three elements add up to Lev 19:18b: 'You shall love | your neighbour | as yourself'. The persecuted ones are thus addressed along the lines of the ancient text, interpreted strictly in its own terms. Of any preoccupation with defining, still less with redefining, the neighbour, there is not the slightest trace. The community to which the editor and his audience belong is therefore not so much a Christian church as Israel. The confession which he and they maintain, the confession of the Son of man, is one which he strives not to allow to bring separation, even though it has provoked vehement opposition inside Israel. It is a confession which must be maintained *within* the ancient community. Every effort is made therefore to be faithful simultaneously to the confession of Jesus and the command of Moses.

4. Reproof in Mercy. Q 6:36–45.

The next saying in the inaugural discourse in Q was a further demand for the imitation of God, and it is overwhelmingly probable that it spoke, as in Luke 6:36, about being 'merciful' (οἰκτίρμων) rather than being 'perfect' (τέλειος) as in Matt 5:48. This is because, first, Matthew may well have been influenced by Deut 18:13, 'You shall be blameless (LXX: τέλειος) before the Lord your God', and have introduced the word here as he did in Matt 19:21 (diff Mark 10:21).[83] The use of the word group in question is well enough attested in Lucan material[84] to make it unlikely that Luke would have dropped the term if he had been confronted by it here. Second, support for the theme of mercy is, as already observed, provided by the beatitude on the merciful (ἐλεήμονες) in Matt 5:7, always bearing in mind that there is no difference of meaning between the two words οἰκτίρμων and ἐλεήμων.[85] Support for mercy is also provided by the presence of ἐλεημοσύνη in Matt 6:2–4, a word found nowhere else in the gospel of Matthew but here occurring immediately after Matt 5:48 (Luke 6:36). For Q the result is a saying which, as often remarked,[86] strikingly resembles the Jewish text, 'As our Father is merciful in heaven, so be merciful on earth' (*Tg. Yer. I* Lev 22:28).

There are two key issues concerning this saying. The first is its meaning as it stands, that is, the significance of its combined reference to mercy and divine fatherhood. The second is the relationship it bears to adjacent material in the Q context, that is, the question of whether, as another *imitatio Dei* saying, it looks back to Q 6:35 (and thus to the whole complex 6:27–35), or whether it relates to some of what

[83]See Schulz, *Spruchquelle* 130.
[84]Thus, τελειοῦν at Luke 2:43; 13:32; Acts 20:24; τελείωσις at Luke 1:45.
[85]R. Bultmann, 'οἰκτίρω', *TDNT* 5.159–61, esp. p. 160.
[86]Cf. Billerbeck II.159; J. Jeremias, *New Testament Theology I. The Proclamation of Jesus* (NTL; London: SCM, 1971) 212; Zeller, *Mahnsprüche* 111.

comes after it. A third possibility is that it might look both backward and forward.

As far as meaning is concerned, the term 'merciful' clearly has covenantal colouring. Occasionally in Jewish traditional material the invocation of God's 'mercy' is accompanied by allusions to the Abrahamic covenant,[87] but more frequently and more firmly the Mosaic covenant is recalled, especially with hints of Exod 34:6, 'The Lord, the Lord, a God merciful (LXX: οἰκτειρμός) and gracious, slow to anger, and abounding in steadfast love and faithfulness'.[88] This means that the demand that the hearers should match God in respect of mercy is in content and also, given the correspondence with Lev 19:2, 'You shall be holy; for I the Lord your God am holy', in form, a demand for human activation of the implications of the covenant relationship. There is more here than mere *imitatio Dei*. Just as God's righteousness is to be matched within the covenant relationship by Israel's righteousness, and just as God's faithfulness is to be matched within the covenant relationship by Israel's faithfulness, so now the same is reiterated in respect of mercy. Such a requirement, an echo through the years of Zech 7:9–10, 'Render true judgments, show kindness and mercy each to his brother, do not oppress the widow, the fatherless, the sojourner or the poor; and let none of you devise evil against his brother in your heart', picks up what is now becoming a familiar theme in this discourse, namely, that the persons being addressed should bring to realization the existence of Israel as the covenant intended. Replication is therefore more than mere imitation, it is the realization of relationship.

This point needs, however, to be made even more pointed. The 'mercy' texts repeatedly set this experience over against the experience of wrath and judgment. Typical in this respect is Sir 5:6: 'Do not say, 'His mercy is great, he will forgive the multitude of my sins,' for both mercy and truth are with him, and his anger rests on sinners'.[89] Thus it comes about that many such texts insist that God shows himself in mercy as one who maintains the covenant in the setting of human abandonment of

[87]2 Kgs 13:23; Mic 7:20; 3 Macc 6:2.
[88]See Pss 40:11; 86:15; 103:8; 145:8.
[89]Cf. also Ps 78:38; Isa 27:11; Jer 13:14; 21:7; Lam 3:31–33; Hos 2:19; Mic 7:19; Zech 1:16; 2 Macc 8:5.

it. The corollary is that from the human side repentance for former sins is necessary if judgment is to be avoided.[90] The exercise of compassion and mercy, and the holding back of judgment, therefore necessarily and repeatedly come to effect in forgiveness.[91]

These themes have been set out at length, not for the sake of stating the obvious, but for the much more positive purpose of insisting that certain key terms bring recurrent associations of ideas with them and must be allowed the freedom to do so. In that light Q 6:36 has profound implications. It implies that the addressees, who belong to a tradition in which breaches of the covenant are commonplace, have responded in repentance and have received forgiveness; at the same time it must be presupposed that any failure to respect the covenant obligation would turn the future into one of judgment and wrath. Inevitably, therefore, there is in this saying a past and a future perspective. Those persons addressed by Jesus have not only responded to his message of repentance in the face of judgment, and his offer of divine mercy in forgiveness, but also his demand for active commitment in the form of compassion towards others, and his warning that failure to do so will reactivate the threatened judgment.

Within the overall presentation of these themes in the complex of mercy/compassion texts there are certain particular nuances which it is important to note for the sake of understanding Q 6.36 fully. First, there is precedent for the linkage with fatherhood. An attribute of the mother (Lam 4:10) or the father (Ps 103:13), compassion is what the orphan finds himself lacking (Ps 109:12). By projection it thus becomes a feature of God's treatment of his people (Ps 103:13; Isa 63:15–16). The linkage of the two ideas in Q 6:36 is therefore not new (cf. *Tg. Yer. I* Lev 22:28, already cited). However, it is important for the understanding of this saying in its Q context to note how rare are the 'your Father' sayings, and that the only other one of which we may be sure in Q is 12:30: 'Your Father knows that you need these things'.[92] This saying, bringing together need for food

---

[90]Cf. 2 Chr 30:9; Neh 9:27–28; Joel 2.13; *T. Levi* 16.2–5.

[91]See Neh 9:17, 19; Pss 25:6; 51:3; 78:38; 79:8; 103:4; Dan 9:18–19; Mic 7:19; Sir 2:11; 3 Macc 2:20; *T. Jud.* 19:3.

[92]On this topic, see Polag, *Christologie* 61–2.

and commitment to the cause of the future kingdom, was probably addressed in the first instance to those who were partners in Jesus' mission, but in its present Q context has (like several other sayings we have examined) been generalized to apply to all disciples. So when Q 12:30 picks up the idea of divine fatherhood it reasserts the theme of compassion and care at the heart of the covenant relationship, compassion or mercy experienced both as support and as obligation. Second, there is well established precedent for an understanding of mercy/compassion in terms of giving and lending.[93] That Q 6:36 was intended to include this understanding may not be doubted in view of Q 6:30. Third, in one of the clearest prophetic statements about mercy/compassion there is a striking use of the 'measure' idea. In Isa 27:11 the prophet declares that as far as an undiscerning people is concerned 'he who made them will not have compassion upon them', this the climax of an oracle of judgment which had earlier affirmed that 'measure by measure, by exile you contended with them' (27:8). It has been shown very clearly that this is one of the foundational 'measure' texts.[94] The principle may be applied either salvifically or judgmentally.[95] Thus we begin to see how naturally Q 6:36 leads into 6:37–38.

In attempting to draw out the meaning of Q 6:36 in its own terms it has several times been natural to refer to the Q context in which it is presently embedded, a context which gives a particularity of meaning to it. We have begun to address the second key issue it raises, namely its precise relationship to the neighbouring sayings.

The case for separating v. 36 from vv. 27–35 has been argued as follows: (i) Although vv. 35c, 36 are the only two cases of *imitatio Dei* in the synoptic tradition, there is a distinction between them, in that the first is unclear and the second clear, and the theme of compassion in the second is not identical with that of love of enemies in the first. (ii) Formally, v. 35c concludes its own unit of tradition and needs no supplement.[96]

The opposite case for attaching v. 36 to what precedes has

[93]Cf. Ps 37:21; Prov 13:11; 21:26.
[94]H. P. Rüger, "Mit welchem Mass ihr messt, wird euch gemessen werden", *ZNW* 60 (1969) 174–82.
[95]Salvation: Zech 1:16; judgment: Isa 27:8.
[96]Thus Schürmann, *Lukasevangelium I* 357–9.

been put forward thus: (i) Thematically, v. 36 fits with the additions within the preceding section, i.e., vv. 30a, 31, 34. (ii) Tension between compassion and love of enemies can be discerned only with difficulty. (iii) Since v. 35c is the less clear of the two *imitatio Dei* texts, v. 36 serves it well by drawing out its meaning more clearly and achieving a final climax. Moreover, there is a further linkage between the two in their common use of the fatherhood/sonship idea. (iv) Several contacts between v. 36 and vv. 37–38 serve to separate the two from one another, i.e., v. 36 is a positive demand, whereas v. 37 is a prohibition; v. 36 refers to the conduct of the Father whereas vv. 37–38 are controlled by the concept of recompense; v. 36 is a demand motivated by reference to the present or even the past, whereas v. 37 looks toward the future action of God; v. 36 asks for conduct which is like that of God, whereas the opposite is involved when v. 37 compares human and divine actions. The conclusion is that the argumentation in vv. 27–28, 32–35 reaches its high point in v. 36, and v. 37 makes a new start.[97]

Which of the two cases is the stronger? Our reconstruction of the pre-Q saying underlying vv. 27–28/35 produced a tradition which was clear, rounded and complete: it had no need of any supplement. Correspondingly, as the parallel Jewish saying, 'As our Father is merciful in heaven, so be merciful on earth', shows, v. 36 is perfectly capable of sustaining a separate existence. The formal separateness of the two sayings is confirmed by the grounding of *imitatio Dei* in creation in the one case and in the covenant in the other, together with the fact that in the one case the love of enemies, although not different in kind, is nevertheless narrower in scope than the unrestricted mercy with no specifying of recipients in the other. The relationship which does indeed exist between v. 36 and what precedes is therefore thematic, probably a shared though independent concern with Leviticus 19 themes, rather than organic, and it exists on the compositional or Q-editorial level.

While v. 36 is capable of standing alone, it does not follow that it always had to do so, and its relationship to vv. 37–38 needs further examination. This is best done in several stages.

---

[97]Thus H. Merklein, *Die Gottesherrschaft als Handlungsprinzip* (FB 34; Würzburg: Echter Verlag, 1978) 223–4.

First, the quite discrepant schemes presented by Matthew and by Luke should be noted. The *imitatio Dei* saying (Q 6:36) in its revised Matthaean form had been used to round off the MattR-constructed antitheses in 5:21–48. The presentation of different themes in Matthew 6 had separated it from the saying in 7:1, 'Judge not, that you be not judged', which thus perforce became the beginning of a new unit. The immediately following saying, 'For with the judgment you judge you will be judged' (Matt 7:2a), has no parallel in Luke and matches so precisely the form of 'with the measure you measure it will be measured to you' (Matt 7:2b), that it is most easily assessed as a MattR creation. It imitates the measure saying, causing Matt 7:1 to be a sort of heading above Matt 7:2ab. It also incidentally suggests that there was in Q something between Matt 7:1/Q 6:37a and Matt 7:2b/Q 6:38c. It is important to note that the measure principle, which could have functioned either salvifically or judgmentally, functions in Matthew only with reference to judgment.

In Luke 6:37ab, 37c–38ab there is an antithesis consisting of two negative demands for the avoidance of judging and condemning, and then two positive demands for forgiving and giving.[98] Since within an antithesis the emphasis normally falls on the second part it comes as no surpise that the promise attached to the positive demands is amplified in the 'good measure, pressed down, . . .' material (v. 38b). In each half of the antithesis there is evidence of pre-Lucan or Q derivation. In the first half, whose judgment saying is already established as Q 6:37a, the verb καταδικάζειν, a verb which is also present in the MattR sayings, 'If you had known what this (i.e., mercy) means, you would not have condemned (οὐκ ἂν κατεδικάσατε) the guiltless' (12:7), and 'By your words you will be condemned (καταδικασθήσῃ)' (12:37). When the first of these sayings contrasts mercy and condemnation it matches the contrast in Luke 6:36–37. The second saying is attached to Matt 12:33–35/Q 6:43–45, which, of course, stood in Q very near the tradition we are discussing. The simplest explanation is that Luke 6:37b stood in Q and was the basis for Matthaean reminiscences in 12:7, 37.[99] In the second half the Palestinian custom of using the

[98]Cf. Sus 52–53 Θ: κρίνων . . . κατακρίνων . . . ἀπολύων. On ἀπολύειν as a term for forgiveness, cf. 1 Macc 10:29–33.

[99]Schürmann, *Lukasevangelium I* 362.

fold of a garment as a container for grain is suggested, something which is unlikely to have been introduced into the tradition by Luke. The aggregate conclusion is therefore that we can justifiably refer to Q 6:36, 37–38ab, 38c. But what is the relationship between the three parts of this Q complex? Could it be an organic relationship through which is discernible a single unit of tradition consisting of an introductory demand, a pair of amplifying clarifications and, finally, a concluding demand which not only restates the initial demand but also draws together both the negative and the positive features of the clarifications?

That the declaration, 'With the measure you measure it will be measured back to you', is capable of performing that summarizing function follows from the way in which the whole measure principle is exploited in ancient Jewish texts. Thus, attached to the virtually verbatim parallel for Q 6:38c in *m. Sota* 1:7 there is a series of illustrations of how the correspondence between a person's action and the matching action of God towards that person actually works. It is evident that the correspondence may sometimes mean the reversal of the human action: thus, 'she (the adulteress, Num 5:11–22) bedecked herself for transgression – the Almighty brought her to shame'. The correspondence may be an exact equivalence: thus, 'she laid herself bare for transgression – the Almighty likewise laid her bare; she began transgression with the thigh first and afterward with the belly – therefore the thigh shall suffer first and afterward the belly'. The divine response may, however, go further than the initial human action: thus, 'neither shall aught else of the body go free'. *M. Sota* 1:8 goes on to provide further illustrations of the second pattern of exact correspondence: thus the case of Samson, whose eyes led him astray, and who was punished by having his eyes put out, or the case of Absalom, who gloried in his hair, took ten of his father's concubines, and stole three hearts, and who was punished by being hanged by his hair, and pierced by spears ten times and by darts three times. There follows in *m. Sota* 1:9 a pair of examples of how the measure principle works out in what are called 'goodly matters': the first correlates Miriam's waiting for Moses for just one hour, and Israel's waiting for her for seven days, while the second correlates the burial of Jacob by Joseph (the greatest of the brothers), the taking of the bones of Joseph by Moses (the greatest in Israel), and the burial of Moses by no less than God himself.

For Q 6:38c to be an apt summary of what precedes it in 6:37, 38ab it is only necessary for the measure principle to cover actions both bad and good (which it clearly does), and for the divine response sometimes to go beyond the initial human action (which it clearly can). At the same time it must be acknowledged that the 'going beyond' in 6:38b is more than a little overpowering: 'good measure, pressed down, shaken together, running over, shall they give into your lap'. That in turn appears to make it entirely appropriate and natural, even necessary, that there should be an introductory heading which places the emphasis in what follows primarily on the positive, even if the negative is by no means excluded. When we recall the inherent connection between mercy and giving, and the frequent complementariness of mercy and judgment, 6:36 seems admirably suited to be that introductory heading. Why then does 6:36 not speak of God's *future* exercise of mercy in order that from the outset the measure principle should be exhibited? Surely for two reasons: First, the actual form chosen deliberately echoes the covenant formulations, which would not have been anything like so clearly achieved through a form like 'be merciful, and mercy will be shown to you'. Second, the measure principle is invoked as a supporting and persuasive argument in favour of mercy, which is ultimately grounded, however, not merely in what God will *do* in future time but rather in what God *is* at all times. The material in Q 6:36–38 therefore emerges as a unity, that is, a unit. And that part of the unit which is by design dominant is the call for mercy.

A dramatic portrayal of the principles set out in this unit of tradition is, incidentally, provided by the parable of the unmerciful servant (Matt 18:23–35), which also happens to be the only other tradition in the synoptic gospels to use the verb ἀπολύειν. That parable very obviously exploits the measure principle (see vv. 30, 33, 34). But that is all in the service of the major theme of mercy (v. 33), mercy which takes effect through forgiveness and release (vv. 27, 32), mercy portrayed in a context sharply contrasting compassion and wrath (vv. 27, 34). Such a parabolic story confirms the naturalness of viewing Q 6:36–38 as a single unit.

The original text thus ran (as in Luke):

γίνεσθε οἰκτίρμονες ὡς ὁ πατὴρ ὑμῶν οἰκτίρμων ἐστίν.
   μὴ κρίνετε, ἵνα μὴ κριθῆτε·
   μὴ καταδικάζετε, ἵνα μὴ καταδικασθῆτε.
   ἀπολύετε, καὶ ἀπολυθήσεσθε·
   δίδοτε, καὶ δοθήσεται ὑμῖν·
      μέτρον καλὸν πεπιεσμένον σεσαλευμένον
      ὑπερεκχυννόμενον δώσουσιν εἰς τὸν κόλπον ὑμῶν·
ἐν ᾧ γὰρ μέτρῳ μετρεῖτε μετρηθήσεται ὑμῖν.

The demands set out in this tradition could without any strain at all fit into the proclamation of the historical Jesus and, in specific terms, with those pre-Q traditions used already in the discourse but probably stemming from him. But, again moving on to the level of the discourse itself, it is worth emphasizing how clearly vv. 36–38 pick up the concerns of vv. 27–35. Both complexes are thoroughly informed by covenantal thinking. Both treat the problem of enmity, that which shows itself in hostile attitudes, actions and speech (vv. 27–28, 29, 35), and that which might provoke judgment and condemnation (v. 37ab). Both call for positive response, whether in loving attitude, action and speech (vv. 27–28, 35) or in the forgiveness which is the presupposition of it all (v. 37c). Both find the required spirit to be most significantly expressed in generous giving (vv. 30, 38a), with the hidden presupposition of the first saying, that the lender can rely on God to repay him, being amply spelt out in the second. Both call for the imitation of God (vv. 35c, 36). Both speak of God's future response to whatever action takes place on the human level (vv. 35c, 37–38). Against this background of common themes one can go on to ask what vv. 36–38 contribute which was not in vv. 27–35, and the answer is the sounding of a warning note and the addition of an extra reason for taking the loving approach which is required. That is, not to respond positively, and instead to respond negatively, is to bring down upon oneself the judgment of God (v. 37ab). Lest this be regarded as the sounding of a negative note, however, the matching of the editorial statement that 'your reward shall be great' (v. 35b) and the emphatic and extraordinarily expansive descriptions of the divine gift 'good measure, pressed down, shaken together, running over' (v. 38b), which are brought together compositionally by the editor, ensure that the cumulative effect is overwhelmingly positive.

From a study of the relationship between Q 6:36–38 and what went before it in the discourse we can now turn to a consideration of how it relates to what comes afterwards. To do this we begin by uncovering a scheme which is present in three relevant texts:

The first of these texts is Lev 19:17–18, two verses which are shown to belong together by their concluding declaration that 'I am the Lord' (cf. vv. 10, 11, 14, 16). In them the love command is coupled with the injunction to 'reason with your neighbour' (MT: *yakah*; LXX: ἐλέγχειν). These two equivalent forms of upright behaviour are set over against a hostile action, namely taking vengeance, and hostile attitudes, namely hatred and bearing a grudge. The concern to tackle the problem by giving attention to the 'heart' is striking; so is the correlation of love with a restoration of ruptured relationships by means of reasoned reproof; and so is the synonymous usage of the terms 'brother' (v. 17) and 'neighbour' (vv. 17–18) to describe a fellow member of the people of Israel.

The second text is Matt 18:15–17, 21–22. This material may well have stood in Q and then survived most substantially in Matthew and in a rather more truncated and damaged form in Luke, but that is an issue to be addressed in the next chapter of this book. For the present the interest is in the detailed conciliation procedure described. The problem under discussion is again that of ruptured relationships within the people of Israel. The offence by a 'brother' is to be met by the offended person's implementing the reproof process. The failure of this three-stage process of attempted conciliation is followed by the offender's being regarded in the same way as the Gentiles and taxcollectors (note the same combination of persons as in Q 6:32–33), though probably being shown unlimited forgiveness. The parameters of this process are through and through Jewish – it is only by the evidently secondary attachment of 18:19–20 that the community consciousness becomes Christian and the perspective christological. But what is additionally fascinating about Matthew's compositional activity is his placing next in the sequence the parable of the unmerciful servant (18:23–35), the parable whose close resemblance to Q 6:36–38 we have already observed. The evangelist's juxtaposition of passages dealing with reproof and with mercy is striking.

The third text is the Testament of Gad. The main subject of reflection is hatred, hatred as exemplified in the reaction of Joseph's brothers to his behaviour. The effects of such hatred are spelt out in a sickly catalogue. It brings a longing for the death of the hated person (2:1–2; 4:3–7); it surfaces in distortion and disapproval of all he does (3:2); evil speaking, envy and arrogance become the order of the day (3:3); the whole person is taken over by evil (2:1); and mercy disappears, along with righteousness and obedience to the law of God (3:1, 3; 4:1; 5:3). What is very significant is the definition of the law which is being infringed (4:2): 'Hatred does not want to hear repeated the Lord's commands concerning love of neighbour, and thus it sins against God.' Clearly this is the rejection of hatred and the requirement of neighbourly love in Lev 19:17–18.

In reflecting on this situation the writer puts into the mouth of Gad an extended explanation of judgment based on the measure principle (5:10–11): 'By whatever human capacity anyone transgresses, by that he is also chastised. Since my anger was merciless in opposition to Joseph, through this anger of mine I suffered mercilessly, and was brought under judgment for eleven months, as long as I had it in for Joseph, until he was sold.' On the positive side, love, already mentioned as synonymous with mercy, is the polar opposite of hatred in thought and act. It brings life into a context of death (4:6); it forms an alliance with the divine law to effect the salvation of men (4:7); as love of the 'brother' (*sic*) it is a matter of combining deed and word and attitude of soul or heart (6:1, 3). But in immediate practical terms it issues in an effort to achieve through direct reproof a state of peace with the offending neighbour. Thus in *T. Gad* 6:3, 6 there emerges an equation between 'to reprove (ἐλέγχειν)' and 'to speak in peace (λέγειν ἐν εἰρήνῃ)'.

The writer goes on to stress the importance of all this if the offender's repentance and confession are not forthcoming. Abandonment of hatred means no anger, no evil speaking and no talking to others. The reproof process is undertaken with peace as the prize of success, but the sequel to failure must be forgiveness from the heart and the recognition of God as sole judge. From this whole panoramic view of the problem of hatred and the process of conciliation it is clear that the controlling principles are to be found in Leviticus 19, in v. 17 as well in v. 18.

The second and third of this trio of texts point us to a significant association of ideas in the mind of Matthew. When *T. Gad* 6:6 set up the equation between reproof and speaking in peace it echoed Prov 10:10: 'He who boldly reproves makes peace (LXX: εἰρηνοποιεῖ)'. The unique occurrence of that verb there in the OT is matched in the NT, leaving aside the one occurrence of the verb in Col 1:20, by a single occurrence of the noun εἰρηνοποιός in the MattR beatitude, 'Blessed are the peacemakers, for they shall be called sons of God' (Matt 5:9). Given the likelihood that Matthew was deliberately echoing Prov 10:10 and simultaneously anticipating Q 6:35, we have further evidence from his work of the suitability of the reproof theme in a context of overcoming enmity through love.

From these three texts we return to Q, and in the association of 6:36–38 with 6:39, 41–42 we find a fourth example of the same scheme. For reasons already mentioned, v. 39 (minus its introductory εἶπεν δὲ καὶ παραβολὴν αὐτοῖς) was not followed in Q by Luke 6:40, and the elimination of the latter permits the relatedness of v. 39 to vv. 41–42 to become evident. This pre-Lucan association is not just a matter of shared imagery or catchword linkage but rather of shared ideas. First, v. 39 speaks of one person's acting as guide to another, and so do vv. 41–42; second, v.39 depends for its cogency on the guide's sharing the same disability as the person being guided, and so do vv. 41–42; third, the specific disability in v. 39 is a sight problem, and the same is true in vv. 41–42; fourth, by contrast with other sayings about leading the blind (cf. *T. Reub.* 2:9), v. 39 is preoccupied with the guide, and the same is true in vv. 41–42. Thus v. 39 interlocks tightly with vv. 41–42, and this latter tradition about the speck and the log discloses the particular concern.

Verbal discrepancies in the Matthew/Luke versions are minor and insignificant and they need not detain us, so the original material emerges clearly:

μήτι δύναται τυφλὸς τυφλὸν ὁδηγεῖν;
οὐχὶ ἀμφότεροι εἰς βόθυνον πεσοῦνται;
τί δὲ βλέπεις τὸ κάρφος τὸ ἐν τῷ ὀφθαλμῷ τοῦ ἀδελφοῦ σου,
    τὴν δὲ ἐν τῷ σῷ ὀφθαλμῷ δοκὸν οὐ κατανοεῖς;
πῶς ἐρεῖς τῷ ἀδελφῷ σου, ἄφες ἐκβάλω τὸ κάρφος ἐκ τοῦ ὀφθαλμοῦ
    σου, καὶ ἰδοὺ ἡ δοκὸς ἐν τῷ ὀφθαλμῷ σου;
ὑποκριτά, ἔκβαλε πρῶτον ἐκ τοῦ ὀφθαλμοῦ σου τὴν δοκόν,
    καὶ τότε διαβλέψεις ἐκβαλεῖν τὸ κάρφος ἐκ τοῦ ὀφθαλμοῦ
    τοῦ ἀδελφοῦ σου.

This material does, however, have two features which certainly should detain us. The first is the term 'brother' which appears here for the first time in the discourse: this is the term which is used uniquely in Leviticus 19 at v. 17, and the term whose only other occurrence in Q is in the reproof passage Q 17:3/Matt 18:15. The second is the exact correspondence with the rabbinic text, *b. Arak.* 16b, which reads,

> R. Tarfon said, I wonder whether there is anyone in this genera-tion who accepts reproof, for if one says to him, 'Remove the mote from between your eyes', he would answer, 'Remove the beam from between your eyes.'

From this it is clear that terminology which is at home in the setting of the reproof process is being employed in Q 6:41–42, and, moreover, that the juxtaposition of vv. 36–38, 39, 41–42 points to the Q editor's use of a well attested scheme. His concern is that each one of those persons who have been wronged and persecuted should not merely avoid a negative response to the wrong but address the problem, take positive steps by means of the reproof process to change the persecutor's mind and restore relationships, renew the peace of the com-munity, but also fulfil the prior condition of being free of any fault which will vitiate and doom to failure that reproof process. This is of paramount importance since a series of texts confirms R. Tarfon's implication that the reproof process was much disliked and most easily repulsed by reciprocal criticism of the character of the reprover.[100] The discourse therefore nears its end by focussing on the integrity and internal condition of each person addressed by it.

[100]See Prov 5:12–13; 12:1; 15:10, 12; Sir 21:6; 32:17.

The final tradition in the discourse which calls for study is that concerned with goodness and its origin. We have already considered Matt 7:15–23/Luke 6:43–45, 46; 13:26–27 from one angle. Now it is necessary to view it from another. But at the outset it must be admitted that the reconstruction of the Q original is complicated by the existence of a pair of Matthaean versions (7:16–20; 12:33–35) alongside the one Lucan version (6:43–45). Each of those Matthaean versions has been heavily edited by the evangelist. In the one case the warning concerns possible intervention by false prophets. From the fact that they do things of which Matthew disapproves he deduces that they are internally evil (Matt 7:15). This warning and charge functions as a heading for a unit framed by the double declaration that 'you will know them by their fruits' (Matt 7:16a, 20). Plainly therefore in vv. 16b-19 Matthew is only interested in the negative side of any apparently balanced proposition, in short the confident insistence that evil fruits will prove that the inner being of the persons concerned is evil. With the two two-liner sayings (vv. 17–18) forming the centre of the unit, it is plain that the thorns and thistles saying (v. 16b) is designed to balance the MattR-positioned quotation from the Baptist (v. 19, cf. Q 3:9). Extensive Matthaean remoulding is thus in evidence in Matt 7:15–20.

Such remoulding is not lacking in the alternative version in Matt 12:33–35. With the saying about blasphemy against the Holy Spirit (Matt 12:31–32/Q 12:10) as a control at the beginning, and the authoritative warning about assessment according to speech in the day of judgment (12:36–37) at the end, the intervening material from Q 6:43–45 again reverberates with an echo of the Baptist's preaching (12:34; cf. Q 3:7b): 'Generation of vipers, how can you speak good, when you are evil?' Whereas Q used the words 'when you are evil' (11:13) to describe the general condition of humanity set over against God, a condition which did *not* prevent good actions, Matthew uses that same phrase in 12:34a to express his conviction that it is an inviolable principle of human life that certain persons, though not all, are evil and that they are in consequence simply unable to produce good speech or good action. In short, here is an assertion of the total depravity of the opposition, whether Christian or Jewish, and the speech of a thoroughgoing sectarian!

For all that the evangelist has made so strong a contribution to the formation of 7:15–20 and 12:31–37 there are schematic agreements with Luke 6:43–45 which suggest that the latter is almost entirely a replica of Q. First, the tree/fruit saying in the form 'good does not produce evil, nor evil good' is followed by the 'knowing by fruit' generalization in Matt 7:18, 20/Luke 6:43, 44a. Second, the treasure saying in the form 'good produces good, and evil evil' comes at the end in Matt 12:35/Luke 6:45ab, and in both cases the generalization about heart and mouth is attached (although it is positioned beforehand in Matt 12:34b and afterwards in Luke 6:45c). Matthew's extensive recasting activity is likely to be responsible for the initial rather than intermediate positioning of the thorns and thistles saying, so after allowance is made for small adjustments in wording the Q source material probably ran as follows:

οὐ ποιεῖ δένδρον καλὸν καρπὸν σαπρόν,
  οὐδὲ πάλιν ποιεῖ δένδρον σαπρὸν καρπὸν καλόν.
ἐκ γὰρ τοῦ καρποῦ τὸ δένδρον γινώσκεταῖ.
  μήτι συλλέγουσιν ἀπὸ ἀκανθῶν σταφυλὰς
  ἢ ἀπὸ τριβόλων σῦκα;
ὁ ἀγαθὸς ἄνθρωπος ἐκ τοῦ ἀγαθοῦ θησαυροῦ προφέρει ἀγαθά,
  καὶ ὁ πονηρὸς ἐκ τοῦ πονηροῦ προφέρει πονηρά.
ἐκ γὰρ τοῦ περισσεύματος τῆς καρδίας τὸ στόμα λαλεῖ.

It is immediately clear that the whole complex belongs to the sphere of secular wisdom. Yet there is a cutting edge to the sayings, the communication of a warning. There must be more intended than the mere setting out of symmetrical statements about good and bad: the reader is challenged to make a decision, to avoid the bad and to achieve the good. But what exactly is the good, and what is the context in which the good comes to expression?

This is where the difficulties really begin! In form there is a correspondence between the two examples of a two-line saying (vv. 43, 45ab) followed by a one-line explanation (vv. 44a, 45c). Nevertheless the two complexes are distinct. First, the term 'treasure' (v. 45a) in the second complex indicates that the saying in question is still in the area of metaphor, a different metaphor (relating to the household? cf. Matt 13:52) from that employed in the first complex. Therefore the second complex is not the interpretation of the first. Second, there is a certain asymmetry between the two two-line sayings: the first works negatively by affirming that good does not produce bad and vice versa, while the second works positively by affirming that good produces good and bad produces bad. Hence, just as v. 45c is the concluding inference for the second complex, so also v. 44a is for the first. At that precise point what would otherwise be little more than a banal truism receives an application which has persons in mind.

Two ambiguities have to be resolved in vv. 43, 44a. One concerns the meaning of the word σαπρός: this could here be qualitative, and thus imply inherent badness, the sort of thing which causes the σαπρός word group to have associations of rottenness, corruption and decay,[101] or it could be generic, the sort of thing which simply makes objects which are satisfactory in their own terms nevertheless useless and unprofitable.[102] If v. 44a is to be true, to work within the terms of reference of v. 43, and to describe a genuine experience of disclosure concerning a tree, 'badness' must be qualitative, for one is not dependent on the fruit for a knowledge of genus. On the other hand, if v. 44a is using the idea of knowledge more in the sense of experience than of disclosure, the generic meaning comes back into the reckoning. And this does seem to be favoured by the presence of the saying, 'They do not gather grapes from thorns, do they, nor figs from thistles?' (v. 44b). We can hardly suppose that v. 44b was intended to be in a state of unresolved tension with vv. 43, 44a, most especially since it appears to pick up the content of v. 43b, 'nor does a bad tree produce good fruit'. As far as thorns and thistles, an idiomatic pairing,[103] are concerned, the reason for their not yielding grapes and figs, another idiomatic pairing,[104] is nothing to do with quality and everything to do with genus. So vv. 43, 44ab as a whole seem to be concerned with the sort of tree and the sort of fruit which can be experienced as good and useful. Doubtless the choice of grapes and figs was deliberate, for text after text indicates that they constitute basic, good and nourishing food,[105] resembling in

[101]Cf. Job 7:5; 17:14; 21:26; 25:6; 2 Macc 9:9; Arndt & Gingrich, p. 749.
[102]Cf. Matt 13:48, and the comment of O. Bauernfeind, 'σαπρός', *TDNT* 7.94–7, esp. p. 97: 'no good as food; biologically . . . quite normal'.
[103]Cf. Gen 3:18; Hos 10:8; Heb 6:8.
[104]Cf. Neh 13:15; Jer 8:13; Hos 9:10.
[105]Grapes: Deut 32:14; Sir 39:26–27. Figs: Deut 8:8; Judg 9:10–11; 1 Sam 25:18.

that respect the bread and fish mentioned elsewhere in Q (11:11–12/Matt 7:9–10) and defined there as ἀγαθά.

The second ambiguity concerns καρπός when that term is made to stand for a feature of human life: it could refer to speech in particular[106] or to actions in general[107] and the consequences of those actions.[108] Nothing within vv. 43, 44a allows a decision, and therefore, as is customary with καρπός sayings, room is left for one to emerge from the associated material. That means v. 45, which in turn means that speech is in mind.

When the two complexes, vv. 43–44 and v. 45, are put together the second simultaneously complements and defines the first. In application they are contrasting persons who have a good and useful effect with those whose effect is the opposite. The first indicates that the human evaluation of a tree is related to its capacity to produce that which is good, necessary and useful, and that correspondingly the true status of a human being is determined by the quality of what is said (thus the generic shades over into the qualitative). The second, working entirely in qualitative terms, indicates that the character of speech is determined by the speaker's inner being. The matter under discussion is therefore how to ensure that speech which is in a certain setting good, necessary and useful may be forthcoming, and the explanation sees the situation ultimately in terms of personal integrity and inner goodness. In short, the only way to speak well is to be good.

What the setting is emerges from a recognition of three factors. The first is the formal consideration that a pair of complementary units (and vv. 43–44, 45 constitute such a pair) is normally preceded in Q by some sort of heading, whether in the form of a single saying or a block. The second is that thematically the material in vv. 43–45 overlaps significantly with vv. 39, 41–42, the language of teaching and instruction being present in both. That is true of the verb ὁδηγεῖν, while the verb προφέρειν (v. 45) can be used in connection with speech which is open, bold and wise.[109] Similarly, in a series of passages

[106]Prov 13:2; 18:20–21; Sir 27:6; 37:22–23.
[107]Prov 31:16, 31; Jer 6:19; 17:10; Hos 10:13; Mic 7:13.
[108]Ps 58:11; Wis 3:13, 15.
[109]Prov 10:13; 3 Macc 1:12; 4:17; 5:39; 7:4, 11.

the metaphor of treasure is used for the resources of wisdom made available through instruction.[110] The third factor is the correspondence between, on the one hand, a section which begins with the subject of reproof and reaches a final climax with the subject of the human heart, and, on the other hand, Lev 19:17: 'You shall not hate your brother *in your heart*, but you shall *reason* with your neighbour . . .'. Consequently, what lies before us is a carefully constructed section which refers to the human precondition for implementing the reproof procedure. Echoing the principle that the reprover must be wise[111] and righteous[112] Q 6:39, 41–45 opts for goodness as the all-enveloping quality needed. The person who sets out to speak in this way, to achieve that which is good, necessary and useful for the community and for each person within it, must give heed first of all to the obligation to be personally beyond reproach. He or she has then attended to the letter of the law of Moses.

5. Conclusions.

Our study is at an end, and it remains only to summarize its outcome. The inaugural discourse of Jesus in Q is an integrated whole in respect of both formal construction and theological texture. The introductory beatitudes ensure that the whole is dominated by the majestic kerygma of Isa 61:1–2, and the concluding parable warns of the serious consequences of inattention to the related didache. Both traditions remind the readers of the supreme authority of the Son of man whom they confess. The centre of the discourse is a spelling out of Lev 19:17–18, and the persons addressed form no community other than that addressed by that ancient law. Given the key role of an inaugural discourse, this is extremely important for the understanding of Q. This is a text for persons belonging to the community of Israel.

Structurally, vv. 36–38 are pivotal within vv. 27–45 as a whole. They gather together the themes of vv. 27–35, where Lev 19:18 dominates. They control vv. 36–45, where Lev 19:17

[110]Prov 2:4; Wis 7:14; Sir 1:25; 20:30; 41:14; Bar 3:15; cf. 2 Cor 4:7; Col 2:3.
[111]Prov 15:12; Sir 20:29.
[112]Ps 141:5.

dominates. They are themselves controlled by v. 36, and thus the discourse is given its keynote, mercy. Members of the audience of this discourse live in the permanent light of divine mercy. They are enabled, indeed obliged, to act mercifully because they have experienced in the past, and they know they will experience in the future, that mercy by which, as adherents of Jesus and members of the community of Israel, they bring to effect what it means to be the community of God.

4

Reproof and Reconciliation

The inaugural discourse in Q served to highlight a strong and vigorous sense of community. The horizon was throughout that of Israel, and this showed in two very important ways. First, the whole nation was brought into view by the initial tradition within the discourse, the beatitudes. The marginalized, those all too easily relegated to the fringes of community life, were revealed as the primary concern of the gospel. Second, the wholeness of the nation was clearly under threat by virtue of polarization and polemic. Those who acknowledged the Son of man were required to respond in a very constructive spirit to the enmity which faced them. Every effort was to be directed towards the achieving of reconciliation on the basis of reproof. In both these two ways, the theme of mercy could be seen to be truly in control: mercy as the keynote of the covenant which makes the people of Israel the people of God, and mercy as the effective attitude which makes for communal peace.

Another tradition, this time one which probably occurred towards the end of Q, picks up these themes: Matt 18:15–17, 21–22/Luke 17:3–4. A study of the tradition history of this material may take a little further forward the ideas of the last chapter.

The presence of Q material in Matt 18:15, 21–22/Luke 17:3–4 is often and quite rightly inferred from the sequence of sayings, agreed by both evangelists, in which the tradition about scandals (Matt 18:7/Luke 17:1) shortly precedes this tradition about disrupted relationships within the community.[1] While there has been a powerful trend towards finding in Luke 17:3–4 the closer approximation to the original Q wording, there has also been a

---

[1]J. Schmid, *Matthäus und Lukas* (BibS(F) 23; Freiburg: Herder, 1930) 309; F. Hauck, *Das Evangelium des Lukas* (THKNT 3; Leipzig: 1934) 211.

striking variety of view about the origin of Matt 18:15–17. Three main suggestions have been put forward. The first is that it is an independent M variant of the Q tradition preserved by Luke.[2] The second is that it is a MattR expansion of the first part of the Q tradition, Luke 17:3.[3] The third is that it is a post-Q but pre-Matthaean expansion of that first part of the Q tradition,[4] and thus an argument for supposing that two different recensions of Q came into the hands of Matthew and Luke. The third of these suggestions has attracted a good deal of support in recent years, but the purpose of this study is to put forward a fourth proposal, namely that Matt 18:15–17 (minus v. 16b) belonged to Q and was both known to, and truncated by, Luke.

A reasonably uncontroversial start to the discussion of Matthew 18 can be made by assembling the arguments in favour of a separation of vv. 15–17 from vv. 18, 19–20, and in favour of regarding vv. 15, 16a, 17 as pre-Matthaean.

First, v. 18 is probably dependent on MattR, not only for its present position but also for its minimal deviations in content from the earlier 'binding and loosing' saying in 16:19. Some writers accept that the position but not the content is MattR;[5] others accept its secondariness in relation to 16:19, but regard it as a pre-Matthaean addition to vv. 15–17;[6] still others regard it as an older version of 16:19.[7] But the arguments for the total responsibility of MattR are surely persuasive. (i) There is the change from singular (vv. 15–17) to plural (v. 18) forms.[8] (ii) Those features of v. 18 which distinguish it from 16:19 are all characteristic of MattR, i.e., the addition of ἀμὴν λέγω ὑμῖν,[9]

---

[2]Streeter, *Four Gospels* 257, 281; W. Grundmann, *Das Evangelium nach Lukas* (THKNT 3; 2nd ed.; Berlin: Evangelische Verlagsanstalt, 1961) 331; T. W. Manson, *The Sayings of Jesus* (London: SCM, 1971) 139.

[3]Schmid, *Matthäus und Lukas* 309; R. H. Gundry, *Matthew* (Grand Rapids, Michigan: Eerdmans, 1982) 367–70.

[4]Lührmann, *Redaktion* 106; Zeller, *Mahnsprüche* 61.

[5]G. Strecker, *Der Weg der Gerechtigkeit* (FRLANT 82; 2nd ed.; Göttingen: Vandenhoeck & Ruprecht, 1966) 223.

[6]Lührmann, *Redaktion* 113.

[7]E. Klostermann, *Das Matthäsevangelium* (HNT 4; Tübingen: Mohr, 1927) 150; W. Pesch, *Matthäus als Seelsorger* (SBS 2; Stuttgart: Katholisches Bibelwerk, 1966) 38.

[8]Pesch, *Seelsorger* 41: 'Die Naht ist am Wechsel der Anrede auch noch aüsserlich erkennbar.'

the movement from ὁ ἐάν to ὅσα ἐάν,[10] the preference for the singular form ἐν οὐρανῷ rather than the plural form ἐν τοῖς οὐρανοῖς as part of a contrast with a necessarily singular γῆ.[11] (iii) The relationship between vv. 15–21 and 16:17–19 is readily explicable in terms of deliberate reminiscence – thus, the common combination of Peter, the church, and the power to bind and loose – and balanced complementariness – thus, the power to bind and loose refers in the one case to the teaching *magisterium* and in the other to the disciplinary process, a combination which is thoroughly appropriate.[12] (iv) The parallels for v. 18 and 16:19 are in rabbinic texts which lack any counterpart for vv. 15–17,[13] while the parallels for vv. 15–17 in *T. Gad* 6, 1QS 5–6 and CD 9 lack any counterpart for v. 18. This indicates two discrete schemes. Overall, therefore, it is overwhelmingly probable that the remodelling of 16:19 in v. 18 and its positioning after vv. 15–17 should be attributed to MattR.

Second, it has frequently been observed that v. 16b is in some tension with its context. The passage quoted, Deut 19:15 (cf. Num 35:30; Deut 17:6; 2 Cor 13:1), refers to formal prosecution testimony rather than an intensification of pressure on the accused to accept his fault and bring the complaint to an end (cf. 1QS 6:1; CD 9:3). The quotation of this passage in v. 16b presupposes v. 17a, the next stage of the process which, at the stage of v. 16a, is still hoped to be unnecessary. The insertion of such an explicit quotation is readily attributable to MattR, but the corollary of the resultant dislocation is that the adjacent material is pre-Matthaean.

Third, the use of the word ἐκκλησία for the local assembly in v. 17a is clearly less developed than its use for the community unrestricted by time or space in 16:18. The latter is Christian (μου ἡ ἐκκλησία), the former is not. The latter is clearly the one

---

[9]Cf. 5:18/Luke 16:17; 17:20 diff Luke 17:6; 19:23 diff Mark 10:23; 24:2 diff Mark 13:2; 25:12 diff Luke 13:25.

[10]Cf. 7:12 diff Luke 6:31; 22:9 diff Luke 14:21; 23:3.

[11]Cf. 5:18/Luke 16:17; 5:34 (Jas 5:12); 6:10 diff Luke 11:2; 11:25/Luke 10:21; 24:35/Mark 13:31; 28:18.

[12]Lührmann, *Redaktion* 113.

[13]Billerbeck I.787; J. Gnilka, 'Die Kirche des Matthäus und die Gemeinde von Qumran', *BZ* 7 (1963) 43–63, esp. p. 55: 'Das diziplinäre Vorgehen gegen den Sünder in der Kirche des Mt besitzt keine Parallele im rabbinischen Judentum.'

in which Matthew has invested theologically, in view of his careful presentation in 16:13–20 as a whole, so that the former is most naturally regarded as pre-Matthaean.

Fourth, for all that the Matthaean community belonged within the flow of traditional Judaism the presence within this gospel of 9:9–13 and 21:43; 28:16–20 implies that its members included Gentiles and tax-collectors. That is not the implication of v. 17b,[14] which therefore also looks like being pre-Matthaean.

Adding all the above arguments together we can conclude that vv. 15, 16a, 17 as a whole are pre-Matthaean. From this conclusion the argument can now be taken forward in a more form-critical direction. This involves a schematic comparison of Matt 18:15, 16a, 17, 21, 22 and Luke 17:3, 4 with *T. Gad* 6:1–7, 1QS 5:25–6:1 and CD 9:2–8. For convenience and clarity these texts are set out in full.

Testament of Gad 6

(1) And now, my children, love each one his brother, and put away hatred from your hearts, loving one another in deed and word and in disposition of the soul.

(3) Therefore love one another from the heart, and if a man sins against you speak to him in peace, after having cast away the poison of hatred; and do not hold guile in your soul. And if he confesses and repents, forgive him;

(4) and if he denies, do not get into a passion with him, lest, when he starts swearing, you sin doubly.

(6) If then he denies, and yet feels shame when reproved, keep silent, lest you provoke him; for the one who denies may repent so as not to offend you again, and he may even honour you and fear and be at peace with you.

(7) But if he is shameless and persists in his wrongdoing, even so forgive him from the heart, and leave to God the avenging.[15]

---

[14]Pesch, *Seelsorger* 41; Lührmann, *Redaktion* 112.
[15]Text in H. W. Hollander and M. de Jonge, *The Testaments of the Twelve Patriarchs. A Commentary* (Leiden: Brill, 1985) 330–1.

1QS 5–6

(25) They shall rebuke one another in truth, humility and charity. Let no man address his companion with anger, or ill-temper,

(26) or obduracy, or with envy prompted by the spirit of wickedness. Let him not hate him because of his uncircumcised heart, but let him rebuke him on the very same day lest

(1) he incur guilt because of him. And furthermore, let no man accuse his companion before the Congregation without having first admonished him in the presence of witnesses.[16]

CD 9

(2) And concerning the saying, 'You shall not take vengeance on the children of your people, nor bear rancour against them' (Lev 19:18), if any member

(3) of the Covenant accuses his companion without first rebuking him before witnesses;

(4) if he denounces him in the heat of his anger or reports him to his elders to make him look contemptible, he is one that takes vengeance and bears rancour;

(5) although it is expressly written, 'He takes vengeance upon His adversaries and bears rancour against His enemies' (Nah 1:2).

(6) If he holds his peace towards him from one day to another, and thereafter speaks of him in the heat of his anger,

(7) he testifies against himself in a capital matter, because he has not fulfilled the commandment of God which tells him, 'You shall

(8) rebuke your companion and not be burdened with shame because of him' (Lev 19:17).[17]

---

[16]Text in G. Vermes, *The Dead Sea Scrolls in English* (3rd ed.; London: Penguin, 1987) 68–9.

[17]Text in Vermes, *Dead Sea Scrolls* 93.

All these texts are reflective of the principle set out in Lev 19:17, and a comparative analysis of their determining features yields the following table:

	Matthew 18	Luke 17	Testament of Gad 6	1QS 5–6	CD 9
A. The brother's sin	15a	3a	3		
B. Direct personal reproof	15a	3a	3	25	6?
C. Approach with love and without hate			1	25,26	4,6
D. Receptivity of reproof	15b	3b	3		
E. Possible denial by offender	16a		4,6		
F. Further reproof before witnesses	16ab		(6)	1	3
G. Submission to assembly	17a			1	3
H. Rejection of assembly decision	17b				
I. Reliance on divine judgment			7		
J. Further sin by offender	21	4	7		
K. Further forgiveness by offended party	21,22	4	7		

This table exhibits a number of important realities about the family of texts.

First, there is the surprising lack of parallel in the Christian texts for the Jewish texts' preoccupation with the spirit in which reproof is undertaken (C). Lev 19:17, 18 probably underlies all versions (explicitly so in *T. Gad* 6:1, 3) but the Jewish texts exhibit its influence much more clearly. In the case of the Testament of Gad the preoccupation with the attitude of the reproving party is mainly responsible for the omission of any reproof beyond the first (F); in the case of 1QS and CD it leads to the total omission of any comment on how the reproved person responds. In the Christian texts it is notable that the only point at which reference is made to the personal attitude of the reprover is Matt 18:17b, 'Let him be to you as the Gentile and the tax-collector.'

Second, Luke and the Testament of Gad both envisage a process only to the extent of including the initial element of personal reproof (B), whereas Matthew and 1QS/CD envisage a three-stage process of personal reproof + reproof before witness + presentation to the assembly (B, F, G). Of the relationship between Luke and the Testament of Gad several things can be said:

(i) Luke does not positively *exclude* further action beyond the initial reproof in the way that the Testament does, and therefore Luke represents something of a middle term between the Testament and the Matthew/1QS/CD scheme.

(ii) A comparison between Luke and the Testament of Gad makes plain the artificiality of the *present* form of Luke 17:4. The Testament closes in 6:7 with a reference to protracted and deliberate sinning by the unresponsive offender. To this corresponds Luke's clause καὶ ἐὰν ἑπτάκις τῆς ἡμέρας ἁμαρτήσῃ εἰς σέ, as parallels demonstrate. A sevenfold repetition gives an action firmness and completeness in Josh 6:15; 1 Kgs 18:43, 44; 2 Kgs 5:10, 14. Prov 24:16, in affirming that 'a righteous man falls seven times, and rises again', means to say that *whenever* and *however often* he falls he will recover. Most significantly, when Ps 119:164 declares that 'seven times a day (LXX: ἑπτάκις τῆς ἡμέρας) will I praise you for all your righteous ordinances', it means that this will happen constantly and without ceasing: it will be a firm and settled behaviour pattern. Now this is what Luke 17:4a is about, but as it stands it is coloured (or, to be more precise, discoloured) by the following phrase in Luke

17:4b, καὶ ἑπτάκις ἐπιστρέψῃ πρὸς σὲ λέγων· μετανοῶ. That phrase has no parallel in *T. Gad* 6:7; it has no parallel in Matthew; it is out of line with Luke 17:3, where the initiative taken by the offended person is shown to be the real subject of concern, whereas 17:4 speaks of a quite extraordinary and spontaneous initiative by the offender; it is extremely artificial, in that a determined and settled pattern of sinning does not square with the repeated claim to repent unless lying or hypocrisy is involved, which we have no reason to suppose. So that whole phrase is secondary, a modification caused by lack of comprehension of the phrase ἑπτάκις τῆς ἡμέρας, and in view of the typical Lucan interest in the theme of repentance, LukeR. The corollary is that we can neither adopt the suggestion[18] that an underlying ἐὰν μετανοήσῃ should be envisaged (to bring the *Vorlage* of 17:4 into line with 17:3), nor follow the counter-argument[19] that while the *Vorlage* did not contain such a phrase it did presume repentance. On the contrary, repentance is not presumed and indeed is excluded.

(iii) The movement in the Testament of Gad 6 from element D to element J serves to show the awkwardness of a parallel movement from D to J in Luke, particularly when the pre-Lucan form of Luke 17:4 is taken into account. In the two sequences a statement about conditional forgiveness, which is a response to repentance (D), is followed by a statement about totally unconditional forgiveness in a setting from which repentance is absent (K). But the Testament at least builds a bridge from one to the other by discussing an ascending scale of reactions by the offender (vv. 3b, 6, 7), and in the process depicting how the desired situation of peace and respect may by varying means be achieved. Luke 17, by contrast, builds no bridge and reads awkwardly and abruptly, and the expectation that something is needed to provide an intervening transition is disappointed. Yet that thoroughly justified expectation remains.

Third, of the relationship between Matthew and 1QS/CD several things may be said:

(i) The most strikingly distinctive feature in Matthew is the offender's rejection of the decision of the assembly, something

---

[18]Schulz, *Spruchquelle* 321.
[19]Zeller, *Mahnsprüche* 61; Merklein, *Gottesherrschaft* 248.

which at Qumran would be unthinkable. In Matt 18:17 indeed we have not only the individual's freedom to ignore the community's decision but also the community's lack of response to such a flouting – note that all terms in v. 17b are not plural but singular, but it is only in the MattR addition in v. 18 that an excommunication is envisaged. The situation in Matthew seems therefore to resemble that in the Testament: the procedure (long or short) is above all concerned for the maintenance of peace and the achievement of reconciliation, and not with the definition of the boundary between those inside and those outside.

(ii) A further distinctive feature in Matthew is the concluding statement about repetitive sinning and unconditional forgiveness (J, K). This follows on from element H and is also a thematic link with *T. Gad* 6:7. But artificiality is again detectable since v. 21 presumes a previous reference to the process of sinning, which is supplied neither by vv. 16, 17, when these describe the negative reaction of the offender, nor by v. 15, where his positive reaction rules it out. The Petrine intervention which shapes the present form of the saying is, however, widely accepted as MattR,[20] and therefore we can draw two conclusions. The first is that it has been necessitated by the insertion of other material (minimally vv. 18, 19–20). The second is that Matthew, like Luke, has obscured the original sense of the concluding saying even though his 7/77 scheme certainly underscores the demand for unrestricted forgiveness of offences.

The implications of all that has been discovered thus far can now be drawn out. Since Matt 18:15–16a, 17 has been shown to be pre-Matthaean, and since Luke 17:4 points to the need for something to intervene between Luke 17:3 and its pre-Lucan *Vorlage*, and since *all* the other texts either describe (1QS/CD) or implicitly recognize as a possibility (*T. Gad*) some action following an initial, unsuccessful reproof, the possibility that Matt 18:16a, 17 figured in Q must be seriously considered. To this we now turn.

Two small considerations can be cleared away quickly. The first is the argument that Luke 17:4 is inconceivable after Matt 18:15–17.[21] This can be set aside once the *pre*-Lucan version of

---

[20]Harnack, *Sayings* 95; Schulz, *Spruchquelle* 321; Zeller, *Mahnsprüche* 62; Merklein, *Gottesherrschaft* 247.

[21]E. Linnemann, *Parables of Jesus* (London: SPCK, 1966) 174.

Luke 17:4 is brought into focus and the above form-critical data included. The second is the observation that Jesus could not have voiced vv. 16, 17 because of the Qumran parallels and because of the attitude to Gentiles and taxcollectors in v. 17.[22] This is entirely right, but it does not affect the issue of whether v. 17 should be included in some particular post-Jesus layer of tradition – for there are plenty of inauthentic sayings in Q!

The issue effectively turns on the requirement ἔστω σοι ὥσπερ ὁ ἐθνικὸς καὶ ὁ τελώνης, and the claim can now be made that the attitude to Gentiles and taxcollectors in v. 17b is exactly the attitude of Q.

First, the ἐθνικός + τελώνης combination occurs elsewhere in the gospel tradition only at Matt 5:46–47 (Q 6:32–33). As argued earlier in this volume, Matthew here reproduces Q, and Luke's word ἁμαρτωλός is an editorial generalization carried out with Gentile readers in mind. Slight reserve on this matter is registered by Schürmann in view of the absence of the term ἁμαρτωλός from Acts and uncertainty about its occurrence in LukeR material in the gospel.[23] The point is, however, secured by LukeR formulations in 15:1–2 (cf. Luke 5:27–32/Mark 2:13–17) and 24:7 diff Mark 16:6. So Matt 5:46–47 does in this respect reproduce Q. Moreover, as already argued, those two sayings look like being a secondary editorial amplification of the demand for love of enemies which is quite securely and sufficiently completed by the statement setting out the incentive, 'and you will be sons of the Most High . . .'. The rejection of a reciprocity ethic in the sayings about Gentiles and tax collectors is an amplification bringing in a quite different pattern of argument. If then Q 6:32–33 derive from Q-editorial work, and moreover in a context where, first, the Lev 19:18 principle of love is being expanded, and, second, the Lev 19:17 principle of reproof is also in mind,[24] then the correspondences with Matt 18:15–17 are arresting and can scarcely be coincidental. Indeed, it becomes difficult to accept, with W. Trilling,[25] that Matt 5:46–47/Q 6:32–33 and Matt 18:17 belong to the same level of tradition, and then forbear to attribute the latter to Q.

[22]Zeller, *Mahnsprüche* 112.
[23]*Lukasevangelium I* 353.
[24]See above, pp. 115, 125.
[25]*Das wahre Israel* (SANT 10; 3rd ed.; München: Kösel, 1964) 115.

Second, further adverse references to Gentiles in two Q passages which are treated at length elsewhere in this book support the suggestion of Q-editorial work in 18:17. In the first, Q 12:30a, 'for all the Gentiles seek these things', issues an appeal for a higher standard of behaviour than that of Gentiles, but does so in a manifestly unoriginal and editorial part of tradition urging freedom from anxiety.[26] In the second, Matt 6:7, the piling up of words by the Gentiles is criticized and a higher attitude in prayer recommended on the part of those to whom the Lord's Prayer is immediately afterwards presented (Q 11:2–4/Matt 6:9–13). Although Matt 6:7 has no exact Lucan parallel it interrupts a section directed polemically at Pharisees rather than Gentiles and appears to be known to the person, i.e., Luke, who edited into the following parable of the friend at midnight the notion of piling on the verbal pressure in prayer (Luke 11:8).[27] Matt 6:7 cannot have been originally associated with the Lord's Prayer, and it corresponds so closely to Q 6:33 and 12:30a, that the possibility of Q editorial work again becomes attractive.

Third, the term ἀδελφός occurs in Q only at 6:41–42 and 17:3. Both passages, as already indicated, treat the reproof idea and clearly derive this 'brother' terminology from Lev 19:17a, where it stands in parallel with 'neighbour' and 'one of the sons of your own people'. Against the suggestion that 'these early Christian community rules describe a Christianizing of late Jewish tradition',[28] or the proposed rendering of ἀδελφός as 'fellow Christian',[29] it is once again necessary to insist that the context presupposed is not specifically that of a Christian church nor, for that matter, a precisely delimited circle of disciples, but rather a community which is, or believes itself to be, the community of Israel.[30] And if that is so, the community awareness behind the term ἀδελφός in Q 17:3 is exactly the same as that behind Matt 18:17b – a strong religious, and not merely national, consciousness of separateness both from Gentiles and from those

[26]See above, p. 26.
[27]See later, pp. 225–6.
[28]R. Hummel, *Die Auseinandersetzung zwischen Kirche und Judentum im Matthäusevangelium* (München: Kaiser, 1963) 58.
[29]Schenk, *Synopse* 31.
[30]Rightly, Zeller, *Mahnsprüche* 62.

who 'make themselves Gentiles'. The coherence of the two sayings articulating this traditional Jewish outlook is a further strong reason for attributing the latter as well as the former to Q.

Fourth, if vv. 16a, 17 belonged to Q it is readily understandable that Luke should have dropped them. Well might W. Trilling exclaim, 'Imagine such a saying in Luke!'[31] The notion of a community which is religiously defined in such exclusive and traditional Jewish terms is not a Lucan notion. When faced with the 'tax collectors + Gentiles' in Q 6:32–33 he changed both to 'sinners', but that was scarcely possible here, so the only feasible alternative was to drop the sayings altogether.

This brings us to the last and most crucial question. What is the significance of ἔστω σοι ὥσπερ ὁ ἐθνικὸς καὶ ὁ τελώνης in itself and in Q?

First, the singular σοί implies that v. 17b is describing a personal and not a community stance. There can therefore be no question of formal exclusion from the community, in spite of recurrent affirmations to this effect.[32] Against such a trend P. Bonnard wrote perceptively, 'La lettre du texte n'impose pas l'idée d'une expulsion de l'Eglise, mais plutôt celle d'une mise en quarantaine dans l'Eglise; le texte ne dit pas 'qu'il soit pour l'Eglise ...' mais 'pour toi (*soi*)'.'[33] That was an important protest against a strong but misleading interpretative tendency, though even the notion of ecclesiastical quarantine may go too far. For the community is, as already seen, not a distinctly Christian one but a Jewish one, and the offender remains a member of the Jewish community of 'brothers'. He has not forfeited his Jewishness, nor could he do so. We note also the absence of any clear definition of his offence, which is here described in exceedingly general terms (ἐὰν ἁμαρτήσῃ, v. 15) and might be anywhere between the criminally serious and the comparatively trivial. Exclusion from the community could scarcely be envisaged without precise definition of the offence. Hence the ultimate situation envisaged by v. 17b has nothing to do with what he *is* and everything to do with how he *is*

---

[31] *Israel* 116.

[32] Thus, Manson, *Sayings* 209: 'He is to be considered no longer a member of the church.' Similarly, Gnilka, 'Kirche', 54; Goulder, *Luke II* 640; Schweizer, *Matthew* 371; Strecker, *Weg* 224; Trilling, *Israel* 115–20.

[33] *L'Evangile selon Saint Matthieu* (CNT; 2nd ed.; Neuchâtel: 1970) 275.

regarded, and that not by the community but by the individual offended person.

Second, similar formulations elsewhere can be brought in to reinforce this understanding. Sir 33:30–31 reads:

> If you have a servant, let him be as yourself,
>   because you have bought him with blood.
> If you have a servant, treat him as a brother,
>   for as your own soul you will need him.

Here the servant does not cease 'really' to be a servant, but because of certain specified considerations his owner's personal attitude is to be defined quite otherwise, i.e., an unreal 'as if' element comes in, so that the new attitude is in line with attitudes to oneself or one's brother which the servant 'really' is not. One might also call upon *b. Sabb.* 105b:

> R. Simeon b. Eleazar said in the name of Halfa b. Agra in R. Johanan b. Nuri's name: He who rends his garments in his anger, he who breaks his vessels in his anger, and he who scatters his money in his anger, regard him as an idolater, because such are the wiles of the Tempter: Today he says to him, 'Do this'; tomorrow he tells him, 'Do that', until he bids him, 'Go and serve idols', and he goes and serves them.[34]

Again, none of the actions described have changed the status of the person concerned: it is just that he is now *regarded* in a new way. In Matt 18:17b, therefore, there is set out a new personal attitude and no more, an attitude conforming to a presumed known attitude to Gentiles and tax collectors.

Third, it is noticeable that the two terms 'Gentile' and 'tax collector' are each bracketed elsewhere with the term 'sinner' (Mark 2:15, 16; Q 7:34; Gal 2:15). And in v. 15 the offending person's actions have been defined by the phrase ἐὰν ... ἁμαρτήσῃ. Hence, the position described in v. 17b represents nothing new, but only a making firm or establishing of the position which is already implicit in his actions.

Fourth, we can in this light paraphrase v. 17b as follows: 'Let your personal attitude to him be the same as that which you adopt to those outside your community, the Gentiles or those

---

[34]Billerbeck I.792.

who make themselves like Gentiles.' And the attitude which is adopted in Q to such persons is easy to determine and to recognize as harmonious with the tradition in Matt 18:15–17/ Luke 17:4. From Q 7:34 it is apparent that friendship with tax collectors and sinners is an allegation levelled against Jesus, an allegation focussed on the practice of table fellowship, an allegation as untrue as the allegation of gluttony and drunkenness, and an allegation expressing traditional Jewish convictions. Since Matt 18:17b stands at the end of a sequence of negative elements, it is likely that 'let him be to you as a Gentile and a tax collector' must have some negative colouring, and therefore involve an abandonment of table fellowship with the offending person. But the two sayings in Q 6:32–33 indicate that within this overtly negative approach there is built something very positive indeed. For Gentiles and taxcollectors are persons whose example is not to be followed: certain characteristic attitudes and actions are exhibited, and these are not to be emulated. In specific terms, they only love or do good to those who love or do good to them, i.e. they adhere strictly to a reciprocity ethic, and if someone treats them badly they do not respond by treating that someone well. On the Q level, Matt 18:17b is a call for something rather different, an attitude of love toward the offender, an attitude which will not permit the relationship to be defined permanently by the offence. The corollary is that v. 17b shows itself to be component C in the scheme set out above.

Fifth, it can now be seen that v. 17b leads directly and without strain into the pre-Lucan version of Luke 17:4. The only attitude which will not permit the relationship between the two persons concerned to be determined by a deliberate and reiterated offence is an attitude of forgiveness. One recalls *T. Gad* 6:7: 'Forgive him from the heart and leave God to do the judging.' So strong is the concern for peace within the community to be, that forgiveness has to be shown to be not merely contingent but also, if necessary, unconditional. The 'if' with which the tradition began has been shown by the way it ends to be an 'only if'. On such a basis it becomes possible to speak, as S. Schulz does, of 'the limitless freedom from boundaries of the brotherly obligation to forgive'.[35]

[35] *Spruchquelle* 322.

148

The reconstruction of the original Q wording of this tradition has been in part carried out already in the course of the above argumentation. A small number of Matthew/Luke variations have to be assessed if the task is to be completed,[36] but none of them involves major differences in content, and with a reasonable degree of assurance the Q text emerges as follows:

ἐὰν ἁμαρτήσῃ ὁ ἀδελφός σου, ὕπαγε ἔλεγξον αὐτόν· ἐὰν σου ἀκούσῃ, ἄφες αὐτῷ. ἐὰν δὲ μὴ ἀκούσῃ, παράλαβε μετὰ σοῦ ἔτι ἕνα ἢ δύο· ἐὰν δὲ παρακούσῃ αὐτῶν, εἰπὲ τῇ ἐκκλησίᾳ· ἐὰν δὲ καὶ τῆς ἐκκλησίας παρακούσῃ, ἔστω σοι ὥσπερ ὁ ἐθνικὸς καὶ ὁ τελώνης. καὶ ἐὰν ἑπτάκις τῆς ἡμέρας ἁμαρτήσῃ εἰς σε, ἀφήσεις αὐτῷ.

This tradition can be seen from a literary- and form-critical angle to be entirely unified. The old suggestion that Luke 17:4 was a secondary expansion of 17:3[37] had not made much headway[38] and now becomes irrelevant in the context of a new reconstruction of the underlying Q source material. The tradition, consisting of six ἐάν-clauses, followed in each case by an imperative demand, reads smoothly. The six form an ascending progression, detailing increasingly adverse actions and reactions by the offending brother, and being held together by two demands for forgiveness. There is a total lack of distinctively Christian colouring and a total conformity to Jewish texts. Given this parallelism, and given the combination of the unity of the tradition and the derivation of v. 17b from Q redaction, it

[36] (1) προσέχετε ἑαυτοῖς is likely to be LukeR in view of Luke 12:1; 21:34; Acts 5:35; 20:28. (2) ὕπαγε is uncertain in terms of word statistics but likely to be Q as a counterpart of παράλαβε Matt 18:16a. (3) ἔλεγξον diff ἐπιτίμησον is likely to be Q in view of its presence in the underlying text Lev 19:17; moreover, ἐπιτιμᾶν is LukeR at 4:39 diff Mark 1:31 and 23:40 diff Mark 15:32. (4) μεταξὺ σοῦ καὶ αὐτοῦ μόνου could be a later MattR clarification, though this is not sure. (5) ἀκούσῃ diff μετανοήσῃ: LukeR is probably involved in view of Luke's interest in the theme of repentance, cf. 15:7, 10; 16:30; 17:4, though it is shown by *T. Gad* 6:3 to be not inappropriate to the context. (6) ἐκέρδησας τὸν ἀδελφόν σου uses language which occurs most similarly in Jas 5:19, 20; the often cited parallels in 1 Cor 9:19–22 are less adjacent. But ἀφιέναι is attested in this context, Matt 18:21/Luke 17:4 as well as in *T. Gad* 6:3, and is therefore probably from Q. (7) The variations in Matt 18:21, 22/Luke 17:4 are covered by the argument set out above in the text.

[37] Bultmann, *History* 86.

[38] See Schulz, *Spruchquelle* 322.

becomes almost impossible to defend the authenticity of any part of the tradition and highly likely that it is *in toto* the product of Q redaction. This would cohere well with the impression conveyed by Q 6:36–45 and 12:58–59 that this whole topic of reproof and reconciliation was of immense concern to the Christians for whom Q was intended. Among such persons, with their entirely and unequivocally Jewish horizon, the process of reflection on how the principles of Lev 19:17–18 should be implemented laid the emphasis above all on the peace of the community, the restoration of relationships, the refusal to be defeated even if the ultimate attempt to change the mind of the offender should fail. Even in this worst case evil was to be overcome with good, and sin met with forgiveness.

5

The Mission Charge

Every study of Q, its theology, its community setting, its purpose, and the history of the traditions it contains, accepts that the mission charge (Q 10:1–16) is both sensitive and significant as a pointer to all those concerns.[1] If it were possible to reconstruct with assurance this Q text, and if the existence of strata within it were demonstrable, then there would be every hope that the history of the tradition would disclose something of the history of the community itself. Realism, however, demands the admission that there is more than a little hazard and uncertainty to be faced along the way to this highly desirable end.

In this connection one does not have in mind simply the familiar difficulty of reaching back behind Matthew and Luke to the Q wording. In this instance it is made more complicated than usual by the existence of an additional Lucan version (Luke 9:1–6/Mark 6:7–13). This complication can certainly be turned into an advantage, indeed a help for believers in Q rather than unbelievers. It allows us to detect LukeR reminiscences of Q even when Mark is the primary source. And while the general tendency to favour Luke's wording as more original than Matthew's is usefully inimical to both Griesbach/Farmer and Farrer/Goulder versions of the hypothesis of Lucan use of Matthew, the suspicion remains that Luke may have created more and Matthew preserved more than tends to be supposed by some exponents of Q. However that may be, the reconstruction of the original Q text is not easy, never has been, and never will be, and the arguments set out below have to be expressed with proper tentativeness.

[1]For a survey of the influence of this tradition on Q research, see R. Uro, *Sheep among the Wolves. A Study of the Mission Instructions of Q* (Dissertationes Humanarum Litterarum 47; Helsinki: Suomalainen Tiedeakatemia, 1987) 21–3.

Another significant issue in the reconstruction of the Q mission charge and its history concerns the singly attested sayings within the double tradition of Matthew 10/Luke 10. Some of these are not uncommonly assigned to Q, and others frequently attributed to one or other evangelist. The length of the list of such single traditions, and the consequent variety of permutations and combinations of those which might be attributed to Q, is a further warning of hazards ahead. Fortunately it is not necessary to carry out an examination of the credentials of each one of these sayings, some of which have scarcely any role of note to play. In this essay it will be accepted that Q probably did contain the prohibition of greetings on the way (Q 10:4b), but not the prohibition of movement from one house to another (Luke 10:7d). On the other hand it will be necessary to mount arguments in support of two particular positions. The first is that Q did contain a saying which placed out of bounds Gentile territory and any Samaritan town (Matt 10:5b). The second is that Q did not include the injunction to eat whatever food is provided (Luke 10:8b).

Of crucial importance for the whole discussion is the vexed issue of Mark's relationship to Q. This has already been addressed in connection with Q 7:24–28/Mark 1:1–8,[2] but it requires renewed and careful scrutiny in connection with the mission charge, and it is to this topic that we turn first of all.

1. Mark and Q.

As part of the discussion of how Q began it was suggested in the second chapter of this book that Q was known to and used by Mark. The opposite view that Mark did not use Q, a view most carefully tested and reaffirmed by Rudolf Laufen,[3] has been incorporated in the work of those who have recently achieved notable advances in the discussion of Q, namely John Kloppenborg and Migaku Sato.[4] The same applies to Risto Uro's investigation of the mission charge in particular.[5] All

[2]See above, pp. 63–70.
[3]*Doppelüberlieferungen.*
[4]Kloppenborg, *Formation*; Sato, *Prophetie.*
[5]Uro, *Sheep.*

these writers have exploited the supposed Marcan independence of Q in order that the Mark/Q overlap may disclose 'the core of the tradition'. Thus for Kloppenborg this 'core' consisted of at least the equipment instruction (Q 10:4/Mark 6:8–9), and instructions about acceptance (Q 10:5–7/Mark 6:10) and rejection (Q 10:10–11/Mark 6:11). For Uro the original 'kernel' consisted of the instructions about equipment and conduct in houses (Q 10:4, 5–7); this was later extended by instructions about acceptance and rejection (Q 10:8–11a) to form an 'early mission code'; the influence of Q 10:4–11a was then exerted in two directions to produce on the one hand Mark 6:7–13 and on the other, after two more developmental stages, the final Q text. These proposals, identifying with a widespread tendency in Q research,[6] would be threatened if Mark's direct use of Q were to carry conviction. Yet this threat does seem to be a possibility requiring to be taken seriously.[7]

The mission instructions exhibit a recurrent phenomenon, namely, that when Q and Mark overlap it is Q which preserves the earlier version of the tradition.[8] In the case of the mission charge Uro accepts this position, except in respect of the 'do not go from house to house' and 'eat what is set before you' sayings. Yet these may not have been in Q at all.[9] There is arguably no detail here in respect of which the Q tradition shows secondary development at the same time as Mark retains the primary version. It would be remarkable that this should be the case after just one further stage of independent development: how much more so if, as Uro proposes, there were two?

Specifically, if we work back from Mark's text, using the normal literary-critical procedures, we find that the pre-Marcan tradition in no way diverges from what seems likely to have figured in Q. Thus, on the equipment rule, the express permission to carry a staff and to wear sandals is gratuitous in view of the natural assumption that a staff would be carried and sandals

---

[6]For a survey, see F. Neirynck, 'Recent Developments in the Study of Q', *Logia. Memorial J. Coppens* (ed. J. Delobel; BETL 59; Leuven: University Press, 1982) 29–75, esp. pp. 41–53; also, Zeller, 'Redaktionsprozesse', 404–5; A. Jacobson, 'The Literary Unity of Q. Lc 10, 2–16 and Parallels as a Test Case', *Logia* 419–23.

[7]See Schenk, 'Einfluss'.

[8]Exceptions to this norm point to the influence of pre-Marcan variants, e.g., in the case of the parable of the mustard seed: see Schenk, 'Einfluss', 144–5.

[9]See below, pp. 176–8.

worn.[10] This 'denial of denials', as Dieter Lührmann has called it,[11] looks like an accidental hint to the discerning reader that such items had in fact been forbidden. This was the case in Q. Similarly, removal of the obviously awkward MarkR attachment μηδὲ ἀκούσωσιν ὑμῶν, discrepant with its context in that it uses a plural rather than a singular form, as well as the typical MarkR explanation εἰς μαρτύριον αὐτοῖς, leaves the statement about the rejecting community (Mark 6:11) in much the same shape as it had in Q.

The instructions presented in direct speech by Mark 6:10–11 read like fragments of something more coherent. As they stand, they could scarcely survive in isolation, and therefore do not appear to support the suggestion that the inconsistency of Mark's version is more primitive than the consistency of the version in Q.[12] Pre-Marcan tradition must indeed lie beneath the surface of Mark's combination of narrative, indirect quotation and direct speech, as Uro has rightly argued,[13] but the range of that earlier tradition has to be uncovered.

When Mark's readers reached 6:6b–13 they were clearly intended, as Uro points out,[14] to recall earlier material, of which 3:13–19 is a prime example. The links between the two traditions are evident: Jesus' calling disciples to himself as the initial move (3:13; 6:7); the designation of those called as 'twelve' (3:14; 6:7); the intention to send stated and then effected (3:14; 6:7); the authority to expel demons/unclean spirits envisaged, then renewed, and finally activated (3:15; 6:7, 13); preaching given prominence first and last (3:14; 6:13, even though not mentioned in 6:7). On the Marcan level, whatever may be the truth about any pre-Marcan level, 3:13–19 and 6:6b–13 are in direct sequence as far as continuity of ideas is concerned.

This direct sequence, however, does not start at 3:13–19. It develops out of 1:16–20, since there the process of assembling

[10]See below, p. 183.

[11]'The Gospel of Mark and the Sayings Collection Q', *JBL* 108 (1989) 51–71, esp. p. 63.

[12]Thus F. W. Beare, 'The Mission of the Disciples and the Mission Charge: Matthew 10 and Parallels', *JBL* 89 (1970) 1–13, esp. p. 2: 'The evangelist has given shape – an uncouth shape, it must be said – to his material.' See also Lührmann, 'Gospel', 62.

[13]*Sheep* 33–6.

[14]*Sheep* 26–9.

the personnel who will make up 'the twelve' begins, and the first hint of Jesus' design for their mission is dropped (1:17). But even before that 1:16–20 is dependent on 1:14–15, and the latter passage is likely to be the first term in the series, controlling all of 1:16–20, 3:13–19 and 6:6b–13. The links are again evident: preaching, specifically preaching of repentance, by both Jesus and his emissaries (1:15; 6:12), with the suffering of the Baptist casting a dark shadow across both complexes (1:14a; 6:14–29). Since the reference in the intermediate tradition to the twelve's being appointed to be 'with him' (3:14) is doubtless intended to establish the basis of their authority within the church and to do so in a context where his mission and theirs are identical and inseparable, the formal announcement by Jesus that the kingdom of God has drawn near and presented itself for belief in the form of the gospel is clearly intended to be what they in their turn will be announcing. For our purpose, Mark 1:14–15, 16–20; 3:13–19; and 6:6b–13 have to be viewed as developing stages in a single unified story. And when that is done Uro's three reservations[15] about Marcan use of the Q mission charge can be met and overcome.

The first is a hesitation over 'why Mark would have left out a positive order to proclaim and heal (cf. Luke 10:9) and at the same time have laid so much stress on the disciples' preaching activity and on the power over demons as he did in his narrative frames (6:7, 12–13; cf. also 3:14)'. The answer is surely that the healing has survived (6:13b) and, most importantly, the proclamation has already been used in direct speech attributed to Jesus (1:15), whence it can in turn define the proclamation of the disciples.

The second concerns 'why Mark would have greatly emphasized the equipment prohibitions (Mark 6:8–9) at the expense of the instructions crucial for the execution of the mission'. The answer this time is that the instructions crucial for the execution of the mission are those which pick up ideas already introduced in 1:14–15, 16–20 and 3:13–19. These do not include the equipment rule, upon which Mark is therefore perhaps not placing such great emphasis.

The third is that 'we may doubt whether (Mark) deliberately

---

[15]*Sheep* 37.

struck out the concrete details from the instructions'. Yet this may well be what Mark has done on Uro's hypothesis, for by itself Mark's final product in 6:6b–13 can only with difficulty be regarded as a complete and rounded whole. If he knew the contents of Luke 10:5–7, that is, what existed at the second of the proposed four stages of development, he was clearly prepared to shorten and even, as we might say, to spoil the balance of the material he received. In other words, there is no issue here between those who accept Marcan use of Q and those who do not.

According to Uro, 'most of the sayings in the Q speech which have no parallel in Mark show signs of being later additions, and this renders it probable that they have grown on to the speech at a stage of transmission which has no contact with the Markan tradition'.[16] Yet three pieces of evidence, collected by Wolfgang Schenk, of the influence of Q 10:13–15 on Marcan material adjacent to the mission tradition remain impressive and can be supplemented by two others.[17]

First, the occurrence of mighty works (δυνάμεις γίνεσθαι) is mentioned in a cluster of passages in Mark which are close to his version of the mission charge. These deal with the healing of the woman with a haemorrhage (5:30), the visit to the home town (6:2, 5) and the summary report of Jesus' activities which reached the ears of Herod (6:14). The same term happens to occur in the woes on the towns of Galilee (Q 10:13–15), present in the mission charge by courtesy of the Q-editor.

Second, repentance and the near kingdom figure together in the Marcan summary of Jesus' initial proclamation (1:14–15). The same association is achieved by the mission charge and the editorially added woes (Q 10:11, 13–15).

Third, there is a parallelism between miracle-inhibiting unbelief or being 'scandalized' by Jesus in Mark (6:3, 6), and that unrepentant hardness of the towns of Galilee which draws those woes from the Jesus of Q (Q 10:13–15). For in Q the woe

[16]*Sheep* 99; similarly Jacobson, 'Literary Unity', 421–2 on Q 10:3, 12, 13–15, 16.

[17]'Einfluss', 150–1. On reflection, a fourth correspondence is perhaps too fragile. Schenk connects the rejection by the πατρίς of Jesus (Mark 6:1), which might be Capernaum (Mark 1:21; 2:1, 15), with the woe on Capernaum (Q 10:15). However, Mark 1:9, 24 probably establish that for Mark the πατρίς is Nazareth.

pronounced on those who *refuse* the message of the miracles is the obverse of the beatitude pronounced on anyone who *receives* it: 'Blessed is the person who is not scandalized by me' (Q 7:23).

Fourth, there is a notable correspondence between the twofold issuing of an Elijah-type call to followers (Mark 1:16–20) in immediate association with the kingdom-centred mission (Mark 1:14–15), and the Q editor's placing of a double Elijah-type call to followers (Q 9:57–60) in immediate association with the kingdom-centred mission charge (Q 10:2–16).

Fifth, it will be argued later in this chapter that the sending saying (Q 10:16) in its Q form contrasted 'hearing' (ἀκούειν) and rejecting (ἀθετεῖν), and that it was added to the mission charge at the editorial stage.[18] An echo of this saying can be discerned in the MarkR editorial phrase μηδὲ ἀκούσωσιν ὑμῶν (Mark 6:11). Mark 9:37 would, of course, use the tradition more fully, and it is easy to see the Mark/Q discrepancies between the two versions as assimilations to the Marcan context: the child as the paradoxical paradigm of leadership (Mark 9:33–35 amplified by 9:36–37), and the phrase 'one such child' drawn in under the influence of Mark 10:13–14; the phrase 'in my name' matching Mark 13:6 and registering a lurking awareness that persons with a message are involved; the verb 'receive' chosen naturally because of suitability in the immediate context and perhaps also as a reminiscence of its earlier use within Mark's own version of the mission charge in 6:11; and finally the removal of the rejection theme (Q 10:16b), again under the influence of the context.

We can sum up the argument thus far as follows. If the presupposition of Marcan independence of Q appears insecure, it is logically no longer possible to use Mark/Q overlaps as evidence of the original and earlier 'core' or 'kernel'.

With this in mind we can now go on to consider the overall content of the Q mission charge, consisting as it clearly does of the harvest saying, the 'sheep among wolves' saying, the equipment rule, arguably the 'Gentiles/Samaritans' saying (Matt 10:5b), again clearly the preaching and healing instructions, the instructions about conduct in houses, the rule concerning reaction to rejection, the woes on Galilean towns, and the sending saying. The main concern of this chapter is the significance of

---

[18]See pp. 178–9.

any material which may be assigned to a later, rather than an original, stratum. More attention will therefore be given to the sayings about the harvest, the Gentiles and the Samaritans, the towns of Galilee, and the sending, than to the rest. On the other hand, those sayings depend upon the others, would not be meaningful without them, and in no way undermine their continuing authority for the transmitting community. Therefore a modicum of discussion of those other sayings will be necessary as well.

2. Workers for the Harvest. Q 10:2.

The two Matthew/Luke versions of the harvest saying are almost identical, and the Q version can be set out without more ado:

ὁ μὲν θερισμὸς πολύς, οἱ δὲ ἐργάται· ὀλίγοι δεήθητε οὖν τοῦ κυρίου τοῦ θερισμοῦ ὅπως ἐκβάλῃ ἐργάτας εἰς τὸν θερισμὸν αὐτοῦ.

Intended to control the mission charge as a whole, this saying is at the same time discrepant with it. Its harvesting metaphor is wholly absent from what follows, and its presumed audience consists of those who pray about mission rather than those who engage in it.[19] Since the praying community asking for a supply of missionaries scarcely belongs to the situation of Jesus,[20] we can infer that Q 10:2 is a Christian construction added editorially. It is intended to define the meaning and context of the main mission charge and to indicate to us how that charge should be read. This fact in itself suggests that it will be specially rewarding to establish with care what Q 10:2 presumes in respect of the character of the community addressed, the christology, the mood and scope of mission, and the underlying eschatological conviction.

[19]Laufen, *Doppelüberlieferungen* 270; D. Zeller, 'Redaktionsprozesse und wechselnder Sitz im Leben beim Q-Material', *Logia. Memorial J. Coppens* (ed. J. Delobel; BETL 59; Leuven: University Press, 1982) 395–409, esp. p. 404; Jacobson, 'Unity', 421; Uro, *Sheep* 99, 113; Kloppenborg, *Formation* 193.

[20]Against Luz, *Matthäus 8–17* 80, who appeals to the optimism of the saying, and its eschatological understanding of the preaching activity, as marks of authenticity.

The well known parallel in Acts 13:1–3; 14:26 serves us well in clarifying the character of the community. There an assembled church engages in worship, variously described as service and fasting (this latter the accompaniment of prayer and preparation for the receipt of revelation, 13:3; 14:23). The worship is directed to the Lord and focussed on his designating already charismatically endowed persons for a new missionary task. The task itself is defined, in conformity with Q 10:2 and wider NT usage, as 'work' (Acts 13:2; 14:26). Altogether the match with Q 10:2 is so close that it is easy and indeed natural to set the latter in the context of the former. The speaker calls upon the Q community to engage in prayer, the outcome of which will be the designation and Spirit-endowment of missionaries. There is just one small, but not unimportant, difference between Q 10:2 and Acts 13:1–3, namely that Acts envisages the pioneering of a new mission whereas Q looks for the reinforcement and expansion of one which already exists and is currently in the hands of the 'few'. Thus the community of Q 10:2 participates in, takes responsibility for, and exercises control over, an established but small-scale mission, which has potential for growth and can in a certain sense be labelled 'church mission'.[21]

Having said that, however, we should probably not drive a wedge between 'the mission of the wandering charismatics', assigned to a Jewish setting, and 'church mission', understood as being aimed at the conversion of Gentiles.[22] It is difficult to accept that the community whose outlook is expressed in Q 10:2 regarded the instructions for the wandering charismatics in 10:3–16 as belonging exclusively to time past, articulating an obsolete pattern, and prescribed for a quite different setting. The sheer quantity of the instructions which follow would suggest a degree of respect for the authoritative past which expressed itself in the contemporary adoption of its patterns. Moreover, although it is a tiny detail, the common use of 'work'/'workers' in Q 10:2, 7b may well imply, as Arland Jacobson suggests, the same stage of redaction and thus an

[21]Uro, *Sheep* 205–6.
[22]Against Uro, *Sheep* 205–6. See the remarks of Lührmann, 'Gospel', 69–71, and Luz, *Matthäus 8–17* 79, on reducing the distinction between, and allowing a combination of, the concepts of 'community' and 'itinerant radicalism'.

identical perspective.[23] The perspective in question would appear to be that of the wandering charismatic missionary (cf. 1 Cor 9:14). So instead of using a wedge we should probably speak of a settled but charismatic church sponsoring a charismatic mission. As far as the contrasting Jew/Gentile settings are concerned, we shall comment shortly.

We now turn to christology. This comes to the fore, but rather subtly, in the term ὁ κύριος τοῦ θερισμοῦ. An instinctive inference that this is a reference to God shows itself in the literature. Is this instinct right, we may ask, or could Jesus himself be in mind? It would not be the only case in Q of Jesus' referring to himself detachedly, as it were, (cf. Q 10:22), and several considerations suggest that an identification with Jesus is not at all impossible. (i) Concentration upon the harvest is conditioned above all in Q by the Baptist's speech in 3:17. Within 3:7–9, 16–17 it is highly likely that (historical) traditions deriving from John have been edited by the insertion of 3:16b.[24] They thus no longer refer exclusively to the work of the coming God but to that which will be carried out by Jesus. Right at the outset, therefore, he is presented as in a certain sense κύριος τοῦ θερισμοῦ. Consistently with this, the saying in Q 11:23, intrusive in its present context, defines being 'with' Jesus as being involved in his (*sic*) missionary 'gathering' (a term used elsewhere in connection with harvesting, cf. Matt 6:26). Similarly, the secondary parable of the talents/pounds (Q 19:12–27), presupposing by its very scheme of the departing and returning κύριος the delay of the parousia,[25] insists on strenuous activity on behalf of the person who 'reaps where (he) did not sow, and gathers where (he) did not scatter'. That κύριος is, by definition, Jesus. (ii) The immediacy of the sending by Jesus himself in Q 10:3 is intended to interpret 10:2. In the sending by

---

[23]'Literary Unity', 421.

[24]Hoffmann, *Studien* 31–3. Kloppenborg, *Formation* 104–5, expresses doubt about this in view of the widespread occurrence of the saying (Mark 1:7; John 1:26; Acts 13:25) and its possible alternative origin in a setting of rivalry between disciples of John and Jesus. However, the consistently favourable attitude of Q to John, and its tendency to value him highly while at the same time imposing a christology upon traditions about him, cf. Q 7:18–35, fits the Q-redactional hypothesis. Direct literary dependence readily explains the Q/Mark/Acts/John distribution.

[25]Cf. Q 12:42–46, on which see pp. 215–6.

Jesus there is effected the sending by ὁ κυρίος τοῦ θερισμοῦ. (iii) The overwhelming majority of κύριος references in Q allude to Jesus; indeed from the specially intense appeal in the probably redactional saying Q 6:46 onwards[26] it becomes clear that this is the dominant christological category. It would therefore be consonant with widespread Q usage for the term ὁ κυρίος τοῦ θερισμοῦ to stand for the exalted and returning one who during the present interval authorizes those who continue and expand upon his own mission.

And yet one must hesitate. To invoke the exalted Jesus in prayer probably implies a christology higher and later than that which could be sustained among the Q Christians. Admittedly, the cry of the Aramaic speaking Christians to their Lord, 'Maranatha' (1 Cor 16:22), is addressed to the exalted Jesus in eager anticipation of his coming, but an ejaculatory cry is different in kind from a measured prayer to the heavenly Lord who supervises the mission during the interval before the end. Moreover, it is perhaps not without significance that a mission charge which is prefaced by a call to prayer to the Lord of the harvest is followed almost immediately by a prayer to the Lord of heaven and earth (Q 10:21), a prayer which is immediately expounded in such a way as to underline the closeness of association between Jesus and God (Q 10:22), but nevertheless a prayer by Jesus to the Lord God.

Are then those straws in the wind which seemed to point to Jesus in Q 10:2 simply to be blown away as light trivia and insubstantial wisps of fantasy? Not at all! They imply, indeed they demand, that a functional equivalence between God and Jesus be recognized. God's authority is experienced in his authority. God's harvest is his harvest. If God's harvest involves separation – and it does – the separation will be visible in his mission. God's sending is involved in his sending. In short, the language may vary but the meaning is the same as in the concluding declaration that 'he who hears you hears me, and he who rejects you rejects me, and he who rejects me rejects him who sent me' (Q 10:16).

Next, the mood and the scope of the mission. These have been closely connected by Uro, who detects in Q 10:2 an

---

[26]See above, pp. 97–100.

optimistic tone and the prospect of a receptive audience, whereas 'it is difficult to believe that the mission among the Jews could have been considered with such optimism at the time of the writing of Q'.[27] He draws a contrast with the supposedly more pessimistic mood of the sayings in Q 10:3, 12–16, which are taken to represent an earlier stage of tradition and experience, and he uses the Acts 13:1–3 comparison to support a Hellenistic setting.[28] It should be noted that Uro accepts in the process that harvest imagery is itself neutral and can be applied to divine intervention in either Jewish (Isa 27:12) or non-Jewish (Isa 24:13; Joel 3:1–13; Micah 4:11–13) spheres.[29] Nevertheless, he takes the frame of reference of Q 10:2 to be the Gentile mission.

While the evidence for a Gentile mission elsewhere in Q remains a matter of dispute, Uro's proposal for the specially sensitive material in 10:2–16 remains unconvincing on several grounds.

First, while leaving 10:12, 13–15, 16 for later discussion in view of the likelihood that the latest stratum of redaction may be discerned there, we may immediately clear away the argument as it relates to 10:3, 'Behold, I send you as sheep in the midst of wolves.' In connection with the activity of wolves the ἅρπαξ word group is used quite conventionally. It is notably employed in Q to describe both the opposition encountered by the kingdom-centred mission from the beginning of the period of Jesus (Q 16:16), and also the fundamental alienation of Pharisees from the principles of the covenant (Q 11:39). The latter saying has been assigned by Kloppenborg[30] to the 'original core' of the Woes tradition, but that proposal should probably be resisted.[31] What is important for our present concern is that Q 10:3 + 11:39 + 16:16 combine to indicate the context of religious polarization in which the Christian mission takes place. The Pharisees and the emissaries of Jesus are locked in conflict, perhaps because of some differences of theological emphasis,

---

[27] *Sheep* 209; Kloppenborg, *Formation* 194, cf. 105–7, where he comments on 3:7–9, 16–17 in similar vein. But does not the audience dictate that the main emphasis should be on warning?

[28] *Sheep* 205, 208.

[29] Against Lührmann, *Redaktion* 60. Similarly Hoffmann, *Studien* 292; Kloppenborg, *Formation* 193.

[30] *Formation* 140–1.

[31] See below, pp. 261–2.

perhaps also because of competition for the commitment of one and the same constituency, but most likely because of the disjunction between the charismatic and the institutional, the prophetic and the priestly (to borrow Max Weber's terminology), and the disturbance caused by the one to the other.[32] Q 10:3 contains the polemical language of alienation and polarization but does not in itself dictate either an optimistic or a pessimistic outlook for the mission itself.

Second, it is fair to say that any mission must as a matter of fundamental principle be undertaken in hope and with optimism. Yet in any context, and most particularly in the context of bringing to Israel a disturbing call not to presume on the covenant as the sure and sufficient basis of security and the enjoyment of the grace of God, sober realism would dictate the need to be prepared for rejection. Social function dictates substance. To divide the traditions into the optimistic and the pessimistic is to risk disturbing a natural and necessary balance. Certainly Q 10:6b, 10–12, 13–15, 16b strike a sombre note, but not excessively so. And such a note of warning is by no means precluded by the use of the harvest metaphor here. After all, John had used it (3:17) and had exploited it both positively and negatively, to warn in respect of the chaff and to reassure in respect of the wheat. That the editor should attach 10:2 to 10:3–16 implies that he regarded each as naturally defining the other. If that is so, we cannot use 10:2 to establish the existence of an unqualifiedly optimistic stage of missionary experience discrepant with the stage represented by any of the following traditions.

Third, against the proposed Hellenistic setting of the 'church mission' must be set the evidence of Gal 2:1–10 (especially vv. 7–8): another community with a strong inbuilt institutionalizing tendency and an emphatic commitment to mission sustained by Spirit-endowed leaders. If the Jerusalem church tried to keep as firm a hold on Antioch-based developments as the Pauline evidence attests, it certainly would have done so in the sphere of Q, and nothing in Q 10:2–16 takes us outside the parameters laid down by that church. Since sayings like Q 17:23 have no

---

[32]The contrast between rejection/persecution (10:3) and mere non-reception (10:10–11) involves different personnel and does not therefore indicate different strata of tradition.

obvious relevance in a Hellenistic setting, but very clear application in a Palestinian context, this latter would seem to be the
background against which 10:2 should be read.

In sum, Q 10:2 provides the interpretative context in which
10:3–16 must be read, and it envisages a reinforcement of an
established small-scale mission led by the 'few' and continuous
with the missions of Jesus and (ultimately) John. As to the
ethnic horizon of the saying, we are not taken beyond
the confines of Israel, and Q 22:30 makes it natural to recollect
the twelve and their mission (cf. Gal 2:7–8). This conclusion will,
however, be underpinned or undermined by whatever conclusions we reach on other editorial elements within 10:2–16.

Finally, the eschatological outlook of 10:2 requires comment.
That the harvest metaphor is used so frequently with the End in
mind must favour the view that Q 10:2 does the same, and in so
doing it could endorse the proclamation of the nearness of the
kingdom which was central to the main body of the mission
charge. While the summary of that proclamation in Luke 10:9
includes the phrase ἐφ' ὑμᾶς, this is absent from the agreed
version in Matt 10:7/Luke 10:11. That agreement makes it
unlikely[33] that the phrase in question should, on the basis of a
correspondence between Luke 10:9 and Q 11:20, be accepted as
original here. It is more likely that the longer version in Luke
10:9 involves a Lucan reminiscence of Q 11:20 and an expression
of the evangelist's characteristic preference in matters eschatological. If that is so, short-term imminence is the contribution of Q
10:11 to the meaning of Q 10:2. That means once again an echo
of the preaching of John, and also the voicing of the conviction
that this mission has a certain ultimacy about it: human responses
to it will determine the final divine assessment of the persons
who hear (cf. Q 6:46, 47–49). To say this is not to forget that Q
presupposes the delay of the parousia; it is simply to recall that
in spite of the delay the Q community found itself in a situation
where it became appropriate once again to revive the stronger
form of expectation for the future. In the situation which gave
rise to the popular prophetic movements against which Q warns,
this was not difficult.

---

[33]So Schulz, *Spruchquelle* 407; Hoffmann, *Studien* 275; Polag, *Christologie* 69.
Contra Uro, *Sheep* 82; Luz, *Matthäus II* 8.

3. 'Gentiles . . . Samaritans . . . Israel'. Matt 10:5b, 6.

The spectrum of opinion about a Q origin for the saying about 'Gentiles . . . Samaritans . . . Israel' (Matt 10:5b, 6) ranges from strong support[34] to equally strong resistance,[35] with those who resist varying in attributing the saying to MattR, or to oral tradition, or even to an alternative version of the mission charge.

The relationship between Matt 10:5b, 6 and Matt 15:24 is an initial complication. It is fairly clear that the latter does not represent an independent or earlier version. Instead, it is either dependent upon 10:6 or, if the latter is MattR, it is that as well. Variations in wording are trivial or easily explained by reference to context, and the attempt by Jeremias[36] to establish a Semitic original for 15:24 on the basis of its distinctive features must be judged unsuccessful.[37] The most notable distinguishing feature of 15:24 is ἀπεστάλην, which makes it not only an I-saying but also (in Laufen's words) 'an even more fundamental and exclusive formulation'.[38] In fact, the positioning of 15:24 inside 15:21–28 forces it to have this form and significance. The verb as such was available in Matt 10:5a/Mark 6:7, and the MattR tendency to create I-sayings completes the picture.[39] We can therefore safely ignore 15:24 when investigating the earlier tradition-history of 10:5b, 6.

Is Matt 10:5b, 6 in accord with Matthew's own theology? The evangelist's theological commitment to worldwide mission is beyond all doubt (21:43; 28:19). Alongside these sayings, which point to a post-passion expansion to the world beyond Israel, we twice find in OT citations a close identification between the mission of the pre-passion Jesus and the mission to the Gentiles: 4:15 (Isa 9:1–2) and 12:18, 21 (Isa 42:1–4). The first text makes the 'Galilee of the Gentiles' allusion a matter of

---

[34]Schürmann, *Untersuchungen* 137–49; M. Trautmann, *Zeichenhaft Handlungen Jesu. Ein Beitrag zur Frage nach dem geschichtlichen Jesu* (FB 37; Würzburg: Echter Verlag, 1980) 200–25.

[35]Hoffmann, *Studien* 258–61; Laufen, *Doppelüberlieferungen* 233–43.

[36]*Jesus' Promise to the Nations* (SBT 24; London: SCM, 1958) 19–20.

[37]See Trilling, *Israel* 99–100; Schürmann, *Untersuchungen* 138; Kasting, *Mission* 110–13.

[38]*Doppelüberlieferungen* 19–20.

[39]Compare the MattR 5.17 with the *Vorlage* underlying Q 16:16.

christological geography and causes the setting of Jesus' own work to be a microcosm of the world.[40] The second text exploits a slightly artificial correspondence between the (Marcan) secrecy motif and the reticence of the Servant, but Matthew has little interest in secrecy and appears to use it merely as a pretext for the exploitation of more favoured ideas within the Isaiah text, namely the endowment with the Spirit, the relief of suffering, and the saving incorporation of the Gentiles. This last element appears twice (vv. 18, 21), and while 'in his name will the Gentiles hope' might be given a post-passion setting (cf. 28:19) the pre-passion setting of 'he shall proclaim justice to the Gentiles' is unavoidable. So Jesus' own mission to Israel is a 'transparent' window for viewing the mission to the Gentiles. In this light two other texts which relate directly to Matthew's version of the mission charge provide assistance. In Matt 10:18 the Israel-centred mission (cf. 10:23) incorporates experiences with Gentiles, and in 15:24 (= 10:6) Jesus provides parenthetic teaching for disciples on how the primary commitment to Israel is to be understood: the 'periodizing' demand that the children first be fed (Mark 7:27) is omitted and the faith-confession of Jesus as Son of David and Lord already opens the door to the Gentiles. Hence, a salvation-historical division of time into successive periods of Israel and the Gentiles, a scheme into which Matt 10:5b, 6 might fit, does not emerge.[41] If the approach to the Gentiles can be attributed to Jesus and, as it were, be overlaid on the approach to Israel, then the sharp antithesis set out in our saying fits very uneasily.

Christology now calls for attention as possibly holding the key to Matt 10:5b, 6. We begin by noting that just as a mission to the world is a function of Jesus' lordship over the universe (28:16–20), so also his mission to Israel is a function of his messiahship.[42] This fits the Syro-Phoenician woman's address to him as 'Lord, Son of David' (15:22), in which the second title is

---

[40]Note the Galilee linkage between 4:15 and 28:16.

[41]Uro, *Sheep* 43–5, draws attention to the mixture of pre- and post-resurrection material within the discourse as a pointer *away from* a salvation-historical resolution of the tension between 10:5b, 6 and 28:18–20. He ends with 'no simple solution' to the tension except an ambiguity and a capacity on Matthew's part to think simultaneously in terms of particularism and universalism.

[42]H. Kasting, *Die Anfänge der christlichen Mission. Eine historische Untersuchung* (BEvT 55; München: Kaiser, 1969) 111–12; Laufen, *Doppelüberlieferungen* 236–37.

MattR. Its relevance to our present enquiry is suggested by Matthew's positioning of the healing of the two blind men just before the mission charge (9:27–31, cf. Mark 10:46–52), with the confession 'Son of David' again having a central place. This was itself followed by the healing of the dumb demoniac (9:32–34), with its double 'choral ending' polarizing two contrary assessments: an event unique in an Israelite context, and one which therefore points to the uniqueness of Jesus (v. 33b), or an event achieved in liaison with the prince of demons (v. 34). From here a signpost points to two later traditions. The first is Matt 12:22–24, where the same polarized assessments reappear, except that 'Can this be the Son of David?' occupies the position of, and provides commentary upon, 'Never was anything like this seen in Israel'. The second is Matt 10:24–25, which is present in the mission charge only because of Matthaean compositional activity, and which, by virtue of 'If they have called the master of the house Beelzebul, how much more will they malign those of his household?', establishes an identification of the missionaries with Jesus, not only in his rejection but also in his Davidic messianic activity. This essential theological insight is suggested by two other features which enable us to approach Matt 10:5b, 6 even more closely, as it were, from either side. The first is the MattR amplification of the disciples' miracle working, so that Matt 10:8 diff Luke 10:9 first matches the miracle working of Jesus (Matt 11:5), interpreted by MattR as 'the works of the messiah', and second builds a bridge between 9:33 and 10:25b by means of 'cast out demons'. The second is the MattR amplification of Mark 6:6 in Matt 9:35–36. This draws in alongside teaching the preaching of the gospel of the kingdom and the healing of disease (cf. 4:23) as a paradigm for 10:7–8, and provides a commentary derived from Mark 6:34. That commentary, referring to the sheep without a shepherd, draws on three OT passages (Num 27:17; 1 Kgs 22:17; Ezek 34:4–6) which understand the wholeness of the nation in terms of the provision of authorized leadership. For Matthew, therefore, the answer to Israel's problem is found in the combination of Jesus' own activity and that of the missionaries. Consequently, there is a deliberate matching of 10:6 with 9:36/Mark 6:34.

In assessing Matt 10:5b, 6 we have to combine the two conclusions reached above concerning Matthaean theology, that is, the interpenetration of the mission to Israel and the mission to the Gentiles, and the interpenetration of the disciples' mission and the mission of Jesus as Davidic messiah. These two conclusions enable us to see Matt 10:6 as wholly consonant with Matthaean thinking and therefore, in view of its proximity to 9:36, very probably dependent upon the same source, namely Mark 6:34. They also enable us to see how uneasily Matt 10:5b, and specifically the antithesis within Matt 10:5b, 6, can fit into Matthaean thinking. It is Matt 10:5b which remains isolated and needing to have its origin determined.

A series of considerations suggests that MattR is not a satisfactory explanation for Matt 10:5b. First, there is no precedent in MattR material for the creation of an essentially negative saying about the Gentiles (τὰ ἔθνη). All other MattR ἔθνη-sayings are positive and inclusive in spirit (cf. 4:15; 12:18, 21; 21:43; 25:32; 28:19). Negative or exclusive sayings derive either from Mark (cf. 10:18; 20:19, 25; 24:7, 9) or from Q (cf. 6:32a; ἐθνικός-sayings in 5:47; 6:7; 18:17). Second, whereas Mark 6:34 serves as the source for Matt 10:6, there is nothing in the Marcan context to serve as the stimulus for Matt 10:5b. Third, there is no evidence elsewhere of any Matthaean interest in Samaritans. Fourth, as it stands, Matt 10:5b, 6 exhibits a nicely balanced symmetry, with its two short negative εἰς-statements in one half followed by a rather longer πρός-statement in the other. It is widely supposed that the two halves must always have belonged together, at whatever stage the saying came into being. Only rarely has the alternative been mooted, as, for example, when Maria Trautmann, after detecting a discrepancy between strictly geographical terminology in v. 5b and theological terminology in v. 6, went on to ascribe v. 6 to the historical Jesus and to view v. 5b as a later attachment within the Q community.[43] Against this: first, when v. 6 is viewed in association with 10:23 it seems doubtful whether the geography/theology discrepancy should be pressed; second, we have already seen grounds for explaining v. 6 otherwise; and third, it is not necessary to see v. 5b as dependent on v. 6. Matthew's fondness for creating antithetical sayings, together with the capacity of v. 5b for separate existence, suggests that it should be considered by itself

[43]*Handlungen* 220–1.

and in its own right. When that is done, much depends on whether this saying, which exhibits parallelism of form, and for which an Aramaic original cannot[44] with any conviction be posited, could fit into Q and, if so, whether it would be dropped by Luke.

There are very good reasons for thinking that Matt 10:5b could fit into Q and that it would be dropped by Luke.

First, immediately Luke begins his travel sequence, and shortly before the mission charge, he tells of the rejection of Jesus in Samaria. This is so close positionally to where Matt 10:5b stands, and so close in terminology (Luke 9:52: εἰσῆλθον εἰς κώμην Σαμαριτῶν / Matt 10:5b: εἰς πόλιν Σαμαριτῶν μὴ εἰσέλθητε) that the suggestion of some literary relationship is almost irresistible.[45] Since there is no strong case for assigning any of Luke 9:51–56 to Q, it is likely that 9:52 is a reminiscence of Matt 10:5b.

Second, Luke gives considerable attention to Samaritans. Luke 10:30–37 and 17:11–17 are not only Samaritan stories but favourable Samaritan stories, stories which place Jewish persons in an unfavourable light. In 9:51–56, for all that the Samaritans reject the approach of Jesus and his associates, it is significant that Luke records an approach to them, places it first in his journey sequence, and has Jesus refuse to allow them to experience the fire of judgment. Since Luke in 10:1, 8b keeps one eye on the mission of the post-Easter church it is clear that the positive and prominent inclusion of Samaria would be on his mind (cf. Acts 1:8; 8:4–25; 9:31). It would therefore have been extremely surprising if he had transmitted any saying like Matt 10:5b.[46]

Third, that which applies to the Lucan treatment of Samaritans applies even more to his treatment of Gentiles. All three of the Q ἐθνικός-sayings are rewritten or removed (see Matt 5:47; 6:7; 18:17). It is surprising that one of the unfavourable ἔθνη-sayings in Q does survive (Q 12:30a), but since for him Israel is an ἔθνος (LukeR at 7:5; 23:2), the phrase πάντα

---

[44]Against Jeremias, *Promise* 19–20.

[45]M. Miyoshi, *Der Anfang der Reiseberichts. Lk 9,51–10,24* (AnBib 60; Rome: Biblical Institute, 1974) 11: 'Ist Lk 9:52 eine Erinnerung an das Samaria-Verbot?'

[46]Rightly, Trautmann, *Handlungen* 204–5; against Kasting, *Mission* 111, who suggests that Matt 10:5b, 6 would have followed very suitably after Luke 9:51–56.

τὰ ἔθνη does not mean to him Gentiles over against Jews but all humanity outside the sphere of faith. In association with Samaritans the ἔθνη of Matt 10:5b could not but be Gentiles as over against Jews, and an evangelist like Luke could not possibly accommodate such a prohibition. Indeed for him Jesus is the light for revelation to the Gentiles simultaneously with being the glory of Israel (2:25); in the mission of the one who is manifested to Israel (1:80) there is a fulfilment of the promise that 'all flesh shall see the salvation of God' (3:6); at the same time as the centrality of Israel is acknowledged in the good works of the centurion (7:5), whom Luke takes to be a Gentile, his incorporation into the community of faith anticipates the decisive outreach to the Gentiles via Peter (Acts 10:1–11:18; 15:7–18).

Fourth, that which applies to both parts of Matt 10:5b does not apply to 10:6. If the word μᾶλλον were removed from the latter, it would fit perfectly into the Lucan scheme in which Jesus is the coming redeemer of Israel (24:21) and the fulfilment of the hope of Israel, which Luke underscores from the infancy narratives onwards. The apostolic proclamation is to 'all the house of Israel' (Acts 2:36; cf. 4:10; 13:17, 24), and Jesus' significance is repeatedly defined with reference to Israel (see Acts 10:36; 28:20). Moreover, the imagery of the lost sheep is accepted easily enough by Luke in his presentation of Jesus' concern for fringe members of Israel (Luke 15:4–7).

Fifth, Matt 10:5b, with its narrow and particularist presupposition, fits rather well with other material in Q which not only depreciates Gentiles but also arguably belongs to a later or editorial stratum. Once again one must recall Q 6:33, where LukeR has removed the original Gentile reference, a saying which is a secondary Q commentary on the earlier demand for love of enemies;[47] Matt 6:7a, a secondary Q introduction to the prayer instruction;[48] Q 12:30a, a secondary expansion of the concluding demand for the avoidance of anxiety about food and clothing;[49] Matt 18:17, which reflects the disciplinary provision in the community to which the Q Christians belonged.[50]

[47]See above, p. 102.
[48]See below, p. 225.
[49]See p. 34.
[50]See above, p. 144.

We conclude, therefore, that the Q mission charge probably contained, along with other prohibitions, the instruction not to go into any way of the Gentiles nor to enter into a town of the Samaritans:

εἰς ὁδὸν ἐθνῶν μὴ ἀπέλθητε,
καὶ εἰς πόλιν Σαμαριτῶν μὴ εἰσέλθητε.

Since it belongs most suitably with redactional material its contribution must be measured along with other editorial additions. Its most important feature is its exclusive and particularist view of mission in a setting where an alternative inclusive and universal outlook is maintained by others.[51] The speaker presumes that the Gentile mission is taking place, but declines to participate in it. We know from Gal 2:7–8 of one community and of one period of time when such a position was maintained.

4. Woes on the Towns of Galilee. Q 10:12, 13–15.

The woes on Chorazin, Bethsaida and Capernaum (Q 10:13–15) belong to the mission charge in Luke and occur shortly after it in Matthew (Matt 11:20–24). In both sequences they occur immediately before the *Jubelruf* (Q 10:21–22), if Luke 10:17–20, itself almost certainly not derived from Q, be set aside. In terms of content, Matthew's version is longer than Luke's, and it is a question whether the original Q version has been expanded or reduced by either of the later evangelists. The introductory Matt 11:20 can readily be assigned to MattR,[52] but the decision about Matt 11:23b–24, the comparison with Sodom, is less straightforward.

The case in favour of Matt 11:23b–24 belonging to Q could be set out as follows: (i) There is the formal parallelism of the two oracles, that is, a denunciation (vv. 21a, 23a), an adverse comparison with notoriously sinful towns (vv. 21b, 23b), and a declaration of grim prospects in the day of judgment (vv. 22, 24).[53] (ii) The absence of vv. 23b–24 from Luke might stem from a concern to avoid repetition. (iii) The numerical

---

[51] See Beare, 'Mission', 9.
[52] Laufen, *Doppelüberlieferungen* 228.
[53] Fitzmyer, *Luke II* 851.

discrepancy in the two references to 'you' in v. 24 (ὑμῖν . . . σοί) might stem from MattR insertion of λέγω ὑμῖν ὅτι into Q source material here as in v. 22 (diff Luke 10:14).

Rather more plausible, however, is the alternative attribution of vv. 23b–24 to MattR. First, on v. 23b: (i) It lacks any reference to repentance and reads like a pale reflection of v. 21b. (ii) It causes v. 23a to focus on miracle (as do the MattR v. 20 and the Q v. 21b) instead of preserving a more comprehensive reference, probably to Capernaum's having been the home base of Jesus, though conceivably to its having set itself polemically over against the totality of what had been happening through him. (iii) It depends for its force upon a phrase μέχρι τῆς σήμερον which is characteristically MattR (cf. 27:8; 28:15). Second, on v. 23a: As it stands, it details an offence and amplifies the threat of judgment. That is, it contains within itself hints of all three formal elements of the first oracle. Finally, Luke elsewhere shows no prejudice against parallelism, indeed quite the opposite. So the marginally more likely conclusion is that vv. 23b–24 did not belong to Q. In that case they are a MattR reminiscence of Q 10:12 and a confirmation that the woes did belong to the mission charge in Q.

The original Q text of the woes can now be set out:

οὐαί σοι, Χοραζίν, οὐαί σοι, Βηθσαϊδά. ὅτι εἰ ἐν Τύρῳ καὶ Σιδῶνι ἐγένοντο αἱ δυνάμεις αἱ γενόμεναι ἐν ὑμῖν, πάλαι ἂν ἐν σάκκῳ καὶ σποδῷ μετενόησαν. πλὴν Τύρῳ καὶ Σιδῶνι ἀνεκτότερον ἔσται ἐν τῇ κρίσει ἢ ὑμῖν. καὶ σύ, Καφαρναούμ, μὴ ἕως οὐρανοῦ ὑψωθήσῃ; ἕως ᾅδου καταβήσῃ.

The secondariness of Q 10:13–15 in its present (Luke/Q) context is beyond doubt.[54] There is a discrepancy of audience between the missionaries and the towns; woes are pronounced before the disciples have even been in action; and it was easy for Matthew to move the woes to a different context. Therefore the position of Q 10:13–15 is due to an editor. And if that is the case, questions arise concerning its presumed setting when existing separately and its present setting within Q 10:2–16.

First, what is the *Sitz im Leben* of Q 10:13–15 when considered

---

[54]Zeller, 'Redaktionsprozesse', 404; Jacobson, 'Literary Unity', 421; Kloppenborg, *Formation* 195: 'formally and materially the most intrusive passage'.

in isolation? It surely must be that of a mission, not to Gentiles but to Israel. The audience is typified by Chorazin, Bethsaida and Capernaum, and belongs to a context in which an adverse comparison with notorious Gentile towns would be particularly galling to the hearers. In this connection the flavour of the material has been well captured by two scholars, both of whom believe that Q as a whole presupposes the existence of a mission to the Gentiles, and both of whom notice the quite different setting within which these woes would function before inclusion in Q. Paul Meyer says of Q 10:13–15, 'It does not seem to immediately reflect the Gentile mission but only (the) parenetic use of Gentiles to condemn Jewish obduracy.'[55] In similar vein Risto Uro observes that 'the emphasis is not on the fact that Tyre and Sidon in reality *are* willing to convert but on the fact that the Israelite towns *are not*'.[56] The setting is therefore a mission to Israel, a mission which calls for repentance and exhibits its essential character in some suitably interpreted δυνάμεις. It is, moreover, a thoroughly prophetic mission. This impression is conveyed by the use of the woe form[57] and the demand for repentance, and is reinforced by the recollection of the most closely related tradition elsewhere in Q, namely 11:31–32. In that tradition the contemporary speaker of wisdom and prophecy has an even higher claim to a response than his illustrious predecessors, but neither hearing nor repentance have been forthcoming. Again Gentile persons serve to enforce an adverse contrast with a presumed Israelite audience.

Second, what is the implication of an editorial insertion of such a tradition as Q 10:13–15 into the mission charge? It can surely be no accident that material with a well-defined Israelite audience was deemed so appropriate. So this editorial intervention seems to have the same horizon as that of Q 10:2 and Matt 10:5b, namely a charismatic mission dedicated to the renewal of Israel. In detail it clearly served to strengthen the miraculous element in the mission (Q 10:9), but also to underline the contrast between a rejecting city and Sodom (Q 10:12).

The unavoidable reference above to the saying which links a rejecting town with Sodom (Q 10:12) makes this the appropriate

[55]'The Gentile Mission in Q', *JBL* 89 (1970) 405–17, esp. p. 417.
[56]*Sheep* 172–3.
[57]Uro, *Sheep* 163.

point at which to say more about that saying, most particularly because its tradition history has a direct bearing on the conclusion suggested above.

This saying follows the statement about dust shaking and brings to a climax the sayings about the mission in the towns (Q 10:8–11). It could not exist separately from those preceding sayings, since 'that city' would then lack definition.[58] It also overlaps very obviously with the woes we have just considered, being 'astonishingly parallel'[59] with the saying which links a rejecting town with Tyre and Sidon. That last fact is the basis for the various competing views about its origin. According to one view, it is a Q-redactional anticipation of the woes on the towns (Q 10:13–15).[60] According to another view, it is secondary but not Q-redaction: the already existing parallelism in vv. 12, 14 was responsible for the connecting of vv. 13–15 to the mission charge.[61] The view taken here is that the saying is not Q-redaction nor even secondary, but an original part of the instructions on conduct in towns. This would not only explain how the woes of Q 10:13–15 came to be placed in the mission charge. It would go further and establish a common setting for the pre-Q instructions on conduct in towns, the pre-Q woes, and the compositional activity of the Q-editor.

The role of the Sodom saying within 10:10–12 must first be examined. V. 11b, the threatening declaration about the kingdom, and v. 12, the Sodom saying, are clearly somewhat in competition with one another in following up v. 11a: the former is a comment reinforcing the messengers' removal of the dust of the rejecting town from their feet, while the latter is a comment intended exclusively for the messengers. The former is best regarded as LukeR, for it assimilates this discourse to others with a 'knowing' or 'being known' climax[62] and characteristically attributes rejection to ignorance.[63] With the removal of the competition represented by v. 11b, the key question is the

[58]Kloppenborg, *Formation* 196.
[59]Lührmann, *Redaktion* 62.
[60]Hahn, *Mission* 43; Lührmann, *Redaktion* 62; Schenk, 'Einfluss', 55; Laufen, *Doppelüberlieferungen* 274–5; Jacobson, 'Literary Unity', 421; Kloppenborg, *Formation* 199.
[61]Zeller, 'Redaktionsprozesse', 404.
[62]Cf. Acts 2:36; 13:38; 15:18; 20:34; 28:28.
[63]Cf. Luke 19:41–44; 23:34 *v.l.*; Acts 3:17; 13:27.

relationship between v. 11a and v. 12. This appears to be very smooth and uncomplicated.

Without v. 12 the mission charge achieves only a weak climax, unless 10:16 be drawn in to provide a final comment on the implications of rejection. We have already begun to see that such is unlikely, given the harmony that exists between 10:16 and the editorially attached 10:2. Now the metaphorical dust removal is certainly, as Jeremias has put it, 'a symbolic breaking off of all community'[64] but it does not spell out the theological consequences.[65] With v. 12, on the other hand, a natural continuation of vv. 10, 11a is achieved, and those consequences are spelt out bluntly. We recall at this point the observation that one of the crying scandals about the Sodomites was their refusal to show hospitality to visiting emissaries. Within the mission charge hospitality is the explicit and open sign of commitment to the message of the kingdom, so v. 12 is more a natural development of what precedes it than an anticipation of what follows. The totality of the whole tradition from Q 10:5 onwards conveys with the utmost clarity the same message as *T. Asher* 7:1: 'Do not become like Sodom, which did not recognize the Lord's angels and perished for ever.'

The extreme radicalism of the saying in Q 10:12 encourages the thought that it is very ancient and indeed authentic. Sodom had long since been viewed as an extreme example of corruption, 'the incarnation of wickedness',[66] the classic example of what provokes judgment by fire.[67] To affirm that any town will fare *worse* than Sodom in the eschatological judgment is truly astonishing. One recalls Lam 4:6, 'The chastisement of the daughter of my people has been greater than the punishment of Sodom, which was overthrown in a moment, no hand being laid upon it', but the eschatological element makes Q 10:12 even more drastic. Such a worse fate must mean final and once for all condemnation (cf. *Jub.* 36:10; Luke 17:28–30). In Christopher Evans' apt words, 'The rejection of what is ultimate

---

[64] *Theology* 238.

[65] It may be conjectured that a sense of this incompleteness underlies the MarkR addition of εἰς μαρτύριον αὐτοῖς, 6:11.

[66] *Encyclopaedia Judaica* 15 (1971) 70–4, esp. 70. See Gen 13:13; 18:20; 19:13; Jer 23:14.

[67] See Deut 29:23; Isa 1:9; 13:19; Jer 50:40; Amos 4:11.

involves ultimate rejection.'[68] And the ultimate which is rejected is the message which stems from Jesus, and that alone! No suggestion is made that classic Sodom-like offences have been committed, such as adultery, lying and the approval of evil,[69] or pride, gluttony, prosperous ease, failure to help the poor and needy, and idolatry[70] – only rejection of the message of Jesus! This message of Jesus, presented by his followers, is the proclamation of the nearness of God's kingdom which, for all that it spells salvation and healing, also by definition implies judgment. Only 10:12 articulates that judgment.

So it seems fair to register some hesitation about the assessment of Q 10:12 as redactional. But whether it is or not, all that was said about the original *Sitz im Leben* of Q 10:13–15 has to be said again for Q 10:12. It belongs to a mission in Israel, and in Israel alone. If the Q editor created it this was his context. If his contribution extended no further than a bringing together of two separate units, each of which belonged to the mission in Israel, the most natural inference is again that this was his own context.

5. Eating without Discrimination. Luke 10:8b.

The instruction to eat whatever is provided, present only in Luke 10:8b, encourages conduct unrestricted by Jewish food laws (cf. 1 Cor 10:27) and therefore belongs to a setting of Christian advance into the Gentile world.[71] It is an item of some sensitivity, both for the recovery of the Q text and for the discussion of Q-redaction. If it is not attributable to LukeR, and was present in Q, it would have to be regarded as redactional at some stage, since the tradition to which it is presently attached antedates the Gentile mission. By the same token, if it turned out to be Q-redactional it would threaten the main proposal of this chapter that Q and its editor belong to a situation in which a Gentile mission elsewhere is known about but not emulated.

[68]*Saint Luke* (London: SCM / Philadelphia: Trinity Press International, 1990) 450.
[69]Cf. Jer 23:14.
[70]Cf. Ezek 16:49; Jude 7; *T. Levi* 14:6; *T. Naph.* 3:4; *T. Benj.* 9:1.
[71]Laufen, *Doppelüberlieferungen* 220; Uro, *Sheep* 67–9, 220–3.

Two arguments against LukeR have been mounted by Uro.[72] The first is that 'Luke avoids introducing a Gentile mission in the teaching of the earthly Jesus'. The second is that 'Luke takes a respectful attitude towards Jewish ritual law (cf. Acts 10; 15:29)'. But against the first argument, Luke does not keep quite so watertight the compartments of the period of Jesus and the period of the Church. One thinks of the Spirit, which is the promise for the post-resurrection community (24:49), and yet is introduced by LukeR at the pre-resurrection stage (Luke 11:13 diff Matt 7:11). One thinks also of the widespread opinion that Luke draws the Gentile mission itself into his construction of Jesus' introductory address by means of a two-level understanding of the word πατρίς (4:25–27),[73] though this is more doubtful. But in any case, if (as Uro suggests) Q presupposes a Gentile mission in its Jesus-sayings, Luke incorporates these sayings within his Jesus-period contentedly enough, and the parallelism between Acts 10 and the redactional Luke 7:3–5 reinforces the point. Against the second argument, Q is just as strong as Luke in maintaining an extremely conservative view of the whole law (Q 16:17), but Philip Esler has shown that a conservative view of the law in general does not prevent a more relaxed approach to the food laws in particular.[74]

Counting more significantly against the inclusion of Luke 10:8b in Q are some structural considerations. Luke 10:8–11 is plainly intended to form an antithetical parallelism, with each of the two subsections beginning εἰς ἣν ἂν πόλιν εἰσέρχησθε/ εἰσέλθητε καὶ (μὴ) δέχωνται ὑμᾶς (vv. 8a, 10a). Each describes certain actions by Jesus' emissaries and concludes with an announcement in direct speech that the kingdom of God is near (vv. 9, 11). This parallelism is contrived, depends upon Lucan data which have no Matthaean support (cf. the earlier discussion of v. 11b), and, since it by no means follows that a reference to rejection in a town (vv. 10, 11) must have been preceded by a reference to acceptance,[75] is most naturally attributed to LukeR.

[72] *Sheep* 69.
[73] See C. J. Schreck, 'The Nazareth Pericope in Recent Study', *The Gospel of Luke* (2nd ed.; ed. F. Neirynck; BETL 32; Leuven: University Press/Peeters, 1989) 399–471, esp. pp. 446–9.
[74] *Community and Gospel in Luke-Acts* (SNTSMS 57; Cambridge: CUP, 1987) 71–109.
[75] Hoffmann, *Studien* 277.

(i) The words καὶ εἰς ἣν ἂν πόλιν εἰσέρχησθε (v. 8a) are supported by Matt 10:11a, itself a preface to material stemming either from MattR or from Mark 6:10. They cannot have stood alone in Q and in principle could have led smoothly into a description of healing and preaching. The words καὶ δέχωνται ὑμᾶς confine the healing and preaching to a setting of reception. This is scarcely conceivable in principle and scarcely in harmony with the Q perspective documented in Q 10:13–15, for there miracles have been part of the appeal for a response and have failed to achieve it. And then the words ἐσθίετε τὰ παρατιθέμενα ὑμῖν conform to Lucan usage (cf. Acts 16:34) as well as to the Pauline slogan (cf. 1 Cor 10:27), and plainly belong to the setting of house rather than town.

We conclude, therefore, that Luke 10:8b is LukeR, and that the Q contribution to Luke 10:8–9 was confined to statements about entry to a town, healings, and the announcement of the near kingdom.

6. The Sending Pattern. Q 10:16.

The sending saying (Q 10:16) at the end of the mission charge has survived in two divergent forms in Matthew and Luke, quite apart from the variants elsewhere in the NT (Mark 9:37 par; John 12:48; 13:20; 1 Thess 2:13; 4:8).

Matthew's shorter form, lacking a rejection statement, is probably a MattR adaptation to a context (Matt 10:40–42) which shows the influence of Mark 9:37–41; in neither Marcan nor Matthaean setting would a rejection statement have been appropriate. Probably under that same influence of Mark 9:37 there occurs at the climax of the saying the declaration that 'he who receives me receives him who sent me', for which Luke has no equivalent except in the rejection part of Luke 10:16. Laufen attributes the longer form to Q,[76] but it is not easy to explain a LukeR shortening. The other major discrepancy is between Matthew's 'receive' and Luke's 'hear'. This time it is easy to adopt the consensus view that Luke's version is the original one. This yields the following text:

[76]*Doppelüberlieferungen* 230–3.

Ὁ ἀκούων ὑμῶν ἐμοῦ ἀκούει,
καὶ ὁ ἀθετῶν ὑμᾶς ἐμὲ ἀθετεῖ·
καὶ ὁ ἐμὲ ἀθετῶν ἀθετεῖ τὸν ἀποστείλαντά με.

The recent reconstruction of the mission of the historical Jesus by Graham Stanton has found in Q 10:16 the epitome of that mission, and it is easy to understand why.[77] It makes explicit the presupposition of so much authentic Jesus material, and it is in evident harmony with the material earlier in the mission charge which we have claimed to be derivative from Jesus. It overlaps with the explicit 'sending' saying, Q 10:3, at the start of the pre-Q tradition. It matches the recurrent pattern of positive and negative elements in Q 10:5–7, 8–12. In and of itself it positively demands a *Sitz im Leben* in mission. But an authentic saying of Jesus whose necessary setting is missionary activity is not thereby shown to be an original and integral part of the pre-Q mission charge in particular. Formally it is self-contained and self-sufficient, could survive without difficulty, and therefore could reach a later editor by other channels prior to being incorporated by him in his own version of the mission charge.

As a saying using antithetical parallelism it is particularly well suited to the end of a mission charge, since the conclusion of a discourse frequently sets out the issues, the choice of human responses, the consequences of that choice. In all these respects it can function in this discourse in just the same way as Q 6:47–49 functioned in the inaugural discourse in Q. As a saying whose major emphasis is in its second half it naturally relates to a mission in Israel where the covenant encourages confidence and even a complacency which it is the prophetic task to disturb. As a saying located at the end of *this* mission charge it is particularly fitting.

7. The pre-Q Mission Charge.

We now turn to the matter of the underlying mission charge. Our discussion of the singly attested traditions has suggested

[77] *The Gospels and Jesus* (Oxford: OUP, 1989) 188.

that the 'Gentiles/Samaritans' saying (Matt 10:5b) figured in Q and was an editorial construction. By contrast, neither the explicit restriction to Israel (Matt 10:6) nor the instruction to eat without discrimination (Luke 10:8b) belonged to Q. Double traditions which did figure in Q as a result of compositional activity by the editor are the harvest saying (Q 10:2), the woes on the towns of Galilee (Q 10:13–15), and the sending saying (Q 10:16). The Sodom saying (Q 10:12) which also belonged to Q was probably not redactional. This leaves the sheep/wolves saying (Q 10:3), the equipment and greeting rule (Q 10:4), and the instructions about conduct in houses (Q 10:5–7) and in towns (Q 10:8–12). It is now necessary to discuss the extent to which this material may have formed a unified pre-Q mission charge.

It is scarcely conceivable that any material relating to mission could exist without a statement of commissioning. Indeed, if we were confronted by the equipment rule (Q 10:4) and instructions on conduct in houses (Q 10:5–7) alone, we would have no idea why this rule and these instructions were issued. In short, they are not self-sufficient and could hardly survive in isolation. Therefore, Q 10:3 is needed as an initial definition, and is unlikely to have been an independent saying added only subsequently to the main mission charge.[78] This text probably ran:

ὑπάγετε· ἰδοὺ ἀποστέλλω ὑμᾶς ὡς πρόβατα ἐν μέσῳ λύκων.

Reference has already been made to the situation of religious polarization which Q 10:3 addresses, and it may be worth amplifying this a little. Wolves habitually feature in contexts which highlight rapacity, destruction and devastation.[79] Harmony between sheep and wolves in the natural world is so inconceivable that it is assigned to the eschatological age when God makes possible the hitherto impossible (Isa 11:6; 65:25). To mention sheep and wolves in the same breath is normally to conjure up a vision of confrontation, threat and danger – one in

---

[78]Against Uro, *Sheep* 99–100, and Kloppenborg, *Formation* 194, who regards Q 10:3 as 'a relatively early accretion to the instructions', while allowing that 'it coheres well with the rest of the speech'.

[79]Cf. Gen 49:27; Prov 28:15; Jer 5:6; Ezek 22:27; Zeph 3:3; *T. Gad* 1:3; *T. Benj.* 11:1–2; Matt 7:15; John 10:12; Acts 20:29.

which there is no fellowship or peace (Sir 13:17–18), one which if brought about by a human shepherd implies negligence (2 Esdr 5:18) or if by divine decision implies judgment (1 Enoch 89:55–56).

What is striking about Q 10:3 is that a metaphor which could be employed in Jew/Gentile confrontation (1 Enoch 90:1–27) is here being applied to a confrontation between Jews, the sharp antithesis being very reminiscent of polarizing Qumran-speak. While the context gives some prominence to the peace theme (Q 10:5), we have presupposed here a dark situation from which peace is absent.[80] Now judgment is not germane, and negligence on the part of the person responsible is clearly not implied, since the emissaries' 'defenceless and unprotected state'[81] is brought about deliberately. But what can be the intention? Surely to make abundantly clear that the mission cannot proceed with imperturbable calm, and at the same time to hint that the missionaries, although potential victims of conflict, are not themselves its initiators. Such an outlook turns out to be consonant with several elements in the following tradition. The first is the lack of a staff (Q 10:4), which is another way of combining vulnerability to danger and non-aggression. The second is the use of the term 'peace' (Q 10:6) to describe the bond between sympathizers, as over against opponents. Clearly peace is in a very special way the essence of what is being done. The third is the warning of rejection by particular communities (Q 10:10–12).[82] So Q 10:3 forms a rather apt introduction to what follows.

Overall it is natural to have recourse to the deuteronomic scheme for the interpretation of prophetic missions to Israel.[83] When we consider the evidence of how extremely widespread was the use of that scheme in early Christianity (cf. Q 6:22–23; 11:49; Mark 12:1–9; Acts 7:51–52; 1 Thess 2:15) and how inevitable and immediate a resource it was for any mission

---

[80]Hoffmann, *Studien* 294.

[81]Jeremias, *Theology* 239.

[82]Jacobson, 'Literary Unity', 422, draws a distinction between non-reception (cf. Mark 6:11) and violent opposition. However, we may compare the dust-shaking gesture in Q 10:11/Mark 6:11 with the sole NT parallel elsewhere, Acts 13:51, where it is the sequel to opposition and persecution.

[83]R. A. Edwards, *A Theology of Q* (Philadelphia: Fortress, 1976) 103; Jacobson, 'Literary Unity', 422.

experiencing conflict, then the presence of this view in the mission charge is less likely to be derived from the final redactional stratum and more likely to mark what is shared with the Jesus-tradition from its very earliest stage onwards.[84] This is the perspective of Q 10:3.

The Q form of the equipment rule probably prohibited the carrying of money, a bag, sandals or a staff (Q 10:4a), and may well have led into a prohibition of greetings on the way (Q 10:4b).[85] This produces the following Q text:

μὴ αἴρετε ἀργύριον, μὴ πήραν, μὴ ὑποδήματα, μὴ ῥάβδον, καὶ μηδένα κατὰ τὴν ὁδὸν ἀσπάσησθε.

There is good reason to suppose that this rule is an authentic element in the very earliest form of the mission charge: it is coherent with other authentic traditions, it picks up themes which are multiply attested, it runs contrary to human instinct, Cynic practice,[86] Jewish assumptions[87] and criticisms of anyone unduly dependent on help from fellow human beings,[88] and it clashes with the tendency of early Christian reflection.[89] This conclusion depends, of course, on the establishing of the original meaning.

First, the lack of money certainly excludes buying and selling (cf. Josephus, *J.W.* 2.8.4 §127) but probably implies far more, namely the ready acceptance of poverty, the abandonment of material concern with the present age, and an identification with those to whom the message of the kingdom is directed. It is not a prophetic sign of what is to come, since poverty is a mark of the present rather than the future. The classic text which gives profound meaning to this rule, and one which shows how well Q 10:4 integrates with Q 10:9, is Q 6:20b, 'Blessed are the poor, for theirs is the kingdom of God.'

---

[84]Laufen, *Doppelüberlieferungen* 273, notes its coherence with the discipleship sayings in Q 14:26–27; 17:33.

[85]Uro, *Sheep* 77–78. The two tunics, mentioned in Mark 6:9, may have figured in Q, but the matter remains uncertain.

[86]C. M. Tuckett, 'A Cynic Q?', *Bib* 70 (1989) 349–76, esp. pp. 367–8.

[87]Cf. Exod 3:5; 12:11; *m. Ber.* 9:5; *m. Yeb.* 16:7.

[88]Cf. *b. Pes.* 113b: 'Treat your sabbath like a weekday rather than be dependent on your fellow beings.'

[89]Cf. the less rigorous Mark 6:8–9.

Second, the lack of a bag[90] means that no food can be carried (cf. Jdt 10:5; 13:10) and consequently, for the person concerned, the expectation of suffering (*Midr. Gen.* 60:11) and what the rabbis, commenting on dependence on a neighbour's table, described as 'life which is no life' (*b. Bez.* 32b). Of course, provision will be made by the 'sons of peace' (thus Q 10:4 connects to Q 10:5–7) or not, as the case may be (thus Q 10:4 connects to Q 10:10, 12), but the reason for the prohibition has still to be found. While Q 12:22–31 (specifically that part of the earlier pre-Q stratum which becomes visible in Q 12:24) clearly corresponds with the promise of divine provision of food, the deliberate plan expressed in μὴ πήραν is most suitably understood as an identification with those to whom the message of Q 6:21a is directed, 'Blessed are the hungry, for they shall be filled.'

Third, the lack of sandals, more drastic than the Essene pattern (Josephus, *J.W.* 2.8.4 §126) and too extreme for Mark (6:9), is shown by parallel texts to mean not only the absence of a basic, even ultimate, necessity but also openness to insult and shame, a life which is worse than being dead and buried.[91] Openness to insult is envisaged elsewhere in Q 6:29 (embedded in the context of passive acceptance of enmity), but this does not suffice as an interpretative guide to the lack of sandals. That is to be found in the association between going barefoot and being in mourning,[92] from which a straight line leads to Q 6:21b, 'Blessed are the mourners, for they will be comforted.'

Fourth, the lack of a staff, without which no ancient oriental traveller would expect to set out, means the absence of support[93] and, more seriously, of the means of self-protection.[94] Not even the itinerant Essenes went this far (Josephus, *J.W.* 2.8.4 §125). These unprotected and vulnerable emissaries of Jesus are, as noted already, compelled to play the part of 'sheep among wolves' in physical as well as religious terms, given the occurrence of the staff in many texts describing the shepherd's instrument for the protection of the sheep.[95] But, as with the other

---

[90]The beggar's bag is not relevant to this saying.
[91]Deut 25:9–10; Amos 2:6; Sir 46:19; *b. Pes.* 113b; *b. Sab.* 129a, 152a.
[92]Cf. 2 Sam 15:30; Isa 20:2–3; Ezek 24:17, 23. See Uro, *Sheep* 119–20.
[93]Cf. Gen 32:10; Ezek 29:6–7.
[94]Cf. 2 Sam 23:21; 1 Chr 11:23; Bel 26.

prohibitions, some more positive intention is to be expected, in this case probably an exhibition of the hallmark of the mission which is peace (Q 10:5–6). That 'peace' is ultimately derivable from Isa 52:7, the announcement of the kingship of God in the Isaianic complex to which the text underlying the Q beatitudes (Isa 61:1–2) looks back. Once again we find a conceptual network holding Q 10:4, 5–7, 8–9 together.

Fifth, the avoidance of greetings evidently coheres with the importance attached to greetings in what follows (Q 10:5–7). It would be perverse to interpret the one otherwise than in the light of the other. Haste (2 Kgs 4:29) in the light of the near kingdom, which might theoretically be present in the one, is absent from the other and therefore ruled out. The very special and loaded significance attached to the greeting in Q 10:5–7 suggests that 'peace' is being given a special meaning to which casual exchanges could not do justice. To this we now turn.

Conduct in houses is focussed on three items in Q 10:5–7, namely the initial greeting (vv. 5–6), the acceptance of hospitality (v. 7abc), and residence in only one house (v. 7d). Apart from minor verbal uncertainties the original Q text has probably been preserved by Luke:[96]

εἰς ἢν δ' ἂν εἰσέλθητε οἰκίαν, πρῶτον λέγετε· εἰρήνη τῷ οἴκῳ τούτῳ. καὶ ἐὰν ἐκεῖ ἦ υἱὸς εἰρήνης, ἐπαναπαήσεται ἐπ' αὐτὸν ἡ εἰρήνη ὑμῶν· εἰ δὲ μή γε, ἐφ' ὑμᾶς ἀνακάμψει. ἐν αὐτῇ δὲ τῇ οἰκίᾳ μένετε, ἔσθοντες καὶ πίνοντες τὰ παρ' αὐτῶν.

In Q 10:5–7 the themes treated give, in association with Q 10:4, a balanced and symmetrical definition of the personal position of the emissaries. During their journey they lack independent provision and establish no relationships by means of greetings: at the end of their journey they experience provision, and are sustained by an established relationship inaugurated by a theologically loaded greeting. In literary terms, there is plainly homogeneity in Q 10:4, 5–7. In religious terms, it is important to dwell on the key function of the greeting. That which might be expected to be part of normal human

[95]Ps 2:9; Mic 7:14; Zech 11:7.
[96]Schulz, *Spruchquelle* 405–6.

interchange[97] is here invested with heavy significance. There takes place a real, but conditional, communication of peace.[98] It may be communicated indeed, though a hostile response will cause its return to its source. When communication does occur it binds the speaker to the 'son of peace'. Elsewhere in Q the phrase 'son of . . .' has both a present (Q 6:35) and an eschatological orientation (Q 13:28), and therefore we should probably envisage here the prospect of eschatological peace, the peace of Isa 52:7,[99] but also a peace which is celebrated in table fellowship and exhibited in personal demeanour. Although the coming kingdom has in the Luke/Q sequence not yet been mentioned, one cannot but recall two other traditions in which that coming kingdom is the future reality in the face of which divine fatherly care brings about the provision of food (Q 11:2–4; 12:22–31). Here the same applies, though with the extra datum that divine provision is brought about by human means. Moreover, the shared table which expresses the fellowship of peace has also itself to be seen as an anticipation of the ultimate meal (Q 13:28–29).

The discussion of the meaning and content of Q 10:5–7 adds to our sense of the close connection between it and adjacent sayings, both those which precede and those which follow it.

The preaching of the kingdom is mentioned in Q (Matt 10:7/ Luke 10:9, 11) but not in Mark. In Luke 10:8–9 it is quite naturally connected with entry to a town but, as we have seen, rather unnaturally attached to a specifically welcoming town where food is provided. The provision of hospitality would be more appropriately connected to a house, and is in any case a reduplication of the allusion to hospitality in Q 10:7, while the linkage with a welcome seems designed only to balance the concluding declaration about the kingdom to an unwelcoming town (Luke 10:11b). LukeR is therefore substantially in evidence. On the other hand, the introductory reference to entry to a city is likely to have been in Q since (i) it is in tension

[97]Cf. Exod 18:7; Tob 5:9; Sir 41:20; 1 Macc 11:6.
[98]F. Hahn, *Mission in the New Testament* (SBT 47; London: SCM, 1965) 45: 'Behind εἰρήνη there stands the Old Testament *shalom*, which denotes salvation in the fullest sense.'
[99]Manson, *Sayings* 257; Schulz, *Spruchquelle* 416; Laufen, *Doppelüberlieferungen* 256–7; W. Grimm, *Verkündigung Jesu und Deuterojesaja* 87. For a helpful discussion see especially Uro, *Sheep* 137–43.

with the following LukeR reference to hospitality; (ii) there is a Matthew/Luke agreement on such an introductory phrase following the proverbial saying about the labourer; and (iii) without any introduction at all the command to preach and heal would follow very abruptly on the instruction detailing conduct in houses. Reference has already been made to the LukeR ἐφ' ὑμᾶς and the MattR expansion of miraculous activity,[100] so when small and insignificant Matthew/Luke discrepancies are tidied up this part of the Q text emerges as:

καὶ εἰς ἣν ἂν πόλιν εἰσέρχησθε, θεραπεύετε τοὺς ἀσθενεῖς,
καὶ λέγετε, ἤγγικεν ἡ βασιλεία τοῦ θεοῦ.

This statement must have figured in the original mission charge if the latter was in any sense coherent and clear. Here alone is a definition of what the mission is all about. Links have already been pointed out between this saying and what precedes and is made meaningful by it. Moreover, if the preceding material has, in terms of its own tradition history, high claim to stem from the historical Jesus, the same applies here. In other words, a stratum of the mission charge later than that of Q 10:4–7 is not in view.

The saying about the rejecting town (Q 10:10–12) has in all probability been worked over by both Matthew and Luke: Matthew introduced μηδὲ ἀκούσῃ τοὺς λόγους ὑμῶν and added the reference to ἡ οἰκία.[101] Luke moved to this stage the idea of entry to the town, added the reference to the streets of the town, and created a new climax with πλὴν τοῦτο γινώσκετε ὅτι ἤγγικεν ἡ βασιλεία τοῦ θεοῦ.[102] The Q text probably ran:

---

[100]See above, pp. 164, 167.

[101]On the former, see above p. 157. The latter, οἰκία, is a MattR assimilation to the earlier but different saying in Mark 6:10, and has no support in Luke 10:11–12.

[102]The first and third of these points have been dealt with above on pp. 174, 178. On the second, Luke's ἐξελθόντες εἰς τὰς πλατείας αὐτῆς is secondary, since πλατεῖαι represent the streets of the town (cf. Luke 13:25), distinguished from the alleys by their width and their suitability for public proclamation and teaching (Matt 12:19; Luke 13:26). One does not go out of the town by merely going into the streets – unless one has mentally fused town and house – and therefore Luke 10 (diff Luke 9) does not in fact get the messengers out of the town at all. This must be LukeR.

καὶ ἐὰν μὴ δέχωνται ὑμᾶς, εἴπατε· καὶ τὸν κονιορτὸν τὸν κολληθέντα ἡμῖν ἐκ τῆς πόλεως ὑμῶν εἰς τοὺς πόδας ἀπομασσόμεθα ὑμῖν. λέγω ὑμῖν ὅτι Σοδόμοις ἐν τῇ ἡμέρᾳ ἐκείνῃ ἀνεκτότερον ἔσται ἢ τῇ πόλει ἐκείνῃ.

In substance this Q saying exhibits a neat balance with the preceding saying about preaching and healing. Q 10:8a describes entry to a town, and Q 10:10a describes departure; Q 10:9 describes the positive approach of the messengers with the proclamation and power of the kingdom, and Q 10:10b, 11a describes the refusal of their approach and their negative reaction; Q 10:8–9 describes what will always happen as a strategy of mission is activated, and Q 10:10–11 describes what may happen simply because a successful outcome of the mission cannot be guaranteed. Thus there is an inherent symmetry and unity about the underlying text of Q 10:8–11. The emphatic sequel in Q 10:12 serves powerfully to reinforce and reiterate for the benefit of the emissaries the eschatological bearing of what is happening. Just as the greeting, which has a more than usually deep theological bearing, is to be offered but may be rejected, so also the effective approach of the kingdom in word and action is to be offered and may be rejected. The first is connected with the micro-community of the house, and has for the emissaries a personal dimension, since it touches on whether their material needs will be supplied; the second is connected with the macro-community of the town, and has a public dimension. The first deals with a response at a deep level ('a son of peace'), which shows itself in the provision of hospitality; the second uses the word 'receive' which can stand for a general and overall response and for the welcome which may particularly express itself in table fellowship. In short,. there is an integrated homogeneity about these different instructions which combine to form Q 10:3, 4, 5–7, 9, 10a, 11a, 12. To separate any one of them from the rest is to damage a carefully judged whole.

8. Conclusions.

We set out to investigate the mission charge as an expression of the self-understanding, and maybe even the history, of the Q community. The results of the investigation are more modest than those recommended by, for example, John Kloppenborg and Risto Uro. In essence, the distinctions which form the basis of a reconstruction of a four-stage evolution in the tradition seem unduly fine, and the associated premise that Mark and Q were independent appears unduly hazardous. In place of such a reconstruction this study has suggested two conclusions.

The first is that an original mission charge, which is an integrated whole stemming from Jesus himself, can be recovered. It is roughly represented by Q 10:3, 4, 5–7, 9, 10a, 11a, 12. This mission charge articulates some of the principles and convictions at the heart of Jesus' own mission: the nearness of God's kingdom which will be effected in salvation and judgment, the anticipation of the power of the kingdom through the experience of healing, the commitment to the poor, the hallmark of peace. All this is set within an unmistakably prophetic framework which becomes visible in the proclamation, the insistence that ultimate issues are involved in human response to that proclamation, the signs, and the hint of a deuteronomic perspective on rejection.

The second is that a single layer of additional material was added by the Q editor. Within that single layer it is possible to distinguish further authentic Jesus material in Q 10:13–15, 16, and inauthentic material in Q 10:2 and Matt 10:5b. The theological position of the editor and the stance of his community thus come into view. First, there is a high degree of respect accorded to the historical Jesus and the traditions which preserve his outlook and missionary principles. Second, there is a christological position which picks up Jesus' own sense of the equivalence between himself and God in the context of his being sent, and then implicitly develops this position further in the direction of his being the Son of man. Third, there is a sense of the eschatological ultimacy of that mission which is carried out in anticipation of the imminent kingdom. Fourth, there is a preoccupation with a mission to Israel, which needs to be expanded by means of yet more charismatically endowed missionaries sent out by a settled but charismatic community with the authority of God himself.

6

The Whole People of God

The parable of the lost sheep plays a key role in both the gospels of Matthew and Luke. For Matthew it alerts the Christian pastor to a matter of life and death, the possible loss of a member of the Christian community who is beguiled away from the true faith and into apostasy. It belongs to a situation of sharp intra-Christian polarization of opposite views about the relationship of the Church to Israel.[1] False teachers who adopt a liberal view of the law (5:18–19) are to be resisted, but it is acknowledged that they may achieve some success and that the pastor's efforts to retrieve the wandering Christians may fail (18:13).[2] Nevertheless, those efforts are to be made. Theologically, just as Paul was inclined to regard the position of his opponents as an abandonment of authentic Christian faith and security,[3] so also the evangelist from a markedly different standpoint viewed such a shift of position as dangerous in the extreme. Salvation is located in the Church, and the Church is located within the continuity of the community of Israel.

For Luke, on the other hand, the parable is a defensive justification of the liberal position of Jesus in the matter of table-fellowship. Therefore, using the principle of 'transparency', there is mounted here a defence of the position of the Lucan community which simultaneously maintains a conservative view of the law as a whole and a relaxed view of the Jew/Gentile table fellowship prohibition in particular.[4] Theologically, repentance is the sole and sufficient requirement for entry to a community

[1]On what might be termed boundary issues like sabbath, food laws, and circumcision Matthew shows traditional respect, cf. G. Barth, 'Matthew's Understanding of the Law', 79–81; R Mohrlang, *Matthew and Paul* (SNTSMS 48; Cambridge: CUP, 1984) 9–12.

[2]The conditional phrase ἐὰν γένηται makes the success of the shepherd (v.13) as uncertain as the risk of the loss of the sheep (v. 12).

[3]Gal 2:21; 5:2–4.

which is not bound by Pharisaic sensitivities, and which has certain sectarian tendencies over against Judaism which the Matthaean community never encouraged.

The question arises, however, as to what the parable conveyed within the community of Q which bequeathed it to Matthew and to Luke. It is possible in theory that the message matched that of the Matt 18:12–14 version in its context, or that of the Luke 15:4–7 version in its context, or that a message different from both was intended. We need to look at the Q content and also at the Q context. The latter will, however, have to be defined rather broadly in terms of recurrent themes. For recent advances in the redactional study of Q, focussing on the structure of clusters of sayings or the reasons underlying the interpolation of extra material in speeches, have had to set Q 15:4–7 on one side with no clear understanding of its contribution, precisely because of the difficulty of determining its original Q setting.[5]

At the outset, the case for assigning the matching parable of the lost coin (Luke 15:8–10) to Q should be noted. Like the parable of the lost sheep, it too is essentially a τίς ἐξ ὑμῶν; parable appealing to an agreed sense of what any human person would do in the circumstances described;[6] it too begins with a quantitative description of property; it too is concerned with the loss of one single part of the property; it too describes a search process which should (even though in Matthew's lost sheep parable, over against Luke's, it may not) continue through to a successful outcome; it too records the joy which accompanies the recovery of the lost possession; and it too transfers from the joy of the earthly celebration to that of heaven.

Faced with such a match it is hard to envisage an independent existence for the two parables, and therefore the options narrow to the parable of the lost coin's having been either present in Q,[7] or created by Luke.[8] The equal derivation of both from Q

---

[4]P. F. Esler, *Community and Gospel in Luke-Acts* (SNTSMS 57; Cambridge: CUP, 1987) 71–109.

[5]Kloppenborg, *Formation* 100.

[6]H. Greeven, 'Wer unter euch . . .?', *WD* 3 (1952) 86–101.

[7]H. Weder, *Die Gleichnisse Jesu als Metaphern* (FRLANT 120; Göttingen: Vandenhoeck & Ruprecht, 1978) 170; J. Lambrecht, *Once More Astonished* (New York: Crossroad, 1981) 40–1.

[8]E. Klostermann, *Das Lukasevangelium* (HNT 5; 3rd ed.; Tübingen: Mohr, 1975) 155; R. Bultmann, *History* 171.

cannot be convincingly resisted by arguing that the parable of the lost coin is weaker than the parable of the lost sheep because the one in ten coins is proportionately more than the one in a hundred sheep; or that the parable of the lost sheep has the concluding application whereas in a pair of parables the application should appear only after the second element (cf. Luke 14:28–33); or that the absence of the parable of the lost coin from Matthew is a fatal drawback. Such resistance can itself be countered:

First, had the lost sheep been one of ten, in order to match the one in ten coins, the shepherd would have been rated a poor man rather than the owner of an average-sized flock, and he would not then have been a rather unexceptional person with whom the hearers of the 'Which of you . . .?' question could identify. Conversely, had the lost coin been one of a hundred the woman would probably have been rated rather prosperous and therefore not unexceptional and typical enough.[9] The point is that both parables are intended to focus on the 'one' and not to provoke any reflection at all concerning the other number involved.

Second, precedents for dual application are provided by Q 11:31–32 and 12.24, 27–28. But this particular form of argument may not be necessary, since there is a real possibility that Luke 15:7 may have been put in place by LukeR, using Luke 15:10 material in advance and adapting that part of the original parable which described the joy of the successful shepherd (Matt 18:13). Precedent for an editorial duplication of a statement at the end of two sub-units of tradition is provided by Luke 10:9, 11 (cf. Matt 10:7).

Third, it is easy to see why Matthew would have dropped the parable of the lost coin. The imagery of the lost sheep parable suited his pastoral purpose and could readily accommodate the loaded religious language of 'being led astray', whereas the latter could not be achieved with the coin imagery. Moreover, the image of the housewife would hardly appeal to this evangelist when depicting concerned church leaders.[10] Matthew was no instinctive sympathizer with the

[9]Cf. Fitzmyer, *Luke I-IX* 1081, commenting that the ten drachmas are 'not a great sum of money'.

[10]Lambrecht, *Once More* 38.

ordination of women! To these considerations can be added some others:

Fourth, a pairing of male + female persons in matching traditions is well attested elsewhere in Q. The men of Nineveh are matched by the queen of the south (Q 11:31–32), those who farm by those who spin (Q 12:24, 27–28), the man with the mustard seed by the woman with the leaven (Q 13:18–20), the two farming men by the two grinding women (Q 17:34–35).

Fifth, the presence of 'the angels' in both Matt 18:10 and Luke 15:10 suggests that either or both were in Q,[11] and it would certainly be typical of Q to support an initial demand with two illustrations, with verbal overlap evident at start and finish.

We are now in a position to comment on the Matthew/Luke discrepancies in order to reach back to the Q originals of these two parables. There is no need to concentrate on trivial verbal variations with no perceptible effect on meaning, but only on those differences which are determinative in some way.

First, Matthew's repeated use of the verb πλανᾶν is likely to be redactional in view of his obvious interest in the theme of religious enticement (Matt 24:4, 5, 11, 24). Luke would have every reason to accept such a term if he found it here, for he too knows the threat of persons' being 'led astray', and the risk of damage to the members of the flock both from outside and from inside (Luke 21:8/Mark 13:5–6; Acts 20:29–30). The term πλάνη itself is unlikely to carry the heavy sense of theological deviation to the worship of other gods,[12] but for someone like Matthew who steers well away from the notion that Jew/Gentile boundary laws like sabbath and food regulations are set aside, and who mounts a fierce critique of ἀνομία, it is likely that the milder sense of straying from the Torah is in mind.[13] One may add that the agreement between Matt 18:14 and Luke 15:4, 6, 8 in using the verb ἀπολλύναι confirms the Luke/Q correspondence.

Second, the less than total certainty that the search will be successful (Matthew diff Luke) probably reflects the disagreeable realities of the pastoral situation. Not all attempts at religious

---

[11] Schürmann, *Untersuchungen* 123.
[12] Cf. Deut 4:19; 11:28; 13:5–6; 30:17.
[13] Cf. Ps 119:110; Wis 2:21; 5:6.

rescue succeed. Could it be that this sombre view antedates the more jubilant outlook of the Lucan version with its vision of success? It is possible, but not probable. For Q clearly emphasized the ultimate joy of the seeker (Matt 18:13/Luke 15:5), but Matthew's stress on the obligation to seek makes the statement about that joy redundant. Put another way, Matthew's point is made by 18:12, 14 alone. Yet if, and we shall return to this point, the thrust of the parable is the parallel between joy on the human level and joy on the heavenly level, the strongest possible basis for that joy seems most appropriate, and it is Luke's version which carries the greater conviction.

Third, there must be serious doubt about the provenance of most of Luke 15:5, 6 from Q.[14] Not only is the Matthew/Luke overlap confined to 'and finding . . . he rejoices', but also the essence of a 'Which of you. . .?' parable is the appeal to common experience, which the return straight home (not to the other sheep!) and the celebratory meal following the recovery of a single sheep certainly are not.[15] Moreover, while the summoning of friends and relations might well be the kind of detail Matthew omits, it is also very much the kind of detail Luke appreciates.[16] The same applies to 'he lays it on his shoulders', an imaginative development of the idea of the journey contained in the basic parable.[17] Once the Lucan text has been, as it were, pruned back to 'and finding . . . he rejoices', together with the application (15:7, paralleled rather more within the parable than its application in Matthew), we are in a position to assess the parallels with Matt 18:13. These consist of an introductory 'finding' clause, a connection between joy and the finding as such, the use of 'I say to you' to preface the affirmation about joy, a repeated reference to the one in contrast to the ninety-nine, and a negative reference to the ninety-nine themselves. If we remove the bulk of 15:5, 6,[18] without which 15:7 could not be an application, and if we simultaneously recognize that Matt 18:13 is superfluous to the evangelist's purpose, which is achieved by

[14]Linnemann, *Parables* 67–8; Bultmann, *History* 171.
[15]Linnemann, *Parables* 68.
[16]Harnack, *Sayings* 93; Schulz, *Spruchquelle* 388.
[17]Linnemann, *Parables* 67: 'a decorative accretion'.
[18]S. Légasse, *Jésus et l'Enfant* (Ebib; Paris: Gabalda, 1969) 57; Linnemann, *Parables* 67; H. Merklein, *Gottesherrschaft* 187.

Matt 18:12, 14 alone, then it begins to emerge that at this point Matthew stands closer than Luke to Q. That is, the final assertion must originally have been (like Matt 18:13) part of the parable itself and not a concluding application. This is confirmed by the extensive evidence of LukeR which emerges in Luke 15:7. There is a match with Mark 2:17/Luke 5:31–32 in respect of the contrast between the righteous and the sinners, the phrase 'to have need', and the repentance theme. Everything adds up to Luke's interest in conversion. With Matthew/Luke agreement in the use of the verb 'to be lost' at the end, it is probable that LukeR imposed an extra stratum on what was originally a simpler statement about 'the one which was lost'.

Drawing together the decisions taken above concerning the Q content of the parable of the lost sheep, and taking account of the close correspondence of the two parables to one another, we may venture the following reconstruction of the earlier versions:

τίς ἄνθρωπος ἐξ ὑμῶν ἔχων ἑκατὸν πρόβατα, ἐὰν ἀπολέσῃ ἐξ αὐτῶν ἕν, οὐχὶ ἀφήσει τὰ ἐνενήκοντα ἐννέα ἐν τῇ ἐρήμῳ καὶ πορευθεὶς ζητεῖ τὸ ἀπολωλὸς ἕως εὕρῃ αὐτό; καὶ εὑρὼν αὐτό, λέγω ὑμῖν ὅτι χαίρει ἐπ' αὐτῷ μᾶλλον ἢ ἐπὶ τοῖς ἐνενήκοντα ἐννέα τοῖς μὴ ἀπολωλόσιν.

ἢ τίς γυνὴ δραχμὰς ἔχουσα δέκα, ἐὰν ἀπολέσῃ δραχμὴν μίαν, οὐχὶ ἅπτει λύχνον καὶ σαροῖ τὴν οἰκίαν καὶ ζητεῖ ἕως οὗ εὕρῃ; καὶ εὑροῦσα αὐτὴν χαίρει ἐπ' αὐτῇ μᾶλλον ἢ ἐπὶ ταῖς ἐννέα ταῖς μὴ ἀπολωλυίαις.

Each of these parables, and particularly the first, must now be examined in isolation for clues as to its original meaning and intention.

First, the nicely balanced unity of that first parable, with its two halves, first a question and then an affirmation, should be accepted. An alternative proposal[19] finds Jesus material in the question and assigns to Q-redaction the responsive affirmation. The latter is said to express the idea of eschatological joy for the encouragement of the Christian community as it separates itself from Israel. Simultaneously, so runs the argument, the idea of judgment on Israel is implied. This proposal is open to some criticism. Above all, the notion of a separation of the Christian

[19]Schenk, *Synopse* 113.

community from Israel in Q is ruled out, first, by the unlikelihood that Q was compiled sufficiently late in time to reflect such a development; second, by sayings like Q 16:17 which suggest that theologically Q was resistant to anything which deviated from a conservative position on the law and which might form a basis for schism; and third, by the definition of the single sheep's lostness as its separation from the rest of the flock, with the implication that its recovery is simultaneously the restoration of the wholeness of the flock. It may be that the proposal is influenced by the fact that the two rabbinic texts often cited as parallels, i.e. *Midr. Gen.* 86.4 and *Midr. Cant.* 1.1,[20] describe searches only, and thus only match what is in the question. Moreover, Matthew more or less ignored the affirmation and used the application (Matt 18:14) as the balancing statement. But he is no sure guide to meaning at the pre-Matthaean stage. Rather, we should be impressed by the distinctiveness of the Q form over against both rabbinic and Matthaean tendencies, and give proper weight to the shared concern with one/ninety-nine which holds the two essential parts of the parable together.

Second, joy emerges as the dominant theme. It is the one element in the second half which exceeds what is in the first half, and moreover it is introduced with the emphatic λέγω ὑμῖν. This joy relates not to the sheep's intrinsic value or distinction[21] but simply and solely to that estimation which obtains exclusively at the moment of recovery,[22] given the presupposition that the totality to which the one originally belonged is of immense importance to the owner.

Third, since joy is the dominant idea it must be the *tertium comparationis* which links story and reality. But which is the level of reality, and whose is the joy on that level? It might be the joy of certain human persons who have engaged in a search and achieved joyful success. That might point to Jesus and/or the disciples, flushed with missionary success and explaining it to some unspecified audience. Alternatively, it might be the divine joy, doubtless experienced as a result of a successful

[20]Billerbeck I.785; II.212.
[21]Contrast *Gos. Thos.* 107: 'because it was the largest'.
[22]Linnemann, *Parables* 66; Merklein, *Gottesherrschaft* 189; Weder, *Gleichnisse* 174.

search carried out by his duly authorized agents. Important for our present purpose is the fact that the parable by itself leaves this choice entirely open: without a context, ambiguity remains the order of the day. To reinforce this observation it is relevant to insist that we cannot opt for divine joy by exploiting the OT usage of shepherd imagery for God,[23] for the parable uses shepherding experience in ordinary life (τίς ἐξ ὑμῶν;) as a basis of argument. With the parable of the lost coin as a sequel using non-theologically-loaded imagery, this point is confirmed. And it is also relevant to note how unrealistic it is to insist that explanations of parables must be supposed *a priori* to be secondary. Again using the parable of the lost coin as an example, we may note how the parable/illustration in the rabbinic parallel, *Midr. Cant.* 1.1, has to be enclosed on either side by a statement of its significance, without which it would not be a teaching aid at all:

> If you seek after words of Torah as after hidden treasures, the Holy One, blessed be He, will not withhold your reward. If a man loses a *sela'* or an *obol* in his house, he lights lamp after lamp, wick after wick, till he finds it. Now does it not stand to reason: if for these things which are only ephemeral and of this world a man will light so many lamps and lights till he finds where they are hidden, for the words of the Torah which are the life both of this world and of the next world, might you not search as for hidden treasures?

So we must conclude that the parable in isolation leaves us unclear as to its meaning, and specifically as to the person(s) whose joy is the main concern.

Fourth, although we await further evidence provided by introduction and/or application, a provisional point can be made in advance about audience. It is frequently urged that, although Luke 15:1–3 is LukeR,[24] the intention of the parable has been correctly sensed there. The theory that the parable of the lost sheep originally functioned as a defence of Jesus' mission in the teeth of Pharisaic criticism is perfectly plausible, though there are no positive grounds for imposing such a restrictive definition upon the audience. All that we are so far permitted to say is that

---

[23]Isa 40:11; Ezek 34:11–16.

[24]Linnemann, *Parables* 69–71; Merklein, *Gottesherrschaft* 187, 190; Lambrecht, *Once More* 44.

those addressed by this parable and the succeeding one are the 'you' among whom there might be a man and a woman in the sort of situation described. The possibility of a role for this material in quite general proclamation, serving the purpose of invitation rather than defence,[25] is worth entertaining seriously. If so, the first corollary would be that the joy is experienced (by whoever) at the moment when the preaching is accepted and when the missionary appeal has been received. The second corollary would be that 'lostness' is not a problem exclusive to one subsection of the community of Israel – Israelites who have fallen away from the Torah, or tax-collectors, sinners and the like – but rather the situation of every person addressed. Every such person must consider himself/herself lost at that moment when he/she is addressed by the gospel, and found at that moment when he/she answers its call. With the covenant with Israel always in the background, this must mean that each person is being warned of the need to actualize all that is implicit in membership of the privileged community, to recognize the implications of a mission's being directed towards those who already rely corporately upon the grace of God, to accept the harsh reality of alienation from God, and to understand the joy which attends the restoration of the relationship. But the question remains: whose is the joy?

Agreement between Matthew and Luke extends to a reference to the angels in the immediate context (Matt 18:10/Luke 15:10), and further references to heaven and to God (Matt 18:14/Luke 15:7,10). Since God appears in Matthew in the typical MattR guise of the Father (cf. Matt 5:45 diff Luke 6:35), and an allusion to the angels is much more likely to have been edited out than edited in by Matthew in the specific saying at the end (cf. Matt 10:32–33 diff Luke 12:8–9), we can safely infer that 'joy in heaven in the presence of the angels of God' was originally in mind.

Unfortunately it is not possible to move with the same confidence towards a decision about the Q definition of the 'one' who occasions such joy among the angels. Matthew's μικρός language could easily be picked up by MattR from Mark 9:42 in the context of the general dependence of Matthew 18 upon Mark 9, though this could be countered by appealing to

[25]Schweizer, *Matthew* 369.

the use of terms used elsewhere like 'babes' (Q 10:21) and 'children' (Q 7:35). If the term μικρός stands for 'une catégorie humaine inférieure et négligeable'[26] and thus very readily for the poor to whom the gospel is preached (Q 6:20; 7:22), it would be possible without any sense of strain to read a reference to 'one of the little ones' as the cause of angelic joy in Q. Luke, on the other hand, refers to one repentant sinner. This could easily be a sign of LukeR here as in Luke 5:32/Mark 2:17, though once again Q does not lack references elsewhere to repentance (Q 3:8; 10:13; 11:32) and to sinners (Q 7:34). To dismiss the Lucan wording by means of the questions, 'Do sheep repent? Does, still more absurdly, a coin?'[27] is almost certainly to press an image too harshly, while the criticism that 'repentance is neither explicit nor implicitly assumed by the text'[28] may extract the parables from their most likely *Sitz im Leben* in a mission which calls for repentance in the face of the coming kingdom.[29] At the end of the day, therefore, we cannot exercise a strong preference for either form of words, because each would express naturally the concerns of the parables themselves and of Q. Those concerns converge in the renewal and wholeness of the people of God. To that end the mission of the Jesus of Q is directed. And the parables acclaim the acceptance of any person in Israel who for his or her own part accepts the call of Jesus which is simultaneously the call of God. Those who accept are themselves accepted. To use the terminology of the other Q saying which introduces the angels (Q 12:8), the person who confesses is confessed.

In conclusion, perhaps a speculative postscript may be added. The two parables are introduced in Luke with some scene-setting which, notwithstanding a recent attempt to establish the presence of some pre-Lucan tradition,[30] looks very much like LukeR throughout. At first sight Matthew's introductory exhortation, 'See that you do not despise one of these little ones; for I tell you that their angels in heaven always behold the face of my Father who is in heaven' (Matt 18:10), seems to call for similar

[26]Légasse, *Enfant* 53, citing 1 Sam 9:21; 2 Kgs 18:24; Isa 60:22.
[27]J Drury, *Tradition and Design in Luke's Gospel* (London: Darton, Longman & Todd, 1976) 158.
[28]Merklein, *Gottesherrschaft* 191.
[29]See the sensible corrective registered by Lambrecht, *Once More* 41.
[30]Weder, *Gleichnisse* 168–9.

evaluation as MattR. This is particularly the case with Matt 18:10a. For καταφρονεῖν occurs elsewhere in the gospels only at Matt 6:24/Luke 16:13 (Q!), but the influence of this last saying on Matt 18:10a becomes a more likely inference when we observe the proximity of the parable of the lost sheep (Q 15:4–7) to Q 16:13 within the Lucan Q sequence. In sense also the despising of little ones could easily be an idea transplanted from Mark 10:13–16, especially when the influence of that pericope has already been evident shortly beforehand in Matt 18:3. Matt 18:10b is, however, much more difficult to explain as MattR.

What is meant by the assertion that 'their angels see the face of God'? As has frequently been observed, 'seeing the face' is often associated with membership of a kingly court.[31] But Matt 18:14b can hardly be saying simply that there is such a court in heaven or even that there is a counterpart-relationship between the members of the heavenly court and the earthly personnel in view. It is much more probable that a more profound meaning of 'seeing the face' as a sign of God's favour and acceptance is involved, and that this in turn is taken to mean that those on the earthly plane enjoy such favour and acceptance. In this connection it may be noted, first, that not seeing the face (especially God's face) is tantamount to experiencing disfavour, refusal, rejection, and judgment because of sinfulness;[32] second, and conversely, seeing the face (especially God's face) is to enjoy unreserved favour and acceptance,[33] that is, a full and unstrained relationship; third, and unsurprisingly, within the large collection of passages which speak about 'seeing the face' there are not a few which attribute the experience to certain distinguished, even mediatorial, figures: Moses, Samuel, Jeremiah, and the like.[34] The vision of God enjoyed by the angels in Matt 18:10b is therefore a sign of great favour and correspondingly a firm indication that their earthly counterparts enjoy acceptance and favour.

Such an affirmation in Matt 18:10 is in serious tension with the ensuing parable in its Matthaean form. For that parable

[31] 2 Kgs 25:19; Esth 1:14; Jer 52:25.
[32] Deut 31:17–18; Ps 88:14; Jer 33:5.
[33] Gen 33:10; Num 6:25–26; Tob 13:6.
[34] Deut 34:10; Jer 15:1; 18:20. Cf also angelic mediators: Tob 12:12–15; *1 Enoch* 15:2; 40:6; 104:1.

addresses the problem of certain persons' having been led astray into religious apostasy and by no means certainly being brought back into the Christian church by the efforts of the orthodox pastor. The introductory affirmation comments on those who are lost, some of whom may never be found. That religious apostates can be said to enjoy the favour of God is simply inconceivable, and an alternative explanation of the data has to be found. This is not difficult. It is, first, that Matt 18:10b preserves part of a pre-Matthaean introduction to the two parables, and describes the situation after all the lost have been found; and, second, that Matthew's redactional activity has shown itself (not for the first time) to be lacking in thoroughness and consistency.

If this proposal commends itself it points to a neat and tidy structure within Q at this point: an introductory assertion referring to the angels, with two parables following, and the second of the two parables ending with another matching reference to the angels. The angels' direct vision of God, and their joy resulting from the retrieval of their previously lost protegés, are two aspects of a single reality.

7

Prayer and the Kingdom

The Q material studied so far has brought to light a community whose faith was personally centred on Jesus as Son of man, but whose commitment to the message proclaimed by Jesus as prophet was intense. The message of Jesus, if the broad range of Q traditions is to be believed, was focussed on the kingdom. And as the kingdom remained the focus of proclamation (Q 10:9), so too did the cause of the kingdom become the pre-occupation of prayer (Q 10:2). Several Q traditions reinforce that impression, notably though not exclusively the Lord's Prayer (Q 11:2–4). But that is not where this study will begin. Instead it will take its cue from the parable of the friend at midnight (Luke 11:5–8), arguing that this parable did indeed figure in Q, and that the Q complex to which it belongs extends our understanding of the concerns and the circumstances which determined the existence of this group of adherents of Jesus.

1. The Friend at Midnight. Luke 11:5–8.

Two contrasting descriptions of this parable expose the central dilemma involved in its interpretation and the reconstruction of its tradition history. According to one description it is 'the parable of the importunate friend', which means that the spotlight is directed at the petitioner.[1] According to another description it is 'the parable of the friend who was aroused in the night by a request for help', which means that this time the spotlight is directed at the petitioned person.[2] Which is correct?

[1] Manson, *Sayings* 267.
[2] J. Jeremias, *The Parables of Jesus* (NTL; London, SCM: 1963) 157. Similarly, J. M. Creed, *The Gospel according to Saint Luke* (London: Macmillan, 1930) 155.

Does the thrust of the parable come from the conduct of the person whose embarrassment at being unable to offer hospitality leads him to turn to his friend for help, or does it come from the conduct of the friend who stirs himself from sleep to provide that help?

Scarcely less of a dilemma is the term ἀναίδεια. This might stand for the conduct of the petitioner, and indeed does so according to the majority view. In this case it normally represents persistence.[3] But there is an alternative. It might relate to the conduct of the person who is petitioned, and in this case the suggestion is that it refers to his anxiety not to suffer shame.[4]

A further complication is created by the evident influence upon interpreters of the parable of the unjust judge (Luke 18:1–8). In detail (i) some even suggest that Luke 11:5–8 and 18:1–8 form a pair, a 'Doppelgleichnis',[5] or that the one is 'almost a doublet' of the other.[6] The symmetry between a petitioning man in 11:5–8 and a petitioning woman in 18:1–8 has attracted attention.[7] But even more influential has been the common theme: the idea of giving way under pressure. B. T. D. Smith, for example, spelt out this parallelism: First, both traditions illustrate the truth that persistence will achieve its purpose. Second, in both the petitioned person acts out of self-interest. Third, in both the argument works, he believes, *ex dissimilitudine*. As Joachim Jeremias later put it: 'If persistence can induce an unwilling neighbour or an unscrupulous judge to grant a request, with what confidence should we persevere in asking when our petitions are addressed to our heavenly Father!'[8] (ii) Others, even when drawing distinctions between Luke 11:5–8 and 18:1–8, still evidently feel under pressure to discuss one when treating the other. Important in this connection is Gerhard Delling.[9] After noting the alleged concern of both traditions with a person who finally, albeit unwillingly, gives

[3] B. T. D. Smith, *The Parables of the Synoptic Gospels* (Cambridge: CUP, 1937) 148.
[4] Jeremias, *Parables* 158.
[5] Grundmann, Lukas 233.
[6] Jeremias, *Parables* 157.
[7] Ernst, *Lukas* 365.
[8] *Parables* 147–8.
[9] 'Das Gleichnis vom gottlosen Richter', *ZNW* 53 (1962) 1–25, esp. pp. 1–4.

assistance, Delling went on to point out three contrasts. First, 11:5–8 is formally a 'question + answer' unit which is designed to bring a response from the hearers, whereas 18:1–8 is a narrative. Second, 11:5–8 is as such a 'question + answer' unit self-contained, whereas 18:1–8 includes an application. Third, 11:5–8 stands content-wise closest to 11:11–13 in the range of parables, whereas the nearest counterpart of 18:1–8 is 16:1–7. It will be necessary later to comment on the similarity *and dissimilarity* of 11:5–8 and 11:11–13, but for the moment it is enough to observe that the problems of 11:5–8 cannot be solved without some reference to 18:1–8. In attempting to solve these problems we shall move forward in several stages.

First of all, the problem represented by the two titles is substantial. It probably ought not to be tackled by supposing that the parable contained a double message. Josef Ernst tried to do this, inferring (i) that there is reward in petitioning God again and again without flagging, and (ii) that God is alert to human need and provides help.[10] Howard Marshall adopted the same approach, referring to (i) God's willingness which is thrown into relief by the householder's unwillingness, and (ii) the need to go on offering prayer despite the lack of an immediate answer.[11] Over against these suggestions one must urge (i) that the splitting of the parable's message into two is in principle questionable and that a decision must be made concerning whether the petitioner or the person petitioned is the focus of interest; (ii) that comparable uncertainties arising elsewhere in the parable material, e.g. in Mark 4:26–29, where the two different proposed titles 'The seed growing secretly' and 'The patient landowner' indicated similar confusion, pointed to the literary character of the problem and therefore to a solution which isolated earlier and later strata within the tradition. Perhaps the same applies to Luke 11:5–8.[12]

The essential requirement for progress in this direction is the clarification of Luke 11:8: 'though he will not get up and give him anything because he is his friend, yet because of his ἀναίδεια . . .'. The LXX usage of ἀναίδεια is an important aid,

[10]*Lukas* 366.
[11]*The Gospel of Luke* (Exeter: Paternoster, 1978) 462.
[12]See H.-W. Kuhn, *Ältere Sammlungen im Markusevangelium* (SUNT 8; Göttingen: Vandenhoeck & Ruprecht, 1971) 106–7.

but not a sufficient one in view of J. D. M. Derrett's quite proper warning that the term may have changed its meaning in the course of time.[13] Therefore, Josephus may as a contemporary of Luke be even more important.

In the LXX the ἀναίδεια word group sometimes conveys the sense of harshness/hardness, a quality explained in terms of 'having no respect for the old and showing no favour to the young'.[14] Elsewhere it can denote ruthlessness.[15] Several times it points to greed or a tendency to grasp.[16] In the remaining passages the emphasis varies, but the general idea is brazenness or mindless inflexibility.[17] Perhaps the text closest to Luke 11:8 is Sir 40:30:

> In the mouth of the shameless (ἐν στόματι ἀναιδοῦς) begging is sweet, but in his stomach a fire is kindled.

In Josephus ἀναίδεια again varies in sense from passage to passage. In some it stands for irresponsibility or a gross absence of honour and integrity.[18] In others the stress is on daring or putting a bold face on a matter.[19] In all these cases it is made clear that ἀναίδεια belongs with effrontery and lack of principle, all in aid of achieving something out of self-interest. A further group of passages brings to the fore an element of stubbornness and persistence, and two of these call for comment with Luke 11:8 in mind.[20] The first such passage is *J.W.* 6.3.3 §199:

> Why tell of the soulless shamelessness (ἡ ἐπ' ἀψύχοις ἀναίδεια) of the famine? For I am about to tell of an act unparalleled in the history of Greeks or barbarians.

The unparalleled act is a mother's eating her son, but ἀναίδεια probably refers back to frenzied grasping after food, to persist-

---

[13]'The Friend at Midnight: Asian Ideas in the Gospel of Luke', *Donum Gentilicum. New Testament Studies in Honour of D. Daube* (ed. E. Bammel, C. K. Barrett and W. D. Davies; Oxford: OUP, 1978) 78–87, esp. p. 84.

[14]Deut 28:50; Bar 4:15.

[15]Dan 2:15; 8:23–24.

[16]1 Kgdms 2:29; Prov 7:13; Isa 56:11; Sir 23:6; 26:11.

[17]Prov 21:29; 25:23; Eccl 8:1; Jer 8:5; Sir 25:22; 40:30.

[18]*Ant.* 20.8.3 §154; *J.W.* 1.14.1 §276; 1.24.7 §490; 2.14.2 §278.

[19]*Ant.* 20.8.8 §181; *Ap.* 1.8 §46; 2.2 §22; 2.2 §26; 2.40 §287; *J.W.* 1.31.4 §616; 6.6.2 §337; *Life* 65 §357.

[20]See also *Ant.* 13.11.3 §317 = *J.W.* 1.3.6 §84.

ence which is indifferent to all normal canons of human behaviour. The second passage is *Ant.* 17.5.5 §119:

> Have you (Antipater) indeed so much confidence in your shame-lessness (τῇ ἀναιδείᾳ πέποιθας) that you ask to be put to the torture and say that the confessions extracted from those already tortured are false, in order that those who would save your father from you may be rejected as not having told the truth, while the words under torture spoken by you may be accepted as trustworthy?

This is clearly a case of extreme self-confidence which produces persistence in maintaining a position under pressure. Finally, there are two passages in Josephus where the persuasive power of much speaking is in mind. The first of these is *J.W.* 1.11.3 §224:

> Malichus succeeded by effrontery (ἀναίδεια) in outwitting Antipater's sons.

The context shows that this involved the intervention of me-diators, Phasael and Herod, who used 'a multitude of excuses and oaths (πολλαῖς ἀπολογίαις καὶ ὅρκοις)'. The second passage is *J.W.* 1.25.3 §504:

> Pheroras observing this quick change in (Herod) the king's feel-ings and the paramount influence exercised on him by his friend Archelaus, despairing of saving himself by honourable means, sought protection in effrontery (ἀναίδεια): he threw himself on the mercy of Archelaus.

Here ἀναίδεια points to a policy of extreme persuasiveness, aiming to press one's case through until a favourable, even if reluctant, decision is achieved. The achieving of success at all costs may require the jettisoning of honour.

When the LXX and Josephus passages are compared with one another it emerges that the latter group differs from the former only in lacking any instance with a specifically sexual conno-tation.[21] But that was only a special case of the general idea of selfish grasping, and therefore the two groups of passages cannot be separated from one another or be shown to demonstrate a change in the meaning of ἀναίδεια. Derrett is therefore not

---

[21]Cf. Prov 7:13; Sir 23:6; 26:11.

correct in suggesting that by the time of Luke the word had lost its pejorative sense.[22] Most interesting is the question of what light these passages might throw on Luke 11:5–8. Here one can comment on some individual passages before dealing with the combined effect of them all.

First, the formulation 'having no respect for the old and showing no favour to the young' (Deut 28:50; Bar 4:15) is formally and in tone rather like 'neither fearing God nor regarding man' (Luke 18:2, 4). If Luke 18:1–8 were shown to be relevant, and if ἀναίδεια in 11:8 were describing the petitioned person, this might be significant. But the comparison proves in fact to be unproductive, for in 11:8 ἀναίδεια brings results, whereas in 18:4 results are achieved in spite of, rather than because of, the comparable attribute.

Second, the notion of intensive petitioning which might match 11:8 in context, is attested by Sir 40:30 and also by *J.W.* 1.11.3 §224; 1.25.3 §504.

Third, a persistent search for food brings *J.W.* 6.3.3 §199 alongside Luke 11:8.

Fourth, the evidence of *J.W.* 1.11.3 §224 is a notable pointer to the similarity between Luke 11:8 and Matt 6:7–8: 'In praying do not heap up empty phrases as the Gentiles do; for they think that they will be heard for their πολυλογία.' This similarity has occasionally been noticed, for example, by T. W. Manson[23] and J. M. Creed.[24] It is not made irrelevant by the difference in the content of the teaching in the two passages, for the occurrence of Matt 6:7–8 immediately before the Lord's Prayer (Matt 6:9–13/Luke 11:2–4) in the Matthaean sequence, and of Luke 11:5–8 immediately after the Lord's Prayer in the Lucan sequence, is a schematic correspondence calling for explanation. To this we shall return.

Most important of all is the fact that all the passages assembled above give an adverse connotation to ἀναίδεια. It is a quality which always calls forth disapproval. This is also the case in Luke 11:8, where two possible bases for action are contrasted, a good one (διὰ τὸ εἶναι φίλον) and an opposite one (διὰ τὴν ἀναίδειαν αὐτοῦ). Hence ἀναίδεια must be how the

[22]'Friend', 84.
[23]*Sayings* 267.
[24]*Luke* 155.

petitioned person characterizes and evaluates the conduct of the petitioner – it is a matter of 'causing trouble' (κοποί, v. 7). Such an evaluation of the petitioner's conduct turns out, of course, to throw adverse light on the character of the petitioned person: it should have been, but was not, sufficient that the petitioner was his friend, and therefore he (the petitioned person) is wicked. This has implications for the structure of 11:5–8. In the light of v. 8, taken in the above sense, v. 7 has to be re-garded as the actual response which he did make to the request in vv. 5b–6. *Aliter*, v. 8 presupposes (i) an initial request, vv. 5b–6; (ii) a rejection, v. 7; (iii) a further persistent repetition of the same request – not specified in the text! – between v. 7 and v. 8. The fact that this scheme is wrong (see below), although required by v. 8, will have important literary consequences.

The next step must be to assess the relationship between 11:5–8 and 18:1–8. This relationship must be taken seriously and cannot be overlooked, even though Delling is right about the difference in form between 11:5–8 and 18:1–8, and almost right about the similarity in form between 11:5–8 and 11:11–13. We shall return to the last point. But meanwhile the important parallels in content ought to be exposed: (i) A petitioner who is in need and who appeals to a person who can meet that need. (ii) Prominence given to the speech, hypothetical or actual, of the petitioned person: 11:7; 18:3b–5. (iii) The κόπος theme: 11:7; 18:5. (iv) The contrasting of the two possible reasons for taking action, one of which would be good but proves insuf-ficient, the other of which is poor but brings success: 11:8; 18:2, 4–5. (v) Emphasis in the present form of the parable on the petitioner rather than the person petitioned: 11:8; 18:1. (vi) Explicit comment on the manner of petitioning: 11:8; 18:1.

In the face of this list, however, the implications for 11:5–8 of the near certainty of LukeR in 18:1–8 must be weighed. In particular, the LukeR introduction in 18:1 changed the original concern and shifted the emphasis from the person petitioned to the petitioner. Specifically, the *manner* of petitioning became crucial and was regarded as a virtue in the petitioner even though it was an exasperation to the person petitioned. This idea had been present already in the parable, but now its prominence was powerfully increased.

Now 11:5–7 forms a unity within which can still be detected, following K. Beyer,[25] the Semitic tripartite combination of (i) an interrogative noun-clause whose subject is τίς, (ii) a relative clause setting out the real presupposition, and (iii) an assertive clause which forms the apodosis in relation to the protasis formed by (i) + (ii). This unity is widely recognized,[26] as is the implication of the question beginning τίς ἐξ ὑμῶν and requiring an answer, 'Of course, no one!'[27] So the response of the petitioned person is regarded as self-evident and certain. That means that any concern with his motives, such as his unwillingness to lose face, is wholly absent.[28] It also means that his words in v. 7 are not what he would or did say but only what he might theoretically have said: thus, entirely rightly, Josef Schmid: 'So könnte er sagen, wenn er nicht wollte, aber er hat es nicht getan.'[29]

A major and determinative discrepancy between 11:5–8 and 18:1–8 has come into view. Luke 11:8 made 11:7 reflect adversely on the character of the petitioned person, but it could only do so because the implication of 11:7, and specifically its role in 11:5–7, was misunderstood. It was taken as an actual and a negative response, whereas it was non-actual; it was taken to reflect adversely on the petitioned person, whereas it was intended to point to a positive response by someone who could be presumed to be honourable and sensitive to need. In short, 11:8 has imposed on 11:7 a scheme contributed by 18:2, 4–5. Correspondingly, κόπος is what brings results in 18:5 whereas it was irrelevant, because ignored, to the outcome in 11:7. That is, the outcome was achieved by means of κόπος in 18:5 but was intended to emerge without being affected by κόπος in 11:7. The natural inference is that LukeR is involved in 11:5–8. This was what changed the focus from the petitioned person to the petitioner, and thus to the manner of petitioning. This was what

[25] *Semitische Syntax im Neuen Testament* I.1 (Göttingen: Vandenhoeck & Ruprecht, 1962) 287–93.

[26] For example, Jeremias, *Parables* 158; Grundmann, *Lukas* 233; Ernst, *Lukas* 366.

[27] This form is paralleled in Luke 11:11; 14:28; 15:4; 17:7; contrast the different OT precedents in non-parabolic contexts, Isa 42:23; 50:10; Hag 2:3. The appeal to the hearer is the appeal of the similitude to everyday life: Linnemann, *Parables* 3.

[28] Against Jeremias, *Parables* 158.

[29] *Lukas* 198.

imported the idea of persistence although it had neither been mentioned explicitly[30] nor suggested implicitly in 11:5–7, itself the *total* description of the relevant data. This was what generated confusion and a twofold interpretation of the parable's meaning. This influence of 18:1–8 upon 11:5–8 can, however, be reversed, and the ensuing problems made to melt away, once we remove as LukeR intervention the words εἰ καὶ οὐ δώσει αὐτῷ ἀναστὰς διὰ τὸ εἶναι φίλον αὐτοῦ, διά γε τὴν ἀναίδειαν αὐτοῦ. Then there is left a thoroughly satisfactory parable in which the concluding declaration, now clear and unmuddled, genuinely does express the hearers' implied answer to the question posed in 11:5–7, 'Of course, no one!'.

τίς ἐξ ὑμῶν ἕξει φίλον καὶ πορεύσεται πρὸς αὐτὸν μεσονυκτίου καὶ εἴπῃ αὐτῷ, φίλε, χρῆσόν μοι τρεῖς ἄρτους, ἐπειδὴ φίλος μου παρεγένετο ἐξ ὁδοῦ πρός με καὶ οὐκ ἔχω ὃ παραθήσω αὐτῷ, κἀκεῖνος ἔσωθεν ἀποκριθεὶς εἴπῃ, μή μοι κόπους πάρεχε, ἤδη ἡ θύρα κέκλεισται, καὶ τὰ παιδία μου μετ' ἐμοῦ εἰς τὴν κοίτην εἰσίν· οὐ δύναμαι ἀναστὰς δοῦναί σοι; λέγω ὑμῖν, ἐγερθεὶς δώσει αὐτῷ ὅσων χρῄζει.

There is another problem which does not melt away, namely the application which the reconstructed parable is designed to support. But before that problem is tackled, some reservations registered by Christopher Tuckett concerning the argument thus far need to be addressed.[31] These reservations are (i) that if vv. 5–7 constitute a single rhetorical question, that question is considerably longer and grammatically more complex than the other τίς ἐξ ὑμῶν questions in Luke 11:11–12; 14:5, 28; 15:4, 8; 17:7; (ii) that 'the detailed way in which the response in v. 7 is articulated seems slightly strange if the response is intended to be only hypothetical in relation to the story'.[32] It is true that the

---

[30]This is recognized from time to time, though its literary-critical significance is left unexplored: Smith, *Parables* 147; Creed, *Luke* 158; Schmid, *Lukas* 198; Marshall, *Luke* 465. Derrett, 'Friend', 79, is almost right when he writes: 'In our parable there is no importunity . . . In fact the sleeper's dilemma arises at the first call.' This would have been entirely correct if Derrett had not retained the ἀναίδεια reference; his understanding of the word as confidence/boldness/unselfconsciousness, as over against lack of conviction, is not obviously encouraged by the details of the episode described.

[31]'Q, Prayer and the Kingdom', *JTS* 40 (1989) 367–76.

[32]'Prayer', 368–9.

rhetorical question is long, but if the question is to produce the answer 'Of course, no one!' it must consist of more than vv. 5–6. If it did not, the hidden presupposition would be that if one were visited at midnight by a friend, and one had no food to put before him, one would certainly not go to a second friend to ask for practical help. One would know that the second friend would definitely (not hypothetically) refuse such help. On that understanding of the parable there would also be no context for the final decision to give (v. 8), because contact between the petitioner and the person petitioned would have been precluded. But that is where v. 7 comes in. It describes vividly, fully and convincingly the constraint upon the petitioned friend arising out of the nocturnal situation, precisely in order to lay the heaviest possible stress on that concern which caused the constraint to be overcome. Because it was overcome it turned out with hindsight to be only theoretical. And what overcame that theoretical constraint was need (χρῄζει, v. 8). So the length and the structure of the single rhetorical question have to do with the storyteller's skill in displaying the principle that *necessitas vincit omnia!*

What is the theological relevance of the reconstructed parable? As things stand, there is not the slightest hint – merely an affirmation of the scarcely riveting or revolutionary idea that a request for help in observing the hospitality conventions will certainly be met on the basis of friendship in the ordinary human situation. This is banal and trivial, so much so that one must not only agree with the judgment that the parable 'lacks an explicit conclusion or application'[33] but also emphasize the scale of the resultant problem. The scale and seriousness of that problem can be underscored by once again returning to the 'sister parable' in Luke 18:1–8 and to the other τίς ἐξ ὑμῶν traditions. That part of the parable of the unjust judge which corresponds to Luke 11:5–8 is 18:2–5: while it is disputed how much of 18:6–8 constitutes the pre-Lucan application and ending, it is still plain that the need for such an ending was realized and met. In other cases of τίς ἐξ ὑμῶν traditions the required application is supplied, by narrative context in Luke 14:5 and by explicit spoken word in Matt 12:11(12); Luke

[33]Fitzmyer, *Luke II* 910.

11:11–12(13);[34] 14:28–32(33); 15:4–6(7), 8–9(10); 17:7–9(10). That means that if Luke 11:5–8 lacks an application it is unique. But does it lack an application? To ask that question is to open up the necessity of taking the further step of investigating the adjacent traditions in the Lucan sequence.

2. Prayer for Food. Q 11:11–13.

Within the Lucan sequence the positional closeness of 11:9–13 to 11:5–8, the remarkable formal similarity of 11:11–13 to 11:5–8, and the frequently asserted unity of 11:9–10 with 11:11–13, make it particularly important to consider the relationships of vv. 5–8, 9–10, and 11–13 to one another.

In Matt 7:9–11/Luke 11:11–13 there are a few variations in wording. Those which are not trivial are ἤ (Matt) diff δέ (Luke); ἄρτος + ἰχθύς (Matt) diff ἰχθύς + ᾠόν (Luke), together with λίθος + ὄφις (Matt) diff ὄφις + σκορπίος (Luke); ἀγαθά (Matt) diff πνεῦμα ἅγιον (Luke). In all three cases it is likely that Matthew reproduces Q, for the following reasons: (i) ἤ functions naturally in introducing the second member as a pair, as indeed it does in Q 11:12. In Luke there is such a pair, the two τίς ἐξ ὑμῶν parables, but in Matthew there is not. The best explanation seems to be that ἤ is a relic, a reminiscence of what was in Matthew's source.[35] The oddity, pointed out by Tuckett,[36] that Matthew should have included such a reminiscence is balanced by the fact that, whatever the explanation, the present Matthaean formulation in Matt 7:9 is itself odd. (ii) It is frequently suggested that Luke describes harmful objects whereas Matthew describes useless ones.[37] This should not be pressed, since ὄφις occurs in both.[38] But two considerations do support a Matthew/Q

---

[34]It is inconceivable that vv. 11–12 ever existed without v. 13, and scarcely possible that v. 13 would exist without vv. 11–12, cf. R. A. Piper, 'Matthew 7,7–11 par Luke 11,9–13: Evidence of Design and Argument in the Collection of Jesus' Sayings', *Logia* 411–8, esp. p. 412.

[35]Otherwise, Schulz, *Spruchquelle* 161.

[36]'Prayer', 369.

[37]Klostermann, *Lukasevangelium* 126; W. Foerster, 'ὄφις', *TDNT* 5.576–82, esp. p. 579; Ernst, *Lukas* 367.

[38]Klostermann, *Lukasevangelium* 126; Foerster, *TDNT* 5.580; Schulz, *Spruchquelle* 162; Schweizer, *Matthew* 173.

correspondence here: first, bread and fish together constitute basic ordinary food (cf. Mark 6:38, 41, 43; John 21:9, 13),[39] while, second, ὄφις + σκορπίος is a combination used shortly beforehand in Lucan material (10:19), which can scarcely be a coincidence since σκορπίος occurs nowhere else in the NT apart from Rev 9:3, 5, 10. (iii) The *a minore ad maius* argumentation of Q 11:13 requires that the Father's gift should correspond to the earthly father's gift, that is, ἀγαθά. Luke's interest in the Holy Spirit makes such an insertion by him explicable.[40] The Q material probably therefore ran:

ἢ τίς ἐστιν ἐξ ὑμῶν ἄνθρωπος, ὃν αἰτήσει ὁ υἱὸς αὐτοῦ ἄρτον, μὴ λίθον ἐπιδώσει αὐτῷ; ἢ καὶ ἰχθὺν αἰτήσει, μὴ ὄφιν ἐπιδώσει αὐτῷ; εἰ οὖν ὑμεῖς πονηροὶ ὄντες οἴδατε δόματα ἀγαθὰ διδόναι τοῖς τέκνοις ὑμῶν, πόσῳ μᾶλλον ὁ πατὴρ ὁ ἐξ οὐρανοῦ δώσει ἀγαθὰ τοῖς αἰτοῦσιν αὐτόν.

Another of the τίς ἐξ ὑμῶν; parables here demands a decision from the hearers: an appeal is again made to an everyday norm with a view to provoking the answer, 'Of course, no one!' The everyday situation is one in which the basic necessities of human life are required and a request for them lodged by a son with his father. This might in itself be thought curious, since it is also an everyday norm that the father has a responsibility to provide food for his family and therefore should not need to be asked. That being so, the use of this scheme clearly has a different purpose: the illustration is moulded by the specific situation of those addressed and not simply by the general and commonplace situation. That means, first, that those addressed need ordinary food, and, second, that God as the provider of ordinary food is going to be seen to do so specifically in his capacity as Father. To make this even more precise, it means that those addressed are disciples committed to the cause of Jesus and the kingdom.

[39]Schmid, *Matthäus* 147; P. S. Minear, *Commands of Christ* (Nashville: Abingdon, 1972) 118: 'a cheap minimal diet for survival in Palestine'.

[40]Schulz, *Spruchquelle* 162. The counter-argument mounted by H.-T. Wrege, *Die Überlieferungsgeschichte der Bergpredigt* (WUNT 9; Tübingen: Mohr, 1968) 108, is that the present Lucan form of the saying presupposes the pre-Easter gift of the Spirit, thus clashing with Luke's pattern of a post-Pentecostal endowment. But Luke is not so meticulous an historian as to keep the Spirit out of the period before Pentecost (cf. 1:15, 17, 35, 47, 67, etc.), and in 11:13 it may well be that 'he *peshers* the original "good things" to the post-Pentecostal reality': E. E. Ellis, *The Gospel of Luke* (NCB; London: Nelson, 1966) 164.

They are the same persons as those to whom the earliest form of Q 12:22–31 is addressed.[41] It also means, first, that the point of the alternative gifts of stone and serpent is not that they are useless or harmful, or that they are deceptive because they look like bread and fish, but simply that they *are not* bread and fish and so leave the original request unanswered and the basic need unmet. Second, the inference must be that the 'good things' given by the heavenly Father are not eschatological blessings or 'the gifts of the messianic age'[42] but present this-worldly food.

This last conclusion has been subjected to searching criticism by Christopher Tuckett, who argues that the 'good things' which the Father will give to those who ask him are 'the gifts of the Eschaton'.[43] In Tuckett's view, the Q Christians have a certain priority laid down for them. They are *not* to be concerned with the material needs of life, but rather to devote their entire energies to the kingdom of God. A consequence of this is that the term ἀγαθά (Q 11:13), reflecting the overrriding importance attached to the kingdom of God, does not stand for ordinary food.

This proposal is in my view correct in its understanding of the priority which is being laid down for the Q Christians, but incorrect about the way that priority is established. On this latter score, resistance can be based on two main patterns of

[41]Jeremias, *Parables* 144–5 (following A. T. Cadoux) argues that the parable is directed at opponents, because (i) πονηροὶ ὄντες is used when addressing opponents in Matt 12:34; (ii) τίς ἐξ ὑμῶν; sayings in general are addressed to opponents; (iii) Luke 11:13 changes from second to third person usage in the phrase τοῖς αἰτοῦσιν αὐτόν. These arguments are not convincing. (i) πονηροὶ ὄντες is designed to describe man (even if he acts well) over against God, so that the *a minore ad maius* argumentation can work, cf. Zeller, *Mahnsprüche* 130, citing Sir 17:31; Mark 10:18. Matt 12:34 is MattR and therefore no firm guide to meaning at the Q stage. Moreover, Q 6:35 also very probably means to say that the whole of humanity is evil. (ii) τίς ἐξ ὑμῶν; material elsewhere in the gospels is not clearly addressed to opponents: the audiences vary between critics (Luke 15:4 diff Matt 18:12), potential followers (Luke 14:28), uncertain (Matt 12:11/Luke 14:5), probably disciples (Luke 17:7), and certainly disciples (Luke 11:5; Matt 6:27/Luke 12:25) – which serves to bring Luke 11:5, 11 particularly close together. (iii) The statement in Luke 11:13 moves to the third person usage because it is setting out a general principle, and in this respect matches Luke 11:11–12 (cf. 15:4).

[42]Jeremias, *Parables* 145; similarly, W. Grundmann, 'ἀγαθός', *TDNT* 1.10–17, esp. p. 15.

[43]'Prayer', 372–6.

argument. The first has to do with how the term ἀγαθά is used in the immediate context and more widely. The second has to do with evidence contributed by other Q traditions.

The first pattern of argument concentrates on the following considerations: (i) The priority of ἀγαθά over πνεῦμα ἅγιον rested upon the correct perception that the gifts of the heavenly and earthly fathers must match. That matching must cover content as well as form if the *a minore ad maius* logic is to be viable. (ii) Many texts in Jewish tradition use τὰ ἀγαθά in the sense of unspecified, not eschatological, blessings.[44] Some place distinct emphasis on the material.[45] A sizable group understands τὰ ἀγαθά as food,[46] alongside those which see τὰ ἀγαθά as God's provision for the needy.[47] Unless the second pattern of argument makes this conclusion impossible the inference would be that the parable is asserting on the basis of an *a minore ad maius* comparison with earthly fatherhood that God as the good and heavenly Father will provide real material food for his needy and praying sons.[48] But does the second pattern of evidence, based on the wider spread of Q evidence, prove supportive?

The Q tradition about anxiety (Q 12:22–31) uses the ravens and the lilies to persuade the hearers to depend entirely on God as the fatherly provider of their material needs. What is specially important here is the redactional addition of no fewer than five extra elements, consisting of (i) the ψυχή/σῶμα saying (Q 12:23), (ii) the argument about life-span (Q 12:25), (iii) the call for conduct superior to that of the Gentiles (Q 12:30), (iv) the kingdom saying (Q 12:31), and (v) the vocative ὀλιγόπιστοι (Q 12:28).[49] In advance of the addition of those five elements the pre-Q tradition had employed wisdom-type arguments to encourage those who were bidden to detach themselves from

[44]Prov 25:22 LXX; Jer 8:15; 14:11, 19.

[45]Sir 32:13; Luke 12:18–19; 16:25.

[46]Pss 34:10; 107:9; Prov 17:1 LXX; Isa 1:19; 55:2; Jer 31:12, 14; Wisd 2:6; Luke 1:53.

[47]Sir 11:12; 39:25–27, 33.

[48]Zeller, *Mahnsprüche* 130–1: 'Nichts deutet darauf hin, dass etwa die erbetenen ἀγαθά erst in der messianischen Zukunft liegen. Vielmehr sollen die Angeredeten ihre alltäglichen, gerade die materiellen Nöte vor Gott tragen.'

[49]Arguments in favour of the secondariness of (i)-(iv) are set out above on pp. 31–35. As far as the word ὀλιγόπιστοι is concerned, it imports an element of rebuke which does not fit the reassuring and encouraging tone of the rest of the pre-Q tradition.

the everyday pattern of work by means of which the resources for food and clothing are normally generated. That the original speaker had been Jesus, and the audience those who were (or had identified with) the poor, in expectation that their fragile and vulnerable present would soon be overtaken by God's powerful exercise of kingship, is not hard to believe. But that is less important than the recognition that it is only with manifest difficulty that Q is able to retain and maintain the outlook of short-term expectancy. For in the five Q-redactional elements distinct evidence of stress and strain is discernible. The introduction of no fewer than three new arguments, (i), (ii) and (iii); the fact that one of them is a distinct weakening of the intellectual force of everything else which is here, that is (i); the addition of even a fourth affirmation that God may be trusted to provide, that is (iv); the introduction of a rebuke, that is (v) – all these elements suggest that in the situation from which or to which the editor of Q speaks, it is proving extremely difficult to keep hope alive and vibrant and to sustain the conviction that God really will, by whatever means, supply not only real clothing but also real food.

Evidence provided by other Q traditions paints in more of the picture which we have begun to sketch. Those with little faith are encouraged to exercise it boldly (Q 17:6). Those who live during a protracted period of time, that is to say, those who are affected by the delay of the parousia,[50] are encouraged to make a choice of life principles which will earn the accolade πιστὸς δοῦλος καὶ φρόνιμος (Q 12:42). Indeed the parable of the faithful and wise servant[51] is specially instructive. First, when compared with its prototypes, the Joseph saga and the Ahikar story,[52] it is distinctive in making the time of reckoning associated with the coming of the Lord a topic of reflection: χρονίζει μου ὁ κύριος. The behaviour described in Q 12:45b is not that of someone who expects the coming to occur, even though that occurrence has been delayed:[53] it is the conduct of

[50]Lührmann, *Redaktion* 69–70.

[51]The second half of the parable should not be regarded as an addition (cf. Q 6:47–49): rightly, Schulz, *Spruchquelle* 274.

[52]Cf. A. Weiser, *Die Knechtsgleichnisse der synoptischen Evangelien* (SANT 29; München: Kösel, 1971) 184–5, 194–5.

[53]Against Weiser, *Knechtsgleichnisse* 190.

someone who regards the delay as so great that the coming is no longer envisaged at all. That is, χρονίζειν here has its strong,[54] rather than its weak,[55] sense. Second, Klaus Beyer[56] and Matthew Black[57] have compared the introduction in Q 12:42 with other examples of the use of an interrogative particle in a conditional statement, and have drawn attention to three defining elements, that is, a noun clause question whose subject is τίς, plus a relative clause setting out the specific promise (these two parts forming the protasis), and an affirmation or rhetorical question (this the apodosis). When set alongside other examples of this scheme, for example, Deut 20:5, Psalm 25:12, Matt 7:9–10 and Matt 12:11/Luke 14:5, the awkward, intrusive and anticipatory character of the words πιστὸς καὶ φρόνιμος in Q 12:42 becomes clear. Their present position stems from a misunderstanding of the grammatical structure, whereby the qualities are understood as the basis of the initial appointment rather than the characterization of the subsequent behaviour. But if they are later additions the permitted inference is that already at the pre-Q stage the delay of the parousia had become an acute problem, and that since at the Q-redactional stage it could scarcely be less so an impassioned plea is being made for the maintenance of πίστις.

[54]Cf. Exod 32:1: 'When the people saw that Moses delayed (LXX: κεχρόνικεν) to come down from the mountain, they said, ". . . as for this Moses . . . we do not know what has become of him".' The associated scheme involving (i) a departure, (ii) a return, (iii) an inference that the person concerned will not come back at all, (iv) a consequent decision to brawl, and (v) final judgment, is remarkably similar to the parable. In Deut 23:21(22) the LXX reads οὐ χρονιεῖς ἀποδοῦναι αὐτήν in connection with a vow, and the issue is not the timing, but the occurrence or otherwise, of the performance. In Tob 10:4 the wife of Tobit says of the absent Tobias ἀπώλετο τὸ παιδίον, διότι κεχρόνικεν, i.e., delay has been so extended that the return itself is no longer expected. Of particular interest is Hab 2:3 LXX ἐρχόμενος ἥξει καὶ οὐ μὴ χρονίσῃ. The context affirms that the expectation of the coming one will certainly be realized, even though the period of waiting might suggest otherwise. Note (i) that the combination of ἥκω, ἔρχομαι, and χρονίζω is common to Hab 2:3 and the parable; (ii) that both Hab 2:4 and the parable counsel πίστις; (iii) that Hab 2:3–4 is used in Heb 10:37 specifically with reference to the delay of the parousia; and (iv) that all Q occurrences of the verb ἥκω, which is comparatively rare in the gospels, are eschatological: Matt 8:11/Luke 13:29; Matt 23:36 diff Luke 13:35; Matt 24:50/Luke 12:46.

[55]Thus, e.g. Gen 34:19; Judg 5:28; Prov 9:18; 31:21 LXX; Tob 5:8; 9:4, etc.

[56]*Semitische Syntax* 287–93.

[57]*Aramaic Approach* 118–9.

An identical situation is, of course, envisaged in the neighbouring Q parables. On the one side, the parable of the watchful householder (Q 12:39–40) does not mention πίστις, but it does describe a situation in which a coming is not expected, rather than one in which it is merely postponed. On the other side, there is the parable of the ten virgins which may well have a Q *Vorlage* in view of (i) the notable agreement between Matt 25:1–13 and Luke 12:35–38; 13:25; (ii) the extraordinary and incoherent combination in Mark 13:33–37 of elements derived from the parables of the householder, the ten virgins, and the talents, a combination suggesting an awareness of earlier tradition. If so, we notice another significant combination of the adjective φρόνιμος and the verb χρονίζειν. Finally, the parable of the talents must assuredly presuppose the same situation as does the parable of the faithful and wise servant, for its concern is also with the interval between the departure and return of the κύριος and with the requirement to be ἀγαθὸς καὶ πιστός during the interval.

When all this evidence is put together it serves to confirm the proposed *Sitz im Leben* of the Q redactional revision of both the ravens/lilies and the bread/fish traditions. Short-term future expectation has been stretched and strained by long-term delay. Yet members of the community must be resolute in πίστις. They must hold on valiantly, even if grimly, to the belief that God will in his own way and in all too real circumstances supply real food. Precisely because, in Tuckett's words, 'the overriding concern, which must dominate the Christians' lives, is the kingdom of God'[58] the rival concern with material survival has to be taken seriously, argued about determinedly, and *then* cleared away to provide space for what was supremely important. The piety of Q was not pietism: it took real problems seriously, and the solution to an all too pressing real problem was to be found, courtesy of the heavenly Father, in real, material, edible 'good things' (Q 11:13).

The relationship between the pre-Lucan versions of Luke 11:5–8 and 11:11–13 can now be clarified as a relationship of quite remarkable parallelism. (i) Both are τίς ἐξ ὑμῶν; formulations leading to an 'Of course, no one!' response. (ii) Both deal

[58]'Prayer', 376.

with petitioning. (iii) Both tackle the lack of the basic necessity of food. (iv) Both emphasize the willing gift of food by the person petitioned. (v) Both use *a minore ad maius* argumentation on the basis of the closest of human relationships.[59] (vi) Both point to a comparable truth about God as willing giver. But here is the critical difference: such an assertion is made in v. 13 but not in v. 8. In other words, the parable of the giving father is complete, but the parable of the giving friend is not. That observation, which is absolutely crucial, means that we have to turn to a consideration of Matt 7:7–8/Luke 11:9–10.

3. Asking, Seeking, Knocking. Q 11:9–10.

With the exception of the uncertain κἀγὼ ὑμῖν λέγω[60] the two versions of this tradition are identical in wording:

(κἀγὼ ὑμῖν λέγω) αἰτεῖτε, καὶ δοθήσεται ὑμῖν·
   ζητεῖτε, καὶ εὑρήσετε·
   κρούετε, καὶ ἀνοιγήσεται ὑμῖν·
πᾶς γὰρ ὁ αἰτῶν λαμβάνει,
   καὶ ὁ ζητῶν εὑρίσκει,
   καὶ τῷ κρούοντι ἀνοιγήσεται.

It is frequently affirmed that Q 11:9–13 is a unity, in spite of occasional suggestions by Rudolf Bultmann and others[61] that

---

[59]The next closest relationship to that within a family is that between friends, hence the pairing of such intimates inside and outside the family in a wide variety of texts: Deut 13:6; Job 19:14; Prov 17:17; Sir 29:10; Luke 14:12; 15:22–24, 29; 21:16; Acts 10:24.

[60]Some say this phrase is consonant with Lucan style, in that ὑμῖν occurs before λέγω elsewhere in Luke 6:27; 12:22 v.l.; 16:7, and add that Matthew would hardly have dropped such a phrase if he had known it: Schulz, *Spruchquelle* 161. Often it is recognized as providing a link with the preceding parable, though there is uncertainty about whether or not that would imply secondariness: Klostermann, *Matthäusevangelium* 125; Marshall, *Luke* 466. It may well be that, in spite of the expectation that Matthew would retain κἀγὼ ὑμῖν λέγω, we should follow Schürmann, *Untersuchungen* 226, in attributing the phrase to Q, since (i) there is no clear case of LukeR, and a strong possibility that Luke 6:27; 12:22 preserve a Q formulation; (ii) no linkage would be possible with the quite different preceding saying in Matt 7:6; (iii) no clash with the λέγω ὑμῖν of Luke 11:8 would be involved, since the latter draws out the logic of the situation previously described, while κἀγὼ ὑμῖν λέγω opens up the application of the whole episode.

vv. 11–13 were originally a separate block of tradition. Dieter Zeller, for instance, sees the overlap in αἰτεῖν + διδόναι as a sign of the unity of v. 9 with v. 13, the latter clarifying for the first time the sense of the former, and the most that he will allow is the possibility that v. 10 might be a redundant and unnecessary restatement of v. 9.[62] But an alternative possibility may be preferable, since (i) the community of theme and language in vv. 9, 11–13 does not necessarily demonstrate original tradition-historical unity, especially since catchword connections are a literary device favoured by Q; (ii) while the αἰτεῖν + διδόναι linkage can be noted, nothing comparable exists for κρούειν + ἀνοίγειν, a curious image to bring in without preparation and then not to follow up; (iii) vv. 11–13 make perfect sense in their own right and, like other units beginning τίς ἐξ ὑμῶν, are self-contained and need nothing by way of introduction. The independence of vv. 11:11–13 is therefore probable. This, however, merely makes the problem of vv. 9–10 more acute. To this problem a two-part solution is available.

First, v. 10 can be regarded as a secondary amplification of v. 9. If the context presumed by v. 10 were secular,[63] then it would be necessary to say that as a generalization πᾶς . . .[64] all its three parts are untrue. It is not generally true in the world at large that all asking, seeking and knocking proves successful. So a secular context can be eliminated. By a shift of main verbal form from present indicative to future passive (ἀνοιγήσεται), v. 10c contains the potential to remove all three parts of the saying away from a secular context into the context where God is at work. Then it is a religious statement about God and his reaction to human asking, seeking and knocking. It is not self-evident whether the future form of the verb is temporal or promissory in intention, but at least it is plain that God is the person whose giving is the petitioner's receiving; he it is who causes seeking to be successful in finding; he hears the knocking

[61]*History* 86–7; Schmid, *Matthäus und Lukas* 242; G. Bertram, 'κρούω', *TDNT* 3.954–7, esp. p. 955; Minear, *Commands* 117.

[62]*Mahnsprüche* 127–8.

[63]So J. Gnilka, *Das Matthäusevangelium I* (HTKNT 1; Freiburg-Basel-Wien: Herder 1986) 262.

[64]Q 11:10 contrasts with partial parallels such as Prov 2:4–5; 8:17; Wis 6:12 where a direct object is provided.

and opens the door. This dangerously optimistic generalization concerning God's working might to a degree be rendered safe by being narrowed to a concern only with eschatological realities, and this is the option which Tuckett selects: asking for and receiving the kingdom, searching for and finding the kingdom, knocking and being admitted to the kingdom.[65] But this will not work on the Q level! For in Matt 25:11–12 (cf. 7:22–23)/ Luke 13:25–26 those who knock in unmistakably eschatological circumstances are by no means admitted. Rather they are summarily dismissed with a melancholy message of exclusion. Consequently, v. 10 would have to be understood religiously but non-eschatologically by the readers of Q.

Once the non-eschatological meaning of v. 10 is established, it can be seen to be wholly tautologous in relation to v. 9. It says no more and no less: it merely uses the indicative in its main verbs, whereas v. 10 uses the imperative. The two together say in effect, 'Ask God, and you will receive, etc., because that is the way things are: when people ask God they receive.' V. 10 ostensibly aims to give strength and support (thus γάρ) to v. 9, but in fact it only restates it. It is insistent but at the same time artificial and redundant. Indeed one might go so far as to say that, if anything, v. 10 is the weaker form of the saying, since an imperative sense, concealed within the indicative in v. 10, is open and clear in v. 9. To say almost the same thing twice, as vv. 9, 10 do, is unlikely in two wholly unrelated sayings and redundant in a single bipartite saying. The natural inference would seem to be that one part is secondary in relation to the other, and that the repetition is to be explained in terms of both the editor's concern and the readership's *Sitz im Leben* in which a need of reassurance about divine provision is keenly felt.

Second, v. 9 has three components which are clearly intended to be synonymous. Curiously, no objects are supplied for the verbs. In respect of the first feature, there is no difficulty in seeing petition as the common topic, since αἰτεῖτε comes first,

---

[65]'Prayer', 375. The tendency to introduce eschatological expectation here is recurrent in the discussion: thus, Manson, *Sayings* 81: 'What is to be sought is the kingdom of God (cf. Luke 12:31); the door to be knocked at is the door which gives entrance to the kingdom of God.' Similarly, Minear, *Commands* 131; Edwards, *Theology* 109.

and since there are parallels elsewhere for metaphorical use of ζητεῖν[66] and κρούειν[67] for petitioning. In respect of the second feature, some object for the verbs is essential, partly because of the unconditionality of the promise of success in prayer (contrast the many OT passages which assert that religious seeking will only lead to finding if it is carried out wholeheartedly),[68] and partly because of the generality of reference (if this were an isolated statement it would be little more than a vague and blithely optimistic expression of prayer ideology, so unprotected as to be readily undermined by counter-examples).[69] As has become clear, this problem cannot be resolved satisfactorily by speculative provision of objects for the verbs, but rather by recognizing that the saying needs a setting which will provide such objects and therefore precision of definition.

Three possible contexts are theoretically available. First, there is that already provided within Q 11:9–13. The objects sought would then be the material necessities of life. But we have already canvassed the reasons for abandoning the unity of 11:9–13. Second, there is the context which might be provided by Q 12:22–31, taking into account the closeness of Matt 6:25–33/Q 12:22–31 and Matt 7:7–11/Q 11:9–13 in Matthew's Q sequence (especially when Matthew 5–7/Luke 6 parallels are set aside). This would make the kingdom of God (Matt 6:33/Q 12:31) the object of petition, and it would strikingly link 6:33 to 7:7 by the common verb ζητεῖν. But quite apart from the flaw already detected in the eschatological interpretation there are other fatal problems here, since (i) the tradition about anxiety is itself self-contained and needs no continuation; (ii) ζητεῖν in Matt 6:33/Q 12:31 extends far beyond prayer, and if prayer alone were to be envisaged by that saying the attitude recommended would be impossibly quietist and passive; (iii) nothing in Matt 6:25–33/Q 12:22–31 prepares for the κρούειν imagery. This brings us by a process of elimination to the third possible context – Luke 11:5–8!

---

[66] 2 Chr 34:21; Cant 3:1; 5:6; Isa 55:6; 58:2; 65:1; Jer 29:12–13. Its use as a synonym for 'to petition/pray' is long established: H. Greeven, 'ζητέω', *TDNT* 2.892–6, esp. p. 893.

[67] Judg 19:22; Cant 5:2; *b. Meg.* 12b: see Billerbeck I.458–9.

[68] Deut 4:29; 2 Chr 15:15; Prov 8:17; Jer 29:13; Wis 1:1–2; 6:12; Sir 6:27.

[69] Cf. Prov 1:28; Amos 8:12.

That Luke 11:5–8, shorn of the LukeR amplification in v. 8, led originally into Q 11:9 and belonged with it in Q, emerges as the solution to the cluster of problems we have reviewed. In its favour are the following points:

First, v. 9 provides the concluding inference from vv. 5–8. The latter passage is incomplete and shown to be so by the formal comparison and contrast with vv. 11–13. What is needed by vv. 5–8 is a statement about God as the giver who responds to petitions for basic human necessities. With its 'divine passives' v. 9 does just that. What is needed by v. 9 is some preceding material which will provide objects for its verbs. With their reference to necessary food vv. 5–8 do just that.

Second, the passage from vv. 5–8 to v. 9 is impressively smooth, for all three metaphors in the latter case – asking, seeking and knocking – are envisaged by the former.[70] Content-wise also, the link is natural, provided we dismiss the somewhat unproductive idea that v. 9 expresses 'beggar's wisdom'[71] born of the conviction that keeping on asking will eventually produce a response.[72] As E. Klostermann observed long ago, the saying contains no idea of *fatigare deos*,[73] and the same must be said of the pre-Lucan version of vv. 5–8.

Third, the two parables separately make the same point, that is, that God will most certainly provide for the material needs of his people. Together they make the same point by varying the scheme, using initially the setting of friendship, vv. 5–9, and then the setting of parenthood, vv. 11–13. An already existing personal relationship is involved in each case (friend/son), and it is this which ensures that human need will be treated with respect rather than indifference.[74] Such a pairing of illustrations is typical of the Q tradition.[75] And in literary terms, as already

---

[70]Against Tuckett, 'Prayer', 370.

[71]Jeremias, *Parables* 159–60.

[72]Similarly, Schmid, *Matthäus und Lukas* 242. Repeated requests for one gift should not be inferred from the present tenses of the verbs in Q 11:9, as the present tense in τοῖς αἰτοῦσιν αὐτόν (Q 11:13) shows. Instead, it is a matter of recurrent prayer, constantly answered, for recurrent necessities.

[73]*Lukasevangelium* 125.

[74]As an appeal for a decision on the basis of everyday known reality this is what brings action (because it defines the relationship between petitioner and petitioned), rather than the obligation of hospitality (which defines the relationship between the petitioner and his guest).

[75]See Q 7:33–34; 9:57–60; 11:31–32; 12:24, 27–28; 13:18–20.

noticed, the particle ἤ hinted at such a pairing at the pre-Matthaean stage.

Following this conclusion it is simply necessary to draw out the consequences for Q 11:10. This saying gives an impression of self-containedness to Q 11:9–10, which may well account for Matthew's dropping of the illustration but retention of its application. But for reasons already noted this impression is an illusion. Instead, Q 11:10 is an interruption. It aims, not very adroitly, to strengthen the argument that God will provide. And that was exactly what the saying, 12:25–26, did when interrupting the two illustrations in Q 12:24, 27–28. That interruption, together with the other secondary and not very adroit interruptions in Q 12:22–31, had the identical purpose of strengthening the argument that God will provide.

4. The Setting of Q 11:5–13.

The conclusions reached concerning the two traditions dealing with the promise of divine provision now need to be reinforced by clarifying the Q context into which they were intended to fit. This means considering briefly three other traditions: the Lord's Prayer, the critique of Gentile prayer, and the call to avoid anxiety.

First, Q 11:2–4. In Luke's use of Q material the pair of parables with which we have been concerned occurred immediately after the Lord's Prayer (11:2–4). Matthew confirms that in this respect Luke preserves Q, since (i) his 7:7–11/Luke 11:9–13 occurs very shortly after his version of the Lord's Prayer in 6:9–13, and (ii) he has adjacent to the Lord's Prayer in 6:7–8 a πολυλογία reference which matches the content of Luke 11:8.[76] If then Luke 11:2–4, 5–9, 10, 11–13 represents the original Q sequence, and if (as is widely agreed) the Q version of the Lord's Prayer involved the Lucan scheme and the Matthaean wording, it becomes possible to spell out the significance of this Q sequence. Crucial here is the interpretation of τὸν ἄρτον ἡμῶν τὸν ἐπιούσιον δὸς ἡμῖν σήμερον. The philological/linguistic discussion of ἐπιούσιος[77] having proved indecisive, it is to other

---

[76]See above, p. 206.

considerations that one must turn to determine the meaning. Several considerations do in fact point away from an eschatological interpretation of ἄρτος,[78] and towards what Schulz has described as 'das notwendige Existenzminimum'.[79] (i) If the eschatological meal were in mind the bread petition would be tautologous in relation to the two synonymous petitions for the hallowing of God's name and the coming of his kingdom.[80] (ii) The qualifying ἡμῶν is inappropriate to the eschatological meal.[81] The problem can scarcely be overcome by explaining that it is 'our' bread because the kingdom is promised to Christians.[82] (iii) Elsewhere, as for example in Q 4:3–4, ἄρτος is not a term which by itself and without qualification can indicate the eschatological meal:[83] all texts normally cited in favour of the latter either do not mention bread or contain a clarifying qualification.[84] (iv) While Christopher Evans has quite rightly pointed out that σήμερον should not be interpreted in such a way as to produce a tautology with ἐπιούσιος,[85] this still does not favour the eschatological interpretation. Rather, the request for *this* experience today would make eschatological expectation altogether too feverish. On the second day when the prayer was used, the problem of unanswered prayer would have arisen! The word 'today' therefore casts doubt on the eschatological interpretation and points to ἐπιούσιος as, in the words of E. Grässer, 'keine Zeitangabe . . . sondern eine Massangabe'.[86]

The bread petition in the Lord's Prayer is the first of the non-eschatological trio in a setting of intense eschatological longing

[77]The options are reviewed in W. Foerster, 'ἐπιούσιος', *TDNT* 2.590–9, esp. p. 597.

[78]Thus Jeremias, *The Prayers of Jesus* (SBT 2/6; London: SCM, 1967) 99–102.

[79]*Spruchquelle* 91.

[80]Schmid, *Matthäus* 131.

[81]Schweizer, *Matthew* 154; A. Vögtle, 'Der 'eschatologische' Bezug der Wir-Bitten des Vaterunser', *Jesus und Paulus: Festschrift für W. G. Kümmel* (ed. E. E. Ellis and E. Grässer; Göttingen: Vandenhoeck & Ruprecht, 1975) 344–62, esp. p. 350.

[82]Thus, R. E. Brown, 'The Paternoster as an Eschatological Prayer', *New Testament Essays* (London: Chapman, 1965) 217–53, esp. p. 241.

[83]Vögtle, 'Vaterunser', 350.

[84]See Matt 8:11; Luke 14:15; 22:29–30; Rev 7:16.

[85]*The Lord's Prayer* (London, 1963) 52.

[86]*Das Problem der Parusieverzögerung in den synoptischen Evangelien und in der Apostelgeschichte* (2nd ed.; Berlin: Töpelmann, 1960) 102. Similarly, Foerster, *TDNT* 2.597.

voiced by the preceding pair of petitions. It is also the only strictly non-religious petition, for the other two members of the trio deal with the religious problems of forgiveness and confessional loyalty under test. As such it stands out as a very special petition for material provision directed to God in his specifically fatherly capacity. It thus becomes the heading or the 'text' for an exposition/commentary which the pair of parables in Luke 11:5–9, 11–13 provides.[87] The association of the petition with the pair of parables is natural in view of (i) the common invocation of fatherhood, vv. 2, 13; (ii) the common idea of petition; (iii) the common reliance on a gift; (iv) the common concern with bread as a basic necessity of life, vv. 2, 5, 11–13; (v) the common awareness that supplies of bread run out and need to be renewed daily, vv. 2, 6, 9, 13. Precisely because there is a situation of need in the background of the prayer, and because the divine response (or lack of it) was critical, the confidence of the petitioners required and received carefully argued support.

Second, Matt 6:7–8. The structure of Matt 6:1–18 is determined by an introductory heading (v. 1) and three formally parallel subsections (vv. 2–4, 5–6, 16–18). The warning in vv. 7–8 against the Gentile practice of prayer, marked by βατταλογεῖν and πολυλογία, stands out not only because it breaks into this formal structure but also because content-wise (i) different persons are singled out for contrast,[88] i.e. not the hypocrites associated with the synagogues (vv. 2, 5) but the ἐθνικοί; (ii) the ground for criticism is not ostentation or hypocrisy in the presence of men but the expectation of gaining an answer to prayer by excessive verbosity; (iii) there is no concern about reward but simply the assurance that the Father knows the need in question. So vv. 7–8 did not originally belong to the parenetic collection which presently surrounds them.

Where did vv. 7–8 originate? MattR is a possibility,[89] but

---

[87]Tuckett is right to point out, 'Prayer', 375, that the bread petition scarcely dominates the prayer as it stands. He finds it odd that the following material should be attached to anything other than the dominant petition, the prayer for the kingdom. Yet the MattR addition of 6:14–15, a comment on the petition for forgiveness, provides a parallel for such a shift in the centre of gravity of the prayer.

[88]The reading ὑποκριταί in B syᶜ (Matt 6:7) is secondary and designed to smooth away the roughness of the transition from vv. 5–6 to vv. 7–8. It is in fact an indirect confirmation of the existence of the problem.

since Matthew is preoccupied with anti–Pharisaic polemic in this context it is somewhat unlikely. If v. 1 is attributed to the evangelist, if Matt 5:20 (which within the structure of Matthew 5–7 prepares for v. 1) is given due weight, if 23:5 contributes clear evidence of whom Matthew is attacking, then his pre-occupations are not only clear but also distinct from those of vv. 7–8. An alternative possibility would be some kind of M tradition, but we would then be faced with a most extraordinary set of coincidences which might better be regarded as pointing in the direction of Q. (i) Vv. 7–8 overlap with Q 12:30a. More important than the bare fact of overlap is the evidence that the combination of an adverse reference to Gentiles and an affir-mation that the Father knows about needs is specifically a Q editorial combination. Furthermore, it counts against MattR and for the link with Q 12:30 that the Q original there referred to ὁ πατὴρ ὑμῶν without addition, as does v. 8.[90] (ii) It is typical of Q redaction to ask for a standard of behaviour which surpasses that of Gentiles, and, moreover, to do so by attributing to Gentiles behaviour which may equally characterize Jews. Thus, first, concern about food and clothing (Q 12:30a) can hardly be exclusively a Gentile concern. Second, βατταλογεῖν/ πολυλογία could just as well be predicated of Jews in view of Dan 3:26–45, 52–90 LXX; 2 Macc 1:23–29; the Eighteen Benedictions and Kaddish material; and the range of evidence set out by Billerbeck.[91] Precisely such warnings had already been directed at Jewish personnel: Prov 10:19 LXX; Eccl 5:2; Sir 7:14. (iii) The links with Luke 11:5–8 are notable. For one thing, χρεία in Matt 6:8 matches δώσει αὐτῷ ὅσων χρῄζει in Luke 11:8. For another, Josephus, *J.W.* 1.11.3 §224 alerted us to the πολυλογία/ ἀναίδεια link.[92] If ἀναίδεια belongs to Luke 11:8 by virtue of LukeR, πολυλογία cannot belong to Matt 6:7 by virtue of MattR, and so must stem from Q. Therefore Luke responded editorially to pressure from both Luke 18:1–8 and Matt 6:8. It is entirely unsurprising that he should have omitted Matt 6:7–8, since the inconsistency between it and the point he was making in 11:8 was clear for all to see.

[89]Bultmann, *History* 133; Klostermann, *Matthäusevangelium* 54.
[90]Schürmann, *Untersuchungen* 119.
[91]I.403–6.
[92]See above, p. 206.

Third, Q 12:22–31. There is ample evidence that independent traditions were grouped in Q on the basis of community of theme: obedience to what is said in Q 6:46–49; 7:1–10, or John and Jesus in Q 7:18–23, 24–28, 31–35, or the unexpected coming of the Lord in Q 12:35–38, 39–40, 42–46. That being so, it is worth exploring the possible literary implications of the remarkable thematic correspondence between Q 11:2–4, 5–13 and 12:22–31.[93] The following points support a very tentative conclusion that in Q there was such a sequence. (i) In the Lucan setting the ravens/lilies tradition does not follow smoothly from the parable of the rich fool (Luke 12:13–21), whose critique of earthly acquisitiveness relates rather more directly to the following tradition about treasures in heaven (Q 12:33–34). Those addressed in Q 12:22–31 are not in the state of prosperity 'enjoyed' by the rich fool. The ravens/lilies tradition also does not follow naturally from Q 12:11–12, even though the verb μεριμνᾶν functions as a long-distance catchword joining 12:11, 22. The objects of anxiety in the two complexes are quite different. Moreover, the phrase διὰ τοῦτο λέγω ὑμῖν, which was in Q 12:22a, requires that there shall have been an identical object of anxiety mentioned immediately beforehand. This suggests that the present catchword-based position of Q 12:22–31 in the Lucan sequence derives from LukeR. It also draws attention to Q 11:2–13 as being the only complex of Q material which could genuinely and without strain provide the argumentative base upon which the ravens/lilies tradition builds. (ii) In the Matthaean setting none of the Q material in Matt 6:19–24 provides the necessary base for διὰ τοῦτο and what follows. Nor indeed does 6:9–13, for all its relatedness of theme, because it contains no argument. On the other hand, isolation of the Q material in Matthew 6–7 which did not belong to the inaugural discourse in Q (Matt 6:9–13; 6:19–24; 6:25–33; 7:7–11; 7:13–14; 7:22–23) serves to show both the closeness to one another of the three traditions we are examining and Matthew's preparedness to set little store on that closeness and to interrupt the natural train of thought. If the intervention of Matthew be set on one side the closeness of Matt 6:9–13, 25–33 and 7:7–11 can be respected.

---

[93]This correspondence is noted by, for example, Schmid, *Matthäus und Lukas* 241 and Manson, *Sayings* 81.

(iii) The correspondence between λέγω ὑμῖν, ἐγερθεὶς δώσει αὐτῷ ὅσων χρῄζει (Luke 11:8) and ὑμῶν ὁ πατὴρ οἶδεν ὅτι χρῄζετε τούτων (Q 12:30) points to an association, and all the more so since χρῄζειν occurs nowhere in the gospels outside these two sayings. Similarly, the adverse comment on the Gentiles, and the insistence on the Father's knowledge of the needs of those addressed, point to an association between Matt 6:7–8 and Q 12:30.

Whether or not the proposed literary association between Q 11:2–13 (with Matt 6:7–8 as its introduction) and Q 12:22–31 be judged convincing, the thematic association remains. And that association is quite sufficient to reveal the human predicament and vulnerability which the Q Christians faced. If they were in such spiritual need of insistent teaching about the Fatherly provision of food and clothing, then truly they were in socio-economic need. In a word, they were poor. No wonder that the inaugural discourse had redirected to the disciples (Q 6:20a) the beatitudes about the poor (Q 6:20b-21). For the present they remained poor, but there was the promise of a better tomorrow. In faith, therefore, the Q Christians held on to, and indeed proclaimed, the imminence of the kingdom of the God they knew as Father. The coming of his kingdom had unmistakably and undeniably been delayed, but in their situation that hope had survived and was now being revived.

8

The Law and the Prophets

Within the diversity of early Christian belief it is clear that purposeful appeal to 'the law and the prophets' was at least one focus of unity. The Christians for whom Q provided guidance in matters of belief and conduct were no exception. Their Jesus was someone whose outlook was unmistakably and to an unusually high degree coloured by scripture. A rough and ready litmus test is the number of allusions to the *dramatis personae* of the Old Testament: eight persons mentioned by name in Mark, of whom three (Moses, David and Elijah) keep on appearing on stage, whereas in Q, a document of arguably no more than one-third the size of Mark, there are nine such persons: Abel, Noah, Abraham, Lot, Isaac, Jacob, Solomon, Jonah and Zechariah.

Rather more significant is the way in which actual verbatim citations of the OT text occur. With formal introduction using the word γέγραπται, scripture is quoted in the traditions of the temptation and Jesus' testimony to the Baptist. In the second of these traditions (Q 7:27), the composite quotation of Ex 23:20 + Mal 3:1 representing the law and the prophets effectively closes the discussion, in that 7:28a and 7:28b thereafter simply clarify and summarize 7:24b-26 and 7:27 respectively. For the editor of Q, who is at work here,[1] it is Jesus' ultimate status in the setting of the future kingdom of God, probably his status as Son of man, which provides the clue to the relationship between himself and John, and therefore to the latter's present role. With a similar introductory formula, widely and rightly seen as indicating that here are two traditions which belong to the same stratum in Q[2] Jesus dismisses the proposals of the devil in the temptations tradition (Q 4:1–12) by citing scripture, specifically

---

[1]See above, pp. 63–70.
[2]Sato, *Prophetie* 35.

by fighting with Deuteronomic ammunition (Q 4:4, 7, 10 = Deut 8:3; 6:16; 6:13). That sequence of quotations is notable in three ways. First, there are three of them, denoting the completeness and decisiveness of the episode. Second, only the third is a positive formulation: 'Man shall not . . . you shall not . . . you shall . . .'. The effect has been, as already noted,[3] significantly damaged by Matthew's addition of 'but by every word that proceeds from the mouth of God', and even more by Luke's reordering of the second and third episodes. Third, the use of Deuteronomic quotations in reverse order, comparable with the presentation in Mark 15 of a set of quotations from Psalm 22 in reverse order (Mark 15:24, 31, 34 = Psalm 22:18, 7–8, 1), must be taken to be deliberate. In Mark 15 an original movement from despair to hope is replaced by a movement, overpowering in its bleakness, down to the depths of despair, and the cry of abandonment becomes a climactic demonstration of the accuracy of the opponents' taunt that 'he cannot save himself'.[4] In Q 4 it must be a similarly deliberate climax which 'You shall worship the Lord your God, and serve him alone' achieves. Here is the ultimate issue: how is the sonship of Jesus, which has been affirmed by supreme authority (Q 3:22), but which is initially placed in doubt and illegitimately required to be demonstrated in one way (Q 4:3, 9; cf. Wis 2:17–18), to be put into effect in another way? Is the mission going to be carried through by an alliance with, or in the aftermath of a rejection of, the authority of the devil? The answer is conveyed to the reader of Q in the longer term by the editorial commentary saying in Q 10:22, πάντα μοι παρεδόθη ὑπὸ τοῦ πατρός μου (cf. εἰ υἱὸς εἶ τοῦ θεοῦ . . . ταῦτα σοι πάντα δώσω), and by the defence against the charge of an alliance with Satan (Q 11:17–20, 21–22). But in the short and immediate term that answer is defined by scripture: the son of God will not live by bread alone, he will not tempt God, and above all he will not enter into his future kingship (note the hint of Ps 2:8 in Q 4:6/Matt 4:9, picking up the echo of Ps 2:7 in Q 3:22) except through the gift of the Father. The temptation tradition is therefore primarily christological, but not in the sense of establishing a christological insight. Rather, it

---

[3]See p. 12.

[4]I am grateful to Professor Vernon Robbins (Emory University, Atlanta) for this observation.

is a matter of reflecting on that insight, exploring how the christological reality will be effected and exercised. The function of the triple citation of scripture is therefore the provision of both a framework of obedience and a means of distancing the son of God from the devil. It is not, incidentally, the achievement of the ultimate victory over the devil. If that were the case the exorcisms would not be needed. But the exorcisms *are* needed, and when they occur (Q 11:14–15) they are but the Spirit-driven anticipation of that future kingship which is God's alone (Q 11:20/Matt 12:28).

These instances of γέγραπται scriptural affirmations belong to the editorial stage in the development of Q. But there occur with striking frequency elsewhere in Q traditions in which Jesus uses a scriptural statement as the 'punchline' at the end of a pre-Q unit of tradition. Thus, in the second of the two woes on the towns of Galilee (Q 10:13–15) Capernaum is scathingly dismissed by means of Isa 14:13, 15: 'Will you be exalted to heaven? You will be brought down to Hades.' The end of the disturbing warning about the inevitable division which will come (Q 12:51–53/Matt 10:34–36)[5] is couched in terms representing a very lightly modified quotation of Mic 7:6: 'The son treats the father with contempt, the daughter rises up against her mother, the daughter-in-law against her mother-in-law; a man's enemies are the men of his own house.' The flimsy inadequacy of a claim to a personal and ultimately significant relationship with Jesus based on human table fellowship and forming an audience for his teaching (Q 13:26–27/Matt 7:22–23) is devastatingly exposed in the words of Ps 6:9: 'Depart from me, all you workers of lawlessness.'[6] The lament over Jerusalem (Q 13:34–35) rebukes and warns of judgment to come, and is indebted for its conclusion to Ps 118:26: 'Blessed is the one who comes in the name of the Lord.' The Q apocalypse (Q 17:22–37) brings together several traditions capable of separate existence, and the one which dominates the collection ends enigmatically with an

---

[5]It is likely that the Matthaean range of relatives is more original: Schulz, *Spruchquelle* 259; Sato, *Prophetie* 294–5.

[6]The overall pattern of Q citations of scripture tends to confirm the view that ἀνομία is original here rather than ἀδικία: Polag, *Christologie* 68; Luz, *Matthew 1–7* 73. Thus the term entered Matthaean vocabulary, though without the full-blown sense of deliberate theologically motivated setting aside of legal demands.

unmistakable echo of Job 39:30: 'Where the slain are, there is he (the eagle).'[7] Other similar instances of OT-based punchlines appear at the end of the parable of the mustard seed (Q 13:19: Dan 4:21), and the end of the judgment warnings appealing to Noah (Q 17:27: Gen 7:7) and Lot (Q 17:29: Gen 19:24).[8]

The range of the OT passages used in these traditions is striking: the law, the prophets and the writings are all quarried. Also striking is the fact that virtually all of these OT-conditioned statements belong to declarations about the judgment or the situation immediately before it. Moreover, virtually all of them belong to attempts to tackle the problem of persons exuding a dangerous confidence and a misplaced complacency: those who quote their closeness to Jesus, those for whom the everyday is everything, those who are close enough to Jesus' cause to nurse high hopes of a peaceful future era, those who prize the presence of God in the house of God, perhaps most tragically of all those who are so proud to be residents of Capernaum. Just two of these traditions seem to be directed at disciples (Q 13:19; 17:37): otherwise their natural setting and function seems to be future-oriented preaching designed to produce repentance – in spite of the fact that nowhere apart from the associated woe against Chorazin and Bethsaida (Q 10:13–14) is the word itself mentioned!

Within this overall purposeful appeal in Q to 'the law and the prophets' certain traditions cry out for special attention. The first is the programmatic statement of principle in Q 16:16.

1. Violence to the Kingdom. Q 16:16.

During the discussion of the existence of Q the Matt 11:12–13/Luke 16:16 relationship received some attention.[9] It was observed, first, that the Matthaean setting of this saying is artificial and, second, that the wording and order of Matt 11:13 are in four respects secondary over against Luke 16:16a.[10] Just one insignificant decision remained outstanding, that between

---

[7]On this saying in more detail, see below pp. 252–3.

[8]For arguments in favour of assigning Luke 17:28–30 to Q, see below, p. 248.

[9]See p. 46.

Matthew's ἕως and Luke's μέχρι. Once this has been made in favour of ἕως,[11] the Q version can emerge as ὁ νόμος καὶ οἱ προφῆται ἕως 'Ιωάννου.

The reconstruction of what gave rise to the two markedly different sayings in Matt 11:12/Luke 16:16b is unusually hazardous, once the easy decision to prefer Luke's 'kingdom of God' to Matthew's 'kingdom of heaven' has been made.

In the case of the competing versions of the timenote, it is Luke who once again appears to preserve the Q wording. His ἀπὸ τότε is unparalleled in Luke-Acts but matched by Matt 4:17, where again Jesus is related to John, and his preaching of the kingdom related to scripture.[12] By contrast, the Matthaean ἀπὸ δὲ τῶν ἡμερῶν 'Ιωάννου τοῦ βαπτιστοῦ ἕως ἄρτι is made up of phrases used elsewhere in MattR.[13]

It is tempting to make out a case, contrary to the usual tendency, in favour of at least Luke's εὐαγγελίζεται. Its presence would produce a natural balance between 'law and prophets' and 'gospel' in the two halves of Q 16:16, and it would be consistent with the declaration in Q 7:22, distinguishing Jesus from John and including in his credentials as the coming one the fact that πτωχοὶ εὐαγγελίζονται. Moreover, its removal by Matthew would prevent the term's being repeated in two very adjacent passages (Matt 11:5, 12), for which there is precedent in the evangelist's avoidance of a double use of εὐαγγέλιον in Matt 4:17, 23/Mark 1:14–15, 39. On balance, however, it is probably better to accept that Matthew's wording is closer to Q. First, the phrase ἡ βασιλεία τοῦ θεοῦ εὐαγγελίζεται is a Lucan favourite.[14] Second, if Matthew replaced it the replacement chosen is curious, given that there is nothing on the theme of

[10]Similarly Schmid, *Matthäus und Lukas* 285; Barth, 'Law', 63; Schulz, *Spruchquelle* 261–2; Polag, *Christologie* 74. Only occasionally do Q specialists dissent from this view: thus Schenk, *Synopse* 44; Kloppenborg, *Formation* 113–4.

[11]ἕως is attested elsewhere in Q (10:15; 11:51; 12:59; 13:21, 35) whereas μέχρι (2–1–1 + 2) is not: given its MattR employment elsewhere (Matt 11:23; 28:15) there would be no reason for Matthew to drop it, and given its presence in Lucan narrative passages elsewhere (Acts 10:30; 20:7) it could certainly be LukeR here.

[12]F. Neirynck, 'ΑΠΟ ΤΟΤΕ ΗΡΞΑΤΟ and the Structure of Matthew', *Evangelica II. Collected Essays by Frans Neirynck* (BETL 99; Leuven: University Press/Peeters, 1991) 141–182.

[13]αἱ ἡμέραι τοῦ, cf. Matt 23:30 diff Luke 11:47; ἄρτι statistics 7–0–0 + 0.

[14]Luke 4:43; 8:1; Acts 8:12.

violence in the section Matt 11:2–11 to which 11:14–15 clamps 11:12–13.

If the statement in Matt 11:12ab is original the amplifying statement can hardly have run as in Luke 16:16bb: καὶ πᾶς εἰς αὐτὴν βιάζεται. The latter follows more suitably a positive statement such as Luke 16:16ba, and a repetition of βιάζεται is scarcely plausible.

The Q text as a whole therefore probably ran as follows:

ὁ νόμος καὶ οἱ προφῆται ἕως Ἰωάννου·
ἀπὸ τότε ἡ βασιλεία τοῦ θεοῦ βιάζεται,
  καὶ βιασταὶ ἁρπάζουσιν αὐτήν.

The first part of the saying, Q 16:16a, is something of a riddle. Does ἕως Ἰωάννου imply a cut-off point and therefore the obsolescence of the old revelation? Such an interpretation is scarcely conceivable (though some have conceived it), certainly not if this enigmatic saying be attributed to the historical Jesus. It is more likely that John is associated with, and then regarded as the last term in the series of, notable persons who figure in the law and the prophets. This would mean that the message is the same as that in Q 7:24b-26, 28a, material which is not only pre-Q in literary terms but also highly likely historically to derive from Jesus.

This brings us to Q 16:16b/Matt 11:12. As a sequel to Q 16:16a it must pick up the idea of John's pre-eminence, which itself stems from the ultimacy of his mission in advance of the coming crisis. It does not say that the crisis has come, or that the kingdom of God has in any sense arrived, but rather that the message of the kingdom has paradoxically been given a hostile reception. This emerges not so much from v. 16ba, since the verb βιάζεσθαι can by itself bear a neutral and even favourable sense.[15] The saying's real sting is in v.16bb, where finally the activity of the βιασταί is defined by ἁρπάζειν. Of a neutral or favourable sense of this term in this setting there can be no chance.[16] The message of the kingdom, very probably voiced

[15]See Gen 33:11; Judg 13:15, 16; 2 Sam 13:25, 27; Jonah 1:13; Sir 4:26; 4 Macc 2:8.

[16]Cf. the frequency with which this activity is associated with the most fearsome and threatening of predatory animals: Gen 37:33; 49:27; Pss 7:2; 10:9; 22:13; 104:21; Ezek 19:3; 22:25, 27; Hos 5:14; Amos 3:4; Mic 5:8; Nah 2:12.

neither by John alone nor by Jesus alone but by both within the essential continuity of their eschatological missions, has been vigorously and violently opposed, and the messengers savaged as if by wild animals. The Teacher of Righteousness had the same feeling: 'I have been iniquity for the wicked, ill-repute on the lips of the fierce, the scoffers have gnashed their teeth . . . violent men have sought after my life . . . mighty men have pitched their camps against me, and have encompassed me with all their weapons of war . . .' (1QH 2:10–11, 21, 25–26).[17] He doubtless had in mind the leaders of the religious establishment of his time, and probably so too did Jesus. So fundamental a reality was it that for the emissaries of Jesus it would be no different (Q 10:3).

To interpret Q 16:16 in its own terms is one thing, to interpret it on the level of Q is possibly another. To do the latter requires some precision about the immediate context in which it was to be found in Q and also any concepts which it may share with other sayings located in the wider context of Q.

In its Lucan setting, 16:16–18, the original Q setting is also probably preserved. This is an inference, not just from Luke's usual respect for the order of his source material, but also from the typical Q catchword connection (νόμος) which attaches it to Q 16:17 and, most significant of all, the schematic Matthew 5/Luke 16 correspondence uncovered by Heinz Schürmann: a trio of sayings about the law and the prophets (Matt 5:17/Luke 16:16), the permanence of the law (Matt 5:18/Luke 16:17), and divorce (Matt 5:32/Luke 16:18).[18]

Luke 16:14–15 has its fair share of *hapax legomena* and Lucanisms.[19] Nevertheless there is a detectable overlap with that same part of Matthew as produced evidence of the Q trio 16:16–18. 'The Pharisees (cf. Matt 5:20) . . . You are those who justify yourselves (cf. Matt 5:20; 6:1) before men . . . (cf. Matt 6:1)'. It is possible therefore that in a no longer recoverable form there exists below the surface of Luke 16:14–15 an introduction which set Q 16:16–18 in an anti-Pharisaic frame. This would achieve a precise definition of the βιασταί, whose activity of ἁρπάζειν in any case links them to the Pharisees of Q 11:39.

[17]Text in Vermes, *Dead Sea Scrolls in English* 169–70.
[18]*Untersuchungen* 130–2.
[19]ἐκμυκτηρίζειν, ὑπάρχειν, φιλάργυρος, ὑψηλός.

Luke 16:17 is liable to reduce commentators to despair,[20] in that the double ἕως ἄν in the matching Matt 5:18 produces a tautology and suggests MattR revision of a source. But the clause introduced by the first ἕως ἄν is matched by Luke, while the second such clause is supported by conformity to a tripartite NT scheme consisting of ἀμὴν λέγω ὑμῖν, οὐ μή + prophetic future, and a temporal clause with ἕως/μέχρι.[21] The least unsatisfactory solution is perhaps to recognize that the form εὐκοπώτερον ἐστιν . . . is elsewhere used by Luke in dependence on tradition,[22] and also to allow for maximum Matthaean creativity. Such creativity involved *him* in introducing the tripartite scheme, in working into a single saying elements which in Mark 13:30–31 belonged to two distinct sayings, and in committing tautology (ἕως ἄν παρέλθῃ ὁ οὐρανὸς καὶ ἡ γῆ . . . ἕως ἄν πάντα γένηται) in the interests of the strongest possible insistence on the permanent authority of all the law. That is exactly the same heavy personal interference with the tradition as appears in 5:17, 19. He may well be responsible for ἰῶτα ἕν as well! Consequently the Q saying probably ran:

εὐκοπώτερον ἐστιν τὸν οὐρανὸν καὶ τὴν γῆν παρελθεῖν ἢ τοῦ νόμου μίαν κεραίαν πεσεῖν.

Luke 16:18 contains two phrases which have no Matthaean counterpart, just as Matthew's phrase παρεκτὸς λόγου πορνείας has no Lucan counterpart and is normally assigned to MattR.[23] Could Luke's καὶ γαμῶν ἑτέραν and/or ἀπὸ ἀνδρός be LukeR under the influence of καὶ γαμήσῃ ἄλλην (Mark 10:11) and τὸν ἄνδρα (Mark 10:12)? Both possibilities are often accepted,[24] but should perhaps be reassessed.

In the first case, a bald declaration that divorce as such is adultery is scarcely credible. One might compare the saying about the lustful look (Matt 5:28) which at least focuses on a recognizable offence which can be defined as equivalent to adultery, but divorce as such cannot be such an offence. More-over, the very use of the term adultery presupposes the involve-

[20]Luz, *Matthew 1–7* 257–8.
[21]Luz, *Matthew 1–7* 258, drawing on the work of K. Berger, *Amenworte* 73–4.
[22]Luke 5:23; 18:25; cf. Mark 2:9; 10:25.
[23]Cf. Schulz, *Spruchquelle* 117; Luz, *Matthew 1–7* 300.
[24]Schulz, *Spruchquelle* 116–7; Schenk, *Synopse* 116.

ment of a third party, and this is what καὶ γαμῶν ἑτέραν introduces. Finally, if adultery is defined in a Jewish context as an offence against a man, Luke 16:18a, as it stands and with Matt 5:28 corroborating it, recognizes the human dignity of the woman and indeed enhances it. This is so, notwithstanding the point that the prohibition in Luke 16:18b of the marriage of a divorced woman would, if understood as a new law, be severely problematic for her.[25] But is it to be understood as law?

In the second case, if each half of the saying refers to both parties to the original marriage and to a third party, whether male or female, there is a symmetry resulting from putting both halves together which suggests originality.

Again therefore it appears likely that Luke has reproduced Q:

πᾶς ὁ ἀπολύων τὴν γυναῖκα αὐτοῦ καὶ γαμῶν ἑτέραν μοιχεύει,
καὶ ὁ ἀπολελυμένην ἀπὸ ἀνδρὸς γαμῶν μοιχεύει.

Q 16:16 was therefore associated in Q with two sayings about the permanence of the law and the impermissibility of remarriage after divorce. At first sight this association appears to be promising theologically: Q 16:16 is a saying which *might* suggest a terminus for the law and the prophets. Q 16:18 is a saying which *might* suggest an undermining of the law of Deut 24:1–4. In between the two, Q 16:17 is a saying which emphatically *does* affirm that the law will last till the end of time. Does this mean that Q 16:16 is now part of an attempt to affirm the essential continuity between law and gospel against a tendency within the Q community to exploit theologically a contrast between the two? The answer must be 'No'. First, as we have seen, Q 16:16 should not be interpreted as depreciating the law and the prophets in any way. Second, as has been pointed out by Ed Sanders,[26] Jesus' treatment of divorce is one of two occasions (the other is Q 9:60) when he seems to have been in tension with Moses, but on the other hand to demand more than Moses demanded is not to promote disobedience to Moses. One might add that while both Mark 10:9 and Q 16:18 have high claim to go back to Jesus their presuppositions are not in harmony. In the former, divorce *should not* occur; in the latter, divorce *cannot*

[25]Luz, *Matthew 1–7* 301–2.
[26]*Jesus and Judaism* (London: SCM, 1985) 256–60.

occur. In the former, a marriage is dissoluble; in the latter, a marriage is indissoluble. But that disharmony simply means that each saying must be read as a demand rather than a law,[27] and that the overarching social function of both must be recognized. That function is a call for absolute faithfulness in and to marriage. If that is the case, Q 16:18 should not be read in anti-Mosaic terms. Third, the need to make the sort of statement we find in 16:17 arose, we may infer, in the setting of the Gentile mission. But Q shows no commitment to the Gentile mission, and the specific legal issue treated, divorce, was in any case not a key 'boundary defining' issue for that mission, in the way that circumcision, food laws and special days were. So we may draw two conclusions. The first is that Q 16:17 suggests that Q is aware of the conservative response to the Gentile mission, endorses it, but does not positively engage in the discussion of the issue. And the second is that Q 16:16, as well as describing the rough and unready response meted out to the messengers of the kingdom, is unreservedly positive about John and 'the law and the prophets'.

We have seen that for Jesus the observation 'the law and the prophets until John' positions John at the climax of the succession of all the persons to whom God had entrusted a mission (cf. Q 7:24b-26, 28a). For Q that remained true, qualified only with reference to John's successor, Jesus who was even greater, the Son of man (cf. Q 7:27, 28b). If we want to see confirmation of that situation we need to look further afield in Q, and such a survey reveals that elsewhere pre-Q tradition affirmed the specialness of what was being achieved by Jesus as the fulfilment of the expectations of the prophets, but without making explicit statements about his person, and that Q-redaction picked up such tradition, developing it christologically in order once again to establish the superiority of Jesus over John. This emerges from Q 7:18–23 in association with Q 10:23–24.

Q 10:23–24 has already been discussed as a classic counter-example undermining the theory that Luke used Matthew.[28]

[27]Cf. the discussion of Luke 16:18b above.
[28]See pp. 54–5. The range of decisions made by Q specialists is repeatedly in favour of Lucan originality: Schmid, *Matthäus und Lukas* 297–8; Schulz, *Spruchquelle* 419–20; Polag, *Christologie* 48; Schenk, *Synopse* 59; Sato, *Prophetie* 260.

Without any great uncertainty the original Q tradition emerges:

μακάριοι οἱ ὀφθαλμοὶ οἱ βλέποντες ἃ βλέπετε.
  λέγω γὰρ ὑμῖν ὅτι πολλοὶ προφῆται καὶ βασιλεῖς ἠθέλησαν
  ἰδεῖν ἃ ὑμεῖς βλέπετε καὶ οὐκ εἶδαν, καὶ ἀκοῦσαι ἃ ἀκούετε
  καὶ οὐκ ἤκουσαν.

Q 7:18–23 can, as we have seen, also be regarded as a classic example of a tradition requiring the Q hypothesis.[29] This time the Q version ran:

ὁ Ἰωάννης ἀκούσας περὶ τούτων, πέμψας δύο τῶν μαθητῶν
αὐτοῦ εἶπεν αὐτῷ· σὺ εἶ ὁ ἐρχόμενος, ἢ ἕτερον προσδοκῶμεν;
καὶ ἀποκριθεὶς ὁ Ἰησοῦς εἶπεν αὐτοῖς· πορευθέντες ἀπαγγείλατε
Ἰωάννῃ ἃ ἀκούετε καὶ βλέπετε·
  τυφλοὶ ἀναβλέπουσιν καὶ χωλοὶ περιπατοῦσιν,
  λεπροὶ καθαρίζονται καὶ κωφοὶ ἀκούουσιν,
  καὶ νεκροὶ ἐγείρονται καὶ πτωχοὶ εὐαγγελίζονται·
καὶ μακάριός ἐστιν ὃς ἐὰν μὴ σκανδαλισθῇ ἐν ἐμοί.

Before the relationship between Q 7:18–23 and Q 10:23–24 is discussed the secondariness of the framework of Q 7:18–23 must first be noted. The intention of this framework is clearly to establish an equation between John's 'coming one', already introduced redactionally in Q 3:16, and Jesus. The one expected by the historical John was God; the 'coming one' expected by the John of Q was the Son of man. That idea therefore represented the *inclusio* for the complex Q 7:18–35, given its implicit presence in Q 7:19 and its explicit presence in Q 7:34, but in no way had it been implicit in the activities of Jesus. Moreover, in no way was it natural to suppose that the fiery judge of Q 3:7–9, 16–17 was Jesus. That this is a christological problem was recognized by the concluding beatitude in Q 7:23: 'Blessed is he who is not offended by me.' The necessary conclusion seems to be that everything in this tradition apart from the six-fold list in Q 7:22 is Q-editorial.[30] That editorial work matches material in the fourth gospel in making John a witness

---

[29]See pp. 43–5.
[30]Of course, we cannot rule out the further possibility, even probability, that some of the actions listed are additions to the original list. This applies particularly to 'lepers are cleansed' and 'the dead are raised up'.

to Jesus (John 1:6–8), subordinating him to Jesus (John 3:30), and using miracle as a means of establishing the superiority of Jesus (John 10:41), so that Q anticipates that gospel's concern to legitimize Christian belief in the face of the continuing existence of the Baptist's movement.[31]

This conclusion can now be connected to another observation, namely that there is a very extensive correspondence in content between the two traditions Q 7:18–23; 13:16–17. Both refer to prophetic promises being fulfilled; both refer to 'seeing and hearing'; both give a predominant role to what is seen, but a striking concluding, even climactic, position to what can be heard; both give pride of place to a beatitude. Commentators tacitly acknowledge the intimacy of the relationship between the two traditions by regularly drawing upon the one when discussing the other. That being so, it is tempting to regard the two traditions as having been adjacent in Q, particularly since the Matthaean position of 'The Blessedness of the Disciples' is evidently secondary, and its position in Luke almost immediately after the Lucan mission charge (Luke 10:1–16) corresponds to the position of 'The Baptist's Question' immediately after the mission charge in Matthew. Two factors combine to prevent this inference:[32] first, there is a typical Q catchword connection between Q 7:34 and Q 9:58 which suggests that those two complexes were adjacent, and second, by relocating Q 7:18–35 to a position after the mission charge Matthew is able to provide in advance examples of every one of the miracles summarized in Q 7:22. An alternative explanation which does justice to the correspondence between the two traditions is, however, to hand. The list in Q 7:22, deprived of its present framework, could hardly survive in isolation, but we can readily account for the phenomena within these traditions if we suppose that at the pre-Q stage it represented the amplification and definition of the presently undefined 'what you see' and 'what you hear'. At the Q stage, if that is right, the tradition was divided and its second half provided with a new framework serving the interests of Christian apologetic vis-à-vis the Baptist movement.

Whatever the problem posed for the Q Christians by the

[31]Similarly, on the purpose of the tradition, Kloppenborg, *Formation* 107–8, though he is not inclined to see any part of the list in 7:22 as deriving from Jesus.

[32]Against Catchpole, 'Law and Prophets', 97–8.

Baptist movement, there is a sense in which his disciples and the disciples of Jesus are placed on a level by the two traditions we have been studying. Q-redaction has allowed the disciples of John to 'see and hear' in just the same way as those addressed by Jesus in Q 10:23. They thus share in the experience of the new era. This corresponds to the fact that John is himself part of the fulfilment of scripture (Q 7:27). And yet in the context of the new era there is a distinction grounded in christology. Jesus must be recognized. He may be, he may not. And that is an ambivalence which is perhaps important for Q. As scripture points forward to the final proclamation of the near kingdom the statement 'the law and the prophets until John' affirms his belonging to the new era. As scripture points forward to the embodiment of christology in the person of Jesus, and as it becomes plain that a decision about the status of Jesus remains to be taken by John (specifically, that is, by his disciples), then the statement 'the law and the prophets until John' affirms his belonging still to the old era.

2. Solomon and Jonah. Q 11:31–32.

When Jesus ben Sirach looked back on the work of his grandfather he saw above all devotion to 'the law and the prophets' as the source of great teachings, instruction and wisdom which redounded to the credit of Israel (Sir, prologue 1, 8). When Judas Maccabeus set about stabilizing the faith of his army, and their confidence that the Gentiles would be worsted and Israel made victorious, it was 'the law and the prophets' which he used for encouragement (2 Macc 15:9). When the father of the seven famous martyrs educated his children he taught them 'the law and the prophets', from which raw material their mother was able to compile, first, a list of named heroes who had faced testing, suffering and/or death (Abel, Isaac, Joseph, Phineas, Hananiah, Azariah, Mishael and Daniel) and, second, a sequence of quotations from named persons confirming the conviction that the inevitable suffering of the righteous will lead to life (Isaiah, David, Solomon, Ezekiel and Moses). Unsurprisingly, there comes to expression in these lists a strong Israel-consciousness and a pattern of encouragement.

In Q, however, the situation is not quite like that. The panorama of Israel's history from Abel to Zechariah in Q 11:49–51 serves the purpose of critical accusation, the deuteronomic view of history being used to establish an association between the persons addressed and the killers rather than those killed. And when the memory of two pairs of famous OT figures is revived, Solomon and Jonah (Q 11:31–32), Abraham and Lot (Q 17:26–30), the note sounded is again no note of encouragement. Just what note is being sounded requires careful definition, and to a study of these two traditions we now turn.

In Q 11:31, 32 two OT stories are invoked as reinforcement for the message to the contemporary generation. The Q text of these two sayings is not in doubt[33] and can be set out immediately:

βασίλισσα νότου ἐγερθήσεται ἐν τῇ κρίσει μετὰ τῆς γενεᾶς ταύτης καὶ κατακρινεῖ αὐτήν· ὅτι ἦλθεν ἐκ τῶν περάτων τῆς γῆς ἀκοῦσαι τὴν σοφίαν Σολομῶνος, καὶ ἰδοὺ πλεῖον Σολομῶνος ὧδε.
ἄνδρες Νινευῖται ἀναστήσονται ἐν τῇ κρίσει μετὰ τῆς γενεᾶς ταύτης καὶ κατακρινοῦσιν αὐτήν· ὅτι μετενόησαν εἰς τὸ κήρυγμα Ἰωνᾶ, καὶ ἰδοὺ πλεῖον Ἰωνᾶ ὧδε.

Side by side in the judgment stand the queen of the south and the inhabitants of Nineveh over against ἡ γενεὰ αὕτη. The agreed criterion of judgment emerges from the two examples. In the first it is hearing the wisdom of the wise man *par excellence*, who according to the tradition instructs foreign rulers, warns of judgment, and also calls for repentance.[34] In the second, rather more plainly, it is repenting at the preaching of judgment by the prophet. The present generation has apparently not passed this test, though the affirmation πλεῖον ... ὧδε indicates that there has been even more reason to do so than was the case in the two OT contexts. The neuter form πλεῖον suggests that the specialness of the contemporary situation is not understood christologically, nor in the present (but not new) preaching of judgment and call for repentance, but rather in the accompanying δυνάμεις which anticipate the dawning new era.

[33]Schulz, *Spruchquelle* 251–2.
[34]See Wis 6:1–11; 11:23; 12:10, 19; Sir 17:24; 44:16; 48:15. Cf. Kloppenborg, *Formation* 133–4.

If so, this bipartite tradition performs the same function as Q 10:13–14 in focussing on miracle as a spur to repentance, which, of course, it cannot do in isolation but only in combination with the message of the near kingdom. The only difference between 10:13–14 and 11:31–32 is that the basis of the argument is what *would have* happened rather than what *did* happen. The same may be said about 11:31–32 in relation to 10:12, where the rejection of a combination of preaching and miracle provokes a warning comparison with Sodom. All these adverse comparisons with Gentile personnel belong to a mission to Israel[35] and have high claim to go back to Jesus himself.

As they stand in Q, however, 11:31–32 are attached to 11:29–30. It has already been observed that Q 11:29–30 is for sure more exactly preserved by Luke than by Matthew.[36] The Matthaean allusion to Jesus' death, burial and resurrection is less easily regarded as original than as a typical OT based insertion by the evangelist. It is an allusion which is distinctly artificial since no one, including the Ninevites, could witness the proposed sign. It is an allusion which Luke would hardly have discarded, had he known it.[37] It is an allusion whose originality is not established by the time note τρεῖς ἡμέρας καὶ τρεῖς νύκτας over against τῇ τρίτῃ ἡμέρᾳ, as is shown by MattR at 27:63, and the evangelist's acceptance of traditional formulations διὰ τριῶν ἡμερῶν/ἐν τρισὶν ἡμέραις at 26:61; 27:40. As a consequence, the final phrase τῇ γενεᾷ ταύτῃ (Luke 11:30) is probably more original and has been supplanted. If the phrases καὶ μοιχαλίς and τοῦ προφήτου (Matt 12:39) are assigned to MattR, as being respectively drawn from Mark 8:38 and designed for clarification, the Q text can be reconstructed thus:[38]

ἡ γενεὰ αὕτη γενεὰ πονηρά ἐστιν· σημεῖον ζητεῖ, καὶ σημεῖον οὐ δοθήσεται αὐτῇ εἰ μὴ τὸ σημεῖον Ἰωνᾶ. καθὼς γὰρ ἐγένετο Ἰωνᾶς τοῖς Νινευίταις σημεῖον, οὕτως ἔσται ὁ υἱὸς τοῦ ἀνθρώπου τῇ γενεᾷ ταύτῃ.

[35]Against Kloppenborg, *Formation* 25, this is not 'too narrow a *Sitz*'.
[36]Lührmann, *Redaktion* 37. This is conceded even by those Q specialists whose general inclination is towards the originality of Matthew's version, cf. Harnack, *Sayings* 37, 137.
[37]Cf. his insertion of an edited version of Mark 8:31 in Luke 17:25.
[38]Schulz, *Spruchquelle* 251–2; Schenk, *Synopse* 71; Sato, *Prophetie* 278.

There is an overlap between 11:29–30 and 11:31–32 in the references to Jonah, the Ninevites and 'this generation'. But there is also unmistakable tension between the two. (i) The first has a personal focus, and the second does not. (ii) The first involves a refusal to give any sign of heavenly authorization, and the second presumes visible manifestations of the near kingdom in the form of acts of power. (iii) The first is concerned only with Jonah and fits awkwardly with a Solomon + Jonah pairing, particularly when in Q that pairing is more likely to have conformed to biblical order; the Matthaean reversal solves that problem but creates another by leaving the Solomon saying hanging over as little more than an appendix. (iv) The first gives no detail of the response of the Ninevites, whereas the second is very specific. (v) The second assigns to the Ninevites a role in the last judgment, whereas the first does nothing of the sort. There may also be (vi): the second envisages Jonah as a preacher calling for repentance, but does the parallelism between Jonah and the Son of man work on that basis? This question forces us towards a decision about the history of the tradition in Q 11:29–30, and to a choice between three main options.

The first option, proposed by Richard Edwards,[39] is that 11:29–30 is *in toto* a Q-editorial revision of the tradition of a refusal of a sign, preserved in its original form in Mark 8:12. On this view the revision centred on 11:30, which Edwards regards as an 'eschatological correlative' saying whose *Gattung* was created by Q. The second option, proposed by John Kloppenborg,[40] is that the earliest version of the refusal of a sign included the phrase 'except the sign of Jonah', which Mark subsequently removed so that Jesus made no such concessions to outsiders (cf. Mark 11:27–33). From the earliest version of the saying refusing a sign there were two further stages of development, the first the addition of 11:30, and the second the attachment of 11:31–32. The third option, proposed by Migaku Sato,[41] varies by taking 11:30 to have been originally an independent tradition. Q 11:30 thus emerges as the key to the discussion.

[39] *The Sign of Jonah* (SBT 2/18; London: SCM, 1971) 71–87, cf. also Lührmann, *Redaktion* 34–42.

[40] *Formation* 128–34.

[41] *Prophetie* 281–4.

That the term 'eschatological correlative' is itself an exaggeration, and that Q did not invent the *Gattung*, has been clearly demonstrated by Daryl Schmidt.[42] Against the background of the 20 OT examples he collected, to which have subsequently been added 2 Qumran examples[43] it is clear that, after separating off the 'sentences of holy law' which correlate what a person does with what will be done to him (Lev 24:20; Jer 5:19: Obad 15), the remaining sayings are better described as 'prophetic correlatives', but not, as Schmidt suggested, LXX-based. Those which are most relevant are not those which simply say that what God has done he will do again,[44] but those which involve a comparison with a distinct reality, everyday or historical[45] or even the prophet himself.[46] From these texts it is possible to draw certain conclusions affecting Q 11:30.

First, in the protasis the reference to a known and experienced reality in the relevant group of texts mentioned above is matched by a reference to something visual in the subgroup of texts in which the prophet himself is a sign. In Isa 20:3, Ezek 12:11, and indeed in Isa 8:18, which speaks of the prophet as a sign even though it contains no precise correlative statement, the essentially visual reality, the 'object of sense perception',[47] consists of the prophet's named children (Isa 8:18), his walking naked and barefoot (Isa 20:3), his acting out the behaviour of someone leaving on a journey into exile (Ezek 12:6). It is each of these visual realities which points forward to the future divine judgment, and it is not the audible speech or the message itself issued by the prophet. In what sense, then, was Jonah personally a sign? The answer is that he was not a sign to anyone! Not even the classification of this saying as a 'riddle' can make him one! His experience in and out of the fish (Jonah 1:17) might qualify, in the light of the attached commentary (Jonah 2), as some kind

---

[42]'The LXX *Gattung* "Prophetic Correlative"', *JBL* 96 (1977) 517–22.

[43]Kloppenborg 130: 'As smoke clears and is no more, so shall wickedness perish for ever and righteousness be revealed like a sun governing the world' (1Q27 i,6), and 'Like the appearance of comets, so shall be their kingdom' (4Q246 ii,1–2). Translation in Vermes, *Dead Sea Scrolls in English* 239, 275.

[44]Thus Isa 10:10–11; Jer 31:28; 32:42; 42:18; Ezek 20:36.

[45]Deut 8:5; Isa 24:13; 41:25; 55:10–11; 66:13; Jer 2:26; 19:11; Ezek 22:20; 34:12; Amos 3:12; the Qumran examples given above (note 43).

[46]Isa 20:3; Ezek 12:11.

[47]K. H. Rengstorf, 'σημεῖον', *TDNT* 7.200–61, esp. p. 211.

of illustration *to him* of a theological truth, but that is not the sense in which a prophet is a sign, and nothing encourages the thought that knowledge of his experience is presumed in his hearers.[48] Equally, his activity in Nineveh itself (Jonah 3) will not qualify, since it lacked altogether any visual features. Consequently talk about the sign of Jonah cannot have his role as a preacher of judgment and repentance in mind. It is effectively the refusal of a sign. The implication for Q 11:30 is clear: a protasis needs to describe a reality which is known and clear in order that the apodosis may work, but this protasis does not, so 11:30 could not exist as a separate saying.[49] At best it leans on 11:29.

Second, the use of the future tense in the apodosis of each of the Jewish texts cited above is, with the sole exception of Deut 8:5, a strict usage. Consequently ἔσται (Q 11:30) too should be taken in a strict sense.[50] The Son of man is central to God's future action, he is not a preacher of judgment and repentance to the contemporary generation. What the future action might be is fairly clear if 11:30 is set alongside the other prophetic correlatives in Q 17:24, 26, 30. The future coming of the Son of man from heaven is the concern of this saying. But that coming is not a sign of anything either. It is what will happen without preliminary signs. The situation to which the saying speaks is therefore a situation which is sign-less and defined simply and solely by the fact that preaching of judgment is taking place and repentance is being demanded.

If 11:30 could not exist by itself and without 11:29, could 11:29 exist by itself and without 11:30? If the original saying concluded with 'the sign of Jonah' and was only later shortened by MarkR to the form it has in Mark 8:12,[51] is it not an oddity that Jonah should be the person singled out in such a saying, and would that original saying have survived in spite of its opaqueness and obscurity? Mark would surely not have been alone in finding the final phrase 'unintelligible'.[52] It seems most

---

[48] Against J. Jeremias, "Ἰωνᾶς', *TDNT* 3.406–10, esp. pp. 409–10.

[49] Against Sato, *Prophetie* 282.

[50] Similarly Lührmann, *Redaktion* 40; Sato, *Prophetie* 283. Against Kloppenborg, *Formation* 132–3; Fitzmyer, *Luke I* 933: 'He comes from afar in the sense of a heaven-sent prophet like Jonah.'

[51] Thus, Kloppenborg, *Formation* 128–32.

[52] Kloppenborg, *Formation* 129.

likely that 11:29 in its present form would not have existed by itself. Whether it originally existed in the form of Mark 8:12[53] does not need to be decided here. The two, rather fragile, supports for that possibility are (i) Jesus' comparable refusal of a reply concerning the source of his authority (Mark 11:27–33 – but a sign is not involved there, and the presentation sounds very Marcan, cf. 6:2) and (ii) the word εἰ, 'a literal rendering of a typical Hebraic oath formula: May this or that happen to me, if such and such . . ., a very forceful way of saying *no* within a Semitic environment'.[54] Whether or not that possibility is true, that is, whether or not there is any pre-Q tradition here, it seems fairly clear that 11:29–30 has been devised in one stage only and with Q 11:31–32 in mind.

The intention of this single-stage editorial activity has now become clear. It was two-fold: first, to say that the present generation must look for no compelling manifestation of divine power in advance of the coming from heaven of the Son of man and, second, to insist that the present generation has all it needs in the form of the preaching of the kingdom, the signs of the kingdom, and the call for repentance. The first of these intentions matches that of Q 17:23–24 with its polemic against the 'sign prophets'. The second has the effect of bringing 11:31–32 under the control of 11:29–30. This causes the word πλεῖον almost inevitably to become personalized in spite of itself, and the Son of man thus takes over as the mouthpiece of wisdom, the prophet, the performer of mighty deeds. In short, editorial work achieved here exactly what editorial work achieved in 7:18–35.

3. The Day of the Son of man. Q 17:23–24, 26–30, 37.

Once again the broad outlines of the Q tradition underlying Matthew and Luke can be discerned in the shape of a warning against localized eschatological expectation, a comparison of the Son of man with lightning, and an appeal to precedent derived from 'the law and the prophets'.

---

[53]Edwards, *Sign of Jonah* 75–6; Lührmann, *Redaktion* 37.
[54]Edwards, *Sign of Jonah* 75.

An initial problem concerns the provenance of the saying about Lot (Luke 17:28–30). In principle this might be assigned to LukeR, or regarded as material 'newly formed within the sphere of Q tradition', [55] or even attributed to L, [56] but in practice it is much more likely to stem from Q, for several reasons. First, the predilection of the Q tradition for pairs is well established by the Gentiles and the tax collectors, the Baptist and the Son of man, Solomon and Jonah, the ravens and the lilies, the mustard seed and the leaven, the farming men and the grinding women. The pair, Noah and Lot, would therefore conform to this Q tendency. Second, judgment by fire, which is the theme of the Lot episode, is important to Q, as the preaching of John at the outset shows (Q 3:7–9, 16–17). Third, the grim precedent of judgment upon Sodom has already been invoked in Q 10:12. Fourth, the occasional omission of Q material by Matthew should occasion no more surprise than his occasional omission of Marcan material. Above all, fifth, the tendency to combine the examples of Noah and Lot is so firmly entrenched in Jewish tradition that pre-Lucan origin in this instance appears much the most probable option. The relevant Jewish texts include Wis 10:3–4, 6–8, which marshals Noah and Lot as the second and fourth in a list of those who were saved by wisdom; Sir 16:7–8, which uses the generation of the flood and the Sodomites to head a list of those whose rebellion and sin incurred the flaming wrath of God; 3 Macc 2:4–5, which mentions the flood and the destruction of Sodom as prime illustrations of the fate in store for the proud and insolent; *Jub.* 20:5–6, which refers to the giants and the Sodomites as those condemned for wickedness and uncleanness; *T. Naph.* 3:4–5, where the Sodomites and the watchers are presented as persons who veer away into committing idolatry and changing the course of nature; and *m. Sanh.* 10:3, which opens with the generalization that 'all Israelites have a share in the world to come', and then proceeds to place the generation of the flood and the men of Sodom in first and third position in the list those who do not.

[55]H. E. Tödt, *The Son of Man in the Synoptic Tradition* (NTL; London: SCM, 1965) 65; Lührmann, *Redaktion* 74: 'die Tradition aus der Lk Q übernimmt'.

[56]Fitzmyer, *Luke X-XXIV* 1165, regards vv. 28–32 as deriving from L, with the statement about Lot's wife in vv. 31b-32 forming an *inclusio* with vv. 28–29. However, v. 31, upon which v. 32 depends, is more likely to derive from Mark 13:15–16, while the formal correspondence betwen vv. 26–27 and vv. 28–30 is impressive enough to suggest common origin.

The conclusion that Q contained the pair of sayings about Noah and Lot[57] can be followed by the observation that while the original wording has been very little altered by either evangelist, Luke several times stands nearer than Matthew does to Q.[58] (i) The substantial introduction, unique to Matthew (24:38a), ὡς γὰρ ἦσαν ἐν ταῖς ἡμέραις ταῖς πρὸ τοῦ κατακλυσμοῦ, spoils the dramatic effect of suddenly introducing the flood after the list of human activities, and is probably secondary. (ii) The phrase ἐν ταῖς ἡμέραις is, however, present in Luke (17:26) in almost the same position as part of the time note ἐν ταῖς τοῦ υἱοῦ τοῦ ἀνθρώπου ἡμέραις. Matthew at this point prefers to speak of the παρουσία, which is a term never used by any other evangelist, a term shown by Matt 24:3 diff Mark 13:4 to be part of MattR usage, and a term clearly being used here by Matthew to integrate the whole discourse. It is not too difficult to infer once again that Luke is preserving Q. This being so, the well known variation between 'day' and 'days' can be explained. The pair of precedents began by comparing the days of Noah with the days of the Son of man. Clearly in each case the period immediately before the crisis was in mind. Then attention moved to the similar period in the experience of Lot. This time the Son of man and his day (*sic*) were mentioned, but only after the day of Lot's removal from Sodom, the day of ultimate crisis, has been brought into view. The whole unit, consisting of the two examples, is thus coherent and symmetrical. (iii) The allusion to the ignorance of Noah's contemporaries (οὐκ ἔγνωσαν ἕως . . .) is a secondary MattR intrusion. In content it differs, and in position it is distanced, from the list of activities 'eating and drinking', 'marrying and giving in marriage'. It prepares for the following separate section Matt 24:42–25:13, framed by exhortations to watchfulness in view of ignorance. So the text in its Q form probably approximated to the following:

καθὼς ἐγένετο ἐν ταῖς ἡμέραις Νῶε, οὕτως ἔσται ἐν ταῖς ἡμέραις τοῦ υἱοῦ τοῦ ἀνθρώπου· ἤσθιον, ἔπινον, ἐγάμουν, ἐγαμίζοντο, ἄχρι ἧς ἡμέρας εἰσῆλθεν Νῶε εἰς τὴν κιβωτόν, καὶ ἦλθεν ὁ κατακλυσμὸς καὶ ἀπώλεσεν πάντας.
ὁμοίως καθὼς ἐγένετο ἐν ταῖς ἡμέραις Λώτ· ἤσθιον, ἔπινον,

[57]Similarly, Kloppenborg, *Formation* 156–8.
[58]Lührmann, *Redaktion* 75–83.

249

ἠγόραζον, ἐπώλουν, ἐφύτευον, ᾠκοδόμουν· ᾗ δὲ ἡμέρᾳ
ἐξῆλθεν Λὼτ ἀπὸ Σοδόμων, ἔβρεξεν πῦρ καὶ θεῖον ἀπ'
οὐρανοῦ καὶ ἀπώλεσεν πάντας. κατὰ τὰ αὐτὰ ἔσται ᾗ ἡμέρᾳ τοῦ
υἱοῦ τοῦ ἀνθρώπου.

What were these two examples drawn from 'the law and the
prophets' intended to convey? The answer emerges when Q
17:26–30 is set alongside the texts which are members of the
same family and which were listed above. A number of form-
critical observations then become possible. First, statements of
principle accompany, and appear to be a normal control on,
such lists.[59] Second, the flood and the fire serve to illustrate the
theme of judgment. Third, a statement of the reason for judgment is normally provided.[60] Fourth, when personal references
to Noah and Lot are included, the main theme of judgment is
tempered by a subordinate theme of salvation. Within these
form-critical parameters Q 17:26–30 can now be assessed. First,
the need for a heading may or may not be met by Q 17:23–24,
37. To this question we must return. Second, the overall theme
of judgment is clear. Third, instead of a list of offences which
provoke judgment there is a list of wholly inoffensive activities
on the part of persons, the list of whose notorious offences
could have stretched far! To this also we must return. Fourth, a
firm hint of divine rescue is dropped. Two items therefore, the
first and the third, call for further study.

The inoffensive activities of the contemporaries of Noah and
Lot should clearly not be adjusted by assimilating 'eating and
drinking' to gluttony. Nor should 'marrying and being given in
marriage' be taken as cover for the doubtful liaisons of Gen
6:1–4. Nor should 'buying and selling' or 'planting and building'
be synonyms for undue prosperity and wealth. Quite the
contrary! All four pairings are repeatedly attested, more or less
idiomatic, and in content entirely and unreservedly honourable.
Elsewhere in Q, however, equally innocent and honourable
pairings, 'sowing and reaping' or 'toiling and spinning' or work
'in the field (and) at the mill', serve to illustrate life which is
ordinary, everyday, even necessary, but unaligned to the great

---

[59]Wis 9:17–18; Sir 16:4, 6; 3 Macc 2:3; *Jub.* 20:5–6; *T. Naph.* 3:2.
[60]Wis 10:3; Sir 16:7; 3 Macc 2:4–5; *Jub.* 20:5; *T. Naph.* 3:3, 5.

eschatological crisis which happens to be very near. That the contemporary generation should be addressed as it is in Q 17:26–30 can only mean that its own life patterns are here being superimposed upon the ancient biblical examples. On the positive side, this generation is therefore *not* being accused of corruption on the ancient model. On the negative side, it *is* being reminded of the danger in which it stands through complacent inattention to the imminent occurrence of judgment, and it *is* being told that in that judgment it will stand with the most notorious and appalling sinners known from the Genesis record. A further hidden, but essential, parallel between the contemporaries of Noah and Lot and the contemporary generation comes to light through the tradition attested by Philo, Josephus and the Targums that the days of Noah and the days of Lot were days of opportunity for repentance.[61]

These form-critical comparisons make possible a further typically form-critical conclusion about the original *Sitz im Leben* of Q 17:26–30. It must be the preaching about an imminent crisis involving salvation and judgment. The accent is placed on judgment, though not on the grounds of wickedness, and the setting for that must be a community whose members view themselves as safe and secure in the favour of God, namely Israel. The demand is for repentance, not in the sense of moral conversion, but in the sense of renewal and openness to the God who will come – or, more precisely, the duly authorized heavenly Son of man who will come. Unless the presently settled and complacent members of the community of Israel open themselves to the message of the contemporary counterpart of Noah and Lot, the imminent event will be shocking in its suddenness and disastrous in its finality.

One element after another in this scheme recalls the message of the historical Jesus. The daring use of the OT, the proclamation of imminent crisis, the call to subordinate the everyday good to the eschatological best, the demand for repentance – these, at the very least, combine to produce a telling echo of Jesus. The use of the term Son of man for an individual coming figure may possibly, though not certainly, be a constraint.[62] In

---

[61] 1. Noah: Josephus, *Ant.* 1.3.1 §74; Philo, *Questions on Genesis* 1.91; 2.13; *Tg. Onq.* Gen 6:3; 7:4, 10. 2. Lot. *Tg. Ps.-J.* Gen 19:24; *Tg. Neof.* Gen 18:21.

these traditions 'Son of man' cannot refer to anyone other than a unique individual. If it should turn out to be a *sine qua non* for authentic Son of man sayings that they should refer to persons over and above the one individual, then the conclusion about Q 17:26–30 would be two-fold. First, the speaker is in general very heavily influenced indeed by the historical Jesus, and belongs to a community which continues to breathe the very atmosphere of his mission. Second, by focussing the preaching on the figure of the coming Son of man a characteristic Q conviction is once again being voiced.

From the content of Q 17:26–30 to its context: was there a 'heading' in Q as in the other Jewish texts? Certainly there was immediately beforehand in Q 17:23–24 the saying comparing the Son of man to the lightning. Quite possibly there was also the saying in Q 17:37b about the corpse and the eagles.

The original wording of that corpse/eagles saying has probably been preserved by Matthew:[63]

ὅπου ἐὰν ᾖ τὸ πτῶμα, ἐκεῖ συναχθήσονται οἱ ἀετοί.

This saying probably did occur in Q where Matthew has it (Matt 24:28), rather than at the end of the complex as a whole where Luke has it (Luke 17:37b).[64] (i) Its unclear connection with Q 17:23–24, together with Luke's wish to insert at this point a quite different passion-oriented saying (Luke 17:25), would explain a Lucan change. (ii) The disciples' question about place in the typically Lucan introduction, 'Where, Lord?' (Luke 17:37a) suggests a reminiscence of the topic of place which had figured in the introduction in Q 17:23. At first sight the corpse/eagles saying seems to interrupt the neighbouring sayings which centre on the Son of man. What contribution does it make? Biblical tradition had frequently used eagles/vultures to represent speed[65] and heavenliness,[66] often (because of adverse associations) as an image of divine judgment.[67] The closest parallel for this saying is Job 39:30, a statement of what is always true as

[62]M. Casey, *Son of Man* (London: SPCK, 1979); B. Lindars, *Jesus Son of Man* (London: SPCK, 1983).

[63]Schulz, *Spruchquelle* 280–1.

[64]Lührmann, *Redaktion* 72; Kloppenborg, *Formation* 156.

[65]Deut 28:49; 2 Sam 1:23; Job 9:25–26; Hab 1:8.

[66]Prov 23:5; Lam 4:19.

[67]Prov 30:17; Jer 4:13; Hos 8:1; Hab 1:8.

part of a design in creation which is divine and not human: 'On the rock . . . (the eagle) spies out the prey; his eyes behold it from afar. His young ones suck up the blood; and where the slain are, there is he.' In Q 17:37b the plural subject and the future tense of the verb do not prevent the saying from remaining a statement of what is always true, though συναχθήσονται may well be intended to assimilate the saying to the future setting in which a sudden descent from heaven brings death and disaster. To that extent Q 17:37b serves as an introduction to Q 17:26–30. Nevertheless, it is Q 17:24 which attracts more attention by virtue of the reference to the Son of man which it shares with Q 17:26–30.

The general thrust of the Son of man/lightning saying, together with its introduction, is clear, though some details of wording are problematic. Luke's reference to the day of the Son of man is widely preferred to Matthew's παρουσία, but otherwise there is a powerful consensus in favour of Matthew's wording.[68] This may be worth questioning in three small details. (i) μὴ πιστεύσητε (Matt 24:26) is reminiscent of Mark 13:21/ Matt 24:23, whereas μὴ διώξητε (Luke 17:23) is more synonymous with the preceding μὴ ἐξέλθητε.[69] (ii) To say that the lightning ἐξέρχεται from the east and shines as far as the west (Matt 24:27) is to use language more appropriate to the sun than the lightning.[70] Given that Luke shows no special fondness for λάμπειν,[71] and given Matthew's frequent use of φαίνειν,[72] it may be that the Lucan ἀστράπτουσα . . . λάμπει is to be preferred. This would yield the following reconstruction:

ἐὰν εἴπωσιν ὑμῖν· ἰδοὺ ἐν τῇ ἐρήμῳ ἐστίν, μὴ ἐξέλθητε· ἰδοὺ ἐν τοῖς ταμιείοις, μὴ διώξητε. ὥσπερ γὰρ ἡ ἀστραπὴ ἀστράπτουσα ἀπὸ ἀνατολῶν ἕως δυσμῶν λάμπει, οὕτως ἔσται ὁ υἱὸς τοῦ ἀνθρώπου ἐν τῇ ἡμέρᾳ αὐτοῦ.

The use of the image of lightning, with its recurrent biblical

---

[68]See Schmid, *Matthäus und Lukas* 336; Schulz, *Spruchquelle* 278–9; Polag, *Christologie* 76.

[69]Sato, *Prophetie* 214, opts for Luke here.

[70]Pss 50:1; 113:3.

[71]Elsewhere in Luke-Acts it occurs only at Acts 12:7.

[72]Statistics: 13–1–2 + 0. MattR at Matt 24:30 diff Mark 13:26. Note the parallelism between ὡς λαμπάδες πυρός and ὡς ἀστραπαί in Nah 2:4 LXX; similarly Ezek 1:13; Dan 10:6; Ep Jer 60–61.

association with judgment, makes it singularly apt in the present Q context. Often theophany is involved.[73] As a component of storm, lightning is often associated with thunder and wind, fire and flood.[74] It is thoroughly understandable, therefore, that in spite of there being no explicit reference to lightning in Genesis 6–7 or 19, Philo should include it in his descriptions of the flood (*De Abr.* 43) and the judgment of Sodom (*De Mos.* 2.56). Similar implicit recognition of the congruence of lightning with what happens in Genesis 19 is shown by Josephus, who uses in his narrative (*Ant.* 1.11.4 §203) the term βέλος which various OT texts use as a synonym for lightning.[75] Within the broader range of lightning passages the association of suddenness or speed merits attention.[76] Speed conveys a sense of the decisiveness, the forcefulness, the finality of judgment.[77] Thus it begins to emerge that the imagery of the Son of man/lightning saying makes it to some extent a suitable heading for the Noah + Lot complex.

As such a heading, was the Son of man/lightning saying from the beginning linked with the Noah + Lot complex? Did the complex never exist separately from the saying, in the same way that the ravens + lilies complex probably never existed separately from the prohibition of anxiety, and the tax collectors + Gentiles complex never existed separately from the demand for love? The answer is almost certainly 'No'. For the affirmation of suddenness in the Son of man saying is more the premise than the main concern, the latter being found in the words ἀπὸ ἀνατολῶν ἕως δυσμῶν λάμπει. These words are wholly appropriate to a lightning saying, since similar passages elsewhere speak of its universal effect when contrasting the earth with the heaven from which God intervenes, comes and reigns. Thus it is that God's 'lightnings lighten the world' (Ps 97:4), or 'the lightning when it flashes is widely seen' (Ep Jer 61), or 'the lightning shone exceedingly, so as to illuminate the whole earth' (2 *Apoc. Bar.* 53:9). In Q 17:24 the universal scope

---

[73]Exod 19:16; Deut 32:41; Pss 18:14; 144:6.

[74]Hab 3:8–12; Wis 5:20–22.

[75]Ps 144:6 is typical.

[76]Cf. the comment on Luke 10:18 by W. Foerster, 'ἀστραπή', *TDNT* 1.505: 'In Lk 10:18 the point of the comparison is the suddenness of the divine working.'

[77]Cf. Mal 3:5.

of the lightning-like appearance of the Son of man answers the problem of location mentioned in Q 17:23. It rounds off a complete and self-contained unit, a unit which needs no amplification, a unit which confronts the ideas associated with the movements of the charismatic-eschatological leaders.[78] Of any concern with those leaders and their movements there was in Q 17:26–30 not the slightest trace.

The situation in Q 17:23–24, 37b, 26–30 turns out to be remarkably similar to that in Q 11:29–30, 31–32. In each case, a pair of OT allusions gives force to sayings whose natural setting is the prophetic proclamation to Israel. In each case a preface is provided which addresses a problem peculiar to the period of some thirty years before the Jewish War, the problem of the charismatic prophets with their preoccupation with particular places where the great act of liberation would occur. Against that whole pattern of thought the Q community sets the coming Son of man, the one whose coming would be visible anywhere and everywhere.

---

[78]Kloppenborg, *Formation* 159–60, infers that 17:23 was not always found alongside 17:24, taking into account (i) the origin of the first in polemic against false earthly messiahs, and that of the second in 'the realm of Son of man speculations'; (ii) the absence of a counterpart for the second in the Marcan version of the saying. But why should not the Q community deliberately use the very different Son of man scheme in polemic against the eschatological leaders? And does not the position of Mark 13:21–23 within the two sections linked by the theme of θλῖψις (Mark 13:19, 24) mean that Mark also sets the concept of the coming Son of man polemically over against the appeal of those leaders?

9

Tradition and Temple

In the course of the discussion so far it has become plain that in terms of the fundamental beliefs of Judaism the Q Christians were a conservative grouping. An antithesis between the gospel of Jesus and the law of Moses held no attractions for them. At the same time they clearly found themselves very much at odds with the Pharisaic movement and engaged in notably bitter polemic against it, notwithstanding the call for love which the inaugural discourse had promoted. This singularly unattractive polemic needs further investigation. So too does the attitude adopted by these Q Christians to the temple. For the temple stood with the law as one of the pillars of Judaism as long as it stood at all. And there is no sign in Q that the editorial process which put the source together post-dated the tragic events of the war with Rome, after which it stood no longer.

On just two occasions the temple is explicitly brought to the attention of the reader of Q. The first is when it serves as one of the settings for the testing of Jesus' identity as son of God (Q 4:9–12), and the second is when it appears as the location of the climactic assassination in the record of 'the law and the prophets' (Q 11:51). The second of these two traditions, and the complex in which it is set in Q, is more revealing than the first concerning the religious tradition to which Q and its community belong. It will form the major concern of this chapter. But it would be as well to draw attention at the outset to a general consideration which may scarcely be doubted, namely, that to the reader of Q the temple could hardly but come to mind as implicit in other traditions beside those two. Thus, whenever legal material with a conservative religious colouring appears (e.g. Q 11:37–52 *in toto*; 16:17), that material necessarily presupposes an appreciative attitude to the temple and its cult. Similarly, when references to Jerusalem appear (e.g. Q 13:34–35), it is not a live option to interpret such references in terms of the city or the community to the exclusion of the temple, for in a striking spectrum of texts[1] we see how important inclusion and association and inseparability were felt to be.[2] This view is given classic expression in the affirmation of 2 Macc 5:15–20 that divine anger with the residents of Jerusalem brought divine disregard of the holy place: 'The Lord did not choose the nation for the sake of the holy place, but the place for the sake of the nation; therefore the place itself shared in the misfortunes that befell the nation and afterward participated in its benefits.' In similar vein, and particularly apposite for our present purpose, is the case of Jesus ben Ananios (Josephus, *J.W.* 6.5.3 §§300–309), whose doom-laden cries took the varied but synonymous forms of 'Woe to Jerusalem', or 'A voice against Jerusalem and the sanctuary . . . a voice against all the people', or 'Woe once more to the city and to the people and to the temple'.

1. Problems of Order.

There are three problems of order to be solved in connection with the traditions we have in view. The first concerns whether the lament over Jerusalem followed the woes against the Pharisees in Q. The second concerns the other traditions which may have framed the woes in Q. The third concerns the sequence of the woes themselves.

First, the legitimacy of attaching Q 13:34–35 to Q 11:37–52 must be affirmed.[3] Doubts about this attachment in Q derive from (i) a predisposition to accept Lucan order in principle; (ii) the argument that 13:34–35 follows entirely suitably on 13:27–30 in view of the shared theme of the judgment upon Israel; (iii) the alleged discrepancy between Q 11:49–51 as prospective in

---

[1] See Tob 14:4–5; *Jub.* 1:17, 28; John 11:48.

[2] Cf. Schweizer, *Matthew* 444, commenting on Matt 23:38: 'Whether "house" refers to the city of Jerusalem or the Temple makes no material difference.' Similarly, A. Sand, *Das Evangelium nach Matthäus* (RNT; Regensburg: Pustet, 1986) 473.

[3] Cf. S. Légasse, 'L'oracle contre "cette génération" (Mt 23,34–6 par. Lc 11, 49–51) et la polémique judéo-chrétienne dans la source des Logia', *Logia. Memorial J. Coppens* (ed. J. Delobel; BETL 59; Leuven: University Press, 1982) 237–76, esp. pp. 238–9.

outlook and 13:34–35 as retrospective; (iv) the ease with which the Jerusalem oracle, as a prelude to the eschatological discourse in Matthew 24 (cf. especially 24:1–3), serves the purposes of Matthaean theology.[4]

Over against these considerations others may be set which support an original Q association between these traditions. (i) It is likely that the Lucan position of 13:34–35 is much more bound up with its dependence upon the LukeR insertion of the non-Q material in Luke 13:31–33, with its interest in Jerusalem as both the end of the journey of the Lucan Jesus and also the allegedly unique setting for the killing of prophets. (ii) In view of the tendency towards thematic grouping of traditions in Q (see, for example, Q 7:18–35), the overlap in content between Q 11:49–51 and Q 13:34–35 makes an original juxtaposition highly likely. (iii) There is the inappropriateness of an oracle against Jerusalem ending a complex set by Luke in one of his typical meal-scenes. (iv) There are verbal connections which are most easily explained as reminiscences in οἶκος[5] and ἥξει.[6] (v) In fact both Q 11:49–51 and Q 13:34–35 contain retrospective and prospective features. (vi) Q 17:34–35 shows that there is nothing more intense and final than the judgment represented by ἀφίεται. (vii) Finally, even those writers who in general favour the originality of the Lucan order are prepared to consider exceptions to that rule. It seems likely therefore that in Q the woes led immediately into the lament over Jerusalem.

Second, we turn to the more extended sequence. In the Lucan sequence of Q material following the woes on the Pharisees there occur the exhortation to fearless confession (Q 12:2–12) and the warning against anxiety (Q 12:22–34), both of which appear in a quite different position in the Matthaean sequence. With the next complex, the parables about watchfulness and faithfulness (Q 12:39–46), we touch material which, in the Matthaean Q sequence, was in exactly the same position relative to the woes (23:1–39 leading to 24:43–51), except that there

[4]D. E. Garland, *The Intention of Matthew 23* (NovTSup 52; Leiden: Brill, 1979) 26–7; D. R. A. Hare, *The Theme of Jewish Persecution of Christians in the Gospel according to Saint Matthew* (SNTSMS 6; Cambridge: CUP, 1967) 94; O. H. Steck, *Israel und das gewaltsame Geschick der Propheten* (WMANT 23; Neukirchen: Neukirchener Verlag) 45–8.

[5]Luke 11:51 diff Matt 23:35: cf. Q 13:35a.

[6]Matt 23:36 diff Luke 11:51: cf. Luke 13:35 diff Matt 23:39.

intervened the tradition about the day of the Son of man (Matt 24:26–28, 37–39, 40–41, 28/Luke 17:22–37). However, when the parable of the unjust judge (Luke 18:1–8) appears immediately after Q 17:22–37 with a secondary Lucan appendix attached referring to the question of whether 'the Son of man will find faith . . .', it strikingly echoes the language of Q 12:40, 42, 43. When these considerations are aggregated the natural inference is that the original Q order was Q 11:37–52; 13:34–35; 17:22–37; 12:39–46. This would mean that immediately after the lament over Jerusalem, with its concluding reference to the one who comes in the name of the Lord, there occurred the warning against those who say, 'He is ἐν τῇ ἐρήμῳ . . . ἐν τοῖς ταμιείοις'.[7] When Luke 12:3 diff Matt 10:27 includes the quite redundant phrase ἐν τοῖς ταμιείοις,[8] it looks very much like a reminiscence of the saying which, on the above hypothesis, originally occurred at this point in Q. We shall return later to discuss the implications of the original Q order for the meaning of the traditions in question.

Third, there is the order in which the woes themselves occurred in Q. This may admittedly be beyond recovery. Nevertheless, adopting the notation of W (= washing: Q 11:39–41), T (= tithes: Q 11:42), S (= chief seats, etc: Q 11:43), G (= graves: Q 11:44), B (= burdens: Q 11:46), P (= prophetic tombs: Q 11:47–48), and K (= keys: Q 11:52), Luke's and Matthew's sequences can be set out as W-T-S-G-B-P-K and B-S-K-T-W-G-P respectively. For Heinz Schürmann[9] these represented edited versions of an original Q sequence S-B-T-W-G-P-K, his reasons being the Matthew/Luke agreement concerning T. .G. .P, the belonging together of T and W (Luke having transposed in order to provide in 11:37–38 a suitable introduction), and the suitability of B. .G as a frame for T-W, with S and K as original introduction and conclusion. In effect, that means that Matthew preserved Q in respect of T-W-G-P, and Luke preserved the original relationship of S. .B. .K. This implicit concession to Matthew has been retracted in the recent

---

[7] On this as the original wording, cf. Schulz, *Spruchquelle* 278.

[8] Schulz, *Spruchquelle* 462: 'das den Parallelismus storënde ἐν τοῖς ταμιείοις'.

[9] 'Das Zeugnis der Redenquelle für die Basileia-Verkündigung Jesu', *Logia. Memorial J. Coppens* (ed. J. Delobel; BETL 59; Leuven: University Press, 1982) 121–200, esp. pp. 174–5.

work of John Kloppenborg,[10] who revives the view of Schulz,[11] for whom the Q sequence consisted of T-W-S-G-B-P-K, that is, only one transposition by Luke, the one which permitted W to serve as immediate response to the LukeR introduction in 11:37–38.

Any alternative proposal has its own hazards, and perhaps the need for one is not very great, but a few considerations may perhaps be ventured. So anticlimactic is K after the use of P as the basis for an extended comment and announcement of judgment (Q 11:49–51) that its Lucan position appears to derive from its generalizing character, which arguably fitted it to conclude the complex and to substitute for Q 13:34–35, following the decision to move the latter elsewhere.[12] An alternative position therefore needs to be found for K. In Matthew's presentation it stands formally as the first of the sayings which uses the actual word 'woe' (Matt 23:13), and as a generalizing statement of basic principle it is admirably suited to do so. On the other hand, P must have come last and, in view of common (catchword) references to μνημεῖα,[13] have been preceded immediately by G. This in turn places a question-mark against B. For Luke B begins the anti-lawyer group of woes, just as for Matthew it begins the catalogue of specific charges against the scribes and Pharisees. This suggests an introductory function for B, which might again be thought appropriate in view of its touching on the very essence, rather than any specific example, of the critique of Pharisaism. What then preceded G-P? The answer must surely be T-W, since W shares with G the charge of inner uncleanness (however we reconstruct the *Vorlage* of G) and combines with T to comment on two definitive features of Pharisaic practice. We thus have an interim conclusion that the last four woes were T-W-G-P, and a decision remains only in

---

[10] *Formation* 139–40.

[11] *Spruchquelle* 94–5.

[12] Garland, *Intention* 197, recognizes the incompatibility of 11:52 and 13:34–35 as endings for this complex, but opts for 11:52 on the ground that it fits Luke's (*sic*) division of the charges. It is precisely that suitability in the Lucan context which makes such a position at the pre-Lucan stage doubtful. The same answer can be made to Schürmann's tentative suggestion that Luke could well have understood K in relation to, and as a conclusion for, 11:29–51 as a whole: 'Zeugnis', 175.

[13] On μνημεῖα as original, cf. Schulz, *Spruchquelle* 105.

respect of S. .B. .K. Of the various possible permutations of
these three, K-B-S would seem to be most persuasive since,
first, K refers to the kingdom, which must be taken to be a
central concept for the speaker, and which is probably presupposed theologically by S; second, K hints at Pharisaic opposition
to the (prophetic preaching of) the kingdom, and in establishing
with P a certain symmetry between the beginning and the end
of the complex would conform to a typical Q form; third, the
recognition by both Matthew and Luke of K's foundational
content and role has already been noted; fourth, a MattR movement forward of B-S is understandable in terms of the
evangelist's redesigning the whole discourse under the control
of 23:2–3, while at the same time feeling the influence of the
Marcan parallel for S in Mark 12:38–39; finally, B is more
closely related to K than S is to either, for B engages with a
matter of fundamental principle while S pinpoints personal
behaviour. To sum up, the proposed reconstruction of the Q
order is K-B-S-T-W-G-P.

When reconstructing the content and exploring the meaning
of the various woes it is important to keep under review proposals which have been made concerning the tradition history of
the complex as a whole and, correspondingly, the history of
the relations of the Q community with Judaism. In the view
of Schulz,[14] all the woes (not including Q 11:49–51) derived
from Palestinian charismatic-eschatological Torah-sharpening
prophets, and no attempt was made by him to uncover strata
representing different stages in the growth of the collection.
Schürmann's reconstruction was more nuanced. For him, T-W
formed the original 'kernel', the viewpoint of law-abiding
Jewish Christians who stressed the love commandment over
against Pharisaic legalism and maintained truly the word and
practice of Jesus; B. .G were added by those who abandoned the
ceremonial law and clashed with the Pharisaic leaders of Judaism,
but had not broken totally with Judaism itself; S. .P. .K were
added at the final 'ecclesiastical-redactional' stage of Q by those
who had become anti-synagogue and had broken with Judaism.[15] Kloppenborg's modification of this view was only

---

[14]*Spruchquelle* 94–114.
[15]'Zeugnis', 174.

slight.[16] For him, T + W belong to an *intra muros* dispute with Pharisaism, recalling the demands of the covenant and by no means rejecting the ceremonial law; B + S reject Pharisaic legal interpretation in practice but not in principle, and presuppose no formal break with Judaism; G + P + K involve an attack on the very existence of Pharisaism and therefore attest a widened gulf. More recently, Christopher Tuckett has registered hesitation about whether the material is patient of so exact a process of differentiation.[17]

2. Entry to the Kingdom. Q 11:52.

K originally accused the Pharisees of neither entering nor permitting others to enter (Q 11:52b).[18] The object of the verb εἰσέρχεσθε was almost certainly 'the kingdom of heaven',[19] and the Pharisees are tacitly accepted as possessing the keys of the kingdom[20] – tacitly, but of course ironically, since in no sense could such a statement be accepted at face value. The saying presupposes that entry to the kingdom, which is synonymous with 'sharing in the age to come' (*m. Sanh.* 10:1), is not the automatic assumption for all Israelites, so the implication must be that it is specifically the kingdom as proclaimed in mission by Jesus or his adherents which is experiencing resistance in the name of the religious convictions maintained by the Pharisees. Those convictions, promoted through their characteristic interpretation of Torah,[21] have gone beyond the will of God and thus have frustrated his purpose as authoritatively effected by Jesus. This sense of the ultimate significance of the mission of Jesus within the purpose of God underlies what will be said in P. On the broader Q canvas, the opposition to the (preaching of) the kingdom recalls Q 16:16b, while the exclusion of those whom Jesus included recalls Q 7:34b.

[16]*Formation* 140–1.

[17]'Q, the Law and Judaism', *Law and Religion* (ed. B. Lindars; Cambridge: Clarke, 1988) 90–101, 176–180, esp. p. 178.

[18]Reconstruction of Q text: Schulz, *Spruchquelle* 110.

[19]Schulz, *Spruchquelle* 110; Schweizer, *Matthew* 433; Garland, *Intention* 124–5; Schürmann, 'Zeugnis', 176.

[20]On Pharisaic usage, see Jeremias', 'κλείς', *TDNT* 3.744–53, esp. pp. 747–8.

[21]Schulz, *Spruchquelle* 111; Garland, *Intention* 127; Sand, *Matthäus* 459.

3. Bearing Burdens. Q 11:46.

B originally responded to a situation in which a corpus of traditional interpretation of Torah already existed.[22] It took up the theological choice facing the contemporary interpreter: to define in ever more detail, to impose ever more precision, to formulate ever more rules, and thus to lay ever more burdens upon those who would conform to the will of God (cf. Acts 15:10), or to ease the burdens, to limit the rules, and to highlight broad principles.[23] It is unlikely that this woe presumes abandonment of the ceremonial law,[24] or that it accuses the Pharisees of resorting to casuistry in order to evade the rulings which they recommend for others[25] (an interpretation unduly influenced by the MattR comment in Matt 23:3b), or that it charges them with teaching one thing and doing another.[26] It is rather more likely that the underlying issue is the same as that in K, in other words, a matter of how the will of God should be defined in relation to the announcement of the kingdom.

4. The Chief Seats. Q 11:43.

S probably did, as has been assumed so far, figure in Q.[27] This follows from the 'minor agreement' in the use of φιλεῖν (Matt 23:6/Luke 20:46; subsequently changed to ἀγαπᾶν by LukeR, cf. Luke 7:5), repeated definite articles, and the order of the items listed. A good case can be mounted for the substance of the charge in Q being undue attention to 'the chief seat at suppers, the chief seats in the synagogues, and the greetings in the market places'. A further case can be mounted in favour of

[22]Reconstruction of Q text: Schulz, *Spruchquelle* 107.

[23]It is thus more critical of Pharisaic principles than is supposed by E. Haenchen, 'Matthäus 23', *ZTK* 48 (1951) 38–63, esp. p. 40, and Schulz, *Spruchquelle* 108. Tuckett, 'Q, the Law and Judaism', 98, regards this woe as the sole exception to the general rule that the woes concern Pharisaic behaviour. Even here he thinks that the main critique concerns '(their failure) to help other people with their burdens'.

[24]Schürmann, 'Zeugnis', 175.

[25]Thus Ernst, *Lukas* 387, *et al.*

[26]Schmid, *Matthäus* 320; D. Patte, *The Gospel according to Matthew* (Philadelphia: Fortress, 1987) 321; Schulz, *Spruchquelle* 108.

[27]Schulz, *Spruchquelle* 104; Schweizer, *Matthew* 431.

the charge's being immediately followed in this Q context by the saying 'Whoever exalts himself will be humbled, and whoever humbles himself will be exalted' (Q 14:11; 18:14b). First, if Luke dropped an original reference to 'chief seats at suppers' in order to exploit the idea in 14:7–10, it is notable that he followed it there with this saying in just the same way as Matt 23:12 followed shortly after 23:6, 7b. Second, a similar reminiscence may be detectable in the secondary addition of Luke 18:14b to the parable of the Pharisee and the taxcollector (18:9–14a), in which terms appearing in the immediate context of the woes like 'extortion' and 'tithes' reappear, and the Pharisaic interpretation of righteousness and sense of security in relation to God are critically scrutinized. As far as the meaning of this woe is concerned, the synagogue as an institution is no more frowned on than supper and marketplace in Q 11:43, while in Q 14:11 the future 'divine passive' points, as Schulz observed, to that community of equals which derives from, and is expressive of, the kingdom of God.[28] The frame of reference for S is therefore the same as that for K + B. One may add that the future 'divine passive' will also be used in the announcement of judgment in P.

5. Tithes. Q 11:42.

T undoubtedly referred to both the tithing of mint and also the practice of judgment.[29] The word κἀκεῖνα (11:42c) indicates that mint did not stand alone, and in view of references to dill and cummin, but not rue, in tithing *halakoth* (*m. Ma'as. S.* 4:5; *m. Dem.* 2:1), together with a typical Lucan generalization in the phrase 'every herb' (cf. Luke 21:29), the original Q combination was probably 'mint and dill and cummin'. On the other side of the antithesis ταῦτα indicates that judgment did not stand alone; the ἔλεος/ἐλεημοσύνη overlap (cf. Luke 11:41)[30] establishes the involvement of mercy; faithfulness, as a traditional covenant

---

[28]*Spruchquelle* 105. It is, of course, a commonplace that in the great new era of the future pride and its effects will be eliminated by God, cf. *Pss. Sol.* 17:41.

[29]Reconstruction of Q text: Schulz, *Spruchquelle* 100.

[30]Luke's is the secondary version, with a rendering which conforms extensively to Acts 10–11: Garland, *Intention* 144–5.

partner of judgment and mercy, probably completed the trio, rather than the love of God, which may have been generated by the recollection of Deut 6:5 (Luke 10:27/Mark 12:30). As far as the verbs are concerned, ἀφιέναι is more likely to be original than παρεῖναι (11:42c), and therefore similarly more original than παρέρχεσθαι (11:42b).

The form of 11:42bc is chiastic: tithes – judgment etc. – judgment etc. (ταῦτα) – tithes (κακεῖνα). Content-wise, the whole saying deals with action and not at all with teaching: ποιεῖν is the opposite of ἀφιέναι, which in turn is the opposite of the *action* represented by ἀποδεκατοῦτε. Finally, 11:42b by itself would be unclear, because it might be attacking the practice of careful tithing as well as failure to practise the fundamental covenant obligations of judgment, mercy and faithfulness. No unclarity at all is left by the combination 11:42bc. What that says is that it was good and appropriate to be careful about tithing, but it is not an alternative to the practice of judgment and the rest, any more than the practice of judgment is an alternative to tithing. In the hierarchy of religious obligation judgment stands well above tithing, and persons are therefore particularly culpable if they neglect the former. Such neglect makes scrupulous care show itself as nothing better than disproportionate concern for small things, whose very smallness is painfully evident within the context of the comparison with judgment and the rest.[31] T therefore attacks Pharisaic inaction, which effectively casts a shadow over one form of Pharisaic action, one which is at the very heart of the movement's existence. But it does not attack Pharisaic teaching or principles.[32] From the point of view of the speaker, Pharisaic shortcoming involves giving more attention to the special obligations of the sect than to the general obligations of the whole people of God, and especially those obligations which have to do with the treatment of the needy, the exposed, the powerless and the vulnerable.[33] Thus the speaker adopts the characteristic

[31]C. G. Montefiore, *The Synoptic Gospels II* (2nd ed.; London: Macmillan, 1927) 301: 'They observe ritual minutiae and neglect ethical fundamentals.'

[32]It is widely agreed that there is no question of an attack on the law (Lev 27:30–33; Num 18:12; Deut 14:22–23). Cf. Hoffmann, *Studien* 170; Kloppenborg, *Formation* 140.

[33]Schweizer, *Matthew* 441; Patte, *Matthew* 325.

perspective of the prophets (Mic 6:8; Zech 7:9–10) and the wise (Prov 14:22), not only in respect of what is affirmed but also in respect of the use of a contrast between religious practices (e.g. sacrifice, Isa 1:10–17) and covenant obligations. In turn, this means that the presuppositions of T and P are in harmony.

6. Washing Vessels. Q 11:39–41.

W arguably began as Matt 23:25 does, apart from minor and unimportant verbal adjustments. Matt 23:26 and Luke 11:40–41, however, differ so markedly that there has been a widespread tendency to see each as entirely MattR or LukeR, as the case may be.[34] Contrary to that inference, while there are grounds for accepting that LukeR is mainly responsible for 11:40–41,[35] it remains likely that Matt 23:26 essentially preserves Q material. First, there is Matthew/Luke agreement on an imperative sequel to the initial charge. Second, πρῶτον links Matt 23:26 and Luke 11:38, and probably indicates a LukeR reminiscence of an original Q saying.[36] Third, the same can be inferred from the Matthew/Luke agreement on an address to a single Pharisee. Fourth, the oft-cited parallel in Q 6:43–45[37] suggests thematic suitability within Q. The question then concerns the meaning of this woe.

Opinions vary as to whether the vessels are real or metaphorical in all or any of this woe, and in addition there is the discussion of whether or not any current Jewish *halakhic* debate about the washing of vessels is in mind. Perhaps one may venture the following proposal. Hyam Maccoby's critique[38] of the proposal of Jacob Neusner[39] that Jesus is contributing to the internal Pharisaic debate, is in general persuasive, and his reminder that any washing process involved total immersion helpful. But the material is not, as he urges, metaphorical throughout. Indeed, it is not metaphorical at all. The pairing of

[34]Bultmann, *History* 131; Schulz, *Spruchquelle* 96–7; Hoffmann, *Studien* 170.
[35]Schulz, *Spruchquelle* 96–7.
[36]Schürmann, *Untersuchungen* 115.
[37]Schürmann, *Untersuchungen* 301.
[38]'The Washing of Cups', *JSNT* 14 (1982) 3–15.
[39]'"First Cleanse the Inside"', *NTS* 22 (1976) 486–95.

'cup and plate' suggests that literal objects are in mind, rather than a single vessel which might correspond to a typical person. Moreover, the situation is that they have been washed, a situation which is accepted as far as the outside is concerned. But the vessels have food and drink in them, and here we must note carefully the formulation ἔσωθεν δὲ γέμουσιν ἐξ ἁρπαγῆς καὶ ἀκρασίας. When this is compared with the similar (probably) MattR formulation in 23:27 ἔσωθεν δὲ γέμουσιν ὀστέων νεκρῶν καὶ πάσης ἀκαθαρσίας it becomes clear that the preposition ἐκ indicates how the food and drink came to be there, and also that descriptions of contents may point not only to actual physical objects (cf. ὀστέων νεκρῶν) but also to the religious status of such objects (cf. πᾶσα ἀκαθαρσία). So the food and drink, which naturally satisfy the Jewish food laws, have been obtained by ἁρπαγή and have thus made the inside of the vessels unclean, though not, of course, in the conventional Jewish sense. Hence, the cleanness of the whole of each vessel, in the new trans-conventional sense, depends on an abandonment of the conduct which has produced the food.[40]

It will be noticed that W is quite remarkably like T in that, first, it is structured chiastically (outside – inside – inside – outside) and draws attention to the problem in the second term; second, the practice of washing is taken for granted and even protected in much the same way as the practice of tithing; and now, third, the descriptions of the offence correspond. The term ἁρπαγή and its cognates is used in Jewish literature as a vivid metaphor for the predatory activities of wolves and lions,[41] and in a transferred sense for injustice done by the rich and powerful to the poor and vulnerable.[42] It represents the unprincipled grasping of the self-seeking who prosper, enjoy good food and high living, and do not give priority to 'judgment and mercy'. So while W concentrates on what is not being done, but should be, T spells out what is being done, but should not be. Thematically, it also matches the profile in S of

---

[40]The word πρῶτον indicates explicitly in W that overriding priority which T leaves implicit.

[41]Gen 49:27; Pss 7:2; 22:13; 104:21; Ezek 19:3, 6; 22:25, 27; Hos 5:14; Mic 5:8; T. Dan 5:7; T. Benj. 11:1, 2; Matt 7:15; John 10:12.

[42]Job 20:19; 24:9; Ps 10:9; Isa 3:14–15; 10:2; 61:8; Ezek 18:7, 12, 16; Mic 3:2.

the upwardly mobile in human terms, as well as engaging in personal polemic of the sort we find in G.

7. Unmarked Graves. Q 11:44.

G is represented by two versions, each of which shows an awareness of Palestinian custom, though not the same custom in each case. The Matthaean version is vulnerable to a series of criticisms: first, that whitewashing was not intended as beautification[43] but rather as a warning of the danger of contracting uncleanness; second, that the application does not fit a warning against such a danger; third, that there is in Matt 23:28 evidence of Matthaean style and interests, and probably some indebtedness to the 'inside .. outside' scheme of W. The Lucan version, which picks up Num 19:16; *m. Ohol.* 17:5, is probably to be preferred.[44] What is its meaning? A strong exploitation of the metaphor of the unmarked graves would lead to the conclusion that 'it portrays them as a source of ritual defilement',[45] but moral rather than ritual defilement must be the topic once the transfer from metaphor to reality has been made. In that case, G is using a different and thoroughly offensive metaphor to make the same point as W, and adding the further charge that outward appearance belies inner reality.

8. The Tombs of the Prophets. Q 11:47–48.

P has with some justice been accused of displaying 'the logic of polemic, not of reasoned argument'.[46] Yet it must be presumed that long-term transmission could scarcely succeed with tradition which is incoherent and unreasonable, so the attempt must be made to reach back to a *Vorlage* which was coherent and rational. Luke's version, for all that it is carefully and chiastically structured (building – killing – witnessing – killing – building), makes little contribution to this attempt,

[43]Garland, *Intention* 152.
[44]Schulz, *Spruchquelle* 106.
[45]Kloppenborg, *Formation* 141.
[46]Hare, *Persecution* 82.

since it hinges on the absurd idea that the building of a tomb constitutes approval of the murder of the person buried in it.[47] Only in two respects does Luke help us: first, by lacking Matthew's τοὺς τάφους ... καὶ κοσμεῖτε ... τῶν δικαίων (the adornment idea is similar to the alien import of whitewashing to make attractive, Matt 23:27, while the inclusion of 'the righteous' anticipates 23:35 diff Luke 11:50[48]) and thus confirming that MattR (in 23:29, contrast 23:31) has created a new synonymous parallelism out of 'you build the tombs of the prophets'; second, by supporting the possibility that Matt 23:30 did indeed appear in Q, in that Luke's central 'witnessing' statement matches positionally the central statement beginning καὶ λέγετε and interpreted ὥστε μαρτυρεῖτε. It is wholly normal for Q to include statements in direct speech[49] and, one may add, the presence of καί in Q 11:49 ('For this reason the Wisdom of God *also* said ...') presumes that the speech of Wisdom is a response to some earlier speech. In sum, therefore, the original P probably contained Luke 11:47 + Matt 23:30, a complementary two-part descriptive statement, with emphasis upon the second part, followed by Matt 23:31, the conclusion exploiting polemically the notion of sonship.[50]

Reconstructed thus, the final woe is notable for the pattern of argument it selects in order to inculpate its audience in the deaths of the prophets. If the members of that audience had literally brought about any such death, guilt by action, rather than guilt by association grounded in so subtle an argument, could have formed the basis of a simple, direct, and compelling charge. This does not happen. Consequently, no actual prophetic death, which might be set to the account of the Pharisees, has taken place. Their guilt rests upon association with their ancestors, based upon the deuteronomic view of Israel's history, and now asserted by the speaker. Their resistance to this view takes the form of a refusal to express repentance in confession.[51] Over

---

[47]Contrast 1 Macc 13:25–30. On Luke's *non sequitur*, cf. Garland, *Intention* 164; Sand, *Matthäus* 461. The verb συνευδοκεῖν is LukeR, cf. Schulz, *Spruchquelle* 109, in view of the similar martyrological context in Acts 8:1; 22:20.

[48]Schulz, *Spruchquelle* 109.

[49]Cf. Q 3:8; 6:42; 12:45; 13:27.

[50]This is a modification of the view of Hoffmann, *Studien* 162–3, that the Q version approximated to Luke 11:47 + Matt 23:31, and a return to that of Steck, *Israel* 28–9.

against what they say as a disclaimer of responsibility, stands what Wisdom said as an affirmation of responsibility and also of judgment.[52]

9. The Speech of Wisdom. Q 11:49–51.

There is no need to rehearse the familiar arguments about the contents of Q 11:49–51.[53] Again and again Matthew/Luke verbal discrepancies have to be resolved in favour of the originality of Luke. Exceptions are the 'apostles', probably inserted to prepare for 'those who are sent' (Q 13:34) as well as to include Christian leaders within the programme here described; 'from the foundation of the world', less Semitic than Matthew's 'upon the ground' (2 Sam 14:14) and brought in to smooth the transition to the Abel reference; and 'the house', less precise than Matthew's 'sanctuary', and probably an anticipation of Q 13:35a.

The meaning of what is said here completes what was begun in P. The past period of Israel's rejection of the prophets is mentioned again. The speech of contemporary persons is balanced and refuted by the speech of Wisdom. The previous assertion of the final answerability of those contemporary persons, based on argument rather than actuality, receives additional and ultimate confirmation from the mouth of even higher authority. Superimposed, one might say, upon all that is the Abel-Zechariah catalogue of rejected ones (Q 11:51a), with its attached repetition of the judgment on this generation (Q 11:51b). Leaving aside all attempts to identify Zechariah as anyone other than the martyr of 2 Chron 24:20–22, we can see in Q 11:51a a panorama of all the martyrdoms of scripture, much like the panorama of experiences of suffering from Abel onwards, which the father of the famous seven sons drew from 'the law and the prophets' (4 Macc 18:10).

---

[51]Steck, *Israel* 281.

[52]The MattR insertion of 23:32, 33 serves as a recognition by the evangelist that 23:29–31 is not an internally complete unit, and that it has to have a new conclusion added if Q 11:49–51 is disengaged. This disengagement was itself necessitated by the transformation of a Wisdom speech into a Jesus speech.

[53]Schulz, *Spruchquelle* 336–8.

10. The Lament over Jerusalem. Q 13:34–35.

The lament over Jerusalem hinges on the contrast beween two wills: ἠθέλησα . . . οὐκ ἠθελήσατε (13:34b). This indicates an underlying call for realignment, in other words, a demand for repentance, in the present. The contemporary refusal of repentance is seen as a projection of that which is a settled and established tendency to kill the prophets, but it is not itself expanded into a contemporary killing. The speaker, whose echoing of imagery used elsewhere for the call of God or of Wisdom, interprets his mission as prophetic and authorized by God and/or Wisdom. In a unit of tradition distinct from Q 11:47–51 he covers the same ground, expresses the same self-consciousness, alludes to the same purpose, and finally affirms the same judgment. Doubtless ἀφίεται points to God and the future, and οἶκος points to the city, the temple, and the community as a three-in-one whole. While a certain sympathy is conveyed by the intense duplication 'Jerusalem, Jerusalem' and the general mood of sorrowful lamentation, judgment forms the climax in Q 13:35a. Superimposed upon that is the more optimistic announcement that the speaker's period of invisibility will end with a joyful welcome back to the city, the temple, and the community.[54]

The history of these traditions, and therefore the manner and extent of their mirroring of the history of the Q community, can now be assessed. As they stand, the woes combine criticisms of the professional principles and the personal character and conduct of the Pharisees, but it has proved difficult to sustain subdivisions of the seven. First, we have repeatedly detected connections, i.e. K/P, B/K, S/K/B/P, T/P, W/S/T, and G/W.[55] Second, recourse to intra-religious polemical texts elsewhere, e.g. *Psalms of Solomon* 4; CD 1.18b – 2.1; 1QH 2.6–14; *Testament of Moses* 7.4–9, serves to confirm how common and instinctive, though doubtless one-sided, is the tendency to combine personal criticisms (with higher or lower coefficients of vitriol!) and assaults on principles of interpretation of the will of God. In these texts we find on one and the same stratum attacks which

[54]D. C. Allison, 'Matt. 23.39 = Luke 13.35b as a Conditional Prophecy', *JSNT* 18 (1983), 75–84.

[55]See above, pp. 262–8.

correspond to those which have been traced by some to different strata of Q. Third, there is the term ὑποκριτής. Its appearance in five out of seven of the woes (in fact all but B and S) could be, and often is,[56] attributed to MattR. But Matthew can also derive it from tradition elsewhere (Mark 7:6; 12:15), including Q (Q 6:42; 12:46), and Luke's generalized warning against the ὑπόκρισις of the Pharisees immediately after his version of the woes (12:1) suggests a reminiscence of the use of the term in the woes themselves. If so, it is relevant that the term ὑπόκρισις encompasses an extremely broad range of meaning: from inaccurate teaching and interpretation (cf. Luke 12:56; 13:15) to downright wickedness and lack of integrity.[57] Such a range of meaning confronts us in the woes, but it does not impede the conclusion that they form a unity.

In principle it is possible that some of the woes have been expanded. Some contain simply an accusation and are irreducible (K, B, G). Others contain a further single sentence, either indicative (S, T) or imperative (W) in form. One only (P) is much more extensive, as befits the last in the series. In the case of S, the saying Q 14:11 is demonstrably capable of existing separately, and Q 11:43 is equally clearly capable of surviving alone. So the former may owe its presence here to editorial work, though it is not clear that it must do.[58] In the case of T, Q 11:42c is regarded by some as redactional, an attempt to guard against the inference that Pharisaic interpretation of the tithing laws is being rejected.[59] Reasons have already been put forward for an alternative view of this woe, and the delicate balance and clarity of 11:42bc, over against the unclarity of 11:42b by itself, tends to make the presence of an editorial comment marginally possible but highly improbable. In the case of W, the situation is not dissimilar, that is, Q 11:39 could

---

[56] Schulz, *Spruchquelle* 96 *et al.*

[57] U. Wilckens, 'ὑποκρίνομαι', *TDNT* 8.559–71.

[58] In a strikingly parallel text, Sir 1:28–30, a warning against hypocrisy and failure to fear the Lord involves the instruction, 'Do not exalt yourself (μὴ ἐξύψου σεαυτόν) lest you fall ... and the Lord will cast you down in the middle of the assembly (συναγωγή).'

[59] Hoffmann, *Studien* 59; Schenk, *Synopse* 76; Tuckett, 'Q, the Law and Judaism', 94. This possibility had already been mentioned by Bultmann, *History* 131, though with the qualification that T and W might preserve authentic sayings of Jesus (p. 147).

be self-sufficient, but in isolation it lacks clarity and coherence to such an extent that the removal of Matt 23:26 would be damaging.

The final woe, P (Q 11:47–51), has almost certainly been expanded.[60] Q 11:51a envisages a sequence of martyrs, but a more extensive one than the sequence of prophetic martyrs; it causes Q 11:51b to reiterate the declaration in 11:50 that blood will be required of this generation. Prophets alone were in view in Q 11:50, so the extra persons mentioned in Q 11:49 must also have been added redactionally. Other Q sayings show an interest in either 'the law and the prophets' as a whole (Q 16:16), or a range of persons more extensive than the prophets as representatives of the pre-John/Jesus period (Q 7:28a; 10:24), and while these other sayings are almost certainly pre-redactional their number suggests a special interest on the part of the editor.

It is widely agreed that the lament over Jerusalem (Q 13:34–35) has been expanded. This expansion probably includes the phrase καὶ λιθοβολοῦσα τοὺς ἀπεσταλμένους, which matches both the similar addition in Q 11:49[61] and also the creation of 11:51, and is, incidentally, further confirmation that in Q the lament did follow the woes. That 'And I tell you, you will not see me again until you say, "Blessed is he who comes in the name of the Lord."' (13:35b) is an expansion is extremely probable.[62] The prospect of judgment forms an appropriate ending for 13:34–35a in form-critical terms, and the hopeful

---

[60]Kloppenborg, *Formation* 144, regards Q 11:49–51 as a whole as 'a secondary construction of Q redaction', on the basis of (i) a discrepancy of audience between Pharisees/scribes and 'this generation'; (ii) the unexpectedness of the apparently pre-mundane speech of Sophia in the midst of the woes attributed to Jesus; and (iii) the difference of character between the reproaches offered by the woes and the retribution threatened in the Sophia oracle. The problem with this analysis is that, as Kloppenborg himself rightly recalls, 11:47–51 corresponds formally to the classic woe oracle form which includes an announcement of judgment. Moreover, dislocation within 11:49–51 makes unitary redaction unlikely. Finally, the broadening of which Kloppenborg speaks has already been implicit in P, since, as has from time to time been observed, for example, by Hare, *Persecution* 83, we cannot suppose that the Pharisees alone were engaged in building tombs for the prophets. Already before Q 11:49–51, therefore, they had become representative figures.

[61]From the range of OT victims of stoning Zechariah ben Jehoiada (2 Chron 24:20–22) is the only one who could, even in the most general sense, be described as having been 'sent'.

[62]Neirynck, 'Recent Developments', 66.

note struck by 13:35b is louder than anything in 13:34–35a. Dale Allison has convincingly demonstrated that 13:35b expresses the conviction that a mission calling for repentance in Israel must continue and will achieve good success.[63] It is this mission with which the Q community is occupied. Although ostensibly addressed to Jerusalem, Q 13:35b is more of a concluding message to the Christian community, in the same way that the whole woe complex is ostensibly addressed to Pharisees, but in fact addressed to disciples (Matt 23:1/Luke 20:45 diff Mark 12:37b).

A further component of the message to the disciples arises from the juxtaposition of Q 13:35b and Q 17:23–24. The one who has gone away (cf. Q 19:12) and who will come (Q 12:43; 19:15) is the Son of man. The Son of man's coming will not be experienced restrictedly either in the sacred settings of desert or inner rooms (of the temple? – the word ταμιεῖον is so ordinary a description of a private room[64] that its particular meaning must be fixed by its context; it is used by Josephus, *J.W.* 4.4.3 §262; *Ant.* 9.7.1 §142; 9.13.3 §274, of a location on the temple site; desert and Jerusalem, the latter viewed at a distance from the Mount of Olives, are the two locations preoccupying the charismatic-eschatological leaders, according to Josephus, *Ant.* 20.8.6 §§167–170; elsewhere in Q 4:3–4, 9–11 desert and temple have been paired as possible locations of christological disclosure). It will not conform to the scheme of the charismatic-eschatological prophets. He will come from heaven to Jerusalem, overwhelmingly and openly for all to see. He will only come when Jerusalem is ready to welcome him because the community there has at last, in response to the Christian mission, repented.

If the foregoing argument has been correct, the material in Q 11:39–52; 13:34–35; 17:23–24 contains a relatively small number of editorial additions. Few and light though they are, those additions do cohere with one another and form a window through which we may view the Q community and its concerns and commitments. The underlying material to which the ad-

---

[63]'Matt. 23:39 = Luke 13.35b', 75–84. Less convincing is his argument that this saying is integral to the oracle and not a secondary expansion.

[64]A room for eating (2 Sam 13:10) or sleeping (Cant 1:4; 3:4) or storage (Ps 144:13; Prov 3:10; Luke 12:24) or hiding (1 Kgs 22:25; 2 Kgs 11:2).

ditions were made is just as interesting, even though the theory of successive stages of literary, and therefore experiential, development has not proved convincing. That underlying material documents the religious tradition upon which the Q community relies, and to which it is answerable.

The woes against the Pharisees have emerged as an originally unified complex attaching supreme importance to the connection between the missions of the prophets of Israel and the contemporary prophetic preaching of the kingdom. Deaths occurred in the former context, but no deaths have occurred in the latter. That means that we can add further strength and precision to the arguments that the woes belong to a pre-70 CE setting by locating them even before the first Christian martyrdom. Inevitably, so early a *terminus ad quem* raises the question whether in these woes we overhear the *ipsissima vox Jesu*.

A distinction between the outlook of Jesus and the outlook of the woes has often been detected in T + W, in that the tithing and purity laws are accepted, rather than being, as in Mark 7, questioned.[65] But recent discussion of Mark 7:15 has severely damaged the view that it supports a conflict between Jesus and Torah, especially when the words εἰσπορευόμενον εἰς αὐτόν are assigned to MarkR and removed. Contrariwise, the way in which T + W, while in no way criticizing the practices in question, nevertheless subordinate them firmly to the primary obligations of justice, mercy and concern for the poor, brings them into the mainstream of what is usually regarded as authentic tradition.

Another supposed discrepancy between the woes and Jesus has been proposed in K. There the idea of the kingdom has been contrasted with Jesus' apocalyptic perspective,[66] and understood in terms of the community, even to the extent of recalling the watchword *extra ecclesiam nulla salus*![67] This must surely be overdrawn, partly because Jesus' debt to apocalyptic must not be exaggerated, and partly because K is most easily understood in terms of a relationship between the kingdom and 'the age to come', and from the point of view of a mission which questions

[65]Hoffmann, *Studien* 170.
[66]Schulz, *Spruchquelle* 111.
[67]Haenchen, 'Matthäus 23', 47; Schürmann, 'Zeugnis', 175–6.

the assumption that all Israelites have a share in that coming age.[68]

Finally, there is in P the confrontation with 'this generation', which Dieter Lührmann has held to be the hallmark of Q[69] and which, if so, might not be traceable to Jesus. What is striking about the other 'this generation' sayings is that they apparently belong to varied strata within the traditions used by Q. Two examples will suffice. On the one hand, there is the sign for 'this generation', the sign of Jonah (Q 11:29–30), which was examined in detail earlier in this volume. It was suggested that Q redaction was alone responsible for that saying. On the other hand there is the denunciation of 'this generation' in the parable of the children in the marketplace (Q 7:31–32). The parable is evidently older than its secondary expansion (7:33–34). As a comment on the obduracy of the audience of Jesus in Israel, presented with a prophetic message which has both celebratory and salutary aspects, this parable rings true to the message of Jesus. It is worth considering whether Q 7:35, which does not seem very obviously integrated with 7:33–34, may have been an original ending for the parable, at once a 'sting in the tail' for opponents and an assurance to those who have accepted the call (cf. the call of Wisdom to the obdurate, Prov. 1:22–27, with comment on that call, 1:28–32, and final assurance about those who are attentive, 1:33.)[70] On any showing the connective καί in Q 7:35 is adversative; the metaphor of children is shared by 7:31–32, 35 but not by 7:33–34; and if the children of Wisdom have 'recognized righteousness' in the call of Jesus, then he must himself be a prophet sent by Wisdom. At all events, the theme of 'this generation', while firmly endorsed by Q, can be derived from Jesus. If so, it is a case of 'from Jesus to Q' rather than 'not Jesus but Q'.

The woes against the Pharisees belong to a setting of conflict *intra muros* within Judaism. Nothing disrespectful of the definitive position of law and temple is said here. But what of the

[68]Similarly in favour of authenticity, Garland, *Intention* 127–8.

[69]*Redaktion* 35–43.

[70]If the 'children of Wisdom' (Q 7:35) are to be equated with the 'babes' (Q 10:21), cf. Légasse, 'Oracle', 246, it would be significant that Q 10:21 itself belongs to an older stratum of the text than the following commentary saying (Q 10:22) and is also worth taking seriously as a possible Jesus-saying.

specific relationship between Christians and Pharisees? Attention has recently and, I believe, rightly been drawn to the closeness of that relationship.[71] It is clear that there were many convictions held in common. How then can we explain the confrontation documented by so many traditions, including the woes? Of course, religious groups which show least sympathy for one another often have most in common in terms of heritage.[72] It's the neighbours who are often nastiest to one another! Nevertheless, the woes do point to a discrepancy of principle as well as a willingness to engage in personalized polemic. In the setting of the prophetic announcement of the kingdom, a missionary message to Israel about which the Pharisees remain sceptical and critical, there is a disposition to stand apart from the process of generating tradition and allegedly burdensome definitions of the will of God, and to insist on the paramount importance of the major principles of the covenant. One corollary of this result would be that we do not (*pace* Tuckett) find evidence in these woes of a tendency to 're-Judaize' within the Q community, nor a claim by that community to be a true part of the Pharisaic movement. The tradition seems throughout to be comfortable within Judaism, uneasy about Pharisaism, and, in view of the rarity of any comment on the authority of the law (Q 16:17), not at all preoccupied with the problem which threatened to tear apart other early Christian communities. Of such controversies Q is aware, but it can afford to pass by on the other side with just that one side-glance.

The Lament over Jerusalem antedates its editorial modification, but by how much? Its nearest relatives, traditionally speaking, are the woes on the cities of Galilee (Q 10:13–15). Indeed there is arguably more than a passing similarity of scheme[73] between Q 10:3–16 and Q 11:39–52; 13:34–35. The similarities extend to early tradition concerned with the preaching of the kingdom and climaxing in the announcement of judgment (10:3–12; 11:39–50, 52); an oracle against specific cities

[71]R. A. Wild, 'The encounter between Pharisaic and Christian Judaism: some early gospel evidence', *NovT* 27 (1985) 105–24; C. M. Tuckett, 'Q, the Law and Judaism', 98–101, with significant modifications of Wild's treatment of Marcan material; K. Berger, 'Jesus als Pharisäer und frühe Christen als Pharisäer', *NovT* 30 (1988) 231–62.

[72]Berger, 'Jesus als Pharisäer', 232.

[73]Similarly Neirynck, 'Recent Developments', 66–7.

(10:13–15; 13:34); and a saying about reception of the one who has come, or will come, with the authority of God (10:16; 13:35b). When 13:34–35a is set alongside 10:13–15, internal similarities also appear.[74] This time the similarities cover, first, the address to cities; second, the historical retrospect (on Tyre and Sidon, and on Jerusalem); third, the reference to the overall mission of Jesus; fourth, a sense of protracted activity (πάλαι . . . ποσάκις); fifth, a demand for repentance; and sixth, the proclamation of judgment. It looks as if these two Q traditions have a common origin.

Once again, the possibility of derivation from Jesus is worth taking seriously.[75] First, the Gentile mission is not presupposed by these sayings in and of themselves.[76] Second, it is hard to see why such obscure places as Chorazin and Bethsaida, which made minimal impact on the gospel tradition, should be singled out in a secondary development. Third, the abrasive radicalism of an adverse contrast between the notorious Tyre and Sidon and any Israelite city is likely to be authentic (cf. the similar contrast with Nineveh, Q 11:32). Fourth, the call to repentance is too deeply embedded in too many traditions for them all to be detached from the mission of Jesus himself. Fifth, the surveying of the whole of a person's activity in a particular place is hardly inappropriate for the person himself: when the emissaries of Jesus engage particular cities with the message and signs of the kingdom, and then feel themselves to be in general unsuccessful, they respond with a final gesture of disassociation and judgment. If the tradition in Q 10:8–11 reflects the original historical situation, it can provide a parallel and support for the two general surveys under consideration. Sixth, the evidence of prophetic self-understanding on the part of Jesus is widespread in the gospel tradition, and the evidence of a sense of overall failure is widespread too. When those two elements are brought together it is entirely unsurprising that the deuteronomic scheme should be adopted. An authentic 'two and two' should not be

[74]Garland, *Intention* 70.

[75]Rightly, C. E. Carlston, 'Wisdom and Eschatology in Q', *Logia* 101–19, esp. p. 117: 'There is no particular reason that Jesus might not have wept over Jerusalem (Lk. 13,34f. = Mt. 23,37–39) for rejecting his message and noted the parallel between his own rejection and the rejection of Wisdom.'

[76]See above, pp. 172–3.

prevented from making an authentic 'four'! Seventh, 'your house (will be) left to you' stands as a final prophetic word of doom over city, community and temple. This is simply a variation on the theme of Mark 13:2; 14:58, a theme which, as Ed Sanders has demonstrated, has a strong claim to authenticity.[77]

The Q community thus inherited some traditions which expressed, on the one hand, a critical view of the Pharisees but a continuing commitment to the covenant, the law, and the temple, and on the other hand, the expectation that Jerusalem and the temple would be abandoned by God. These were held in balance. The fate of the temple in the future was not taken to imply its religious irrelevance in the present. On the contrary, the future was taken seriously and exclusively as future. And thus we have a picture of a community whose outlook was essentially Jerusalem-centred, whose theology was Torah-centred, whose worship was temple-centred, and which saw (with some justice) no incompatibility between all of that and commitment to Jesus.

---

[77]*Jesus* 71–6.

10

Faith

The language of faith occurs only rarely in Q. When an uncertain instance (Matt 24:26 diff Luke 17:23) is set aside, as it almost certainly should be,[1] we are left with a very small selection of sayings. There is Q 11:42, whose original form exposed the essence of true religious commitment as 'judgment, mercy and faith'. Faith, in that sense of faithfulness to the covenant, was viewed as the overall context for faithfulness to the departing Jesus who would return as Son of man, according to some of the parabolic material in Q: 'Who is the faithful and wise servant? . . . Well done, good and faithful servant, you have been faithful over a little . . .' (Q 12:42; 19:17). Unfaithfulness might be a matter of doing evil (thus Q 12:45) or, more tellingly, it might be a matter of simply doing nothing at all (thus Q 19:20–21). But faith would show itself as goodness, faithfulness and wisdom, and it would be oriented in a very special way towards Jesus. It would be an acknowledgement of his status as the κύριος and would be defined as obedience to his word.

One of the most striking references to faith occurs in Q 17:6, the saying whose original wording probably ran:

ἐὰν ἔχητε πίστιν ὡς κόκκον σινάπεως, ἐλέγετε ἂν τῇ συκαμίνῳ ταύτῃ· ἐκριζώθητι, καὶ ὑπήκουσεν ἂν ὑμῖν.[2]

This promise is all the more arresting and dramatic for its bringing together in a single saying the proverbially tiny mustard seed[3] and the extremely deep rooted sycamine tree.[4] The faith of which Jesus speaks is extraordinary in its effects but not, in view of the 'divine passive' ἐκριζώθητι, autonomously

---

[1]Matt 24:26 is a reminiscence of Matt 24:23/Mark 13:21.
[2]See Schulz, *Spruchquelle* 466–7.
[3]*m. Nid.* 5:2; *m. Tohar.* 8:8; *b. Ber.* 31a.
[4]Billerbeck II.234.

so. Faith is by definition an appeal to the God through whom all things are possible. The context in which such faith is exercised, however, remains unclear in this saying without a definitive setting. It could belong to some quite general setting[5] or to the more specific setting of miracle-working activity by early Christian charismatics.[6] Only by correlating it with other traditions on the same subject in the same source can we determine what it meant in Q.

The classic Q passage in which reflection occurs on the notion of faith is that concerning the centurion (Q 7:1–10). It is scarcely possible to overestimate the importance for Q of this apophthegmatic miracle story and the theology it aims to articulate. The preceding inaugural discourse of Jesus in Q is, as we have seen, held together by an *inclusio* (6:20b-23, 46–49) in which the redactional layers (6:22–23, 46) draw attention to the one who is to be confessed and obeyed, the Son of man and Lord. The following unified complex (Q 7:18–35) is held together by redactional elements (7:18–19, 23, 27, 28b, 33–34) which also concentrate on Jesus, this time as coming one and Son of man. Wedged between these two complexes, both heavy with one and the same christology, stands the tradition about the centurion. To make sure that the reader of Q understands this the editor not only positions it where he does but also takes care to set up narrative links between it and the material on either side. At the beginning of the centurion tradition such a link lies beneath the surface of Matt 7:28a; 8:5a/Luke 7:1. And beneath the surface of Matt 11:2a/Luke 7:18a there lies a further significant link. The latter indicates that John's question, and therefore the christological issue of Jesus as coming one and Son of man, arises directly from what has just happened, namely the miracle described in Q 7:1–10. That miracle, so it would emerge, is intended to be typical of a range of miracles which have not been explicitly narrated but which are now listed for the Baptist's benefit (Q 7:22). Not surprisingly the two polar opposites of πίστις and σκανδαλίζεσθαι (cf. Mark 6:3, 6) are present as alternative responses to Jesus and his status in the two adjacent passages (Q 7:9, 23).

[5]Schenk, *Synopse* 119.
[6]Thus Schulz, *Spruchquelle* 468; Zeller, *Mahnsprüche* 131.

A rather different angle on this tradition has been suggested by John Kloppenborg.[7] His thesis has several constituent parts: (i) The links between Q 7:1–10 and what precedes are mere catchwords. The verbal links are through λόγος (6:47, 49; 7:7) and κύριε (6:46; 7:6), with no strong christological connotations – indeed nothing beyond 'sir' – being involved in κύριος in either case: 'otherwise intrinsic affiliation is quite tenuous'. Specifically, the recognition of Jesus' authority in 7:1–10 is by outsiders, not by members of the community. (ii) The significant links are between Q 7:1–10 and what follows, where the shared concern extends to miracle (7:18–23) and 'the implicit criticism of Israel's lack of response to Jesus' ἐξουσία' (7:31–35). (iii) The centurion's identity as a Gentile is 'crucial to the story as it stands'. The idea that the counterpart figure in John 4:46–54, the βασιλικός, is someone, either official or soldier, either Jewish or Gentile, attached to the court of Antipas is 'plausible' in that context, but in Q it is different. (iv) While the story may not in isolation be evidence of a Gentile mission it is made such by 'other factors . . . in the context of Q redaction'. In the light of Q 10:13–15; 11:31–32, 'similar examples of real or predicted Gentile response', and also 13:29, 28; 14:16–24, it becomes 'an apology for Gentile inclusion'. Whereas faith had not been expected among Gentiles it is now forthcoming, indeed 'the story stresses not only the fact of his faith but its exceptional quality', and so Gentile participation in the kingdom is no longer restricted to the eschatological pilgrimage. So, Kloppenborg concludes, the reception of this story into Q 'is to be seen in the context of Q's polemic against Israel's lack of recognition of the authority of Jesus and his message, and Q's interpretation of Gentile faith as an *Unheilszeichen* for Israel'.

This proposal provokes a series of questions. (i) Is it really the case that 'Why do you call me κύριε, κύριε . . .?' is so non-christological and so open to being paraphrased 'Why do you call me "sir, sir . . ."'?[8] Why should there be so strong an expecta-

[7]*Formation* 117–20.

[8]By contrast Sato, *Prophetie* 178, considers several possible *Sitze im Leben* for this saying and concludes that, whatever its origin, its meaning on the Q level envisages Jesus as the exalted one with divine authority. U. Wegner, *Der Hauptmann von Kafarnaum*, (WUNT 2/14; Tübingen: Mohr, 1985) 381–3, prefers to see κύριος as expressing Jesus' status as the divinely empowered emissary of God.

tion of obedience attached to the use of the term 'sir'? Is it clear and firm that the centurion's recognition of the authority of Jesus relates exclusively to the latter's power in miracle and not to his issuing of authoritative words in a wider sense? And is the centurion one of 'the outsiders, not members of the community'? How should 'the community' be understood? (ii) If we were to favour a stronger christological link between Q 7:1–10 and what follows, would that not be supported by the data assembled above? Is there not some danger of exaggerating the theme of Israel's rejection in 7:18–35 when being 'scandalized' is mentioned only as a theoretical possibility in the first unit (7:23), ignored altogether in the second in which an agreed *positive* response to John is recorded (7:26), and tempered in the third by the concluding affirmation that in spite of everything the children of Wisdom have recognized both John and Jesus (7:35)? To this we shall need to return. (iii) Is it so clear that the ἑκατοντάρχης is a Gentile? If the term were to turn out to be ethnically neutral, and if it might stand in Q, just as much as βασιλικός in John, for someone attached to Antipas,[9] and if, as Kloppenborg allows, it is not so much the *fact* of his faith as its *exceptional quality* which is being hailed, might it not be necessary to revise a widespread assumption? (iv) Is not the mission to *Israel* the natural *Sitz im Leben* of the traditions to which appeal is made in the interests of interpreting Q 7:1–10 in terms of Gentile mission, in spite of itself being intrinsically unable to provide that support? The Gentiles mentioned in Q 10:13–15 are not models of actual response but simply means to an end of rebuking the presumed audience in Israel. The Gentiles mentioned in Q 11:31–32 are models of response but only as means for rebuking those who have not responded, those who, on the level of Q redaction (Q 11:29–30), seek a sign in the way which is typical of *Jews* (1 Cor 1:22). So we have a collection of questions to answer in what follows, questions which all converge on one major question: Is the ἑκατοντάρχης a model of Gentile faith?

The answers to these questions emerge slowly as the process of establishing the original Q text gathers momentum. But at

---

[9]Luz, *Matthäus 8–17*, 14, while presuming overall that he is a Gentile, allows for the possibility of an Herodian connection.

the outset one must pause to resist occasional denials of a straightforward Q solution to the problem of Matt 7:28a; 8:5–13/ Luke 7:1–10; 13:28–29. First, the verbal overlap is intense, the only contrary impression being created by the most probably LukeR intervention with the delegation of Jewish elders. Second, after Matt 8:1–4 is set aside as being derived from Mark, there is Matthew/Luke agreement in the position of this tradition immediately after the discourse.[10] Only when there is a reluctance to assign Luke 7:3–6a, 7a to LukeR do different recensions come into consideration,[11] and only when Matt 8:5–13 is regarded as a MattR construction out of Mark 2:1–12; 5:21–43[12] is a stronger Marcan connection mooted. Neither of these positions carries conviction, and the evidence seems rather to favour a straight Q-based treatment of the material. The reconstruction of the Q tradition and the attempt to recover its original meaning need then to recognize the following realities:

First, the agreement in order which aligns the tradition with the Matthew 7/Luke 6 parts of the preceding Q discourse is qualified by a further agreement in order which aligns Matt 8:11–12/Luke 13:28–29 with the Matthew 7/Luke 13 parts of the preceding Matthaean discourse. This, together with the difficulty of explaining why Luke should disperse the traditions, confirms the widespread view that Matt 8:11–12 owes its present position to MattR activity.

Second, the healing of the leper (Matt 8:1–4/Mark 1:40–45) is followed in Matthew by the story about the centurion and in Mark by the tradition of the healing of the paralytic (Mark 2:1–12). The latter passage was left over by Matthew until later, Matt 9:1–8, but the correspondence suggests that Matthew may have regarded the two as in some way equivalent. This may be entirely correct in the sense that there is an underlying tradition historical relationship between the two stories, even if not one of direct literary dependence, and as far as Matthew is concerned it may enable details to move to and fro, as it were, between the two. In a not dissimilar fashion we note that after following the Marcan sequence exactly in Matt 8:23–27, 28–34 (Mark

[10]Lührmann, *Redaktion* 57.
[11]Thus Wegner, *Hauptmann* 161–98; Sato, *Prophetie* 55.
[12]E. Wendling, 'Synoptische Studien II. Der Hauptmann von Kapernaum', *ZNW* 9 (1908) 96–109; Goulder, *Midrash* 319.

4:35–41; 5:1–20), the evangelist broke off instead of using Mark 5:21–43 immediately afterwards – he saved it for Matt 9:18–26 – and returned to the Marcan sequence of Mark 2:1–12, 13–17 (Matt 9:1–8, 9–13). Thus his version of Mark 2:1–12 occurred where his version of Mark 5:21–43 would have occurred if he had been following the Marcan order strictly in one of the ways open to him. Again, this may encourage the inference that there is an underlying tradition historical relationship between the traditions about the centurion, the healing of the paralytic and the raising of Jairus' daughter, and it provides the setting within which details may move around between all three traditions. When the further possibility[13] that the discussion of Matt 8:5–13 ought to draw in Mark 7:24–30, the story of the Syro-Phoenician woman, is recalled, then the range of possibly related traditions has become quite wide. And the comparable Johannine and rabbinic stories must also not be forgotten![14] In the case of John 4:46–54, where John's direct literary dependence upon the synoptic gospels has been established by Frans Neirynck,[15] the Johannine story can be used simply as one example of how the synoptic tradition was handled.

Third, the discussion cannot be made too dependent on any conclusions which may be reached about either the verbal minutiae of the transition from the discourse (Q 6:20b–49) or the original conclusion which doubtless confirmed the occurrence of the cure. At the one end of the story, it is not difficult to envisage the Q transition as καὶ ἐγένετο ὅτε ἐτέλεσεν ὁ Ἰησοῦς τοὺς λόγους τούτους, εἰσῆλθεν εἰς Καφαρναούμ, thus matching OT precedents (Num 16:31; Jer 26:8 and especially Deut 32:45), and taking seriously the Matthew/Luke agreements in substance: (i) a time clause referring to (ii) the completion of (iii) the sayings of Jesus in · (iv) the hearing of the audience, followed by (v) a movement into Capernaum.[16] Similar formulations in Matt 11:1; 13:53; 19:1; 26:1 do not negate this proposal, since there are several examples of Matthew's repeated

[13]Bultmann, *History* 38.

[14]John 4:46–54; *b. Ber.* 34b; *b. B. Qam.* 50a = *b. Yebam.* 121b; *b. Pes.* 112b; *b. Ta'an.* 24b–25a.

[15]'John 4,46–54: Signs Source and/or Synoptic Gospels', *Evangelica II. Collected Essays by Frans Neirynck* (ed. F. Van Segbroeck; BETL 99; Leuven: University Press, 1991) 679–87.

[16]Schürmann, *Lukasevangelium I* 391.

usage of phrases attested singly in one of his sources.[17] At the other end of the story, a good case could be made on the basis of general Matthew/Luke agreement in content, and Matthew's overall tendency to be faithful to Q in this tradition, for the following as the conclusion: καὶ εἶπεν ὁ Ἰησοῦς τῷ ἑκατοντάρχῃ· ὕπαγε, ὡς ἐπίστευσας γενηθήτω σοι. καὶ ἰάθη ὁ παῖς ἐν τῇ ὥρᾳ ἐκείνῃ. But this conjectural conclusion adds nothing to, and is totally dependent for meaning upon, the body of the tradition where the original content is subject to much less uncertainty.

1. Help Requested and Promised. Q 7:2–6.

Following his arrival in Capernaum Jesus receives a request for help. This request is very differently portrayed in the two versions: it is direct in the one case and uses intermediaries in the other. If, as will be argued, the latter is LukeR, the reconstruction of the underlying Q version is not so complicated. The standard MattR προσῆλθεν and the Lucan favourite παραγίνομαι[18] probably replace an ἔρχομαι formulation, supported by the redactional Luke 7:7a and by the frequency with which such a MattR replacement takes place.[19] The verb παρακαλεῖν is agreed by Matt 8:5/Luke 7:4 and extremely suitable in the context of a miracle[20] or an approach to a person in authority.[21] Direct speech by the centurion in the presence of Jesus is suggested by (i) Matthew/Luke agreement in having *some* direct speech by someone, (ii) the greater suitability of Matt 8:8–9/Luke 7:6b, 7b-8 as the speech of someone who is present,[22] and (iii) the overall tendency of Q to reduce narrative to a minimum.

---

[17]'There shall be weeping and gnashing of teeth' (Q 13:28) became the prototype for five other Matthaean occurrences: Matt 13:42, 50; 22:13; 24:51 diff Luke 12:46; and Matt 25:30 diff Luke 19:27. The 'little ones' (Mark 9:42) became the source of the characteristic Matthaean discipleship terminology. The Marcan reference to 'your Father who is in heaven' (Mark 11:25) stimulated many such Matthaean references.

[18]Statistics: 3–1–8 + 20.

[19]See Matt 8:2; 9:14, 18, 20; 14:12; 21:23; 22:23; 26:7; 26:69.

[20]See Mark 5:23 (Jairus); Matt 14:36/Mark 6:56; Mark 7:32.

[21]See Josephus, *Ant.* 8.8.1 §213.

[22]Harnack, *Sayings* 76.

If then the description of the approach to Jesus was καὶ ἦλθεν αὐτῷ ἑκατόνταρχης παρακαλῶν αὐτὸν καὶ λέγων, what was the verbal exchange like? Here it is necessary to be more precise, and to consider four possible small constituent parts.

First, the address κύριε (Matt 8:6 only). In spite of the linkage to Q 6:46, the only other κύριε address in Q outside this tradition,[23] and the agreement with Q 7:7, it is easier to attribute this term to MattR than to explain why Luke would have dropped it.

Second, the sick person: ὁ παῖς μου (Matt 8:6) or δοῦλος . . . ὃς ἦν αὐτῷ ἔντιμος (Luke 7:2). The final phrase in Luke, using a term which occurs elsewhere only at Luke 14:8, and conforming to the evangelist's tendency to make personal details more specific (cf. Luke 8:42 diff Mark 5:23), is necessary only when the concern of the centurion needs to be explained.[24] This is so in the case of a servant, but not in the case of a son, so much hinges on whether παῖς is original and whether it stands for a son. The answer is probably 'yes' on both counts, for the following reasons: (i) Q 7:7 uses παῖς, and Luke's change would be explicable in terms of his 'studied variation of phrase and exchange of synonyms'.[25] For Luke,[26] as for a minority of instances in Josephus,[27] παῖς can stand for a servant. (ii) The terms παῖς and υἱός are equivalent in normal Josephus usage, and in Matt 17:15, 18/Luke 9:38, the retelling of Mark 9:14–29. Significant above all is the use of παῖς/παιδίον with a clear sense of one's own child in the related traditions of Jairus and the Syro-Phoenician woman: Mark 5:39–41/Luke 8:51, 54; Mark 7:30. The appeal of the parent, not the master, seems to be a standard feature of this family of traditions, so in this case the sick person should probably be taken to be a παῖς, that is, a son of the centurion.

Third, the terms describing the illness. (i) The phrase κακῶς

[23]Lührmann, *Redaktion* 58.

[24]Manson, *Sayings* 64; Schulz, *Spruchquelle* 237; Schürmann, *Lukasevangelium I* 391.

[25]H. J. Cadbury, 'Four Features of Lucan Style', *Studies in Luke-Acts* (ed. L. E. Keck and J. L. Martyn; London: SPCK, 1968) 87–102, esp. p. 92; similarly, Schürmann, *Lukasevangelium I* 391.

[26]Luke 12:45 diff Matt 24:49 σύνδουλος; Luke 15:26 παῖς = Luke 15:22 δοῦλος = Luke 15:17, 19 μίσθιος.

[27]*Ant.* 18.6.6 §192; *J.W.* 1.3.6 §82.

ἔχων cannot with safety be attributed to Q.[28] Not a normal Lucan term,[29] it occurs elsewhere in Luke-Acts only at Luke 5:31/Mark 2:17. But in that context he also introduced ὑγιαίνειν, present also in Luke 7:10, so he may in both contexts be redactionally setting up a pairing. Certainty is elusive. (ii) More promising is the phrase ἤμελλεν τελευτᾶν. The verb μέλλειν is a Lucan favourite but, in view of Q 3:7 usage and its being needed here to qualify τελευτᾶν, not thereby shown to be LukeR.[30] Much depends, therefore, on the verb τελευτᾶν itself. This is rare in the synoptic gospels:[31] leaving aside OT quotations there remain only the two non-relevant cases in Matt 2:19; 22:25 and the two very relevant cases in Matt 9:18 diff Mark 5:23 and Luke 7:2, i.e., Matthew's Jairus story and Luke's centurion story! Since Luke did not know Matt 9:18, the 'coincidental' overlap must be a reminiscence by Matthew of what was in the related tradition.[32] This serves once again to confirm the flow of details between one and another member of this family of traditions. On this basis the same can be said of Matthew's παραλυτικός, derived directly from the related healing story in Mark 2:1–12,[33] probably the source of all NT παραλυτικός references. (iii) The phrase ἐν τῇ οἰκίᾳ could certainly be a reminiscence of οἶκος in Mark 2:1, 11, or even drawn from Mark 1:29 in view of the next tradition in Matthew's sequence being Mark 1:29–31/Matt 8:14–15. However, οἶκος/οἰκία is a natural element in the story, especially since Q located the conversation with Jesus away from the centurion's home, and the occurrence of οἰκία in Luke 7:6 is better understood as a Lucan reminiscence of a Q detail than as evidence that Matthew knew some text approximating to Luke 7:1–6.[34] (iv) The verb βέβληται. The use of βάλλειν in a description of a sick person before recovery is extremely rare in the gospels and confined to two cases of MattR, both in traditions adjacent to this one.[35] Therefore βέβληται seems likely to be MattR as

[28]Otherwise, Schürmann, *Lukasevangelium I* 391.
[29]Statistics: 5–4–2 + 0.
[30]Against Schulz, *Spruchquelle* 236.
[31]Statistics: 4–2–1 + 2.
[32]Against Wegner, *Hauptmann* 143–5.
[33]Against Schulz, *Spruchquelle* 237; Schenk, *Synopse* 37.
[34]Otherwise, Schürmann, *Untersuchungen* 121.
[35]Matt 8:14 diff Mark 1:29; Matt 9:2 diff Mark 2:3.

well. (v) The extreme and striking phrase δεινῶς βασανιζόμενος probably did figure in Q. The word δεινῶς is expressive of great intensity.[36] It occurs elsewhere in the NT only at Luke 11:53, so word statistics prove nothing. With βασανίζειν, however, more can be said. It occurs in Matt 8:29/Mark 5:7/Luke 8:28 and Matt 14:24/Mark 6:48, while βάσανος occurs at Matt 4:24 diff Mark 1:28, 32, 34. Its presence in Matthew can therefore derive from a source or from MattR. The former is more likely, in Matt 8:6, for four reasons. First, the βάσανος group normally stands for extreme agony/torture/torment, which does not fit well content-wise with the MattR παραλυτικός. Second, the use of βασανίζειν to describe dangerous and potentially fatal illness not only goes beyond παραλυτικός but matches ἤμελλεν τελευτᾶν extremely well. It frequently occurs elsewhere in contexts involving fatal illness or suffering when the judgment of God or the torture of martyrs is in view.[37] Given the intensity conveyed by δεινῶς, the point is clear. Third, the use of such language would fit particularly well the exorcistic pattern regarded by many as involved in Q 7:7b-8.[38] Fourth, some such language would go far to explain why, contrary to the norm, the sick person is not this time brought to Jesus.

Finally, the words of response by Jesus: direct speech in Matt 8:7 ἐγὼ ἐλθὼν θεραπεύσω αὐτόν, and in Luke 7:6 a narrative statement about Jesus' moving towards the scene of the problem. The tendency is to find Q in Matthew's wording,[39] and this is perfectly safe in respect of θεραπεύειν,[40] but ἐγώ is less safe, and a good deal hangs on whether it was in Q and, if so, what meaning it conveyed.

It is often argued that Jesus is here asking a question which refers either to how his entering a Gentile's house would infringe

[36]Cf. intensity of anger (Job 19:11), of terror (Wis 17:3; 18:17), or of verbal reproach (4 Macc 12:2).

[37]Wis 11:9; 12:23; 16:1, 4; 2 Macc 7:15; 9:6; 4 Macc 6:5, 10, 11; 8:2, 5, 27; 9:7, 15, 27, 30–31; 11:16, 20; 12:4, 13; 13:27; 15:22; 16:3, 15; Josephus, *Ant.* 2.14.4 § 304; 9.5.2 §§100–101; 12.10.6 §413.

[38]Cf. Mark 5:7; the exorcism involved in the related tradition Mark 7:24–30; *T. Asher* 6:5: βασανίζεται ὑπὸ τοῦ πονηροῦ πνεύματος.

[39]Wegner, *Hauptmann* 153–4.

[40]When Matthew uses θεραπεύειν he normally draws it from a source; occasionally, when it is MattR, the context demands it or a comparable word. It occurs in Q at 10:9 and is probably original here, too.

the purity laws[41] or, if the purity laws are not in mind, to his self-understanding as the emissary of God sent primarily to his own people.[42] In the former case such reticence would, so it is said, conform to the Q community's conservative position in favour of radicalized obedience to the law. In the latter case support for a strong sense of mission, specifically a mission to Israel, would conform to other Q material such as 10:16; 22:30. Support for a more or less indignant question is chiefly found in (i) parallel expressions of reluctance in the related Mark 7:27; John 4:48;[43] (ii) the emphatic ἐγώ, which is unnecessary in a straight promise by Jesus to come and help;[44] (iii) the absence of any explanation of why Jesus does not actually come and instead performs an unprecedently powerful miracle, if Matt 8:7a contains a statement rather than a question;[45] (iv) the need for a statement of reserve to provide the basis for the centurion's declaration of unworthiness in Q 7:6b and his extremely energetic attempt to gain Jesus' help in Q 7:7b-8;[46] (v) Luke's apparent awareness of the idea that Jesus' scruples have to be overcome.[47]

These arguments cannot, however, be considered compelling. (i) It is important to take seriously the continuity of the story. In his first speech in Q 7:2/Matt 8:5-6 the centurion describes the problem, asks for help, but does not ask Jesus to come. In Matt 8:7a it is *Jesus* who introduces the idea of coming (ἐλθών), an idea which is picked up in the centurion's second speech (Q 7:6b: ὑπὸ τὴν στέγην μου εἰσέλθῃς). Following his explanation that this was not what he meant, it becomes a matter for reflection in what follows. Had Jewishness as such, and therefore the purity laws, been in mind in Jesus' initial response, there would have been no reason to use the word ἐλθών and every reason to formulate instead ἐγὼ 'Ιουδαῖος θεραπεύσω αὐτόν. One might cite as an analogy Gal 2:14 εἰ σὺ 'Ιουδαῖος ὑπάρχων . . . On the other hand, had Jesus' exclusive role as the emissary

---

[41]Luz, *Matthäus 8–17* 14: 'Jesu Antwort, eine erstaunte Frage, weist die Bitte ab: Als Jude kann Jesus nicht das Haus eines Heiden betreten.'

[42]Wegner, *Hauptmann* 380.

[43]Jeremias, *Theology* 163; Wegner, *Hauptmann* 377.

[44]Held, 'Miracle Stories', 194; Wegner, *Hauptmann* 376.

[45]Klostermann, *Matthäusevangelium* 74; Wegner, *Hauptmann* 376.

[46]Schulz, *Spruchquelle* 238, 243; Wegner, *Hauptmann* 376.

[47]Bultmann, *History* 39; Wegner, *Hauptmann* 380.

to Israel been in mind, there would have been every reason to expect the centurion's reply to recognize that fact. But of such recognition there is none. So within the continuity of the story it is the going or not going of Jesus which forms the essential thread. This impression is confirmed when another parallel is drawn in, one which is at least as adjacent and important as those commonly cited. Mark 5:23–24 reads παρακαλεῖ αὐτόν . . . ἵνα ἐλθὼν ἐπιθῇς . . . καὶ ἀπῆλθεν. Jairus' plea explicitly involved ἐλθών. The centurion's did not, but it was a natural assumption. Consequently, in the same way as his response to the one was registered in ἀπῆλθεν, his response to the latter included ἐλθών. Between the two there is no difference. (ii) Care does, of course, have to be exercised in the use of parallels. Whether Luke's version can accurately be said to envisage the overcoming of reluctance is doubtful. The more the centurion's good deeds associate him with godfearers, the less distanced is he, the precursor of Cornelius, from the saving intervention of God. On the other hand, Mark 7:27 certainly does document reluctance. There, however, the main concern of the story as a whole is the Jew/Gentile distinction. That concern is introduced by Jesus in Mark 7:27, but then in Mark 7:28 first acknowledged (ναί, κύριε) and then argued around (καὶ τὰ κυνάρια . . .) by the Syro-Phoenician woman. Nothing in the centurion's speech corresponds to the latter element. There must therefore be some considerable doubt about whether Jewishness in either of the suggested forms is a concern of this story at all, and arguments will shortly be mounted to show that it is not. What is of concern is πίστις, as Q 7:7b–9 establishes. In that respect the later version of the same tradition in John 4:46–54[48] is a closer parallel. John 4:48 succeeds in making πίστις the central concern in a setting whose horizon is from start to finish so Jewish that the Jew/Gentile distinction simply does not arise. (iii) While ἐγώ may well be emphatic in Matt 8:7a, though in view of Q 19:23 it does not have to be, it only seems unnecessary and therefore striking if we ignore the instances of its presence in several authority statements elsewhere: the sending out of the emissaries with ἐγὼ ἀποστέλλω ὑμᾶς (Matt 10:16 diff Luke 10:3), the explanation of exorcistic activity with ἐγὼ ἐκβάλλω τὰ

---

[48]Cf. p. 285, n. 15.

δαιμόνια (Matt 12:28 diff Luke 11:20), and the sending of the prophets and others in ἐγὼ ἀποστέλλω πρὸς ὑμᾶς ... (Matt 23:34 diff Luke 11:49). These MattR insertions of ἐγώ alert us to the twin dangers of over-interpreting the term and of discounting the likelihood of MattR in Matt 8:7. (iv) There is no need for a statement of why Jesus does not come, other than that which the centurion himself furnishes. Jesus, having indicated his willingness to come, is restrained precisely by that statement of unworthiness and the recognition of authority contained in the centurion's words in Matt 8:8–9.

In view of the unconvincing character of the arguments for understanding Jesus' response as a deliberative question, better inferences can now be drawn. The first is that ἐγώ is MattR. The second is that Jewishness, whether represented by purity laws or by the scope of Jesus' mission, is not in mind. The third is that Jesus responds unquestioningly, immediately and clearly in the normal way. The last is that such an entirely conventional introduction serves to highlight the dramatically unexpected next speech by the centurion, and to show that everything is thereby oriented towards the discussion of authority, which thus emerges as the supreme concern of the Q story.

These considerations make it possible now to reconstruct the Q text of the request for, and provision of, help:

καὶ ἦλθεν αὐτῷ ἑκατοντάρχης παρακαλῶν αὐτὸν καὶ λέγων, ὁ παῖς μου ἐν τῇ οἰκίᾳ δεινῶς βασανιζόμενος μέλλει τελευτᾶν. λέγει αὐτῷ. ἐλθὼν θεραπεύσω αὐτόν.

That text having been reconstructed, and the typical form of a miracle story starting to become evident, there is just one unusual feature which is worthy of comment. This is particularly so in view of all the arguments about whether or not the Jew/Gentile distinction is intended to be formative for our understanding. The question may be posed tersely: is the ἑκατοντάρχης a Gentile at all? The answer will depend in part on how we evaluate the description of the intermediaries in Luke 7:3–6a, 7a, and on how we understand the climactic declaration about 'faith in Israel' (Q 7:9b). But at this stage it is worth affirming that the term in itself stands simply for 'an officer commanding 100 men' and is in itself ethnically neutral.[49] The NT usage is dominated by Lucan examples, where a Gentile person is unmistakably in mind (cf. Acts 10:1, 22), but it does not have to be so, and it may not always be so. In the LXX it is not so.[50] Similarly in Josephus it is often not so.[51] None of the passages in the LXX and Josephus which use ἑκατοντάρχης for Jewish personnel figure in Uwe Wegner's otherwise extremely comprehensive review of the multitude of texts in which the term appears,[52] but their importance should not be discounted. They demonstrate that the matter of nationality has in each particular case to be made clear in the context. We shall examine in due course the crucial saying in Q 7:9b, but in advance of that it is worth asking why this Q story, a member of a family of related traditions whose leading figures may be a ruler of a synagogue (Mark 5:22), or a rabbi (*b. Ber.* 34b), or a βασιλικός whose nationality is not normally regarded as non-Jewish (John 4:46), should have as its leading figure a centurion. The answer is surely that the choice of such a person facilitates the declaration about authority in Q 7:8. If so, one must take seriously the fact that the declaration about authority could be made by any military officer irrespective of nationality.

2. The Intermediaries. Luke 7:3–6a, 7a.

The Lucan central section, describing the delegation which presses Jesus for help, has no parallel in Matthew 8, but has nevertheless occasionally been claimed for Q. Josef Schmid, for example, set the shorter version of the story in Matt alongside shortened versions of other stories and claimed that a similar shortening had happened here. His three parallels were Matt 8:28–34/Mark 5:1–20; Matt 9:18–26/Mark 5:21–43; and Matt 11:2–6/Luke 7:18–23.[53] These three examples, the third of which

---

[49]This is implicitly recognized when commentators turn from the term itself to Luke 7:9 for confirmation that the soldier is a Gentile: thus, Fitzmyer, *Luke I–IX* 651.

[50]See Exod 18:21, 25; Num 31:14, 48, 52, 54; Deut 1:15; 1 Sam 8:12; 22:7; 2 Sam 18:1; 2 Kgs 11:4, 9, 10, 15, 19; 1 Chr 13:1; 26:26; 27:1; 29:6; 2 Chr 1:2; 23:1, 14; 25:5; 1 Macc 3:55.

[51]*Ant.*, 6.3.5 §40; 7.10.1 §233; 7.14.8 §368; 9.7.2, 3, 5 §§143, 148, 151, 156; 9.9.1 §188; *J.W.* 2.20.7 §578.

[52]Hauptmann 60–9, 372–5.

[53]*Matthäus und Lukas* 252–4.

is particularly problematic, almost certainly do not suffice to establish Schmid's position. Luke 7:3–6a, 7a is shot through with Lucan verbal and stylistic features,[54] though that by itself is also not sufficient. After all, Luke often edits Mark drastically so that his verbal and stylistic tendencies are very much in evidence, but there is still the Marcan source in the background. More important as supplementary and confirming evidence are the conformity of the extra Lucan material here to Lucan theological concerns, and also the awkwardness in its relationship to its present context.

More recently support has been attracted to the proposal that Luke 7:3–6a, 7a is a post-Q but pre-Lucan development. Uwe Wegner, for example, believes that there were four stages in the evolution of Luke 7:1–10:[55] (i) The primary formation in Q. (ii) The adoption and modification of the Q tradition by the tradents of Lucan *Sondergut*. (iii) The adoption and redactional modification by Luke of the version in the *Sondergut*. (iv) The Lucan displacement of the Q version in favour of the *Sondergut* version. However, in an extended investigation of Luke 7:3–6a, 7a Wegner is able to find almost no formulations to which the conclusions 'lk Red möglich' or 'lk Red nicht unmöglich' do not apply. His explanation of the choice made by Luke involves an appeal to the very considerations which would support the attribution of Luke 7:3–6a, 7a to LukeR of Q, namely, the centurion's pious Jewish-style performance of good works and his humble demeanour.

The effect of Luke 7:3–6a, 7a is to draw out and amplify ideas which were already given prominence in the Q version. In particular, the theme of the worthiness of the centurion is developed in a distinctive way. In v. 6b the centurion affirms through a second set of mediators that he is not worthy to have Jesus come into his house, but this is developed in a highly elaborate fashion: in v. 7a it is extended so that he states his unworthiness *even to come* to Jesus, which implies that he is in some way inferior to both the Jewish elders (v. 3) and the friends (v. 6a). Since there is some content correspondence between the centurion's friends (φίλοι) and his love (ἀγαπᾷ) of

[54]Schulz, *Spruchquelle* 238.
[55]*Hauptmann* 161–88, 250–5.

'our nation' it is evident that the friends are as Jewish as the elders, and therefore that (un-)worthiness does not relate to modesty and self-deprecation in general but to the Jew/Gentile distinction in particular. It is this general correlation of 'worthiness' and Jewishness that the speech of the elders takes up. In spite of the self-awareness of the centurion they affirm that he is, on account of his active benevolence towards the nation and its religion, to be regarded as genuinely worthy of a salvific intervention by Jesus. He has, in other words, to be regarded as typical of at least a trend towards the position of the godfearer. And Jesus, by responding to the plea of the elders, and therefore to the argumentation upon which it is based, already sets his own work within the continuity of the salvation history of Israel.

The substance of all this is, of course, entirely in line with Luke's concept of salvation history, a fact which naturally reinforces the suspicion of LukeR, but the manner of its achievement is with some cost and difficulty as far as detail and coherence are concerned. The notion of worthiness in v. 6b could certainly be interpreted in terms of the Jew/Gentile distinction, along the lines of the oft quoted *m. Ohol.* 18:7, 'The dwelling places of the Gentiles are unclean',[56] but (i) the initial request of the elders presumed that Jesus would come to the sick person, that is, that he would enter the house, and (ii) the Jew/Gentile distinction in no way provides the basis for the attitude, articulated in v. 7a, that he would not even make a personal approach to Jesus because of unworthiness. Point (ii), which can be reinforced by the observation that an awareness of the Jew/Gentile distinction had not prevented personal contact between the centurion and either the friends or the elders or the nation (vv. 3, 5, 6), points towards a second and alternative basis for his sense of unworthiness – that is, christology.[57] If his worthiness is to be defined in Jewish terms his unworthiness is to be defined in Christian, specifically in christological, terms. The experience of salvation (διασώζειν) which he directly and uniquely needs (his asking is essentially different from the third-party asking by the elders) is therefore a matter of grace and nothing but grace –

[56]Cf. Fitzmyer, *Luke I-IX* 652.
[57]See K. H. Rengstorf, 'ἱκανός', *TDNT* 3.293–6, esp. p. 294.

again a characteristic Lucan article of belief about salvation transcending the Jew/Gentile division: 'We believe that we shall be saved through the grace of the Lord Jesus *just as they will*' (Acts 15:11). So the centurion's sense of unworthiness in *both* its manifestations, his suggestion that Jesus should not enter his house and his decision not to come to Jesus in person, coupled together as they are by διὸ οὐδέ (v. 7a), is grounded not in an awareness of ethnicity but in a christological conviction about who Jesus is.

The theology which underlies the Lucan version of the tradition is wholly in line with the evangelist's outlook. It is not, however, put across without artificiality. First, the message brought by the first delegation specifically asked that Jesus would come (v. 3: ἐλθών). That message is mentioned before the direct speech of the elders and came ultimately from the centurion himself. There could be, therefore, at that stage no expectation of a second delegation asking Jesus not to come under his roof, nor of such remarkable faith as that which envisages Jesus' acting by word alone and at a distance. So the section dealing with the first delegation is essentially out of harmony with the rest of the story. And while the second delegation *need* not have been persons other than the centurion himself, it is clear that there would have been no deflection away from Jewish and towards Christian considerations if v. 7a had not been included, that is, if the centurion himself had come at the second stage. Second, there are several factors which make the second delegation problematic. (i) It presumes an awareness of the success of the first delegation in persuading Jesus to come, something which the reader of the story knows but which the centurion does not. (ii) It represents a change of mind about Jesus' coming, though no reason is given for the change. (iii) It presents the words of the centurion himself in such a way that one would normally have assumed that he personally was the speaker. (iv) It presumes a considerable journey from the start, where Jesus is when asked to help, to the finish, where the sick child lies, whereas this is a very odd follow-up to the initial very precise geographical note that 'he entered Capernaum'.

These very artificial schematic features are not only accommodated within a totality which aims to articulate Lucan theology. They can also be seen to match very closely, and therefore

very probably to originate in, two related traditions, namely
Acts 10–11 and Mark 5:21–43. With the first in mind Charles
Talbert rightly observed, 'It is precisely in vv. 3–5 that the
details of the correspondence with Acts 10 are found.'[58] This
was made easy for Luke by the presence in the Q material of (i)
a centurion, cf. Acts 10:5, who (ii) approaches a man of God, cf.
Acts 10:5, with (iii) attention being drawn to the problem of
entry to his home, cf. Acts 10:22, 28; 11:3, 12, and finally (iv)
great prominence being given to faith, cf. Acts 10:43; 11:7. On
the basis of these common elements it became possible to
develop within Luke 7:3–6 a series of other features which have
counterparts in Acts 10, namely, (v) the catalogue of pious acts
by the centurion, including his treatment of the Jews, cf. Acts
10:2, 4, 22; (vi) the sending of a delegation, cf. Acts 10:5, 8, 17;
and (vii) the agreement of the person concerned to come to the
centurion's house, cf. Acts 10:20. The second related tradition,
the Jairus story, is in certain respects more interesting and in
many ways a more determining influence than any other on
Luke 7:1–10. Again, a recollection of it was made easy for Luke
by several matching features: (i) a man in authority, the
ἀρχισυνάγωγος, Mark 5:22, with (ii) a child, cf. Mark 5:23, who
is (iii) on the point of death, cf. Mark 5:23, so that (iv) the
anxious parent journeys, in order (v) to appeal, παρακαλεῖν, for
help, cf. Mark 5:36. Given so extensive a correspondence it is
readily understandable that Luke should move over from the one
story to the other a series of details: (i) From the ἀρχισυνάγωγος
(Mark 5:22) there develops the συναγωγή reference in Luke
7:5. (ii) From ἵνα ἐλθὼν ... σωθῇ (Mark 5:23) there develops the ὅπως ἐλθὼν διασώσῃ in Luke 7:3. (iii) From ἀκούσασα
περὶτοῦ 'Ιησοῦ, sandwiched inside the Jairus tradition (Mark
5:27), there develops ἀκούσας δὲ περὶ τοῦ 'Ιησοῦ/αὐτοῦ in Luke
7:3. It is striking that there are no other exact ἀκούσας περὶ τοῦ
'Ιησοῦ/αὐτοῦ formulations anywhere else in the synoptic tradition except in Mark 7:25, part of the Syro-Phoenician woman
tradition. (iv) From the idea of the journey by Jesus from the
point of meeting to the house where the child lies (Mark 5:24)
there develops the idea of the journey which is so essential to

---

[58]*Literary Patterns, Theological Themes and the Genre of Luke-Acts* (SBLMS 20;
Missoula: Scholars Press, 1974) 19; similarly, though with a different understanding of the provenance of Matthew's version, Goulder, *Luke I* 376–8.

Luke 7:3–6. (v) From the double approach to Jesus, first by Jairus and then by members of his household (Mark 5:22, 35), there develops the idea of the double approach by the elders and the friends in Luke 7:3, 6. The influence of this material is confirmed by μὴ σκύλλου in Luke 7:6, cf. τί ἔτι σκύλλεις (Mark 5:35): σκύλλειν occurs in the NT only at Mark 5:35/ Luke 8:49, at Matt 9:36 which, in view of its proximity to Matthew's Jairus story (Matt 9:18–26), is clearly a reminiscence of Mark 5:35, and at Luke 7:6. In sum, therefore, we can observe that there is no feature of Luke 7:3–6 which lacks a counterpart in Mark 5:21–43 or Acts 10:1–11:18. Given the formal, verbal and theological relationships we have uncovered, it can be inferred without risk that Luke 7:3–6a, 7a do indeed owe their existence to LukeR. They did not belong to Q or to any pre-Lucan recension of Q.

3. The Centurion's Speech. Q 7:6b, 7b–8.

Few and insignificant are the points of doubt about the reconstruction of the Q text at this stage. The centurion's direct speech, like that of Jesus (Q 7:9), was probably introduced by εἶπεν (cf. λέγων, Luke 7:6), since Matthew's ἔφη is repeatedly attested in MattR[59] and never attested in Q. But it really doesn't matter! Luke's μὴ σκύλλου has already been considered and attributed to LukeR. It is theoretically possible to defend Matthew's μόνον, and to explain its absence from Luke, on the ground that in Luke's version, where the expectation is from the outset that a healing would take place at a distance, it would not be needed.[60] But (i) in Luke the centurion only expects Jesus to heal from a distance from the time of the second delegation onwards, and μόνον would be wholly appropriate within a contrast between Jesus' *coming* to heal (v. 3) and his *speaking* to that effect (v. 7b); (ii) in contexts where a μόνος reference is appropriate Luke will insert it,[61] so it would be odd for him to drop it here where it is so obviously useful and emphatic; (iii) MattR insertions are well attested.[62] Next,

[59]Matt 14:8; 21:27; 22:37; 26:34, 61; 27:11.
[60]Schulz, *Spruchquelle* 239.
[61]See Luke 5:21; 6:4; 9:18.

Matthew's ἰαθήσεται, is probably more original than Luke's ἰαθήτω: the latter fits the fact that now for the first time the centurion himself 'speaks' and voices his plea, but Matthew's verb form matches the following verbs πορεύεται, ἔρχεται, and ποιεῖ, which comment upon it. Finally, the Lucan τασσόμενος is probably a redactional clarification.[63] To sum up, therefore, the text of Q 7:6b, 7b-8 probably ran:

ἀποκριθεὶς δὲ ὁ ἑκατοντάρχης εἶπεν,
  κύριε, οὐκ εἰμὶ ἱκανὸς ἵνα μου ὑπὸ τὴν στέγην εἰσέλθῃς· ἀλλὰ εἰπὲ λόγῳ, καὶ ἰαθήσεται ὁ παῖς μου.
  καὶ γὰρ ἐγὼ ἄνθρωπός εἰμι ὑπὸ ἐξουσίαν, ἔχων ὑπ' ἐμαυτὸν στρατιώτας. καὶ λέγω τούτῳ· πορεύθητι, καὶ πορεύεται, καὶ ἄλλῳ· ἔρχου, καὶ ἔρχεται, καὶ τῷ δούλῳ μου· ποίησον τοῦτο, καὶ ποιεῖ.

Nothing could demonstrate more firmly the absolute centrality of this saying of the centurion than the reaction of Jesus to it: 'When Jesus heard this he marvelled ...' (Q 7:9). As Wolfgang Schenk has observed, the reaction of amazement normally follows a miracle and represents the response of the onlookers, but this amazement is the reaction of the miracle worker to the petitioner and it precedes the cure.[64] To the form-critically sensitive reader the amazement is indeed amazing. All the more care is therefore needed in interpreting what has been said.

A syntactical difficulty immediately arises in v. 8. As J. Wellhausen put it many years ago, 'Statt εἰμί erwartet man ein Partizipium und statt ἔχων ein Finitum.'[65] Wellhausen's solution was to suppose that an infelicitous translation had occurred, and in this respect he although dead still speaks. For Wegner envisages 'dass εἰμί eigentlich konzessiv-partizipial durch ὤν, während ἔχων indikatisch-präsentisch durch ἔχω urspr wiederzugeben waren'.[66] With regard to the sense of the statement the same path has been trodden by those who suggest that

[62]See Matt 12:4; 18:15; 24:36.
[63]Schulz, *Spruchquelle* 239. It reinforces the subordination of the centurion, cf. also the correlation of τάσσειν and ἐξουσία in Tob 1:21 (aleph).
[64]*Synopse* 38.
[65]*Das Evangelium Matthaei* (Berlin: 1904) 36.
[66]*Hauptmann* 274.

the preposition ὑπὸ (ἐξουσίαν) is a rendering of *tahoth* (= in the place of), so that the original text spoke of the superiority rather than the subordination of the centurion.[67] The difficulty with all these approaches is that, as Eduard Schweizer observed, we have no reason to suppose that there ever was an underlying Aramaic text.[68] We have to do the best we can with the Greek text and, if necessary, settle for some slight awkwardness in the formulation.

The dominant view of what is intended in v. 8 is set out by Siegfried Schulz: As with the centurion's being under authority so that he has power to issue commands which are obeyed, so also Jesus' authority which derives from God implies that he needs only to speak and the demons of sickness will obey.[69] The subordinationist christology implicit in this scheme, which sets in parallel the two chains of command God-Jesus-demons and superiors-centurion-soldiers/servant, is not universally accepted, especially in view of the absence of any reference to Jesus' being under the authority of God and the presence of the reference to him as κύριος.[70] Progress with this vexing problem can perhaps only be made by taking cautiously a series of small steps forward:

First, the centurion's words καὶ γὰρ ἐγώ have the effect of associating rather than dissociating, of comparing rather than contrasting. This can be seen clearly illustrated in the forms καὶ γὰρ οἱ ἁμαρτωλοί (Luke 6:32) in connection with their loving only those who love them, and καὶ γὰρ αὐτοὶ ἀφίομεν (Luke 11:4) in connection with forgiving as God does. An even closer parallel is καὶ γὰρ αὐτὸς ἄνθρωπός ἐιμι (Acts 10:26), paralleling the positions of Peter and Cornelius and, like Q 7:8, using the word ἄνθρωπος. At first sight that word ἄνθρωπος is quite unnecessary in Q 7:8. Could not the interpretation proposed by Schulz and others stand if that word were absent? To ask is to answer and consequently to affirm that it must be all the more vital to give it some definite role.[71] If we

[67]Manson, *Sayings* 65; Black, *Aramaic Approach* 159.
[68]*Matthew* 214.
[69]*Spruchquelle* 243. Cf. also Manson, *Sayings* 64-5; Tödt, *Son of Man* 257; Jeremias, *Theology* 164.
[70]See Schürmann, *Lukasevangelium I* 393.
[71]As an equivalent, suggested by Wegner, *Hauptmann* 275, τίς/jemand would be much too weak.

take our cue from Acts 10:26 the contrast there between two orders of existence is arresting. Significantly for our present enquiry, Ernst Haenchen commented on 'I too am only a man' as Luke's way of illustrating Peter's exemplary humility in the face of Cornelius' treating him as 'a being of some higher order'.[72]

There are in consequence two impressions created by this formulation in Q 7:8. (i) The centurion is associating himself with other persons and not with Jesus. They must be persons occupying a subordinate position, specifically the soldiers and the servant. This interpretation has the merit of both permitting the phrase ὑπὸ ἐξουσίαν to have its straightforward meaning '*under* authority' (cf. 2 Macc 3:6) and also allowing the two phrases ὑπὸ ἐξουσίαν and ὑπ' ἐμαυτόν to be genuinely parallel in meaning. (ii) The centurion is *as a man* contrasting himself with Jesus. In that case we can take the word γάρ to point directly back to the statement of unworthiness/humility in Q 7:6b; we can take seriously the centurion's address to Jesus as κύριος; and we can recognize the structural parallelism between the two statements of subordination in vv. 6b, 8a, and also the parallelism between the two statements about the word and its effectiveness in vv. 7b, 8b.

Second, the participle ἔχων can easily be taken in a concessive sense, that is, 'although I have . . .'. This readily supports the proposed interpretation.[73] In that case the sense is 'Although I have soldiers under me, who come and go at my bidding, and a slave, who does what I say, I as a man am like them under authority'.

Third, the term ἱκανός is interpretable with the greatest of ease in terms of christology rather than the Jew/Gentile distinction. Using ἱκανός as the equivalent of the Hebrew *shaddai*,

---

[72] *The Acts of the Apostles* (Oxford: Blackwell, 1971) 358.

[73] Parallels cited by C. F. D. Moule, *An Idiom-Book of New Testament Greek* (Cambridge: CUP, 1963) 102, are 1 Cor 9:19 ἐλεύθερος γὰρ ὢν . . . ἐμαυτὸν ἐδούλωσα (although I am free . . . I subject myself); 2 Cor 10:3 ἐν σαρκὶ γὰρ περιπατοῦντες οὐ κατὰ σάρκα στρατευόμεθα (although we walk in the flesh we are not fighting according to the flesh); Gal 2:3 οὐδὲ Τίτος, . . . Ἕλλην ὤν, ἠναγκάσθη (although Titus was a Greek, he was not forced . . .); Phlm 8 παρρησίαν ἔχων ἐπιτάσσειν . . . μᾶλλον παρακαλῶ (although I am bold to command . . . yet I prefer to appeal); Heb 5:8 ὢν υἱός, ἔμαθεν . . . (although he was a son . . . he learned).

several LXX texts not only use the term for God himself but also set up a ἱκανός/κύριος equivalence.[74] Human expressions of lack of ἱκανότης are provoked, or remedied, by their being set against the overwhelming reality of God.[75] Therefore a ἱκανός statement such as Q 7:6b necessarily resonates with a sense of the great gulf fixed between the human and the divine. Absolutely no encouragement can be found here for a subordinationist christology.[76] Rather it is the exalted position of Jesus which is envisaged. Similarly, as K. H. Rengstorf has correctly observed, there is in mind 'not the ritual uncleanness which Jesus as a Jew would incur by entering a non-Jewish house' but 'the majesty and authority of Jesus which lifts him above everything human'.[77]

Fourth, the structure of the centurion's description of his exercise of authority is instructive. He gives three instances, the first two of which are symmetrical and therefore preparatory for the climactic third instance: 'I say to my servant (δοῦλος), 'Do this', and he does it.' This one naturally hints at the antonym of δοῦλος and thus to his status as a κύριος. And yet his inferiority to another κύριος has to be explained. The line of thought is remarkably close to that in 1 Esdr 4:1–12, where the three servants of Darius produce rival answers to the question of where supreme strength is to be found.[78] Wine, the king himself, and women: they each have their claims to the possession of ἐξουσία (4:28, 38), the receipt of obedience (4:12) and the status of κύριος (4:3, 14–16, 22), but ultimately those claims wilt in the face of the power of truth. The case for the king is mounted in terms very reminiscent of Q 7:8:

> If he tells them to kill, they kill; if he tells them to release, they release; if he tells them to attack they attack; if he tells them to lay waste, they lay waste; if he tells them to build, they build; if he tells them to cut down, they cut down; if he tells them to plant, they plant.

---

[74]See Ruth 1:20–21; Job 21:15; 31:2; 39:32.
[75]Exod 4:10; Joel 2:11; 1 Cor 15:9; 2 Cor 2:6, 16; 3:5, 6.
[76]Against Tödt, *Son of man* 257.
[77]'ἱκανός', *TDNT* 3.293–6, esp. p. 294. Similarly Schürmann, *Lukasevangelium I* 393.
[78]Cited by Grundmann, *Lukas* 158. This is a much closer parallel than Epictetus I.25.10, which he also cites.

And when the claim of women is mounted third in the sequence the tactic employed is quite explicitly to concede all that has been claimed on behalf of the king, and then to claim that *in spite of it all* women are κύριος (4:14), women rule (4:22), women have strength (4:32). Similarly the centurion: he can exercise effective authority, but in spite of all that he recognizes an even higher authority to which he now submits, the authority of Jesus himself.

Fifth, two other Q passages provide important support. (i) In the redactional statement in Q 3:16c the Baptist affirms that he is not ἱκανός in the face of the coming one.[79] His inferiority has nothing to do with cleanness regulations but is again christologically and eschatologically grounded.[80] It has everything to do with the status of the one who will come as lord and judge, the one whom Q defines as Jesus implicitly there and explicitly in Q 7:18–23. (ii) In Q 7:24–28 there is again an antithesis, introduced by redaction[81] and setting John as one who belongs to the human sphere ('born of woman') over against the one whose status is determined in relation to the kingdom of God. The pre-Q text had contained no contrast, had set John in a human context (ἐν γεννητοῖς γυναικῶν), and had given him a position of supremacy over all others, specifically over all others who had received a mission (ἐγήγερται) from God; the Q text introduced a contrast so that, for all his superiority in the human context, his inferiority to Jesus in the ultimate context was unmistakable. That is exactly the way the centurion is made to think: for all his superiority in the human context, his inferiority to Jesus in the ultimate context is the overpowering reality. The similarity of the formulations in Q 3:16c; 7:6b, and the positional closeness of Q 7:6b, 24–28, make it almost inconceivable that the centurion's statement of inadequacy should be understood otherwise than with reference to the authority of Jesus as Lord and Son of man. As someone who understands what lordship means, and as someone who acknowledges the Lord and Son of man, he is indeed a 'paradigm of faith',[82] and a model for those

[79]See Hoffmann, *Studien* 31–3.
[80]Cf. the carrying or untying of sandals as the task of the servant, Billerbeck I.121.
[81]See above, pp. 63–70.
[82]Lührmann, *Redaktion* 58.

who would answer the question posed by the preceding inaugural discourse, 'Why do you call me "Lord, Lord," and not do what I tell you?'

4. Jesus' Pronouncement. Q 7:9.

With the concluding pronouncement of Jesus the transformation of the tradition from a miracle story into a pronouncement story or, more strictly, an 'apophthegmatic miracle story'[83] is complete.

The specific audience for that pronouncement was probably οἱ ἀκολουθοῦντες without further qualification, for two reasons. (i) An association between ἀκολουθεῖν and ὄχλος (thus Luke 7:9) occurs sufficiently often in MattR[84] to make it unlikely that Matthew would pass over such an association if he had found it in his source. (ii) Such an association occurs just once in Mark, specifically in the Jairus story (Mark 5:24) whose influence upon the centurion story has already been detected. The most likely explanation for the combination used in Luke 7:9a is therefore LukeR.[85]

As for the pronouncement itself two decisions have to be made. The first concerns Matthew's ἀμήν, a disputed matter but perhaps just more likely to have been inserted by Matthew than excised by Luke.[86] The second concerns παρ' οὐδενί diff οὐδέ.

The case for παρ' οὐδενί has been put by Paul Meyer,[87] and again more recently by Uwe Wegner.[88] (i) Luke's οὐδέ conforms to the scheme which gives priority to Jesus' mission to Israel and positive acclaim there, rather than a scheme involving sharp antagonism towards Israel. (ii) Matthew's version is in line with many other Q texts – 10:13–15; 11:29–32; 13:28–29; 14:15–24[89] – condemning the faithlessness of 'this generation' and viewing Gentiles as 'instruments by which the Jews may be convicted and repent'.[90] (iii) The Matthaean importation of Q

[83]Wegner, *Hauptmann* 343.
[84]Matt 4:25; 8:1; 19:2; 20:29; 21:9.
[85]Note also the occurrence of ἐπιστράφεις in Mark 5:30.
[86]Schulz, *Spruchquelle* 239; Schenk, *Synopse* 37.
[87]'Gentile Mission', 410–11.
[88]*Hauptmann* 216–20.
[89]Wegner, *Hauptmann* 220 even cites Luke 4:25–27.

13:28–29 does not prove that a MattR alteration has occurred in
Matt 8:10, but rather indicates a Matthew/Q theological agreement that 'the Jews' unbelief was subject to condemnation when
compared with the faith Gentiles were manifesting'.[91] In the
Matthaean context the παρ' οὐδενί saying is 'somewhat
contradictory' because faith in Jesus' ability to work miracle has
been confessed in the healing of the leper (Matt 8:1–4).

By way of comment, several observations may be made: (i)
The difference between Matthew and Luke has been greatly
exaggerated. The key to the saying must be the agreed word
τοσοῦτος, representing for both Matthew (cf. Matt 15:33 diff
Mark 8:4) and Luke (cf. Luke 15:29; Acts 5:8) one amount
rather than another. By 'another' neither evangelist would understand 'nothing'. Therefore neither evangelist would take ἡ
τοσαύτη πίστις to mean that no faith at all had previously been
encountered. Consequently, far from a discrepancy between
Matt 8:1–4 and 8:10 there is a simple consistency. By way of confirmation, the faith which is shown in 'bringing' (προσφέρειν)
the sick to Jesus in Matt 9:2/Mark 2:5 is also anticipated in
advance of the centurion episode in the same 'bringing' in Matt
4:24/Mark 1:32. Similarly for Luke the faith of those who bring
the sick to Jesus has already been on view in Luke 5:20/Mark
2:5. Consequently, whichever of παρ' οὐδενί and οὐδέ stood in
Q, the implication is not that faith has been absent thus far in
Israel. It is rather that in the context of a mission to Israel faith
has indeed been present, but never on the scale or of the quality
presently being exercised. (ii) What then of the argument from
parallel material in Q, including that which refers to 'this
generation'? Here again exaggeration is all too liable to occur.
Q certainly envisages the present generation in general as
misguided or obdurate, but there are qualifications and many
exceptions. How otherwise can the criticism of 'this generation'
as 'evil' (Q 11:29) and unrepentant (Q 11:32) coexist with the
testimony of Q that the call for repentance (Q 3:8) has been
heeded (Q 3:16b), as well as the implication that general human
'evil' (Q 11:13) by no means excludes all true goodness? How
otherwise can a denunciation of 'this generation' in Q 7:31–32

[90]Meyer, 'Gentile Mission', 410.
[91]Meyer, 'Gentile Mission', 411.

be interpreted in a seemingly unqualified fashion as the rejection of John (Q 7:33) as well as Jesus (Q 7:34), and yet the preceding tradition make abundantly plain that 'crowds' (Q 7:24) have recognized him as a prophet (Q 7:26), and the concluding affirmation end on a resoundingly positive note in recording the recognition accorded by Wisdom's children (Q 7:35)? (iii) As to the Matthew/Q theological agreement centred on the use of Q 13:28–29, there is more than a little evidence that the saying in question referred to the diaspora Jews who would come 'from east and west' and displace certain other persons.[92] The 'sons of the kingdom', almost certainly the term used by Q to describe those persons,[93] cannot stand for all Jews resident within the boundaries of the land but rather for those Jews who have witnessed the mission of Jesus and kept their distance. Alongside them must be set those who, according to Q, receive the revelation as 'babes' (Q 10:21–22), or see and hear the present eschatological realities (Q 10:23–24), or address God as 'Father' (Q 11:2–4), or have some faith even if it is 'little faith' (Q 12:28). Indeed, one might add, even in the present story the audience consists of οἱ ἀκολουθοῦντες, and who are they but persons, Jewish persons indeed, who satisfy the conditions of discipleship (cf. Q 9:57–60; 14:27)? (iv) Word-statistical evidence is not decisive:[94] παρά + dative formulations are attested in MattR,[95] while οὐδέ formulations are well attested in LukeR.[96] But the slightest of slight preferences may favour Matthew's παρ' οὐδενί, given the overall closeness of the Matthaean text to Q, the correspondence with Lucan formulations in similar settings (Luke 4:25–27; 14:24), and the agreement between Luke's οὐδὲ ἐν τῷ Ἰσραήλ and the LukeR intervention in his vv. 3–6a, 7a.

[92]D. C. Allison, 'Who will come from East and West? Observations on Matt. 8.11–12 – Luke 13.28–29', *IBS* 11 (1989) 158–70.

[93]Its synoptic usage is confined to Matt 8:12 diff Luke 13:28 and Matt 13:38. The two cases are related in that Matthew is in both contexts drawing on Q 13:18–30, but unrelated in that the sense of the term varies between those who participate in the kingdom and those who are excluded from it. One (Matt 8:12), but not the other (Matt 13:38), is therefore pre-Matthaean. See my article 'John the Baptist, Jesus and the Parable of the Tares', *SJT* 31 (1978) 557–70, esp. p. 566.

[94]Wegner, *Hauptmann* 216–21.

[95]Matt 6:1; 22:25; 28:15.

[96]Luke 6:3; 12:26; 20:36; 23:15, 40.

A tentative reconstruction of Q 7:9 therefore runs:

ἀκούσας δὲ ὁ Ἰησοῦς ἐθαύμασεν καὶ εἶπεν τοῖς ἀκολουθοῦσιν· λέγω ὑμῖν, παρ᾽ οὐδενὶ τοσαύτην πίστιν ἐν τῷ Ἰσραὴλ εὗρον.

The groundwork has been done for the interpretation of this climactic saying on the level of Q. It has been suggested above that the term ἑκατοντάρχης is ethnically neutral, which means that something decisive is needed to overturn the natural expectation that a story about Jesus belongs to the setting of Jesus, namely the land and people of Israel. It has also been argued that the initial response of Jesus ἐλθὼν θεραπεύσω αὐτόν is not a question expressing an unwillingness based on Jewish ethnic sensitivity. Moreover, the centurion's speech, developing from οὐκ εἰμὶ ἱκανός is oriented to christology and not to any sense of Gentile inferiority. Consequently, Q 7:9 stands entirely isolated and alone as a possible support for the view that the Q version of this story has to do with Gentile faith. Yet by itself it is not capable of so striking an achievement. At this point the related acclamation in Matt 9:33 can be recalled: οὐδέποτε ἐφάνη οὕτως ἐν τῷ Ἰσραήλ. Following the centurion tradition the only Q material used by Matthew in advance of Matt 9:32–34 had been Q 9:57–60, which he intercalated within his version of the Marcan stilling of the storm tradition. There can be little doubt that the ἐν τῷ Ἰσραήλ saying in Matt 9:33 is generated by Q 7:9. But Matt 9:33 certainly does not intend to contrast two spheres of activity, one Jewish and another Gentile. It simply declares that what has just happened (in Israel, of course) is greater in kind than anything which has previously happened (also in Israel, of course).

Q 7:9 assumes that there are different strengths of faith, as it were. This is no surprise since it has already been shown to be the logical implication of Q 17:6, and indeed also of ὀλιγόπιστος in 12:28. When the centurion is praised for his quite remarkable faith it is within the setting of the mission of Jesus to Israel. He has done what no one in Israel has previously done. He has exhibited faith of a quantity and therefore quality far exceeding faith in Jesus as a miracle worker. His faith is outstanding because it is focussed on Jesus as the authoritative Son of man. Such faith is exactly what the mission to Israel is directed towards achieving. It is something of a tribute to, and confirmation of, that faith that, as is not usual in Q, he should have a story told about him. But in a sense the point could probably only be communicated by means of a story, for his faith was expressed in his speech, and his speech was facilitated by means of the distinction between Jesus' coming and his not coming.

The tradition which Q sets between the inaugural discourse of Jesus and the material relating Jesus to John is a tradition which exposes the power of the word of Jesus. And yet it is the word of the centurion which is, if anything, more arresting. For his word supremely witnesses to Jesus' word, and if the word of Jesus is the direct cause of the miracle it is the word of the centurion that is the indirect cause. As an implicit confession of the earthly Son of man this word is the confession which the mission to Israel seeks. It is a word of faith even more significant than that which, even though no larger than a mustard seed, can under God root up a sycamine tree.

Select Bibliography

Allison, D. C., 'Matt. 23:39 = Luke 13:35b as a Conditional Prophecy', *JSNT* 18 (1983) 75–84.

Beare, F. W., 'The Mission of the Disciples and the Mission Charge: Matthew 10 and Parallels', *JBL* 89 (1970) 1–13.

Berger, K., 'Jesus als Pharisäer und frühe Christen als Pharisäer', *NovT* 30 (1988) 231–62.

Black, M., *An Aramaic Approach to the Gospels and the Acts* (3rd ed.; Oxford: OUP, 1967)

Bornkamm, G., Barth, G., and Held, H. J., *Tradition and Interpretation in Matthew* (NTL; London: SCM, 1963).

Bultmann, R., *The History of the Synoptic Tradition* (Oxford: Blackwell, 1963).

Davies, W. D., and Allison, D. C., *The Gospel according to Saint Matthew I* (Edinburgh: T.& T. Clark, 1988).

Degenhardt, H.-J., *Lukas Evangelist der Armen* (Stuttgart: Katholisches Bibelwerk, 1965).

Delling, G., 'Das Gleichnis vom gottlosen Richter', *ZNW* 53 (1962) 1–25.

Delobel, J., ed., *Logia. Memorial J Coppens* (BETL 59, Leuven: University Press/Peeters, 1982).

Derrett, J. D. M., 'The Friend at Midnight – Asian Ideas in the Gospel of St. Luke', *Donum Gentilicium. New Testament Studies in Honour of D. Daube* (ed. C. K. Barrett, E. Bammel and W. D. Davies; Oxford: OUP, 1978) 78–87.

Dibelius, F., 'Zwei Worte Jesu', *ZNW* 11 (1910) 188–92.

Dibelius, M., *Die urchristliche Uberlieferung von Johannes dem Täufer* (FRLANT 15; Göttingen: Vandenhoeck & Ruprecht, 1915).

Downing, F. G., 'Towards the Rehabilitation of Q', *NTS* 11 (1964) 169–81.

Dungan, D. L., ed., *The Interrelations of the Gospels* (BETL 95; Leuven: University Press, 1990).

Dupont, J., *Les Béatitudes I-II* (Ebib; Paris: Gabalda, 1969).

Edwards, R. A., *The Sign of Jonah* (SBT 2/18; London: SCM, 1971).

Edwards, R. A., *A Theology of Q* (Philadelphia: Fortress, 1976).

Ernst, J., *Das Evangelium nach Lukas* (RNT; 5th ed.; Regensburg: Pustet, 1977).

Esler, P. F., *Community and Gospel in Luke-Acts* (SNTSMS 57; Cambridge: University Press, 1987).

Farrer, A. M., 'On Dispensing with Q', *Studies in the Gospels. Essays in Memory of R. H. Lightfoot* (ed. D. E. Nineham; Oxford: Blackwell, 1957) 55–88.

Fitzmyer, J. A., 'The Priority of Mark and the "Q" Source in Luke', *Jesus and Man's Hope I* (Pittsburgh: Theological Seminary, 1970) 131–70.

Fitzmyer, J. A., *The Gospel according to Luke* (2 vols; AB 28–28A; New York: Doubleday, 1983–85).

Friedrichsen, T. A., 'The Matthew-Luke Agreements against Mark. A Survey of Recent Studies: 1974–1989', *The Gospel of Luke* (ed. F. Neirynck; BETL 32; 2nd ed.; Leuven: University Press, 1989) 335–92.

Garland, D. E., *The Intention of Matthew 23* (NovTSup 52; Leiden: Brill, 1979).

Gnilka. J., 'Die Kirche des Matthäus und die Gemeinde von Qumran', *BZ* 7 (1963) 218–34.

Goulder, M. D., *Midrash and Lection in Matthew* (London: SPCK, 1974).

Goulder, M. D., 'On putting Q to the Test', *NTS* 24 (1978) 218–34.

Goulder, M. D., 'The Order of a Crank', *Synoptic Studies* (ed. C. M. Tuckett; JSNTSup 7; Sheffield: JSOT Press, 1984) 111–30.

Goulder, M. D., *Luke. A New Paradigm I-II* (JSNTSup 20; Sheffield: JSOT, 1989).

Green, H. B., 'Matthew 12:22–50 and Parallels: An Alternative to Matthaean Conflation', *Synoptic Studies* (ed., C. M. Tuckett; JSNTSup 7; Sheffield: JSOT, 1984) 157–76.

Greeven, H., 'Wer unter euch ...?', *WD* 3 (1952) 86–101.

Grimm, W., *Die Verkündigung Jesu und Deuterojesaja* (ANTJ 1; 2nd ed.; Frankfurt am Main/Bern: Lang, 1981).

Grundmann, W., *Das Evangelium nach Lukas* (THKNT 3; 2nd ed.; Berlin: Evangelische Verlagsanstalt, 1961).

Guelich, R. A., *The Sermon on the Mount* (Waco, Texas: Word Books, 1982).

Gundry, R. H., *Matthew* (Grand Rapids, Michigan: Eerdmans, 1982).

Haenchen, E., 'Matthäus 23', *ZTK* 48 (1951) 38–63.

Hahn, F., *Mission in the New Testament* (SBT 47; London: SCM, 1965).

Hahn, F., *The Titles of Jesus in Christology* (London: Lutterworth, 1969).

Hare, D. R. A., *The Theme of Jewish Persecution of Christians in the Gospel according to St Matthew* (SNTSMS 6; Cambridge: CUP, 1967).

Harnack, A., *The Sayings of Jesus* (London: Williams & Norgate, 1908).

Hawkins, J. C. 'Probabilities as to the So-called Double Tradition of St Matthew and St Luke', *Studies in the Synoptic Problem* (ed. W Sanday; Oxford: Clarendon, 1911) 95–138.

Hoffmann, P., *Studien zur Theologie der Logienquelle* (NTAbh NF 8; 2nd ed.; Münster: Aschendorff, 1972).

Hoffmann, P., '"Selig sind die Armen ..." Die Auslegung der Bergpredigt I (Mt 5,3–16)', *Bibel und Leben* 10 (1969) 111–22.

Hoffmann, P., 'Die bessere Gerechtigkeit. Die Auslegung der Bergpredigt IV (Mt 5,38–48)', *Bibel und Leben* 10 (1969) 264–75.

Hollander, H. W., and de Jonge, M., *The Testaments of the Twelve Patriarchs* (Leiden: Brill, 1985).

Horsley, R. A., '"Like One of the Prophets of Old": Two Types of Popular Prophets at the Time of Jesus', *CBQ* 47 (1985) 435–63.

Horsley, R. A., *Bandits, Prophets and Messiahs* (New York: Harper & Row, 1988).

Humbert, '"Laetari et exultare" dans le vocabulaire religieux de l'Ancien Testament', *RHPR* 22 (1942) 185–214.

Jacobson, A., 'The Literary Unity of Q. Lc 10, 2–16 and Parallels as a Test Case', *Logia. Memorial J. Coppens* (ed. J. Delobel; BETL 59; Leuven: University Press, 1982) 419–23.

Jeremias, J., *Jesus' Promise to the Nations* (SBT 24; London: SCM, 1958).

Jeremias, J., *The Parables of Jesus* (NTL; London: SCM, 1963).

Jeremias, J., 'Ἰωνᾶς', *TDNT* 3 (1965) 406–10.

Jeremias, J., *New Testament Theology I. The Proclamation of Jesus* (NTL; London: SCM, 1971).

Kasting, H., *Die Anfänge der urchristlichen Mission. Eine historische Untersuchung* (BEvT 55; München: Kaiser, 1969).

Klein, P., 'Die lukanischen Weherufe Lk 6,24–26', *ZNW* 71 (1980) 150–9.

Kloppenborg, J., *The Formation of Q. Trajectories in Ancient Wisdom Collections* (Studies in Antiquity and Christianity; Philadelphia: Fortress, 1987).

Klostermann, E., *Das Matthäusevangelium* (2nd ed.; HNT 4; Tübingen: Mohr, 1927).

Klostermann, E., *Das Lukasevangelium* (3rd ed.; HNT 5; Tübingen: Mohr, 1975).

Lambrecht, J., *Once More Astonished* (New York: Crossroads, 1981).

Laufen, R., *Die Doppelüberlieferungen der Logienquelle und des Markusevangeliums* (BBB 54; Königstein/Ts.- Bonn: Hanstein, 1980).

Légasse, S., *Jésus et l'enfant* (Ebib; Paris: Gabalda, 1969).

Légasse, S., 'L'oracle contre "cette generation" (Mt 23,34–36 par. Lc 11,49–51) et la polemique judéo-chretienne dans la source des logia', *Logia. Memorial J. Coppens* (ed. J. Delobel; BETL 59; Leuven: University Press, 1982) 237–56.

Linnemann, E., *Parables of Jesus* (London: SPCK, 1966).

Lührmann, D., *Die Redaktion der Logienquelle* (WMANT 33: Neukirchen: Neukirchener Verlag, 1969).

Lührmann, D., 'The Gospel of Mark and the Sayings Collection Q', *JBL* 108 (1989) 51–71.

Luz, U., *Matthew 1–7* (Edinburgh: T&T Clark, 1990).

Luz, U., *Das Evangelium nach Matthäus (Mt 8–17)* (EKKNT 1/2; Zürich/ Neukirchen-Vluyn: Benziger/Neukirchener Verlag, 1990).

Maccoby, H., 'The Washing of Cups', *JSNT* 14 (1982) 3–15.

Manson, T. W., *The Sayings of Jesus* (repr.; London: SCM, 1971).

Marshall, I. H., *The Gospel of Luke* (Exeter: Paternoster, 1978).

Merklein, H., *Die Gottesherrschaft als Handlungsprinzip* (FB 34; Würzburg: Echter Verlag, 1978).

Meyer, P. D., 'The Gentile Mission in Q', *JBL* 89 (1970) 405–17.

Miyoshi, M., *Der Anfang des Reiseberichts. Lk 9,51–10,24* (AnBib 60; Rome: Biblical Institute, 1974).

Neirynck, F., 'Recent Developments in the Study of Q', *Logia. Memorial J. Coppens* (ed. J. Delobel; BETL 59; Leuven: University Press, 1982) 29–75.

Neirynck, F., 'Introduction: The Two-Source Hypothesis', *The Interrelations of the Gospels* (ed. D. L. Dungan; BETL 95; Leuven: University Press, 1990) 3–22.

Neirynck, F., 'Matthew 4:23–5:2 and the Matthean Composition of 4:23–11:1', *The Interrelations of the Gospels* (ed. D. L. Dungan; BETL 95; Leuven: University Press, 1990) 23–46.

Neirynck, F., 'Response to the Multi-Stage Hypothesis: I The Introduction to the Feeding Story. II The Healing of the Leper. III The Eschatological Discourse', *The Interrelations of the Gospels* (ed. D. L. Dungan; BETL 95; Leuven: University Press, 1990) 81–93, 94–107, 108–124.

Neirynck, F., *Evangelica II* (BETL 99; Leuven: University Press, 1991).

Neusner, J., '"First Cleanse the Inside"', *NTS* 22 (1976) 486–95.

Patte, D., *The Gospel according to Matthew* (Philadelphia: Fortress, 1987).

Pesch, W., *Matthäus als Seelsorger* (SBS 2; Stuttgart: Katholisches Bibelwerk, 1966).

Polag, A., *Die Christologie der Logienquelle* (WMANT 45; Neukirchen: Neukirchener Verlag, 1977).

Rengstorf, K. H., *Das Evangelium nach Lukas* (NTD 3; Göttingen: Vandenhoeck & Ruprecht, 1966).

Rengstorf, K. H., 'σημεῖον', *TDNT* 7 (1971) 200–61.

Rüger, H. P., '"Mit welchem Mass ihr messt, wird euch gemessen werden"', *ZNW* 60 (1969) 174–82.

Sand, A., *Das Evangelium nach Matthäus* (RNT; Regensburg: Pustet, 1986).

Sanday, W., ed., *Studies in the Synoptic Problem* (Oxford: Clarendon, 1911).

Sanders, E. P., *Jesus and Judaism* (London: SCM, 1985).

Sanders, E. P., and Davies, M., *Studying the Synoptic Gospels* (London: SCM, 1989).

Sato, M., *Q und Prophetie. Studien zur Gattungs- und Traditionsgeschichte der Quelle Q* (WUNT, 2/29; Tübingen: Mohr, 1988).

Schenk, W., 'Der Einfluss der Logienquelle auf das Markusevangelium', *ZNW* 70 (1979) 141–65.

Schenk, W., *Synopse zur Redenquelle der Evangelisten* (Düsseldorf: Patmos, 1981).

Schmid, J., *Matthäus und Lukas* (BibS(F) 23; Freiburg: Herder, 1930).

Schmid, J., *Das Evangelium nach Lukas* (RNT; 4th ed.; Regensburg: Pustet, 1960).

Schmid, J., *Das Evangelium nach Matthäus* (RNT; 5th ed.; Regensburg: Pustet, 1965).

Schmidt, D., 'The LXX *Gattung* "Prophetic Correlative"', *JBL* 96 (1977) 517–22.

Schneider, G., *Das Evangelium nach Lukas 1–10* (Gütersloh: Mohn, 1984).

Schulz, S., *Q. Die Spruchquelle der Evangelisten* (Zürich: Theologischer Verlag, 1972).

Schürmann, H., *Das Lukasevangelium I* (HTKNT 3/1; Freiburg: Herder, 1969).

Schürmann, H., *Traditionsgeschichtliche Untersuchungen zu den synoptischen Evangelien* (Düsseldorf: Patmos, 1968).

Schürmann, H., 'Das Zeugnis der Redenquelle für die Basileia-Verkündigung Jesu', *Logia. Memorial J. Coppens* (ed. J. Delobel; BETL 59; Leuven: University Press, 1982) 121–200.

Schwarz, G., 'Lukas 6.22a, 23c, 26. Emendation, Rückübersetzung, Interpretation', *ZNW* 66 (1975) 269–74.

Schweizer, E., *The Good News according to Matthew* (London: SPCK, 1976).

Smith, B. T. D., *The Parables of the Synoptic Gospels* (Cambridge: CUP, 1937).

Stanton, G. N., *The Gospels and Jesus* (Oxford: University Press, 1989).

Steck, O. H., *Israel und das gewaltsame Geschick der Propheten* (WMANT 23; Neukirchen: Neukirchener Verlag, 1967).

Stendahl, K., *The School of Saint Matthew* (ASNU 20; 2nd ed.; Lund: Gleerup, 1967).

Strecker, G., *Der Weg der Gerechtigkeit* (FRLANT 82; 2nd ed.; Göttingen: Vandenhoeck & Ruprecht, 1966).

Strecker, G., 'Die Makarismen der Bergpredigt', *NTS* 17 (1971) 255–75.

Streeter, B. H., 'On the Original Order of Q', *Studies in the Synoptic Problem* (ed. W. Sanday; Oxford: Clarendon, 1911) 141–64.

Streeter, B. H., 'St. Mark's Knowledge and Use of Q', *Studies in the Synoptic Problem* (ed. W. Sanday; Oxford: Clarendon, 1911) 165–83.

Streeter, B. H., 'The Original Extent of Q', *Studies in the Synoptic Problem* (ed. W. Sanday; Oxford: Clarendon, 1911) 184–208.

Streeter, B. H., 'The Literary Evolution of the Gospels', *Studies in the Synoptic Problem* (ed. W. Sanday; Oxford: Clarendon, 1911) 209–27.

Streeter, B. H., *The Four Gospels* (rev. ed.; London: Macmillan, 1930).

Tödt, H. E., *The Son of Man in the Synoptic Tradition* (NTL; London: SCM, 1965).

Trautmann, M., *Zeichenhafte Handlungen Jesu. Ein Beitrag zur Frage nach dem geschichtlichen Jesu* (FB 37; Würzburg: Echter Verlag, 1980).

Trilling, W., *Das wahre Israel. Studien zur Theologie des Matthäusevangeliums* (SANT 10; 3rd ed.; München: Kösel, 1964).

Tuckett, C. M., *The Revival of the Griesbach Hypothesis* (SNTSMS 44; Cambridge: CUP, 1983).

Tuckett, C. M., with Goulder, M. D., 'The Beatitudes: A Source-Critical Study', *NovT* 25 (1983) 193–216.

Tuckett, C. M., 'Q, the Law and Judaism', *Law and Religion* (ed. B Lindars; Cambridge: James Clarke, 1988) 90–101, 176–180.

Tuckett, C. M., 'Q, Prayer and the Kingdom', *JTS* 40 (1989) 367–76.

Tuckett, C. M., 'A Cynic Q?', *Bib* 70 (1989) 349–76.

Tuckett, C. M., 'Response to the Two-Gospel Hypothesis: I. The Position Paper. II The Eschatological Discourse', *The Interrelations of the Gospels* (ed. D. L. Dungan; BETL 95; Leuven: University Press, 1990) 47–62, 63–76.

Uro, R., *Sheep among the Wolves. A Study of the Mission Instructions of Q* Dissertationes Humanarum Litterarum 47; Helsinki: Suomalainen Tiedeakatemia, 1987).

Vermes, G., *The Dead Sea Scrolls in English* (3rd ed.; London: Penguin, 1987).

Weder, H., *Die Gleichnisse Jesu als Metaphern* (FRLANT 120; Göttingen: Vandenhoeck & Ruprecht, 1978).

Wegner, U., *Der Hauptmann von Kafarnaum* (WUNT 2/14; Tübingen: Mohr, 1985).

Weiser, A., *Die Knechtsgleichnisse der synoptischen Evangelien* (SANT 29; München: Kösel, 1971).

Wild, R. A., 'The Encounter between Pharisaic and Christian Judaism: Some early Gospel Evidence', *NovT* 27 (1985) 105–24.

Zeller, D., 'Redaktionsprozesse und wechselnder Sitz im Leben beim Q-Material', *Logia. Memorial J. Coppens* (ed. J. Delobel; BETL 59; Leuven: University Press, 1982) 395–409.

Zeller, D., *Die weisheitlichen Mahnsprüche bei den Synoptikern* (FB 17; Würzburg: Echter Verlag, 1977).

Index of References

10:20	297		28:20	170
10:22	293, 297		28:28	174
10:24	218			
10:26	300–301		**Romans**	
10:28	297		1:3–4	5
10:30	233		2:20	69
10:31	21		3:25	5
10:35	20			
10:36	22, 170		**1 Corinthians**	
10:38	44		1:22	283
10:43	46, 297		5:2	85
11:3	297		7:10	5
11:7	297		9:14	160
11:9	22		9:19	301
11:12	297		9:19–22	149
12:7	253		10:27	176, 178
13:1–3	159, 162		11:23	5
13:2	159		15:3	5
13:3	159		15:9	302
13:10	20		16:22	161
13:17	170			
13:24	10, 74, 170		**2 Corinthians**	
13:25	72, 160		2:6	302
13:27	174		2:16	302
13:38	174		3:5	302
13:38–39	20		3:6	302
13:51	181		4:7	133
14:23	159		10:3	301
14:26	159		13:1	137
15:7–18	170			
15:10	263		**Galatians**	
15:11	296		2:1–10	163
15:18	174		2:3	301
15:29	177		2:7–8	163–164, 171
16:26	45		2:14	290
16:34	178		2:15	147
19:4	10, 74		2:21	189
19:11–12	31		3:26–28	5
19:12	13		5:2–4	189
20:7	233			
20:19	21		**Philippians**	
20:24	116		2:6–11	5
20:28	149			
20:29	42, 180		**Colossians**	
20:29–30	192		1:20	127
20:34	174		2:3	133
21:14	30			
22:20	269		**1 Thessalonians**	
23:6–8	12		2:9	32
25:4	13		2:13	178
26:20	10			

336

Index of Modern Authors

342